Crowning The Animal Kingdom

To swim and run and fly, across the water, land and sky

This project started with two authors and ended up with over 200!

This effort constitutes a commitment toward global conservation. Together we can make a world of difference.

You have to love the novel literary approach which is embarked upon within this project. No one has ever taken the threads of zoological conservation, the history of animals, and animal humor and fed them through the eye of a single needle as happens here. This is the ultimate blending of entertainment and education! It's like, "Hello Science, we'd like to introduce you to Pop Culture!" This is a meeting not to be missed.

For the Animals

Crowning The Animal Kingdom

All Creatures, Great and Small

by

Tim & Deb Smith

Pandamensional Solutions, Inc.

Mendon, New York

This book contains both original and previously published work. Some material contained herein represents the opinions of the individuals quoted and not necessarily the opinion of the authors. In some cases, for metaphorical purposes, this work contains fiction. In such circumstances, names, characters, places and incidents are either the product of the authors' imagination or are used fictitiously. Any resemblance to actual events or locales or persons, living or dead, is entirely coincidental.

Limit of Liability/Disclaimer of Warranty: While the publisher and the authors have used their best efforts in preparing this book, they make no representations or warranties with respect to the accuracy or completeness of the contents of this book and specifically disclaim any implied warranties or merchantability or fitness for any particular purpose. No warranty may be created or extended by sales representatives or written sales materials. Neither the publisher nor author shall be liable for any loss of profit or any other commercial damages, including but not limited to special, incidental, consequential or other damages.

COPYRIGHT © 2024 BY TIM & DEB SMITH

Published by Pandamensional Solutions, Inc., Mendon, NY

Cover artwork by Svetas

Back cover photos by Scott and Savanna Smith

Cover design by Catarina Carosa

ALL RIGHTS RESERVED
INCLUDING THE RIGHT OF REPRODUCTION
IN WHOLE OR IN PART IN ANY FORM

ISBN-10: 1-938465-17-2
ISBN-13: 978-1-938465-17-8

What others are saying about Tim & Deb Smith's

Crowning The Animal Kingdom

We're impressed by your dedication to informing the public about the importance of wildlife conservation, and we share your goal of valuing, respecting, and conserving wildlife. Your approach of mutual collaboration aligns with our mission, and we would be honored to be part of your efforts. We appreciate the opportunity to collaborate and support your cause and look forward to being a part of your impactful project. ~ Marketing Director, Samantha Hansen, Shark and Marine Research Institute

A BIG mahalo for supporting and recognizing the conservation efforts of zoos! Aloha! ~ General Curator Laura Debnar, Honolulu Zoo

Thank you for making an impact for the animal kingdom. Wishing you good luck with your book and keep up your engagement! Highly appreciated. ~ Marketing and Communication Director Jana Saure, Turtle Foundation

Thank you for reaching out and considering us to be a part of your project. My team and I are very excited to represent our country (Jamaica) in your upcoming book project. You're embarking on a great project and we appreciate the opportunity to contribute. We look forward to work with you and your team and we are excited to see your story unfold. ~ Paul Fearon, Jamaica Zoo Attraction Ltd.

Thank you for reaching out; what a fun premise! ~ Executive Director Jeff Ewelt, Zoo Montana

Thank you for thinking of our zoo! This project sounds amazing, as it will shed more light on modern zoos' missions – protecting endangered species through the conservation process. We are all about education and science, moving away from the ancient concept that the whole purpose of zoo is entertainment. ~ Public Relations specialist Elīza Lindāne, Riga Zoo, Latvia

I love your humor and writing, it is great. Thank you so much for getting the word out about pinniped entanglements! We all really appreciate it! ~ Kim Raum-Suryan, Pinniped Entanglement Group

[This book] was a joy to read! Marina Wright, Lion Guardians

(And perhaps our most unexpected response considering that it came from a war zone ...) We take pride in participating and would like to provide the following information about the animals. ~ Director Volodymyr Topchy, Mykolaiv Zoo, Ukraine

The power of this project is pulling in a parade of experts who engagingly espouse upon their areas of expertise with relentless rigor. With the Smiths' style of irreverent humor and pop culture consciousness serving as the thread linking the animal analysis this is a zoological masterpiece which can boast a never-before-taken approach and brag never-before-achieved results. Consider the animal kingdom crowned! ~ Animal enthusiast, Cory Dupree

Here's a sampling of contributions from Africa... We would be happy to appear in this book alongside our friends from the Pan-African Sanctuary Association. Lékéid Park, Gabon... ~ We would be very grateful if Tacugama can appear in this project. Tacugama Chimpanzee Sanctuary, Sierra Leone... ~ Thank you very much for including us in your new book. Lion Park Harare, Zimbabwe.

What an exciting project. We are happy to have Germany join in and provide a few fun facts about our animals. ~ Director Katharina Heinroth, Berlin Zoo

What you have here so far looks great and it really made my day reading it this morning! ~ Global Animal Welfare Specialist Liam Hodgson, Humane League

This book is an engaging way to get a purposeful perspective on an array of animal species in an informatively humorous manner – not like you're reading a biology book or a Wikipedia entry. Communicative, concise, and comical. I'm actually feeling pretty good about myself now that I now know the difference between a sea star, a sea urchin and a sea cucumber, all part of the echinoderm family. But of course at this point, I'm just showing off. ~ Dr. Fred Marra

Thank you for reaching out to us for feedback regarding your upcoming book. The team was very excited to see what you are working on and look forward to seeing the finished product when it is released. We love the approach you have taken and were happy to fact check for you. ~
Programs Director Candace Hansen, Amphibian Survival Alliance

We look forward to being featured in your book and hope that this will bring more attention to the importance of wildlife preservation. We also hope that it will inspire readers to take an interest in the rich and diverse wildlife that Africa has to offer. Thank you for considering us for this exciting project. We're eager to see the final product and how it will contribute to the cause of wildlife conservation globally. ~ Social Media Manager Georgie Bristow,
Lion Park Harare, Zimbabwe

Every component kicks off with a killer hook. You absolutely never feel like you're reading a reference book. No, no, not at all. ~ Historian Mike McGory

We are excited about your initiative to raise awareness about wildlife conservation and we're longing to see the result. ~ Marketing Director,
Maria Ordinaria, Parco Natura Viva, Verona, Italy

Your information about seals looks great and thank you for supporting the seals! ~ Dr. Jane Reldan, President, Seal Conservancy

Let me thank you for this amazing project. We are happy and excited to be included in your book. ~ International Relations Specialist Sona Serobyan, Yerevan Zoo, Armenia

As literally "The most photographed squirrel in the world" I am honored to bestow my blessing and endorsement upon the Smiths' tribute to the Animal Kingdom. Of course I was most fascinated with the Squirrel component of the book and I salute my fellow squirrels who join me in the countdown. ~ Sugar Bush the (real-life) squirrel

Thank you for your invitation to contribute to your book and the impressive content. ~ Director Richard Østerballe, Givskud Zoo, Denmark

Thank you for reaching out to Big Life Foundation. It's encouraging to know that your upcoming book aims to shine a light on conservation issues, a cause close to our hearts. ~ Outreach Associate, Traci Walter, Big Life Foundation

We feel honoured that you chose us as an Austrian zoo to participate in this interesting project. We agree that is a great idea to create the book with a lot of humour, which is one of the best ways to awake interest and to sensitize [people toward] animals. Therefore we enjoy to support you. ~ Kurator Dirk Ullrich, Alpenzoo Innsbruck, Austria

Looking forward to seeing the book when it is published! ~ Goodwill Ambassador/Communications Director Ron Macgill, Zoo Miami

Thank you so much for including us in this book, it's such a clever (and fun) idea. Hopefully it will bring more awareness to many of these unique and sometimes misunderstood animals. ~ Brian Kleinman, Riverside Reptiles

There are hundreds of components here that are all engaging entities in and of themselves. It has the appeal that you can pick it up and put it down without having to reconnect the dots when you re-engage, but it's all held together by this overall vision, an engaging embrace of the animal kingdom. If you're not an animal lover, you probably haven't even read this far, so playing upon the hunch that you are blessed with an animal affinity, this book offers the unique opportunity to allow you to constantly change directions on your skis, slaloming back and forth between fiction and reality. You're going to learn much, laugh often, and cry occasionally. It's an animal carousel off of which you won't want to climb down. ~ Educator Bob Caulkins

In *Crowning The Animal Kingdom,* the first global anthology of stories from animal organizations, co-authors Deb and Tim Smith, gather over 200 contributors from around the world in a passionate blend of sublime science and ample doses of irreverent pop culture and wit. ~ Author Karen Mireau

Dedication

~ For the Animals ~

All Creatures, Great and Small

and especially our beloved
Chynna Cat Sunflower Smith
who died of cancer at just 1 ½ years old,
on February 6, 2024,
having lived just long enough to serve as our muse
through the completion of this book

TABLE OF CONTENTS

LET'S KICK OFF THIS BALLYHOO, WITH OUR LEAD-OFF OVERVIEW

CHAPTER 1 ~ STORYLINE SAMPLER

IN THE JUNGLE THINGS DO RUMBLE, IN THE WOODS IT'S ROUGH AND TUMBLE

CHAPTER 2 ~ LIONS & TIGERS & BEARS, OH MY!
pg. 11 ~ Lions   pg. 18 ~ Tigers   pg. 22 ~ Bears

CHAPTER 3 ~ THE FOREST NOW ROCKS, WITH THE WOLF AND THE FOX
pg. 30 ~ Wolves   pg. 36 ~ Foxes

CHAPTER 4 ~ COMING TO TERMS WITH THOSE PACHYDERMS
pg. 40 ~ Hippopotamuses   pg. 46 ~ Rhinoceroses   pg. 52 ~ Elephants

CHAPTER 5 ~ GRACEFUL MOVES UPON THEIR HOOVES
pg. 60 ~ Giraffes   pg. 67 ~ Zebras   pg. 72 ~ Deer

CHAPTER 6 ~ THERE'S NO SHORT SUPPLY MATES, IT'S TIME FOR THE PRIMATES
pg. 76 ~ Monkeys & Apes

EVERYTHING'S BETTER, DOWN WHERE IT'S WETTER

CHAPTER 7 ~ IT'S TO THE BEACH WE HEAD, WITH OUR FAVORITE PINNIPED
pg. 83 ~ Seals & Sea Lions   pg. 84 ~ Walruses

CHAPTER 8 ~ SALUTING OUR FAVES, FROM BENEATH THE WAVES
pg. 90 ~ Fish   pg. 93 ~ Sharks   pg. 98 ~ Dolphins   pg. 103 ~ Whales

CHAPTER 9 ~ CRUSTACEAN ELATION, DOWN-UNDER SENSATION
pg. 109 ~ Shrimp   pg. 109 ~ Crabs   pg. 110 ~ Lobsters

CHAPTER 10 ~ GETTING TO KNOW THE CEPHALO
pg. 112 ~ Octopuses   pg. 113 ~ Squids

CHAPTER 11 ~ COMING TO TERMS WITH ECHINODERMS
pg. 116 ~ Sea Stars   pg. 117 ~ Sea Urchins   pg. 118 ~ Sea Cucumbers

WE'LL SWIM AND WALK AND FLY, THROUGH THE WATER, LAND AND SKY

CHAPTER 12 ~ AMPHIBIANS IN LOADS, LET'S BRING ON THE FROGS AND TOADS
pg. 121 ~ Frogs & Toads

CHAPTER 13 ~ WE'VE GOT LOTS OF TOOTHY TALES,
                WHEN THOSE REPTILES FLASH THEIR SCALES
pg. 127 ~ Turtles   pg. 132 ~ Snakes   pg. 136 ~ Alligators & Crocodiles   pg. 142 ~ Dinosaurs

CHAPTER 14 ~ NEVER AT A LOSS FOR WORDS, WITH THE CHICKENS, DUCKS & BIRDS
pg. 147 ~ Chickens   pg. 150 ~ Ducks   pg. 153 ~ Birds

FINAL ROUND UP, SEARCH THE ANNALS,
CLOSING STORIES STARRING MAMMALS

CHAPTER 15 ~ HERE'S THE PART WHERE WE REGALE YA,
　　　　　　　WITH OUR STORIES FROM AUSTRALIA
pg. 161 ~ Kangaroos   pg. 162 ~ Tasmanian Devils   pg. 163 ~ Platypuses
pg. 165 ~ Wombats

CHAPTER 16 ~ WRITING OPTIONS BLOSSOM WITH THE GOPHER, SKUNK & POSSUM
pg. 171 ~ Gophers   pg. 172 ~ Skunks   pg. 174 ~ Opossums

CHAPTER 17 ~ HERE'S SOME TALES IN A FLURRY,
　　　　　　　'BOUT SOME CRITTERS SOFT AND FURRY
pg. 179 ~ Rabbits   pg. 184 ~ Squirrels   pg. 190 ~ Chipmunks   pg. 192 ~ Mice

CHAPTER 18 ~ HERE COME STORIES FULL OF CHARM,
　　　　　　　FOR OLD McDONALD ON HIS FARM
pg. 198 ~ Pigs   pg. 203 ~ Cattle   pg. 207 ~ Horses

CHAPTER 19 ~ IT'S RAINING CATS AND DOGS
pg. 214 ~ Cats   pg. 220 ~ Dogs

ADDENDUMS

Pg. 231 ~ Addendum #1 ~ U.S. Zoos & Aquariums
Pg. 243 ~ Addendum #2 ~ International Zoos & Aquariums
Pg. 259 ~ Addendum #3 ~ Animal Sanctuaries & Wildlife Preserves
Pg. 279 ~ Addendum #4 ~ Animal Advocacy Groups
Pg. 283 ~ Addendum #5 ~ Best Zoo Logos
Pg. 285 ~ Addendum #6 ~ Longest-Living Animals
Pg. 289 ~ Addendum #7 ~ Animals in the Olympics
Pg. 293 ~ Addendum #8 ~ How Fast Can That Animal Move?
Pg. 295 ~ Addendum #9 ~ The Bible's Top 6 Animal Acts
Pg. 297 ~ Addendum #10 ~ Animal Accolades
Pg. 299 ~ Addendum #11 ~ Top 10 Endangered Species Comeback Stories
Pg. 303 ~ Addendum #12 ~ Presidential Pets
Pg. 315 ~ Addendum #13 ~ Timeline of Animal History
Pg. 323 ~ Addendum #14 ~ Sports Mascots
Pg. 329 ~ Addendum #15 ~ Oldest Zoos in the U.S.
Pg. 333 ~ Addendum #16 ~ Top 35 Overall Rankings
Pg. 335 ~ Addendum #17 ~ Chynna's Eulogy

Foreword

By Brianna Silva

This is a book that started out with two authors and ended up with over 200!

What in the world kind of feeding frenzy comes to such fortuitous fruition? My referencing "the world" in the previous sentence is particularly purposeful because what has evolved from this endeavor is a global networking of animal organizations the likes of which has never before been achieved. Check out the library, search Amazon, avail yourself of any archive at your disposal, and then confirm the credibility of the claim that this is truly a zoological zenith.

Allow me to elaborate on the evolutionary process which fell into place as Tim and Deb Smith embarked upon writing their 6th book. It all started with a love of animals, so while pondering the possibilities for book #6, the Smiths thought that was a topic they could rally around. Then, replicating an approach they've previously employed, the goal became to entertain, as well as educate.

Bubbling in this biological cauldron is the perfect blend of sublime science stirred together with ample doses of irreverent pop culture humor. Lots of facts and lots of thoughts factored through a prism of scientific accuracy and sardonic wit.

Then the idea is spawned that if they can engage some zoos to share their actual stories, connections can be made that generate material that is right from the horse's mouth, so to speak. Notice how the dominoes begin to line up and strategically fall at this point.

A sensible succeeding analogy would be that what zoos are to land, aquariums are to water, and next they find several of the world's finest such aquatic facilities climbing aboard to be a part of the project.

Following that, a message comes in from the Ngamba Island Chimpanzee Sanctuary in Uganda asking the Smiths if they would be interested in including an African wildlife preserve and sanctuary in the project. These sanctuary stories are powerfully different in that they deal with animal rescue and survival as opposed to animal exhibition.

The idea is embraced and, like the water rushing over Victoria Falls, a dozen Dark Continent dominoes fall into place. The Pan African Sanctuary Alliance embraces this effort with powerful tales where the passion is palpable. For example, what do you do when you come across a bar in Tanzania where a chimpanzee has been taught to drink beer and smoke cigarettes so as to serve as a tourist attraction?

As the literary contributions are flowing in from all over the world, the final layer of depth that is lavished upon this crowning achievement is the importance of the expertise provided by the abundant array of animal advocacy groups which spring up to support their specific species. From the Amphibian Survival Alliance to the Australian Platypus Conservancy, if you are an animal walking, swimming or flying on this planet, rest assured that there is a group somewhere looking out for your best interests.

With this project developed to the level the Smiths had accomplished, it's probably not surprising that these animal advocacy groups would generously join the team, more than willing to contribute their knowledge to this noble cause. So if you thought my opening line of this review seemed suspect, now you know the nuances of how a book that begins with 2 authors can end up with more than 200!

The number crunch conclusion on *Crowning The Animal Kingdom* is that the Smiths have succeeded in the global networking of over 100 countries, all 50 states, 40 wildlife sanctuaries, and dozens of animal advocacy groups. With this book you will laugh, learn, and love. The goal of simultaneously informing and entertaining is realized here beyond anyone's expectations...

ACKNOWLEDGEMENTS

As you begin to read this project of passion, please allow us to kick off with some opening background notes. We are two retired school teachers who have published 5 books which are all available on Amazon. We also write two weekly columns, as well as frequent additional features, for our local paper in Rochester, NY. A restful retirement was not to be our destiny.

At this point we thought it appropriate to share a bit about our process, which actually underwent multiple levels of evolution along the trail from inception to completion. It all started with a love of animals which, if you're reading this at all, you probably share with us.

So while pondering the possibilities for book #6, we thought that was a topic we could get excited about. Let's run with it. A goal with all of our books has been to look for an approach that's a bit different from anything previously attempted. Subsequently we settled on the notion of trying to simultaneously serve science while cultivating pop culture.

We weren't trying to write a biology book and we weren't trying to write a media encyclopedia. (Even though the sound of the latter does have a nice ring to it.) We were just trying to employ a term that some reviewers have applied to our style which is "irreverent research". Lots of facts and lots of reflections filtered through a prism of scientific accuracy and sardonic wit.

Then the idea occurred to us that if we could engage some zoos and aquariums to share their stories, we could begin to connect some organizations while gleaning some material that was right from the horse's mouth, so to speak.

While remaining open to any input offered, we thought it would be advantageous to present the animal care facilities we contacted with some kind of consistent format they could use to participate in the project. Just unloading a request to, "Tell us about your zoo," seemed too dauntingly open-ended.

So we thought we'd come up with a template of questions which would prompt responses that would be interesting, but not so time consuming that people might be averse to completing the assignment because hey, they've got a job to do already!

We ultimately landed on a 3-part questionnaire asking each zoo or aquarium to share with us one of their...
Most unique animals
Oldest animals
Animals with a clever name

It seemed to be the perfect formula with some respondents offering answers that were short and sweet while others took the opportunity to share in depth about their facility's stories. It was all good and all now compiled as a part of this project.

With things on a roll, our next evolutionary leap came when a wildlife preserve in Uganda reached out to ask if we could share their story. Why not, right? And let us tell you, that Dark Continent is by no means light on laughter or devoid of drama! The stories came spilling in like waters rushing over the rapids.

Then we embarked upon what we would consider our final phase of evolutionary engagement, which was to bring in the various animal advocacy groups which are devoted to specific species. Our proposition basically went like this… "We have a chapter on your species and you obviously have a deeper level of expertise than we do. If you'll proofread and fact check our chapter, we'll acknowledge you by including your organization and mission statement in the book."

It struck us that this had to be one of the most mutually symbiotic concepts we'd ever come up with! The concern for environmental conservation is spread, the animal advocacy groups are acknowledged, and the expertise displayed in our material is heightened. This book uniquely started out with two authors and ended up with over 200, certainly validating the concept that there is strength in numbers.

Perhaps, not surprisingly, we received an unbelievably positive response from the animal organizations with whom we engaged. After all, these are people who have devoted themselves to their cause and tend to be more than willing to share, especially in the environment we have created of connecting the dots and networking the people who are passionate about *Crowning The Animal Kingdom*. Hey, that could be a title for the book!

And so it is.

Here's a nutshell summary of this book with which you are about to engage. Covering a wide variety of species, we offer a fun and factual introduction and then count down our list of the most renown animals in each species, fictional or real-life. The criteria which we considered in calculating our countdowns will be delineated below.

Conservation status is addressed where appropriate and the end product is a unique combination of history and humor, education and entertainment. We are telling some stories which strive to support animals, zoos, aquariums, and wildlife preserves while cultivating a world that values, respects, and conserves wildlife. Our hope is that there is a corps of people, who might not otherwise be exposed to the environmental and conservation topics we raise here, that will attain a level of interest through delving into this global zoological project.

IUCN Red List ~ While conservation status is assessed by many different organizations on a global level, the IUCN Red List has ascended to recognition as the preeminent system by which species status is assessed. From the organization's website, here is some background and the nine levels of assessment into which all species are categorized...

Established in 1964, The International Union for Conservation of Nature's Red List of Threatened Species has evolved to become the world's most comprehensive information source on the global conservation status of animal, fungi and plant species.

The IUCN Red List is a critical indicator of the health of the world's biodiversity. Far more than a list of species and their status, it is a powerful tool to inform and catalyze action for biodiversity conservation and policy change, critical to protecting the natural resources we need to survive. It provides information about range, population size, habitat and ecology, use and/or trade, threats, and conservation actions that will help inform necessary conservation decisions. Here are the 9 different classifications, along with the associated color coding:

NE: Not Established ~ white
DD: Data Deficient ~ gray
LC: Least Concern ~ dark green
NT: Near Threatened ~ light green

VU: Vulnerable ~ yellow
EN: Endangered ~ orange
CE: Critically Endangered ~ red
EW: Extinct in the Wild ~ purple
EX: Extinct ~ black

Our Rating System ~ In this project, as we outlined earlier, we have endeavored to take a unique approach to our animal countdowns by taking each species and counting down its most significant members. Obviously there is a certain level of subjectivity in play but slight nuances in the numbers are secondary to our primary goal which has been to inform as well as entertain. Nothing is life or death here with these ratings; let's just all have some fun!

That being said, we will share the basis by which we arrived at our admittedly-subjective ranking results. For each species of animal, we implemented a five-prong template of analysis upon which we rendered the rankings of our candidates. Those 5 elements we assessed were the animal's level of 1) fame, 2) humor, 3) importance, 4) influence and 5) intrigue. Obviously there's some overlap, but you get the idea.

The types of candidates available for consideration vary by species. The "Horses" component, for example, combines five rather distinct and mutually exclusive categories of candidates. There are race horses (Secretariat), live movie/TV star horses (the Lone Ranger's Silver), live non-movie star horses (the Clydesdales), animated horses (Bojack Horseman), and historical horses (the Trojan Horse).

Ranking horses within the same category can be done with some level of objectivity, for example race horses can be compared by times and/or victories, and movie/TV stars can be compared by the number of films and/or shows they appeared in. Those are, in a sense, apples-to-apples comparisons, but when it comes to apples-to-oranges comparisons, then it becomes totally subjective and, as we said, our goal was to just make logical decisions that people could have some fun with.

Tim & Deb Smith
Mendon, New York
February 1, 2024

Always looking for the opportunity to segue, we'll default to Walt and do Disney to transition out of the appetizers and into the main course. Here's our transition statement from a studio stalwart.

"So perhaps the best thing to do is to stop writing introductions and get on with the book." ~ Winnie The Pooh

LET'S KICK OFF THIS BALLYHOO, WITH OUR LEAD-OFF OVERVIEW

CHAPTER 1
STORYLINE SAMPLER

We felt a little bit like Noah as we embarked on this project of gathering up the animals and collecting them in a process of preservation. We wanted to make absolutely sure that every base had been covered and no stone was left unturned. It was a resolute goal to avoid what happened to Noah when the flood waters receded and he docked the ark to find that hoof-written note reading...

Dear Noah,
We could have sworn you said you were leaving at 2:00.
Sincerely,
The Unicorns

This ark is surely sailing into uncharted waters from a literary standpoint, attempting something heretofore unattempted. There are books out there on animals in the media and there are even more books out there on animals in general, which deal with endangered species and environmental concern issues to varying degrees, but if you scroll through your Amazon options you can confirm what we shared earlier; no one has ever taken the threads of zoological conservation, animal history, and animal humor and fed that trilogy through the eye of a single needle as happens here.

For this work in progress, one early reviewer coined a phrase we liked, referring to *Crowning The Animal Kingdom* as "A science book for humorists and a humor book for scientists." Over the next several hundred pages prepare yourself for some spontaneously succulent slices of laughter and learning. That's always a delectable combination and here's an assorted sampling of what's to come.

ZOO QUESTIONNAIRE ~ As we were in the research phase of this book, we had one unique notion occur to us that came to fruition on an even grander scale than we had anticipated. We thought we would reach out to zoos around the country, and around the world, with a similar set of questions, the responses to which would spark some interest, draw some comparisons, and provide some entertainment.

As we honed the concept, we landed on three as the perfect number of questions, not too few and not too many, and looked to craft questions that would satisfy the criteria stated in the previous sentence while not being too time consuming to answer. Our three-part query for each zoo was to share with us one or more of their...

Unique animals:
Older animals:
Animals with a clever name:

We will sample some of those responses in this opening chapter and we thought we'd lead with one response in its entirety, answering all three questions, and following this opening contribution, our Chapter 1 "storyline sampler" will cherry pick our favorite individual components from several submissions.

This sample submission, from the Givskud Zoo in Denmark, we liked because it features concision, conservation and comedy. Certainly a hat trick to herald! Givskud gave us...

More unique animals: Mountain Bongo. With about 400 animals in breeding programs in zoos worldwide, there are more captive bongos [a type of antelope] than there are bongos left in the wild.
Older animals: Plateosaurus trossingensis, 227 million years old (in our dinosaurpark ☻) or our white rhino "Sophie" who is 42 years old.
Animal with a clever name: Our pygmy hippo male is called "Microchip." His father was "Chip."

EARTH DAY ~ Perpetuating our passion for possums, we'll take you back to the first Earth Day when the premiere poster for the environmental initiative featured Pogo Possum from the classic *Pogo* comic strip. We are actually going to have to take you back to the War of 1812 for the setup on this one when, after winning the Battle of Lake Erie, Naval Commander Oliver Perry declared, "We have met the enemy and they are ours." Over a century and a half later, on April 22, 1970 when 20 million people attended inaugural events for the first Earth Day, the organizing committee retooled the quote for their poster. The image featured Pogo Possum standing amidst a patch of litter-strewn land about to attempt a clean-up.

The caption read, "We have met the enemy and he is us." It effectively made the point that people were responsible for the pollution problem and only people could solve it. A lasting legacy was launched.

SMOKEY BEAR ~ Here's our hypothetical story of what happened to Smokey while living at the Washington Zoo, which the iconic fire-fighting bear actually did from 1950-1976. This would have been the era during which Smokey achieved fame for his original environmental catch phrase of, "Only you can prevent forest fires." So the story goes...

One day Smokey hears a knock at the door of his cage and it's a ram from the sheep enclosure around the corner. The ram goes on to tell Smokey that he and his sister have just opened a flower store and he wants to share with Smokey a list of specials their store will be offering.

Smokey informs the ram that he cannot accept the list from him, but he can accept it from the ram's sister. When the confused ram asks why, Smokey says the reason should be obvious. It is, of course, that, "Only ewes can present florist fliers."

A GLOBAL ZOO ~ A major drive in this initiative was our global outreach to zoos which resulted in multiple moments of exhilaration upon being blessed with nuggets of knowledge and stirring stories from all over the planet. We heard from zoos who literally had bombs flying overhead while animals were giving birth on the ground, as well as zoos that exist at the bottom of the ocean. How can that happen?

Travel with us to the middle of the Indian Ocean, halfway between Africa and India, where you'll find the small island nation known as the Republic of Maldives. The native Maldivians proudly boast of their "Tiger Zoo" which is the heart of their primary tourist attraction… people deep sea diving to enjoy their large colony of offshore tiger sharks.

We pretty much circumnavigated the globe writing to animal care facilities in every location we could find. In light of the current situation in the world, one location we felt sure we would never hear from was Ukraine. Imagine our surprise when the following submission was received from Volodymyr Topchy, Director of Mykolaiv Zoo.

In response to our question about unique animals at the zoo he wrote, "We take pride in participating. Amur leopards are among the rarest animals kept and bred in our zoo. We have a pair of leopards, Rayo and Eva, who have been breeding regularly in Mykolaiv Zoo since 2014. Even in March 2022, during the war, when Mykolaiv was actually under siege, during daily shelling, a male cub of the Amur leopard was born in our zoo, he was named Aldan."

ZOO TV ~ Returning to some highlights from our zoo questionnaires, here are some responses linked by virtue of having movie/TV references. Two zoos opted for the macabre dark comedy of *The Addams Family* for their black vultures with the Colchester Zoo in England naming theirs Gomez and Morticia and the 3 Palms Zoo in Delaware going with Morticia and Lurch, both vividly employing vulturous vernacular.

Entertainment-themed names for animal groups also provided some raucous results with Zoo Miami cruising down *Sesame Street* to name their vultures Bert, Ernie, Grover, Oscar, and The Count. At Roger Williams Park Zoo in Providence, RI, their flock of scarlet ibises are named after the Pink Ladies in *Grease*… Marty, Rizzo, Frenchy and Jan. "Very fitting due to their bright pink color," added marketing director Vicki Scharfberg.

We hope to slay you with the last gasp on our Zoo TV component. In the "cleverest name" category the Wildlife World Zoo, Aquarium & Safari Park in Arizona nominated, "Our striped skunk named Buffy the Vampire Sprayer".

HOLIDAY BOOKENDS ~ We will have for you the story of the record-breaking cow who also just happened to be blessed with the most incredibly ironic birth and death dates. Check these out. This girl, named Big Bertha, is born in Ireland, on St. Patrick's Day, 1945 and then proceeds to live until New Year's Eve 1993.

Could there possibly be a better lifespan scenario that could assure people would be partying just as hard on the day you were born as they were on the day you died? We think not. The story gets even better when you find out how she makes it into Guinness World Records not once, but twice!

WHERE IN THE WORLD ZEBRAS? ~ If you were working without any inside information, one trivia question that would be pretty tough to nail would be, "Where on the planet could you find the largest herd of wild zebras outside the continent of Africa?" The answer to that question would be Central California, and we'll share the story of how the zebras who escaped from William Randolph Hearst's private zoo almost a century ago have not only survived, but actually thrived.

DAREDEVIL DEBAUCHERY ~ In the long and risky history of daredevils going over Niagara Falls in a barrel, there have been exactly two times when the humans chose to involve their pet animals. The animal lovers in our audience will probably be pleased to hear that in such situations the survival rate of the animals actually exceeds that of the humans. And if you go to the actual site of these historic events, you'll find yourself only a 5-minute walk away from Bird Kingdom, the largest indoor aviary in the world.

LONGEVITY LEVITY ~ Taking a look at animal longevity, sometimes can bring you some genuine levity. Worthy of note would be a species called the Greenland shark which can live over 400 years. Here's a strange-way-to-look-at-it shark stat... a Greenland shark that saw the Pilgrims dock the Mayflower at Plymouth Rock in 1620 could still be out there swimming off the coast of Massachusetts today.

That would make for a pretty nice run, or perhaps we should say swim, but the real heavy hitters remain as yet unnamed. You've got your red coral which, rallying around the cry of "Better red than dead" can stay alive, if immobile, for 500 years. There's a species of sponge that can soak up water for over 10,000 years.

But in *Crowning The Animal Kingdom*, as we profess to do in this book, the true legend of longevity in this category is a species of jellyfish which is actually immortal. Upon determination that the current life has run its due course, they revert to an earlier stage of their life cycle and proceed to just do it again.

SPANNING CENTURIES ~ Knowing that naturalist Charles Darwin lived from 1809-1882, and "The Crocodile Hunter" Steve Irwin lived from 1962-2006 would it surprise you to know that there was a specific animal, named "Harriet", that was actually handled by each of these two men? How that could actually happen sets us up to tell an amazing story you'll enjoy in Chapter 13.

PAVLOV'S DOGS ~ We're going to lead off this paean to Pavlov by quoting the rock group Barenaked Ladies from their hit song "Brian Wilson"…

> *It's a matter of instinct*
> *It's a matter of conditioning*
> *And a matter of fact*
> *You can call me Pavlov's Dog*
> *Ring a bell and I'll salivate*
> *How'd you like that?*

The Russian scientist Ivan Pavlov (1849-1936) is famous for his experiments on what he called, "classical conditioning". You all know the basics. You've got Pavlov, the dogs, the food, the salivation, and so on. But, believe it or not, one of the facts that you've read in this brief teaser is wrong. Do you know or can you guess which one?

FOOD FIESTA ~ While we've just established a focus on alliterative "F" words how 'bout we fly in with a flamboyance of flamingos. Yes, "flamboyance" is the word for a herd of that bird. The Nashville Zoo has Chilean flamingos named after chili peppers including Jalapeno, Ahi, and Cayenne. If you'd like some beans with your chili then head to Albuquerque where the ABQ BioPark is the home to their cheetah "beans", Garbanzo, Pinto & Borracho.

Staying in the states, Riverbanks Zoo & Garden in Columbia, SC pops with a corn snake named Kettle. Zoo Atlanta sizzles with Australian tawny frogmouth birds named Tater Tot and Hashbrown and Pennsylvania's Lehigh Valley Zoo is home to a wildcat named Shishka Bobcat.

Moving overseas to visit war-torn countries past and present, the Vinpearl Safari in Vietnam shares with us that they have "three white rhinoceros born in our zoo, named Cà Phê, Sữa, Đá (which means Coffee, Milk, Ice in English respectively). While hoping the bombs continue to miss them, Ukraine's Mykolaiv Zoo reports that "Interesting 'sweet, milky' names have our polar bears. They are Sour Cream (Smetanka) and Marshmallow (Zephyrka)."

CRAZY PARADE ~ Okay, it's 1826 and we want you to picture yourself in small-town France, before the advent of even nominal modern-day advances such as trains or electricity, let alone cars. The only vehicles that might have been advancing through your village would have been horse-drawn carriages and perhaps the most primitive versions of the bicycle which had recently been invented.

Suddenly you see some movement, down the road, on the horizon. There's not much else to look at so you keep your gaze focused on the approaching entourage which, as it draws closer, is seen to include an elderly French scientist, a middle-aged Black Arab animal keeper, three cows, and a giraffe. This might be the spot, if history were seeking an apropos opportunity, for the French to first invoke their classic interjection of surprise, "Sacré bleu!" Details are forthcoming…

AFRICAN ANTICS ~ One somewhat unexpected direction this project took occurred when wildlife preserves and animal sanctuaries in Africa began reaching out to us with requests to tell their tales. Up to that point most of the zoos and aquariums with whom we'd been in contact had been sharing stories of serene settings with engaging exhibitions of animals created upon a conservational foundation.

These dedicated folks in Africa are facing situations of rescue and survival as they deal with predatory poachers and illegal animal traffickers who are maniacally motivated by money alone and whose hearts are absolutely devoid of all compassion for the creatures you must love if you're reading this book in the first place.

One moving example comes from the Chimfunshi Wildlife Orphanage Trust where they told us of their chimpanzee, Mila whose story is guaranteed to "fill your heart with sorrow." Captured and purchased as a baby in Cameroon, she was taken to Tanzania at the age of three and taught to be a tavern attraction by drinking beer and smoking cigarettes for the purpose of entertaining patrons.

Made aware of the situation the legendary anthropologist Dr. Jane Goodall personally intervened, initiating an endeavor which would lead to Mila's relocation to Chimfunshi in Zambia, and a story which we will complete later. And while we do have ample African accolades to bestow, heroic efforts to save the animals are not limited to this continent.

ASIAN ANTICS ~ Next, we'll take you to Asia where the Lao Conservation Trust for Wildlife works to fulfill a mission purpose of eradicating the illegal wildlife trade while improving wildlife education and welfare in Laos. In responding to the older animal question, they shared the story of Keaw Khun, their 48-year-old elephant who, while she did adeptly dodge the desire to run away and join the circus, trudged the trail of life from logging elephant, to riding elephant, to zoo elephant before eventually being transferred to LCTW's care, "where she was freed from her chain and given an enclosure."

"Last year, she was transferred to the specialized Elephant Conservation Center (ECC) where she is part of a reintroduction program, learning to live in the forest and live with other elephants. If all goes well, she will be fitted with a radio collar and live as a free elephant for the remainder of her life."

In working their way through the questions we posed, our friends from Laos adeptly moved from this heartwarming rescue story to wreaking some humorous havoc in their version of the name game. In terms of a series of thematic plays on words, we found the naming efforts of the team at LCTW to be a particularly stellar rock 'n roll revival. With zoos around the world making music a common theme for intriguing names, we felt a need to wax poetic and deliver the following global analysis…

> *While musical names were a common endeavor*
> *We found those Laotians exceedingly clever*
> *With those pun battles raging all over the house*
> *There were none could compete with those punsters from Laos*
> *Challenging wordplays they conquered like hurdles*
> *With ingenious musical names for their turtles*

Prompting the promenade down a musical path from…
Elvis Presley→Elton John→Alice Cooper→Alice in Chains→Shania Twain, those musical magicians from Laos coined a turtle shell shellacking shining the spotlight on…
Shellvis→Shellton John→Shellice Cooper→Shellice in Chains→Shellia Twain

ZOO MUSIC ~ Returning to some highlights from our zoo questionnaires, here are some responses linked by having musical themes. The aforementioned small Indian Ocean island nation of the Maldives is particularly proud of its Tiger Zoo which isn't exactly what it sounds like on the surface, a topic which we'll tackle in a bit. On its roster the Maldives boasts a trio of tiger sharks named Rhianna, J.Lo, and Shakira.

Meanwhile, over at the North Carolina Zoo they are rockin' and rollin' with Bat Benatar while Zoo Idaho counters with Tina Turtle. Back at 3 Palms in Delaware their Indian blue peacock struts his stuff as Elton John and if they could just teach that peacock to sing "Crocodile Rock" they would really have an animal hit on their hands!

LEFT SHARK ~ One of our more surprising stories comes from the 2015 Katy Perry Super Bowl half-time show. During an expansively choreographed performance of "Teenage Dream" Perry finds herself immersed amidst a stage backdrop of surfboards, dancing beach balls, and at the key point in question, flanked by two supersized costumed dancing sharks.

It is what happens when the choreography is intentionally abandoned by the shark to the left of Perry that makes this moment become one of the most viral in Super Bowl history. Full details are swimming on the horizon but sample reactions include Snoop Dogg tweeting, "If you were wondering, that was me inside the Shark costume!!" Alas, a confession.

HEARTFELT REALITY ~ "Until you have loved an animal, part of your soul will have remained dormant." Doesn't this quote tug at your heartstrings? It appeared in the email tagline we received from the Bear Creek Exotic Wildlife Sanctuary in Canada, which also happens to be the only place in the world where you can find a live jaglion (offspring of male jaguar and female lion). What's not to love?

OLYMPIC MASCOTS ~ If you love a story where the irreverent, rebellious, underground rises up against the establishment, and uses the establishment's rules to beat them at their own game, then you'll want to buckle up for our joyous ride to the 2000 Summer Olympic games in Australia.

Here, our storyline features the two hosts of a sports/comedy TV show creating an unofficial Olympic mascot to compete with the official native Australian mascots created by the country's Olympic committee which were Syd (a platypus), Millie (an echidna), and Olly (a kookaburra).

So what did our irreverent comedians conjure up for the competition? How 'bout Fatso the Fat-Arsed Wombat! Brace yourself for the fun and games when the wombat is totally embraced by the athletes and media casting a truly fat-arsed shadow over the official mascots.

HOLLYWOOD HIJINKS ~ We will be heading out to Hollywood for a few stories. In the category of most accomplished casting, we'll reveal the group of animated female characters whose voice artists included Christina Applegate, Kaley Cuoco, Anna Faris, and Amy Poehler.

Simultaneously switching gears and genders, we'll share the story of what live animal George Clooney was sharing his bed with when his supermodel girlfriend issues the ultimatum, "Either the animal goes or I go!" The animal lovers in our audience will enjoy this ending much more than the supermodels will. Which is probably not a bad thing for us.

DISNEY DYNAMOS ~ Trying to take advantage of every animal allusion opportunity afforded, let's piggyback on the movie theme to see what kind of a Disney deep-dive delve we can do into the zoo-pool of animals named after this studio's stars. In our Disney disclaimer, we'll let you know we're saving the best for last. Think fateful fire.

But before the blaze, let's head to La Palmyre Zoo in France where, "Our twins, Bearded Emperor tamarins (monkeys) named Tic and Tac, are the French names for the famous Walt Disney characters Chip 'n Dale." In Kentucky, at the Louisville Zoo, they have four black swans named after Disney princesses Ariel, Aurora, Jasmine, and Mulan.

And heading back to France for our fave, let's visit Zoo de Doue-la-Fontaine where we'll return to the day of April 15, 2019. Late tax filer or not, do you remember where you were that day? Maybe we can help you. That was the day the Notre-Dame Cathedral in Paris caught fire and burned.

As the staff at Zoo de Doue-la-Fontaine watched footage of the fire on CNN, a baby female giraffe was born at their zoo which had not yet been named. Seizing the historical moment, the staff decides to default to the Disney feature *The Hunchback of Notre Dame* and use the name of the film's female heroine to bless their new baby giraffe with the beautiful name of Esmerelda.

MISCELLANY ~ Right now we're going to rapid fire some scattershot short and sweet quick-hitting questions at you…

* Did you know that the teddy bear is named after an actual famous person named Teddy? Do you know which Ted, and/or would you like to proffer your guess?

* In over 100 years of Disney history, there have only been three snake protagonists. Walt was never sold on snake heroes.

* "Which came first, the chicken or the egg?" If you'd like to crack this one open for the last time, we've got *National Geographic* on the line to provide you with the definitive answer once and for all.

* If you had to pick one example to be the "Best Oxymoron in the Book" would you go with "jumbo shrimp" or "pygmy hippopotamus"?

QUOTATION SENSATION ~ You may, or may not, be familiar with the *Kung Fu Panda* franchise, but either way, we have two wonderful quotes we'd like to share. The overarching sage and spiritual leader of the franchise, was the elderly Galápagan tortoise Grand Master Oogway.

Oogway addresses the philosophical from a platitude of perspectives, acknowledging the realities of life by saying, "One often meets his destiny on the road he takes to avoid it." Our favorite however is when he pontificates that, "You are too concerned with what was and what will be. There's a saying: Yesterday is history, tomorrow is a mystery, but today is a gift. That is why it is called the present."

SECTION ONE
IN THE JUNGLE THINGS DO RUMBLE, IN THE WOODS IT'S ROUGH & TUMBLE

CHAPTER 2

LIONS & TIGERS & BEARS, OH MY!

LIONS

The King of the Beasts and the Lord of the Jungle, the lion certainly reigns as regal. Visually awe-inspiring, they are the embodiment of superbly esteemed characterizations such as bravery, loyalty and strength. Time for them to roar.

Size ~ In terms of size, male lions can exceed 500 pounds and grow to 10 feet long. Females can weigh as much as 350 pounds and reach lengths of 8 feet. Their roar is used to announce their presence to others as well as to communicate amongst themselves, and when they really give it their all, that roar can resonate over distances of up to 10 miles.

Speed ~ Lions are not as fast as cheetahs, but they can hit a top speed of 50 mph which, if maintained throughout a hypothetical all-animal 100-yard dash race, would result in a 100-yard dash time (hereafter referred to as a "100-YDT") of 4.1 seconds.

Life ~ In terms of lifespan, lions live to an age of 15 to 19 in the wild, and 25 or more in captivity. The oldest documented life span of a captive lion was that of Arjun who lived his entire life at the Indian Animal Rescue Center at the Indira Gandhi Zoological Park in Kolkata, India. He passed away at the age of 29 on May 17, 2018. According to Lion Guardians co-founder and Director of Science, Dr. Stephanie Dolrenry, "The oldest known wild lion was Loonkiito who lived in the Amboseli ecosystem of southern Kenya. He lived to the age of 19."

Lions live in groups called prides which can include up to 40 members consisting of a select handful of adult males, several related adult females and an assortment of mixed cubs. Upon reaching the age of about 2, the males disperse out from their family group and traverse a wide area looking for suitable habitat and available females to form their own prides.

Dr. Dolrenry noted that prides can change day to day/hour to hour. Within the pride a sense of community exists whereby the females will communally protect and nurse each other's cubs sharing the burden of motherhood.

They usually hunt at night, when their visual acuity affords them an advantage, and/or during storms when the noise and wind make them less discernable to their prey. It is the females that do most of the hunting and they even have "positions," so to speak, that are reminiscent of a hockey team with a "center" flanked by right and left "wings". And it is the job of the wings to drive the prey into the center.

So if you wanted to find a lion in the world today, where would you go? There is a relatively small pocket of them in western India, but for the most part you'd want to head to sub-Saharan Africa. Your top 6 picks for lion licks would be the countries of Tanzania, Kenya, Botswana, South Africa, Zambia, and Zimbabwe.

Conservation Status ~ There are estimated to be less than 20,000 lions left in the world, as compared to 450,000 elephants, so it's time to act for the preservation of our golden-maned feline friends. The International Union for Conservation of Nature (hereafter referred to as IUCN) has listed their status as "vulnerable" since 1996.

Right now let's let out a roar for our Nine Fine Lions…

 # 9) CECIL ~ Here's a lion that makes the list for all the wrong reasons, the victim of a compound bow and arrow shooting in the African country of Zimbabwe in July of 2015. The villain of the story would be an American dentist and recreational hunter named Walter Palmer who paid two native guides $50,000 to enable him to shoot and kill a lion. Here's what happens…

On the evening of July 1st, the pair of unethical natives lures Cecil out of the Hwange National Park into territory where he is unprotected. Around 10:00 pm that evening Palmer shoots and wounds Cecil, then tracks him until the following morning when he kills the lion with a second arrow. Cecil is then decapitated and skinned before his body is left to be scavenged by vultures.

When the news breaks to international outrage, Palmer skedaddles back home to his dentist office in Bloomington, Minnesota and basically plays dumb, proffering the perspective that he doesn't realize he has done anything wrong. Unfortunately, the particulars of how the poaching has played out, make it impossible to prosecute Palmer in Zimbabwe.

Subsequently Palmer finds himself targeted by the general wrath and outrage of the American public which for the most part finds his hunting escapade to be reprehensible. Before scrambling out of the country, Palmer had returned Cecil's head and skin to Zimbabwe officials in an attempt to quell the international furor that had arisen over his actions. So ends the story of the most infamous African lion of the 21st century.

Liaison Lindsey ~ At this point it's time for an introduction. In the course of our research on this project we found ourselves in communication with biology professor John Koprowski, who is also the Dean of the Haub School of Environment & Natural Resources at the University of Wyoming. Dr. Koprowski had emerged as the nation's #1 expert on squirrels. (We'll hear from him in Chapter 17.) After reviewing our material, he told us he had a student he would like to connect with us, describing her as, "Supremely talented, experienced with zoos and wildlife more generally, and on my top 10 list of most pleasant people that I know!"

Well, it's rather difficult to walk away from an endorsement like that, so therein lies the backstory of Lindsey Mitchell's entrance into this zoological project. While we call in a guest expert or two for almost all of the species in our book, Lindsey will, as of this moment, assume the role of color commentator for the remainder of this book.

She's knowledgeable, she's funny, and she certainly knows her way around the animal kingdom. Prepare to be both entertained and informed by her contributions on a regular basis moving forward. You're going to be so impressed that you'll want to know a little bit about her, so here's the story.

Lindsey graduated from the University of Wyoming in 2024, having introduced herself by saying, "I am now a senior at the University of Wyoming, and I am double majoring in Wildlife Biology and Management, along with Environment and Natural Resources, with a minor in American Politics! I was the vice president of our student chapter in The Wildlife Society, and I have been working in Dr. Koprowski's lab for a little over a year now, helping with one of his grad student's projects!

I think this project and what you are both doing is incredible!"

At this point the podium will be turned over for the first time to Lindsey Mitchell, hereafter referred to as "Liaison Lindsey", and enable her to put a final perspective on the story of Cecil.

Part of this we're going to have to describe in our own words because they are based upon charts which will not appear in the book. These charts, shown to us by Lindsey, tracked hits on Facebook and Twitter before and after Jimmy Kimmel delivered a scathing rant decrying the actions of Dr. Palmer. It was an appeal so impassioned that Kimmel actually teared up during the delivery.

So the charts showed a tremendous outpouring of conservational outrage with a graph line that looked like the Empire State Building, peaking and fading almost instantly. In assessing these charts Lindsey said, "I was shown these figures in a class and found them interesting because it shows there **was** public concern and uproar, but it didn't last long and didn't translate into individuals becoming involved with lion conservation. When things like this happen, there is an increased awareness, but this does not always translate into increased conservation action."

 # 8) SNAGGLEPUSS ~ How can you not love this 1960's Hanna-Barbera concept… We've got a snazzy pink mountain lion, wearing a bow tie, along with upturned collar, and cuffs, who loves to quote Shakespeare. And while he had a few notable catch phrases, his signature salutation of jubilation was one the writers coined specifically for him. Before Snagglepuss no one had ever exclaimed, "Heavens to Murgatroyd!" Now let's "exit stage left" and head to #7 in the countdown.

 # 7) SCAR, from Disney's *The Lion King* ~ When it debuted in 1994, awash with themes of treachery, betrayal and death, *The Lion King* was destined to be one of Disney's darker endeavors, and no character cast a more sinister shadow than the scurrilous Scar. With hints of *Hamlet* and Hitler the character evokes imagery laden with historical stature.

The channeling of the play *Hamlet*'s brother-killing-brother-in-order-to-usurp-the-throne plotline casts Scar in the role of Hamlet's evil Uncle Claudius, thus sliding Simba into the slot of Hamlet. In both storylines, of course, the deposed son of the rightful king will eventually avenge the murder of his father and assume the throne.

What's inherited from Hitler has more to do with style than story. At the height of the rise of Nazism, Adolph Hitler held a huge rally in Nuremburg in 1934 which was documented in the 1935 propaganda film *Triumph of the Will*. Disney animators actually used that film as a model to create the goose-stepping march of Scar's hyena henchmen during the song "Be Prepared".

Scar has certainly ascended the ranks of most reviled villains. Publications which list him in their "Top 10" of villainy include *E!*, *Yahoo*, and *Entertainment Weekly*. In the *Huffington Post*'s "A Definitive Ranking of 25 Classic Disney Villains" Scar scores the #1 position.

 # 6) DANIEL'S LIONS, from the Bible ~ It was quite possibly the worst sleep-over ever and we've got the down-and-dirty details for you. Let's set the Wayback Machine with the following coordinates... Time: about 250 B.C.; Location: Persia. The era is pre-Jesus and pre-Muhammad, so there's no Christians or Muslims. Your two teams in the game are the Jews and the Pagans so you can pretty much guess who Vegas has listed as the early favorite to win this one.

So here's what happens. Darius is the King of Persia and Daniel is a devout Jew who has risen to a high rank in the court of Darius. Some Pagans, who have grown jealous of Daniel, convince King Darius that it would be in his best interest to sign an edict which decrees that for 30 days no man should pray to any power other than Darius with "being thrown to the lions" established as the penalty for violation of said edict.

Devout Daniel continues to pray to his God, subsequently enabling the Pagans to call upon Darius to enforce the edict he has established. Valuing Daniel's service to Persia, Darius does not want to enforce the punishment but he has essentially painted himself into a corner. Led to the lions' den for an overnighter, Daniel prays to God who sends an angel to close the jaws of the lions.

When Darius goes to the den in the morning and finds Daniel alive this is viewed as evidence of Daniel's righteousness, and the King commands that the conspirators who opposed Daniel be thrown to the lions along with their families.

You know what they say about payback! The long version of this story can be found in the Book of Daniel, Chapter 6.

 # 5) THE MGM LION ~ This one lion claws his way to a lofty perch on the countdown tree by virtue of the fact that if you're reading this book, despite the lack of immediate name recognition, you've probably seen the MGM lion at least a hundred times. He became the iconic mascot for the Hollywood film studio Metro-Goldwyn-Mayer (MGM) when it was formed in 1917.

Various lions have appeared during the intro of MGM films over the years, but from *Casablanca* to *Rocky* to *The Terminator* to *The Wizard of Oz,* you've seen the lion roar in every opening.

For the first decade the lions just looked around in the opening sequence as the era of sound, or the "talkies", was not ushered in until 1927. MGM used multiple lions to fill the bill over the studio's first four decades, but it has been Leo the Lion who has roared during the opening of most every MGM film since 1957.

 # 4) MUFASA, from Disney's *The Lion King* ~ "Look at the stars, the great kings look down on us from those stars... And so will I." Perhaps no voice resonates deeper in Disney canons than that of James Earl Jones bringing the character of Mufasa to life, as well as to death, in both the 1994 original and the 2017 remake.

It is on a morning outing to survey the kingdom from the symbolic perch atop Pride Rock that the conversation takes place. "A king's time as ruler rises and falls like the sun," says Mufasa. "One day, Simba, the sun will set on my time here and will rise with you as the new king."

"I'm going to be King of Pride Rock," responds Simba. "I want to be brave like you."

Discouraging false bravado, Mufasa's response is, "I'm only brave when I have to be." Mufasa's impactful presence in the film remains powerful beyond the relatively short period of time while he is alive. After Scar brings about Mufasa's death, and Simba's exile, Mufasa must exert his influence over Simba from the heavens.

 # 3) CHRISTIAN ~ Okay, admittedly, this one scores high in the ratings because, while you probably haven't heard it yet, the story is so good we guarantee you'll be moved.

There are multiple occasions in this book where we suggest that you watch a video related to the writing, but we only have one opportunity to say that this is **the** one you should absolutely check out on YouTube at "Christian the Lion: Original Viral Video". Here's the story…

In 1969, Australians Ace Bourke and John Rendall, who are then living in London, purchase a lion cub from Harrods Department store which is dealing in exotic animals at the time. They name the cat Christian and frivolity ensues… for the next year.

Christian leads a high-profile life being driven around in their Mercedes, hanging out at the beach, attending glamorous parties, and eating the finest food. The men obtain permission from a local church to use their adjacent enclosed graveyard as an exercise site and they adapt the basement of the furniture store they own into living quarters for Christian. The name of the store is actually Sophistocat, so it's almost as if the universe has aligned for the pet and his owners.

But alas, as Christian grows older, and more importantly larger, it becomes apparent that a "Plan B" is in order. As fate would have it, actors Bill Travers and Virginia McKenna who have recently starred in the movie *Born Free* stop by their store to see the lion, and Christian's owners share their dilemma.

Subsequently Bourke and Rendall share their connection with George and Joy Adamson who were in charge of the lions in *Born Free* and also operate a lion compound at the Kora National Reserve in Kenya. The Adamsons had reintroduced *Born Free*'s Elsa to the wild and offer to do the same for Christian. With no other viable option on the table, the Adamsons are taken up on their offer.

Obviously men of means, one year after Christian's move to Kenya, Bourke and Rendall decide to pay their old pet a visit and head off to Africa, all the while thinking, "Maybe we'll make a documentary movie about the reunion." Upon arrival in Kenya, Adamson advises the men that he is skeptical about whether or not Christian will remember his former owners an entire year after having last seen them.

If you'd like to enjoy seeing how this plays out live, before we give it all away, you should go to the video right now and be forewarned, it may well bring a tear to your eye. With the cameras rolling, Bourke and Rendall venture out into the reserve calling Christian. Upon making eye contact, the lion initially approaches them with caution as if he's thinking, "Is that really who I think it is?"

When the recognition is confirmed, Christian charges the men for one of the most magical movie moments ever. The lion stands on his back legs and alternately embraces each man. The way he wraps his arms around their shoulders, nuzzles their faces and kisses them is just heavenly heartwarming.

Turning the whole thing into the ultimate family affair, Christian summons his two lioness partners, Mona and Lisa, as well as their cub, Supercub, to share the love. It's all documented in the film *Christian, The Lion at World's End*.

There would be one more reunion, the following year. When Bourke and Rendall reveal to Adamson their plan to return, he tells the men it is likely to be a wasted effort as Adamson has not seen Christian in nine months. Then, almost as if the result of some kind of divine animal intervention, Christian and his family return to the reserve the day before the arrival of his previous owners.

On this occasion Rouke, Rendall and Christian spend nine days together, their final nine days, before the lion hears the calling that it is his time to return to the wild. Gathering his family, Christian walks away one morning and the men would never see him again.

 # 2) THE COWARDLY LION, from *The Wizard of Oz* ~ Here we have the ultimate jungle paradox, a scaredy-cat lion. That is the conundrum which connects the Cowardly Lion to the Oz entourage looking to solve his problem as well as those of Dorothy, the Scarecrow and the Tin Man.

Upon their initial encounter, the lion displays a false sense of bravado challenging the Scarecrow and the Tin Man to, "Put 'em up, put 'em up!" It is only when Dorothy defuses the situation with a slap-in-the-face submission on the part of the lion, that he is exposed as cowardly. In his own words, the lion details his psychological status as follows…

I'm afraid there's no denyin'
I'm just a Dandy-Lion,
a fate I don't deserve!
But I could show my prowess
be a Lion, not a mouse
If I only had the nerve!

Playing upon the premise that there's probably not a lot of prerequisite plot summary necessary on this one, suffice it to say that the lion is actually pre-possessed of the qualities of bravery, a fact of which he is only made aware in the film's dramatic conclusion.

 # 1) SIMBA, from Disney's *The Lion King* ~ After defeating Scar, Simba channels his father Mufasa by reflecting upon the prophetic words the elder had once spoken to him… "Somebody once told me that the great kings of the past are up there, watching over us."

The storyline has Simba (Swahili for lion) being born a prince destined to one day be king before having that destiny seemingly taken away from him. When ultimately faced with the recognition of what he must do, Simba reflects upon his impending return reluctantly acknowledging, "But going back means I'll have to face my past. I've been running from it for so long."

Let's defer to producer Don Hahn's thoughts on Simba's plight at this stage of the story… "So that idea of redemption, that idea of that day in your life that you have to take responsibility for yourself, that you're no longer a child, you're an adult; all those themes resonated with us when we were making the movie and, thankfully, the audience appreciated them, as well."

Speaking of the filmmakers, while much was made of the plot similarities to Shakespeare's *Hamlet*, director Roger Allers revealed that it was totally unintentional. He commented that, after one brainstorming session had altered a few storylines, someone out of the blue "announced that its themes and relationships were similar to *Hamlet*."

That was not considered to be a bad thing so obviously they went with it, but here's an alternate take on the story's origins that provides some historical humor. Based upon the plot involving the death of a protagonist's parent, and prior to any reference to *Hamlet*, some in the room had been joking that an alternate title for the film in progress might be *Bambi in Africa*.

TIGERS

Here's the craziest tiger revelation we came across in our research... hold on to your safari hats, folks! There are now approximately three times as many tigers living in captivity as there are in the wild. Yep, you read that right! While sources regarding tiger counts vary, the average from our research lands at about 12,000 in captivity (mainly the U.S. and China) and less than 4,000 still roaming free in the wild (all in Asia).

As we began our process of reaching out to animal advocacy experts, our first response on this tiger component came from Carole Baskin, CEO of Big Cat Rescue. She told us, "While it may be more detail than you want to give regarding the number of captive tigers vs. wild tigers, I'd love it if you could include something like: But get this – only about 500 of those caged tigers in the U.S. were calling legit zoos home; the rest were hanging out in Aunt Sally's backyard or some dodgy roadside attraction. That was until the Big Cat Public Safety Act swooped in like a superhero on December 22, 2022, making it illegal for Aunt Sally – or anyone not running a legitimate zoo – to possess these majestic creatures. This law also put an end to the cub petting industry, which was basically the tiger version of a puppy mill. So, hats off to progress!"

An alternate take on this situation was provided by Mindy Stinner, President of the Feline Conservation Foundation who told us, "You should probably also be aware that the Big Cat Public Safety Act did not actually make it illegal for someone to own a big cat as a pet; it requires a registration process for those animals and prohibits additional acquisition of new animals. Since FOIA, [Freedom of Information Act] requests have made it clear that only a small number of cats have been registered (fewer than 20 owners), we must assume that the thousands of tigers once estimated to be owned by private individuals simply don't exist. While the registration process is imperfect and we must assume there are still some illegal cats out there, large numbers seem highly unlikely."

We'll follow that up with crazy tiger revelation #2. Right now, raise your hand if it surprises you to find out that tigers do not now, nor did they ever, live in Africa. Okay, if you want to split tiger hairs, about two million years ago some tiger ancestors were living on the dark continent before ambling over to Asia where they could replace lions at the top of the food chain. But in anything even slightly connected to the modern era, Africa had no tigers.

So where do you find them in Asia? Their habitat spans southeast Asia, starting in Thailand and spreading through India, Bangladesh, Bhutan and Nepal into northeastern regions of the continent in China and Russia. They can also be found in the island nation of Indonesia. Let's move on to some tiger stats.

Life ~ Carole Baskin (Big Cat) also added that, "Regarding life expectancy, it's interesting to note the numbers. Now, let's be clear: wild tigers don't fill out surveys or have a say in their living conditions. But just for laughs, let's imagine if they could understand these statistics. In the wild, a tiger's life expectancy is about 7-10 years. Compare that to captivity, where those numbers can stretch to 16-23 years, and you might think a tiger would invest in a 'retirement cage-fund' – if they had any idea what that was or any desire for such a thing, which, of course, they absolutely don't."

We'll need to travel to the Kanpur Zoological Park, the largest in north India, to cover the story of the longest living tiger ever. On January 15, 2014 Kanpur mourned the death of the male tiger Guddu who had lived to be 26 years old.

Size ~ In our various literary endeavors, we often opt for clusters of three in exemplifying the myriad of concepts we cover, so right now we'll defer to that approach and offer up crazy tiger revelation #3. Okay, it's not exactly crazy, but let's at least call it surprising. If, before picking up this book, you were asked to guess which species of cat was the largest, would you have chosen lions or tigers?

By now you can certainly see where we're going with this. What with all that "King-of-the-Jungle" clamor clanging in the background, one might be inclined to assume that the lions were the big boys on the block, but not so fast. Tigers are actually the big dog on the big cat size-monitor. They weigh up to 700 pounds and can reach 11 feet in length.

Speed ~ While they could not outrun a lion or a cheetah, they could definitely outrun you. With a top speed of about 45 mph tigers have a 100-YDT of 4.5 seconds.

Conservation Status ~ In 2010 the 13 Asian countries with extant tiger populations came together for "The St. Petersburg Declaration on Tiger Conservation" and established July 29th as Global Tiger Day. The proclamation was issued that in "the past century, tiger numbers have plummeted from 100,000 to below 3,500, and continue to fall. Tiger numbers and habitat have declined by 40 percent in the last decade alone, lost largely to habitat loss, poaching, the illegal wildlife trade, and human-tiger conflict. Three subspecies have already disappeared, and none of the other six are secure." (Population is now back to 4,000.)

Species Research ~ Mindy Stinner (Feline Conservation) added, "It [would be interesting to cover] the re-categorization of tiger subspecies. It's not often that the taxonomy of a whole species is called into question, but genetic research conducted over the past decade has made a strong argument that all of the mainland tigers in the world are one subspecies, with some variations in size and coat texture across geographic ranges."

"Separate from the mainland, tigers found on Sumatra, Java, and Borneo make up their own subspecies. They have been separated from the mainland for potentially a million years, which means their evolutionary track is very independent. These cats are smaller and well adapted to island life. It completely turns on its head the idea that tigers from India and Siberia are only distantly related… It's the same cat with some minor adaptations."

And in closing, we'll share that tigers are also capable of altruism; male tigers will often let their mates and cubs eat before they do. The lion kingdom is not capable of such compassion. Now strap on your racing stripes and we'll charge into the countdown of our Top 5 Tigers.

 # 5) HOBBES, from *Calvin and Hobbes* ~ Waxing philosophical, while also flashing a clear consciousness of capitalism, Hobbes once pointedly pontificated the theory that, "Van Gogh would've sold more than one painting if he'd put tigers in them." Processing that comment, you can't be sure how talented Van Gogh was at painting animals as opposed to painting nature scenes and starry nights, but there is one unavoidable truth in Hobbes' statement; he couldn't have sold many fewer paintings. Moral: In trying times, attempt a tiger.

From 1985-1995 Bill Watterson published his *Calvin and Hobbes* comic strip, the retirement of which was mourned by many. The title characters were a precocious adventurous 6-year-old boy and his stuffed animal tiger who would come to life in the mind of Calvin, but not to any of the other humans they would encounter. Hobbes' de facto duty was to provide the voice of reason to calm Calvin's calamitous urges and eccentricities. Sometimes a tough task to tackle.

 # 4) MANACORE, the Siegfried & Roy tiger ~ The date was October 3, 2003 when the bite was taken out of the act, or perhaps put into the act may be the more appropriate description. This is the story of the only real-life tiger prominent enough historically to make our countdown. Reflective of the two men behind the show, this is a story both magic and tragic.

This one perhaps resonates more than most because not only are there real people involved, the zenith of the story occurred within the memories of most of our readers. Siegfried Fischbacher and Roy Horn were a pair of magicians and entertainers who began their Las Vegas stage act in 1967. Eventually they became most famous for introducing white tigers into their act which sets up this saga.

Here's what happens… during a performance at the Mirage Resort and Casino, Horn is attacked on stage by a 7-year-old white tiger named Mantacore. In the best spontaneous response to the time-honored tradition that "the show must go on" Horn holds his mic to the mouth of Mantacore with the hopeful suggestion that the tiger "say hello to the audience."

At this point, with neither the man nor the tiger following the script, Mantacore grabs Horn by his neck and drags him off stage. Worst exit ever. While Horn has suffered injuries from which he will never fully recover, his words upon being loaded into the ambulance are, "Mantacore is a great cat. Make sure no harm comes to Mantacore."

Horn's request was honored and while he did survive, the Las Vegas gig was essentially over forever for multiple obvious reasons.

 # 3) SHERE KHAN, from *The Jungle Book* ~ A hatred of man is the common thread linking all incarnations of Shere Khan, although the nuances of the antagonist character vary slightly from one treatment of *The Jungle Book* to the next. And there have been at least a dozen takes on the story beginning with Rudyard Kipling's 1894 version, continuing through the Disney interpretations, and most recently with Netflix.

 # 2) TONY THE TIGER ~ Originally it was a 4-way competition. Simultaneously breaking out of the starting gate in the race to become the mascot for Kellogg's signature cereal in 1952, we had Elmo the Elephant, Katie the Kangaroo, Newt the Gnu and Tony the Tiger. Clearly the preeminent participant prevailed. The final design came from a former Disney artist who would go on to develop other iconic characters ranging from the Jolly Green Giant to the Baltimore Orioles mascot.

In the career of an advertising icon that spans seven decades one would expect some changes to occur, and with Tony the most notable were connected to society becoming more health conscious. Even the name of the product changed with the original brand of "Sugar Frosted Flakes" eventually deleting the word "Sugar".

Tony's body also got a buff-up. Originally designed like a real tiger, he morphed into a more human-looking physique, even sporting a bit of a body-builder vibe with a thinner waist and broader shoulders, about which it could be said, "They're Gr-r-r-eat!"

Animal Planet ranks Tony the Tiger as #19 on its list of "50 Greatest TV Animals."

 # 1) TIGGER, from *Winnie the Pooh* ~ "Look at those beady little eyes, that preposterous chin, and those ridiculous striped pajamas," serves as a perfect piece of self-deprecating self-description when Tigger sees his own reflection in a mirror and does not realize he's looking at himself. Facial features and wardrobe woes notwithstanding, Tigger still manages to bounce his way into the #1 spot on our tiger countdown.

That being said, keep in mind the word "tiger" is totally banned from the world of Winnie the Pooh. It literally never comes up, even once. And in case you might need a pneumonic device to remember how to avoid the spelling faux pas of using "tiger" in a Pooh piece, we'll share the following Tigger quote. "Glad to meet ya! Name's Tigger. T-I-double 'guh'-er! That spells Tigger!"

BEARS

If you've been looking forward to this one so fervently you could almost taste the eucalyptus leaves, brace yourself for the bad news... koala bears are not actually bears. Furthermore, the entire continent of Australia is bear deprived. They don't have any in the wild.

Moving on to the continents that these creatures do call home, let's lead with the acknowledgement that bears are smart. Their brains are large and complex, enabling them to perform an impressive array of tasks. In hunting and foraging, because bears consume large quantities of fruits and vegetation, they have superior navigation skills and have been known to remember fertile feeding grounds they last visited a decade earlier. While being hunted, grizzly bears occasionally employ the strategies of covering their tracks and hiding behind large objects like rocks.

Bears are compassionate and capable of displaying a wide range of emotions including grief. Young cubs have been known to cry and moan, sometimes for weeks, when they lose or are separated from their mothers. They are known to fight till the death in order to save a family member. They are also good problem solvers and are able to open car and house doors.

Turns out there are just 8 species of bears in the world, few enough that we can provide a quick rundown for you here.

* **North American Black Bears** ~ while this is the most prominent species in North America, one misnomer would be the "black" title as they can be brown, blond or even white.
* **Asiatic Black Bears** ~ can be black or brown in color and are sometimes called moon bears because of the white crescent-moon marking on their chest.
* **Brown Bears** ~ are the world's most prevalent species, living in all four of the continents that have bears... Asia, Europe, and North & South America. According to our guest expert David Meanwell at Bear Conservation (BC), these animals used to live in Africa but, "Brown bears went extinct there in the 1870's." For the record, if you're looking at this list and wondering, "Where are

the grizzly bears?" the answer would be that they are a subspecies of brown bears.

* **Polar Bears** ~ are the largest in size, meeting the parameters we will outline below. That being said, according to David at BC, "Generally they are the largest but the Kodiak bear, a brown bear subspecies, can be even bigger." Because of their natural habitat, they are the most vulnerable to global warming. The "best guess" numbers as to global population estimates there are about 26,000 polar bears in the world with Canada having the most, about 16,000, with the others spread throughout Alaska, Russia, Greenland, and some northern islands owned by Norway, such as Svalbard.

* **Andean Bears** ~ South America's only bears, living in the Andes Mountains, are called "spectacled bears" because the cream-colored markings around their eyes look like glasses. They are agile climbers and make leafy platforms in trees to rest and feed, bear "nests" so to speak.

* **Giant Pandas** ~ are endemic to China. There are about 2,000 of them living in the wild and 500 in zoos, but China owns them all. If you see them in a zoo they are on loan. When China retrieved its panda bears from the National Zoo in Washington in November of 2023, it made the Atlanta Zoo the only remaining zoo in the U.S. with pandas, and there are mixed signals and an ongoing conversation assessing China's future plans in this regard.

* **Sloth Bears** ~ live only in Asia with their habitat being the grasslands and forests of India, Nepal, Bhutan and Sri Lanka. Their main foods are ants and termites, but they also love honey and are sometimes called honey bears.

* **Sun Bears** ~ are the smallest species, half the size of black bears, with a habitat that ranges from continental southeast Asia (Thailand/Vietnam) to the Pacific islands further south (Indonesia/Malaysia). They live in forests and, as well as being the smallest, they are also the rarest bear and they can be the most aggressive.

Size & Speed ~ Bears are big and fast. The largest species can be 10 feet long, stand 11 feet tall on their hind legs, and weigh 1,500 pounds. Certainly more than enough to cover the bare necessities. Brown bears are the fastest, able to reach a maximum speed of 35 mph giving them a 100-YDT of 5.8 seconds. From a standing start they can reach that max speed in 7.5 seconds.

At this point, we'll hand the mic back over to our college collaborator Liaison Lindsey who we definitely admire for her ability to turn a phrase. Connecting some dots between size and speed, she summed things up by saying, "Bears, standing on their hind legs and swatting is a 'scary movie bear'. Bears really only stand on their hind legs to access food, scratch themselves, or look at their surroundings. A truly 'scary bear' is one running on all fours towards you, which is where they get to their top speed." Nobody is able to describe true fear like our Lindsey!

Life ~ When it comes to life expectancy for bears there are some variations in place depending on species… in the wild they're looking at 15-30 years, and in captivity that range expands to 30-50 years. Polar bears tend to be on the lower range of that spectrum and the one of this species who achieved the longest recorded lifespan would be Debby who reached the age of 41 (one month shy of 42) at the Assiniboine Park Zoo in Winnipeg, Manitoba, Canada. Our overall winner in the bear longevity record book is a grizzly named Brownie who reached the ripe old age of 56 at the Sunset Zoological Park in Manhattan, Kansas. (This zoo proudly represents Kansas in our state-by-state addendum) **Conservation Status~** We are going to hand this one off to David at Bear Conservation and allow him to flash his expertise… "The polar bear is not the most endangered, at least not right now. Only brown bears are not classified as 'Vulnerable'. The other seven species are ['Vulnerable'], with the panda having an increasing population, the polar bear not having enough data to specify population status, and the other five all having falling populations. Despite the depletion of the Arctic ice, the polar bear could very easily outlive the sun bear and maybe the Andean bear."

Lured out of their lairs, here's our 10 Favorite Bears…

 # 10) THE COCA-COLA POLAR BEARS ~ Over the past few decades Coca-Cola has put together one of the more spectacular advertising campaigns in history which has featured a series of computer animated commercials starring a captivating cast of polar bears. Check out 2005's "Christmas Party" on YouTube for the best of the bunch. Animal Planet ranks the Coca-Cola Polar Bears as #38 on its list of "50 Greatest TV Animals".

 # 9) FOZZIE BEAR, from *The Muppet Show* ~ Fancying himself as quite the comedian, Fozzie's cue to the audience that his one-liner had been delivered was to punctuate his act with the interjection, "Wocka wocka!" Brownish-orange in color, Fozzie's attire consists of a pink and white polka-dotted necktie, complemented by a brown pork-pie hat atop his head. Often insecure, he considered Kermit his BFF and… final fun fact… he gets quoted by Don Henley of the Eagles in his song, "Johnny Can't Read."

 # 8) THE THREE BEARS ~ One thing about fairy tales is that many of them have very violent origins, which have often been softened over time. That would be the case with "Goldilocks and the Three Bears". Earliest versions of the tale featured a promiscuous old woman and three bachelors. Not a lot of debate over porridge temperature in that one.

That version morphed into one where the old woman was replaced with the young girl named Goldilocks, hence introducing child endangerment as a new theme. Ultimately they clean this one up for the kids by bouncing the bachelors and bringing in the bears. Don't we all feel a little better now?

Speaking of kids and fairy tales, our collegiate zoological guru Liaison Lindsey offered a timely comment to help put this one into perspective. "Fairy tales and movies often give people perceptions of animals they have for the rest of their lives," she said, "this being a prime example for bears. Other examples are the wolf in "Little Red Riding Hood", the hyenas in *Lion King* (people grow up afraid of them), or the constant portrayal of vultures being bad (like in *Jungle Book* or also *Lion King*).

On that note, we'll close with a cute one-liner... At a party last week, Goldilocks and the Seven Bears met Snow White and the Three Dwarfs; they exchanged numbers.

 # 7) BERENSTAIN BEARS ~ How's this for the moment when you know you've made it big. You get a message from Dr. Seuss saying, "[Forget the penguins], we're selling the hell out of the bear book." Let's rewind to the beginning of the story...

In 1962 Stan and Jan Berenstain have written a children's book called *The Big Honey Hunt* for Random House Publishing Company where Dr. Seuss heads the children's literature department. Initially sales are mediocre which prompts the advice from Dr. Seuss that, "There are already too many bears ... Sendak's got some kind of bear. There's Yogi Bear, the Three Bears, Smokey Bear, the Chicago Bears ... for your next book you should do something as different from bears as possible."

So the Berenstains start their next kids book with a playful plan for plentiful penguins, which brings us back to our opening line of this component. Suddenly, *The Big Honey Hunt* takes off prompting Dr. Seuss to issue the change of strategy expressed in the lead paragraph above. The penguins are purged, the bears are back, and the Berenstain Bears take the kid-lit world by storm launching a career which would sell 260 million copies of over 400 different books.

 # 6) THE TEDDY BEAR ~ You may or may not know that the first teddy bear was actually named after President Theodore Roosevelt and the substantiating story surely inspires. Here's the scoop... In 1902, Roosevelt is invited on a black bear hunting trip to Mississippi, but comes up empty. Hating to have his president return to the capital disappointed, one member of the hunting party uses dogs to corner an older bear and tie it to a tree for Roosevelt to shoot. Obviously there is no sport to be had in this opportunity and the president refuses.

The story goes viral and a toymaker in New York asks Roosevelt if he can make and market a stuffed animal black bear which would be called a "Teddy Bear". Roosevelt gives his blessing to the initiative and the success of the Teddy Bear becomes the impetus for the formation of the Ideal Toy Company.

 # 5) PADDINGTON BEAR ~ In his introduction by Michael Bond in the 1958 book *A Bear Called Paddington*, this character arrives in England in a lifeboat from South America wearing a broad-brimmed red bucket hat and crisply-clasped blue coat. Despite that trickle of jelly leaking out of the corner of his mouth, he has gone on to sell over 30 million children's books featuring his ensemble of enchanting English adventures.

We have a uniquely interesting backstory on this one. You're actually reading about Paddington a little later than you might have been because of the 300 animals this book rates in our collective countdowns, Paddington was the only character to emerge with a lobbyist advocating to boost his countdown rating!

Remember David Meanwell from Bear Conservation in the U.K. who served as our bear expert in the intro to this chapter? Well, Dave did **mean well** when he read our draft of this entire chapter; not only did he provide his expertise for the introduction, he campaigned on behalf of his "best bear", voicing the opinion that Paddington should have placed higher in the rankings than the #8 at which we had him placed.

Initially commenting upon the jelly trickling from Paddington's mouth, David wrote that it was, "'Marmalade', not Jelly (aka jam)! And only number eight! Your choice, of course. I'd have him at number 2 just behind Pooh! Have you seen the film of when Paddington met our late Queen Elizabeth II?" You can find the film to which David alludes on YouTube under the title "Ma'amalade sandwich Your Majesty?"

At this point, anxious to allay the fears of another international incident between the colonies and the mother country, the judges retired to their chambers to view the video. Check it out yourselves and we think you'll agree that Paddington deserves a better fate than #8. A compromise was clearly in order, hence the current appearance of Paddington in the #5 slot.

 # 4) YOGI BEAR ~ As he was oft-inclined to let the audience know, Yogi had no doubt that he was "smarter than the average bear." He debuted in the 1958 Hanna-Barbera TV series *The Huckleberry Hound Show*, but soon found himself more popular than Huck, and by 1961 he was given his own show. In 1964 *Hey There, It's Yogi Bear!* became the studio's first theatrical movie release.

Yogi was a brash and boisterous bear who roamed Jellystone Park in his green pork pie hat and matching tie searching for food, most frequently in the form of what he could purloin from people's picnic baskets, the key word being one he always pronounced in 3 syllables as "pic-a-nic". The character's name was basically lifted from the 1950's New York Yankees catcher Yogi Berra, with the studio's defense that it was all just a coincidence. This was found by most not to be credible. Berra sued at one point, but then just decided to drop the whole thing.

The rest of the cast consisted of Yogi's sidekick and voice of reason Boo Boo, girlfriend Cindy and finally Park Ranger Smith whose job it was to pull in the reins on Yogi's antics. His typical greeting of, "Hello, Mr. Ranger, sir!" provided a thinly veiled attempt to convince the authority figure that his behavior would be on the up-and-up, but of course, that never lasted for long.

Yogi's personality and voice mimicked that of Ed Norton's character (played by Art Carney) in *The Honeymooners* sitcom which was widely popular at the time. Referencing the medieval hero to whom he likened himself, Yogi said,

"What's not to like about Robin Hood? I'll steal from the rich and give to a poor bear... me." Recognizing the foibles of his ways he acknowledged that, "Pic-a-nic baskets may be delicious on the lips, but they're a lifetime on the hips!"

His legacy is carried on through the Jellystone Campgrounds franchise which can be found throughout the U.S. and Canada. Animal Planet ranks Yogi as #37 on its list of "50 Greatest TV Animals".

 # 3) SMOKEY BEAR ~ Do you know how the iconic catch phrase of this valuable public servant has changed since we were kids? It now reads, "Only You Can Prevent Wildfires" with the shift being in the final word(s). Those were changed from "Forest Fires" to "Wildfires" in 2001 because of the increase of fires in non-forested natural areas like grasslands. So essentially the purpose of the word change was to make the fire prevention message more universal.

When the concept originated in 1944, Smokey existed only as artwork on posters with the dedicated purpose of educating the public about the dangers of forest fires. Then in 1950 a real-life event sparked the idea (no pun intended) that the advertising character might be more impactful if it also had a living, breathing animal to serve as the embodiment of the concept.

That event we mentioned was a fire in the Capitan Mountains of New Mexico where an American black bear cub was heroically rescued from a tree, with significant burns, particularly on all four of his legs and paws. Obviously those circumstances provided the perfectly appropriate scenario to anoint the cub as the official firefighting poster bear.

Not so obviously perfect was the work of the naming committee which initially decided to dub the cub as "Hotfoot Teddy". That's a little bit like pouring salt on the wound, isn't it? Or perhaps the more apt cliché would be to say it was a little bit like pouring gasoline on the fire. Immersed in temperature-appropriate verbiage, we'll close this by saying that cooler heads prevailed and the decision was made to replicate the name of the cartoon bear for the live bear bringing "Smokey Bear" to life for the first time.

Along with his new name, Smokey was also awarded some new accommodations. There would be no more scavenging for food and dodging the flames in the remote mountains of New Mexico; Smokey was set up with new digs at the National Zoo in Washington D.C. where his popularity soared to the point where he was receiving so much fan mail they had to give the bear his own zip code! Even President Truman was jealous. Smokey enjoyed his capital stay through the Reagan administration, passing away in 1976.

 # 2) BALOO, from Disney's *The Jungle Book* ~ "Look for the bare necessities, the simple bare necessities, forget about your worries and your strife." Those were the signature lines from this character, in the signature song from the 1967 Disney feature *The Jungle Book*. And it's hard to hear those words without feeling an infectious lifting of your spirits while also putting a special little skip to your step. If you think about it, Baloo's "Bare Necessities" was Disney's version of Timon and Pumba doing "Hakuna Matata" a quarter century before *The Lion King*.

Returning to the '67 Disney film, after the dramatic ending where Baloo contributes to saving Mowgli from Shere Khan, he does suffer a sliver of disappointment when Mowgli follows the young human girl into the man-village to begin a new life. He does, however, realize it is in the best interest of everyone involved. And what better way for the whole thing to end than to have the blustery Baloo and the stoic black panther Bagheera strolling down a jungle path with their arms around one another singing a reprise of "The Bare Necessities", with Baloo contributing the encouragement of, "Come on, Baggy, get with the beat!"

 # 1) WINNIE THE POOH ~ "Did you ever stop to think, and forget to start again?" Such unique takes on life were amongst the musings that enabled Winnie the Pooh to winsomely and wistfully win the hearts of such an immense audience. And another wonderful Winnie quote that lumbers into our brain right now as we describe our pet passions propelling this project would be the thought that while we were writing this book, "We didn't realize we were making memories, we just knew we were having fun."

So when did all this fun begin? A. A. Milne published the Pooh debut, *Winnie-the-Pooh* in 1926 and certainly had a nice run with the character until his death in 1956. Walt Disney always had his eye on Winnie the Pooh and upon the passing of the patriarch, he struck a deal to buy the rights to the franchise in 1961.

The Milne family actually sold out rather reluctantly because Disney had acknowledged that the classic characters would be redesigned to appeal to a more modern-day audience. The original character designs are still featured through artwork on cards, books, and memorabilia which fall under the designation of "Classic Pooh". If you've ever noticed related artwork that shows the characters you recognize with different, more crudely drawn, representations... those would be the "Classic Pooh" character designs.

Sometimes the characters own words describe themselves better than we could have and we are going to allow this to become one opportunity when we allow the character to write his own story. If you were ever one to feel that Winnie the Pooh was just all about cute, with no thoughtful substance to substantiate his wisdom, prepare to be educated.

The general characterization of Winnie the Pooh would be to establish him as the most gentle, kind and compassionate bear on the block. Part of what sets Pooh apart is the innocent sagacity with which he shares his sentiments. What follows is our attempt to convey Pooh's personality through the use of his own words...

* When life throws you a rainy day, play in the puddles.
* There must be somebody there because somebody must have said, "Nobody."
* The sun still shines, even when it's hiding.
* Rivers know this: There is no hurry. We shall get there some day.
* If you live to be 100, I want to live to be 100 minus one day so I never have to live without you.

Here's our poem to that one special someone you have in your life that you truly would not want to live a day without.

If it rains on your parade, puddle playing
Is one thing you shan't be delaying
And please know all the while I'll be praying
As the rivers they always flow true
I'll not live one lone day without you

Chapter 3

THE FOREST NOW ROCKS, WITH THE WOLF AND THE FOX

WOLVES

In this component we're going to go from fairy tale wolves like the Big Bad Wolf, to movie star wolves like Two Socks (a story you're going to want to hear), to biblical wolves. We'll start off by sharing some fun facts on this brave and noble animal.

You can find some on every continent except Australia and Antarctica. While humans can hear the piercing howl of a wolf from a six-mile distance, the more acute hearing of a wolf enables it to detect more subtle sounds from that same six-mile distance in the forest, as well as hear sounds from up to 10 miles away in open country.

Wolves mate for life and, as you'll see in the upcoming component on White Fang, they can also mate with dogs. It is estimated that there are 300,000 wolfdogs in the United States. For the most part their only predator is man, who wolves try to avoid. Serving as our guest export for this component, wolf curator Giselle Narvaez Rivera from the International Wolf Center added, "Humans hunting wolves are one of the sources of mortality for wolves. Given the opportunity though, bears, tigers, mountain lions, can also prey on wolves. Interpack lethal aggression is also a common source of mortality for them."

Now do wolves ever turn the tables on humans? As confirmed by Curator Rivera, in North America during the 21st century there have only been two recorded wolf attacks that have led to human deaths, one in Alaska and one in Canada.

Trophic cascade ~ Let's break this one down. "Trophic" means "related to feeding" and the "cascade" definition pertinent here would be to "happen in a series or sequence". Environmentally speaking, trophic cascades occur when predators limit the density and/or behavior of their prey and thereby enhance the survival of the next lowest trophic level. Our Liaison Lindsey noted the relevance of wolves to this concept pointing out that, "Yellowstone is a great example with wolves balancing ungulate (deer, elk, pronghorn, and bison) populations which then restored native plants and waterways."

Size & Speed ~ Gray wolves are the most prevalent species in North America and also the largest with adult males averaging 100 pounds, while occasionally reaching 130 pounds. Females weigh about 20% less. The smallest species is the Arabian wolf where adults may weigh no more than 30 pounds. Their top running speed peaks out at just over 35 mph, giving them a 100-YDT of 5.8

seconds, and they are also great swimmers, able to cover as much as 8 miles in a single session.

Life ~ The upper range of their life expectancy would be 13 years in the wild and 16 years in captivity. The all-time record for a wolf's life span was achieved by Madadh who died in 2017 at the Wolf Watch UK reserve at the age of 19. This story follows immediately below.

Next we'll continue with the countdown of our 9 Fine Wolves…

 # 9) MADADH ~ We're heading across the drink to visit the animal advocacy group Wolf Watch UK for this next component. Madadh was just eight days old when she and her brother Kgosi were discovered in 1998 by Tony Haighway, the founder of Wolf Watch UK. "From 8 days old, she slept in a sleeping bag with me in the kitchen for the first two months of her life, being bottle fed every two hours," said Haighway. "We were spending probably 12 hours a day with her. Hence, she remains well socialized to people in general, but to me in particular."

It was the beginning of a pretty sweet run for the wolves as well as the Wolf Watchers. Madadh and Kgosi had the run of a 2½-acre expanse of lush forest land where they would spend most of the next two decades. You would have to say this pair of wolves obviously came from a strong gene pool because by the beginning of the year 2017, Wolf Watch UK found itself the home of the two wolves who had each lived longer than any other wolf in recorded history.

When Kgosi passed away at the age of 18 in May of 2017, Madadh assumed the mantle of the wolf with the longest life ever. She died five months later in October of 2017. We are going to allow Tony Haighway to close this segment with his own words in a quote that we found particularly passionate. Regarding Madadh and Kgosi he said, "They probably did more in their lifetimes to educate the public and dispel the myths that surround the wolf, touching the hearts of everyone that they came into contact with and were in every sense true ambassadors for the whole of their species."

 # 8) WHITE FANG ~ If you're an animal person then Jack London might be an author you've explored. His two most famous novels were *The Call of the Wild* (1903) and *White Fang* (1906) and the plotlines of these two may be viewed as clever inversions of one another.

One motif that links the two books is London's striking ability to write from the perspective of the animal. In each case London explores the animals' perceptions of the violent world of humans as well as their own violent worlds.

The inversions of which we spoke above would be that in *The Call of the Wild*, the dog Buck (St. Bernard/sheepdog mix) begins as a pet, but when interjected into the rugged world of sled dogs in the Yukon he begins to revert to the behavior of his ancestors, the wolf, in order to survive and thrive.

In *White Fang*, the title character is a wolfdog, born of a wolf mother and a dog father. He was originally bred to fight but would eventually undergo a life transformation after he is purchased by a man named Weedon Scott. White Fang's new owner becomes a loving master who essentially domesticates the wolfdog and makes him a part of the family in Santa Clara Valley, California.

 # 7) WOLF IN SHEEP'S CLOTHING ~ Okay, we are taking an idiomatic and biblical approach on this next component. The proverbial use of the "wolf in sheep's clothing" phrase can be traced back to the man who had one of the greatest speech writers in history, namely Jesus Christ.

The line in question can be traced back to the Sermon on the Mount, which of course was a great show. You couldn't ask for a better stage, the mountain was packed, Jesus taught his audience the Lord's Prayer, and he did the Beatitudes for an encore. The crowd was going crazy.

The Wolf in Sheep's Clothing idiom was used to designate those who would play a role contrary to their actual character for deceitful self-serving purposes. Let's go right to the transcript to cue up a few quotes. According to attendee Matthew, Jesus said (in Matthew 7:15), "Beware of false prophets, which come to you in sheep's clothing, but inwardly they are ravening wolves… by their fruits shall ye know them."

Even with the best sheep costume money could buy, you could not sneak one by Jesus. God's only son could never be accused of being a poor judge of character.

 # 6) LUPA ~ We're going to go all biblical on you again and announce that we're allowing Lupa to hoist her Mother of the Millennium Award for the year's 1000 B.C. – 0, but only because the Virgin Mary actually gave birth to Christ in the year 4 AD. Check our previous book *Walking in a Women's Wonderland* for full details, but trust us… that's the facts, Jacks; Jesus was born in 4 AD. So what did Lupa do, and when?

According to legend, in around 750 B.C., the mother wolf was walking the banks of the Tiber River when she happened across the pair of abandoned royal twins Romulus and Remus who had been left to die by an evil king. Lupa adopted the humans and suckled them to survival where they grew up with a huge hand of destiny historically hanging over their heads. The world needed an empire to dominate it and these twins would get the ball rolling. After a dispute arose regarding location, location, location; Romulus killed Remus and made the proclamation, "We are going to build Rome right here!"

So everything went according to plan and Rome went on to conquer most of the known world. If it weren't for the she-wolf Lupa, history might have taken a very different course. But keeping history's actual course in mind, what about the full-circle concept of the Romans erecting the cross upon which Jesus was hung, essentially creating Easter. Turns out that without our #5 wolf, we never would have landed our #1 rabbit, namely the Easter Bunny who will top

the charts in the upcoming rabbit chapter. Just to directly connect the dots for you on this one...
* The #5 wolf Lupa saves a human's life, hence we have Romulus.
* Romulus founds Rome, hence there are Romans.
* Romans crucify Christ, hence he must rise from the grave.
* Christ rises, hence we have Easter.
* Easter needs a secular mascot, hence the Easter Bunny.

It certainly makes for the best wolf-begats-rabbit story known to man. So if you really want to confuse your kids next Easter, when they name the Easter Bunny as the animal they would like to thank, throw them an historical curveball, and let them know that the animal they really deserves the kudos is the wolf called Lupa who lived in 750 B.C. Then let the egg hunt begin.

#5) TWO SOCKS, from *Dances with Wolves* ~ Allow us to introduce the titular star. When Kevin Costner made his epoch Native American film, 1990's *Dances with Wolves*, Two Socks would be the wolf with whom Costner's character danced. In the movie he plays Lt. John J. Dunbar a U.S. soldier who comes to live with and marry into the Native American Sioux tribe in South Dakota.

Dunbar befriends a wolf who he names "Two Socks" because the animal has white forepaws which look like socks. When the Sioux see Dunbar and Two Socks frolicking and playing together, they bestow upon him the Native American name of "Dances with Wolves" so the movie title is also a man's name, which you may not have known.

Two different real-life wolves alternated in playing Two Socks in the movie, namely Buck and Teddy. Wolves are temperamental and not naturally inclined to patiently perform for the movie cameras so the trainers used a lot of patience, and meat scraps, to coax them through their scenes.

In general, harsh realities are not avoided in *Dances with Wolves*, and such is the case with Two Socks. The storyline has the Army charge Dunbar with desertion when he refuses to act as an interpreter between the government and the Native Americans. When he's arrested and transported back east, Two Socks loyally attempts to follow his friend and is shot and killed by U.S. soldiers, leaving Dunbar with only remembrances of the dances.

 # 4) THE WOLF FROM LITTLE RED RIDING HOOD ~ One interesting aspect of medieval fairy tales (as well as nursery rhymes) would be that in centuries past, when society in general was more violent and devoid of censorship standards in that regard, even stories intended for children often took on a level of violence and depravity which modern-day standards have toned down to reflect current societal values. This fairy tale is certainly a case in point.

Here's the original story... Little Red Riding Hood is walking through the woods with a basket of food to be delivered to her sickly grandmother. The Wolf intercepts Red on the path and, upon coaxing from her the purpose and

destination of her trip, the Wolf enacts a plan which will hopefully avail him of a three-course meal consisting of...
1) Granny
2) Red
3) the food in the basket

To that end, he suggests that Red pick some flowers for Granny which delays Red long enough that the wolf can make his way to Granny's house, eat Granny, dress in Granny's clothes, and hide in the bed waiting for Red's arrival. High drama ensues when Red enters Granny's home to find her looking a bit out of sorts. The all-too-familiar dialogue follows...

Red: What a deep voice you have!
Wolf: The better to greet you with.
Red: Goodness, what big eyes you have!
Wolf: The better to see you with.
Red: What a big mouth you have!
Wolf: The better to eat you with! responds the Wolf, at which point the Wolf jumps out of the bed and eats her too, before crawling back into the bed and falling asleep.

Next arriving on the scene we have the heroic hunter who, while displaying no medical license whatsoever, takes his axe and performs a precise incision upon the belly of the wolf, before carefully extracting the intact bodies of both Granny and Red. Glory hallelujah, with a happy ending, but of course there's one nagging question left to be answered. Did these medieval wolves have no ability whatsoever to chew their food?

 # 3) PETER AND THE WOLF ~ This may well be the most-often-heard piece of classical music in existence and its raison d'être certainly serves to clarify why. In 1936 Russian composer Sergei Prokofiev tasked himself with writing a piece of music that told a story and took a calculated approach to expose children to the various sounds and instruments comprising a classical orchestra.

To this end, a masterful tale is crafted with different instruments representing the characters of Peter (violins), his Grandfather (bassoon), and various animals including the Wolf (French horns), Duck, (oboe) Bird (flute), and Cat (clarinet). Finally, it's the hunters (kettle drums) who march in at the end to secure and assure the happy ending. If you haven't enjoyed this since your childhood, we suggest you give it a whirl!

 # 2) THE BOY WHO CRIED WOLF, from *Aesop's Fables* ~ This is certainly one of the classic Aesop's Fables, especially because the point is made to such poignant perfection. A young boy, looking for attention, makes multiple runs into his village falsely reporting wolves threatening the sheep he is in charge of guarding.

After the threats have become so numerous the boy's credibility has been compromised, wolves do actually appear. At that point however, when the threat is reported, it's ignored by the villagers who logically assume it is yet one more false alarm. Subsequently, the sheep are all eaten. If you're looking for a silver lining to this cloud, here it is. No one will have to count the sheep before going to bed that night; they're all gone.

The moral Aesop states at the culmination of his fable is, "This shows how liars are rewarded: when they do tell the truth, no one will believe them." Expanding upon our animalistic examination of the English language, let us add the allusion that this is the literary thread that gave birth to the idiom "to cry wolf". Okay, no tears allowed as we head on to #1.

 # 1) THE BIG BAD WOLF, from "Little Red Riding Hood" ~ So, how do we differentiate between equally evil wolves in equally famous fairy tales? Why exactly does Wolf #1 surpass Wolf #4 in this fairy tale face-off? We were hoping you'd ask because we're armed with an answer. Actually, we have three answers as to why the wolf in "The Three Little Pigs" trumps the wolf in "Little Red Riding Hood".

1 – Film success ~ While both stories have received multiple film treatments, the 1933 Disney short "The Three Little Pigs" is rated as the #11 cartoon of all time.

2 – Musical success ~ The song from that film, "Who's Afraid of the Big Bad Wolf," was a huge hit, peaking at #2 in 1933.

3 – Name game ~ Not only does the "Little Pigs" wolf have a name, it's a savagely scary-good name… "The Big Bad Wolf". The "Little Red" wolf is just called "the Wolf"… no pizzaz there.

So now that we've justified the cred of our #1 wolf, let's quickly reset the story. The three pigs leave home to embark upon their independent lives and each starts by building a home. In balancing ease of construction vs. degree of safety, the range of responsibility reflected results in the homes being built of 1) straw, 2) sticks, 3) bricks. Enter the Big Bad Wolf who reaffirms his #1 status by having the best fairy tale catch phrase whereby, upon being denied entry into house #1, he announces his intention to "huff and puff and blow your house down!"

After the obliteration of the straw and stick houses, the three pigs find themselves holed up in that last bastion of safety, the brick house which stood with huff-and-puff-proof resolve. Unable to broach the bricks with heavy breathing alone, the wolf goes all Santa Claus and opts to enter the abode by descending the chimney.

As we know, this is destined to end ugly for the wolf. Depending upon the level of violence employed by your fairy tale version of choice, here is the range of your alternate endings…

Wolf's worst case scenario: He falls into the bubbling cauldron trap set by the pigs where he is cooked and consumed as a porcine picnic.

Wolf's best-case scenario: He receives a well-deserved butt-scalding before scrambling up out of the chimney and skedaddling back into the woods.

As we continue to play with poetry, we're going to see what happens if we juggle the rhyme scheme of a limerick. Rather than the typical **aabba** pattern, we're going to challenge ourselves and go with an **abbaa** rhyme scheme.

Big Bad Wolf finds himself in a scrape
What is he gonna do?
Outcomes number just two
Does a nice cooked-wolf dinner take shape?
Or does he make a narrow escape?

FOXES

We are going to turn over our introduction to Mikalah Singer, the founder and Executive Director of Fox Protection International. Mikalah wrote, "Foxes are represented in literature, myths, and media from many cultures throughout history. They are often portrayed as tricksters or painted in a negative light. However, foxes are generally shy and play an important role in pest control and seed dispersal. I would recommend saying that many people only recognize fox species that belong to the genus *Vulpes* as 'true foxes', but most people would not be able to distinguish between which species of foxes fall into which category by looking at them."

Though they are members of the animal family that includes wolves, dogs and jackals, in many ways foxes are more like cats. They are nocturnal with vertical pupils to enhance night vision, they use their whiskers to navigate and some have retractable claws enabling them to climb trees. Even their gait is catlike as they stride elegantly on the balls of their feet.

You can find them all over the world, every continent except Antarctica, and they thrive in a large range of habitats. You can find Arctic foxes living north of the Arctic Circle and the smallest foxes of all, the fennec which is just over one foot long, is found strictly in the desert of northern Africa. This is the most surprising fox picture you can Google because they're small little critters with humungous ears (which enable them to dissipate body heat and hear prey).

In North America the two most prevalent types are the red fox and the gray fox. Species titles notwithstanding, they both appear in a wide range of colors, from black to gray to red to white. The red fox (actually orange) is the most common and certainly the image most people first conjure when they think of a fox.

Size & Life ~ Adult red foxes can weigh 35 pounds and stand 20 inches tall and 3-4 feet long including the tail. Gray foxes are smaller, having a more cat-like face and are only half the size of red ones. Average life span in the wild is 3-4 years while in captivity they can live up to 12 years. The longest recorded life of a fox goes to a vixen who Corinne Shaw, Zoo Boise's registrar at the time, documents as having died in January 2007 at the age of 23 years, seven months. In a recent conversation with Zoo Boise's Interpretation Coordinator Austin Reich, he confirmed that the fox arrived at Zoo Boise in 1985.

Speed ~ The fastest species is the gray fox which can hit a top speed of 42 mph which calculates to a 100-YDT of 4.9 seconds.

Foxes & Folks ~ Foxes share a long history with humans which leads us to the single most surprising fox fact we came across in our research, this one coming from a 2019 article in *Bare Ground Solutions* called "The Amazing Fox". That website reports that in 2011 in the country of Jordan, a 16,500-year-old grave was discovered in which a man was buried with his pet fox. That would be 4,000 years older than the earliest-known example of a man being buried with his dog.

We've got one more we think you'll like involving the research of a Soviet scientist during the 1960's. Using silver foxes, he selectively continued to breed only the ones who showed the greatest tolerance of humans. Ten generations into the experiment the foxes were displaying domestic almost dog-like behaviors; they were seeking the attention of humans, barking, wagging their tails and licking hands.

Here's our countdown of Fab 5 Foxes…

 # 5) SAMSON'S FOXES, from the Bible ~ In the Old Testament's Judges 15, Samson catches 300 foxes, pairs them in two's, ties their tails together and sets them on fire. They are subsequently released into the land of the Philistines as an act of revenge. Clearly, there is no PETA in the Old Testament.

This storyline can't help but leave one wondering what this kind of vengeance was being sought for… turns out it was the Philistines who sent Delilah to cut off Samson's hair, which of course was the source of his power.

 # 4) NICK WILDE, from Disney's *Zootopia* ~ Of the multiple movies we reviewed as part of our research on this project, we'll go on record as saying the most pleasantly surprising was this 2016 film. The long-story-short is that the land is populated by animals who were formerly divided into two groups as being either "predators" or "prey". They all now live in relative Zootopia peace, but their original ancestry and underlying differences occasionally emerge.

Nick Wilde is a cynical streetwise con artist fox whose life takes a turn toward the positive when his path crosses that of the energetically irrepressible, buoyantly optimistic, and fiercely independent rabbit police girl Judy Hopps. The characters' chemistry sparkles as each imparts their most valuable qualities upon the other while collaborating to conquer the crime wave that threatens to take the utopia out of Zootopia.

Their final scene in the film sees the following words exchanged as they drive away in their car…

Nick: You know you love me.
Judy: Do I know that? Yes. Yes, I do.

 # 3) TOD, from Disney's *The Fox and the Hound* ~ "We'll always be friends forever, won't we?" is the quote which embodies the theme of Disney's 1981 feature film. Turns out, that question has two answers driven by the overlap of the laws of nature and society. Those words are spoken by fox cub Tod to puppy Copper early on in this story which is guaranteed to have a tear welling up in your eye by movie's end.

A chance meeting between the fox and the hound leads to an unlikely friendship between two characters who strive to maintain their relationship despite emerging instincts coalescing with societal demands which label them as natural enemies. Both man and nature have a profound impact upon the relationship as the story evolves.

Lifesaving efforts are exchanged in this mutually symbiotic relationship where ultimately nature must take its course when Tod encounters his future mate Vixey. After a final euphoric moment, as the parties prepare to part, Tod and Copper exchange one final smile, symbolically cementing their friendship which, while it will never end, must now traverse separate paths. The movie culminates with parallel tributes of acknowledgment to the special friendship.

Once home, Copper curls up outside the doghouse for a nap and daydreams about the occasion upon which he first met Tod, prompting a sleepy smile to spread across his face. Simultaneously, Vixey joins Tod high atop a hill in the forest. As Tod looks down, he can actually see the curled-up Copper in the distance prompting Tod's own daydream. After a moment of reflection upon his past, Tod is ready to begin the walk with Vixey toward his future.

 # 2) THE FOX AND THE GRAPES, from *Aesop's Fables* ~ This is certainly one of Aesop's more famous fables as it gives birth to a commonly used idiom in the English language. The story involves a hungry fox coming across some grapes hanging from a vine which he cannot reach.

After multiple efforts to leap high enough to pick the enticing fruit, the fox abandons his efforts and leaves remarking, "Oh, you aren't even ripe yet! I don't need any sour grapes."

Thus the expression "sour grapes" has come to apply to any situation where a person speaks disparagingly of someone or something they truly want, but pretend they don't want, because in actuality they don't possess the ability to attain the object of their pursuit.

 # 1) ROBIN HOOD, from Disney ~ In the 1973 Disney feature *Robin Hood*, Friar Tuck seeks to counsel our hero by saying, "Oh, for heaven's sake, Son, you're no outlaw. Why, someday you'll be called a great hero." And keep in mind this was not your typical mild-mannered milquetoast friar; at one point, this dude even gets into a fist fight with the villainous Sheriff of Nottingham!

No surprises on the basic plotline here... Robin steals from the rich and gives to the poor, but you knew that. So we'll flesh this thing out with some of the more minor character nuances and a few personal perspectives. The other character in the story who's worthy of a whoopin' is the antagonist, Prince John, who earns this well-deserved disdain by virtue of his excessive taxation of the residents of Sherwood Forest to line his personal coffers.

Robin Hood sees the inequity in his community and makes the efforts necessary to rectify the situation, establishing himself as the embodiment of the spirit of the people in the process. Upon leaving the home of a family of rabbits who had been royally robbed, his departing words are, "Keep your chin up. Someday there'll be happiness again in Nottingham, you'll see."

The romantic highlight of this story occurs at an archery contest which Prince John has arranged to lure Robin Hood out of hiding and orchestrate his capture. With the contest prize being a kiss from his heart's desire Maid Marian, Robin Hood enacts a plan to enter the competition in a disguise, which initiates the following conversation…

Friar Tuck: Wait a minute, Rob. Hold it. That place will be crawling with soldiers.
Robin Hood: Ah, but remember, faint hearts never won fair lady. Fear not, my friends. This will be my greatest performance.

And indeed it was. Robin Hood wins the contest, marries the girl, defeats the bad guys, and saves Sherwood Forest. All in a day's work for a medieval hero.

They say crime doesn't pay but it could
Just one guy who could make robbin' good
If we could just name him we would…
Meet the dude that they call Robin Hood

Chapter 4

COMING TO TERMS WITH THOSE PACHYDERMS

HIPPOPOTAMUSES

We need to lead with a disclaimer on our chapter title for this one, defaulting primarily to the San Diego Zoo with most of the next two paragraphs quoting their website. The class of "Pachydermata" was originally used in the late 18th century "to describe what was considered to be a group of related animals [which included elephants, hippos, and rhinos]; they were all large bodied and had thick skin, in comparison to other mammals. As taxonomy progressed, it became clear that some of these animals were [not properly classified]. Elephants were found to come from a lineage not related to either."

"As a result, the Pachydermata classification was abandoned. But by then, the term pachyderm had been established in common use, and it continues to be used as a generalized word referring to animals with thick skin. These days, it is mostly used when referring to elephants, but it can still apply to hippos and rhinos, just not in a scientific way." So there's the explanation for our umbrella title and do take note that "pachyderm" is applied in a non-scientific usage.

Living primarily in a sub-Saharan African habitat, spending 16 hours a day mostly below water avoiding the heat, with just their eyes extending above the surface, one might assume that the hippopotamus leads a pretty laid-back life. But here's one hippo stat that slayed us, so to speak. On the list of animals that take human lives in Africa, hippos rank at #2. This of course throws down the gauntlet as to the question of who's #1 on that list? In terms of size, we'll have to travel to the other end of the animal spectrum to answer that question... turns out the African animal that takes the most human lives would be the mosquito.

Despite their somewhat docile demeanor, along with the fact that they are herbivores, hippos initially pose as perhaps a somewhat unlikely candidate to come in at #2 on the list of African death threats, but there is a rationale. We had originally written that male hippos fiercely defend what they deem to be their territory and female hippos defend their babies with equal ferocity. Our guest expert on this hippo component was Dr. Rebecca Lewison, Professor of Biology at San Diego State University and she tweaked our comment by saying, "All hippos respond aggressively to human encroachment. And female hippos can display aggressive behavior even without an offspring present." So any human who happens to encroach upon their home turf could be looking into the mouth of some piercing canines and very powerful jaws.

Liaison Lindsey is longing to wrap up this component with some hippo fun facts. From the world of zoological academia, her shares include that, "Hippos can open their mouth up 180 degrees! Enough to eat a full watermelon or pumpkin. One of my other favorite hippo facts is that they have "blood sweat", which is a red tinted liquid that comes out of their skin clear, but turns red and acts like sunscreen."

Size ~ In terms of size they are the third largest land animal, behind elephants and rhinos. They average about 4-5 feet tall and 15 feet long with an average weight of 3,500 pounds. That being said, there are hippos who have approached 6,000 pounds.

Now is probably the time to bring up the fact that there are two different species of hippos and there is a considerable difference in size. The most common type, and the type we've been talking about so far, is the river hippopotamus which has a much smaller cousin called the pygmy hippopotamus. This would be one of those scenarios where "smaller" becomes a somewhat relative term. The pygmy hippos are 3 feet tall, 6 feet long, and weigh 600 pounds.

Conservation Status ~ In addition to size, the other major difference between the two types is the degree to which they have become endangered. While there are 125,000-150,000 river hippos left in the world, they are losing population to illegal hunting and habitat loss leaving their survival status classified as "vulnerable". Pygmy hippos on the other hand have seen their population decline to about 2,500 remaining in western Africa (Sierra Leone, Liberia, and Cote D'Ivoire) and are officially classified as "endangered".

Life ~ Moving on to life expectancy, both species of hippos can hang out for a while. They're good for 30-40 years in the wild and 45-50 in captivity. There are, of course, some outliers with the longest-living hippo on record being Lu, who lives at the Homosassa Springs Wildlife State Park and recently turned 64 on January 27, 2024. Lu has set herself up to make a run for the record which is currently held by a hippo named Bertha (1952-2017) who lived to be 65 at the Manilla Zoo in the Philippines.

Speed ~ While the river hippos are winning the race for survival with the pygmy hippos, let's check the comparison charts if we could set the two types of hippos up at the gates for a competition in the hundred-yard dash. We'll give you a bit of time to formulate your favorite. Would you pick the larger and stronger river hippo or would you opt for the lighter and leaner pygmy hippo?

Well, if you're reading this book as a family and there is currently money on the table, you can all pick it up and put it all back in your pockets. No harm, no foul. Turns out they both have a max speed of 19 mph which gives them equal 100-YDT's of 10.2 seconds. They can hit maximum speeds of 10 mph in the water.

Let's kick off the countdown of our Super 6 Hippos...

 # 6) WILLIAM JOHNSON HIPPOPOTAMUS ~ In 1927 U.S. President Calvin Coolidge learned that he was about to become the recipient of an unusual gift from tire mogul Harvey Samuel Firestone who had taken advantage of his African connections in the country of Liberia to procure for Coolidge a pygmy hippopotamus. For the president that has everything, how 'bout a gift of the ultimate oxymoron?! Wouldn't you agree that "pygmy hippopotamus" is bigger and better than "jumbo shrimp"?

Only on occasion was Billy, as his friends called him, able to enjoy free range roaming in the White House. The "pygmy" part was of course a relative term, as Billy tipped the scales at 600 pounds. Most of his time was spent at the National Zoo in Washington D.C. where he was able to attain legendary status. In the sidebar of his Wikipedia entry, his "Occupation" is listed as "Stud". Tough job, but somebody's gotta do it.

How studly was he? Billy sired 23 baby pygmy hippos, a darn fine performance in anyone's book. Led by Billy's stellar efforts, the pygmy hippo breeding program at the National Zoo has been a sweet success story with the birth count now numbering 58, almost all of whom are direct descendants of Billy.

William Johnson Hippopotamus managed to outlive his original owner Calvin Coolidge by 23 years, continuing to raise a ruckus at the National Zoo until October 11, 1955. His last child was born just five months before he died. Going back to the stud status for which he was known, the eulogy from the zoo official confirmed that, "He carried his work on to the end."

 # 5) HIPPOPOTHAMES ~ Okay, imagine you're with friends in London, standing on the banks of the Thames River, and you hear someone say, "Don't look now, but I want you to guess what is coming down the river behind you." As the options run through your mind, from raft to canoe to boat, a potential answer that probably does not shoot to the top of your list would be a hippopotamus.

Well, that actually might be more of a possibility than you may have suspected thanks to Dutch artist Florentijn Hofman. During a summer of 2014 festival celebrating the Thames River, Hofman made a most unusual contribution to the festivities. What might that have been? How 'bout a colorful 101-foot-long floating wooden sculpture of a hippopotamus called HippopoThames.

The huge hippo art had been a request from the organizers of the annual river festival called Totally Thames. For the record, the river is pronounced "Tems" so the festival name is alliterative. This may beg the question, what kind of a resumé is Hofman sporting to be on the receiving end of such a request? Well, his previous project had been a huge 105-foot-high inflatable rubber duck that had attracted crowds while floating through the waterways of countries as far flung as Australia, Brazil, Japan, Hong Kong and New Zealand.

About his unique artwork, Hofman said, "The purpose of setting my sculptures in the public domain has always been to give members of the public a break from their daily routines, to inspire conversation, and to cause astonishment." Certainly there would have been no shortage of astonishment and conversation when Londoners saw that brightly painted 101-foot hippo majestically floating down their river.

From an historical perspective there was a time when a hippopotamus in the river would not have been surprising at all. Going back 125,000 years, the Thames was teeming with hippos and, for the record, there were also herds of elephants hydrating themselves at the river bank.

 # 4) OBAYSCH & ADHELA ~ When something happens in England that hasn't happened since the days of the Roman Empire, there's certainly a chance that it might become newsworthy. Well, we've got some news for you here. Let's set the Wayback Machine with the following coordinates... Time: May 25, 1850, Location: London, England.

Our story begins with the Port of London welcoming a ship that is arriving from Cairo, Egypt with a very special passenger on board. Who would that be? It's none other than Obaysch, the first hippopotamus to set foot anywhere in Europe since the days of the Roman Empire!

And, Great Caesar's Ghost, doesn't the hippo take London by storm. Obaysch, who was named after the Nile River location where he was captured, achieves such celebrity status that he even warrants a visit from Her Majesty, Queen Victoria. One can only hope Obaysch was not offended by the Queen's comment that his swimming looked like that of a porpoise. It was Victorian Hippomania at its most manic.

Explaining the close connection, Egypt was a British colony at the time and the next stage of the story has the Viceroy of Egypt sending a follow up gift of a second hippopotamus in 1854, a female named Adhela, in hopes that the two would breed. We'll get back to that in a minute after a quick unrelated story.

While kind to his new mate, Obaysch was not particularly enamored with humans. To illustrate, on one occasion he managed to escape his enclosure prompting the London Zoo superintendent to implement a most unusual strategy to recapture him. There was one zookeeper for whom Obaysch bore a decided disdain and the plan was for this man to show himself and attract the hippo's attention at a location in between the animal and his cage.

The plan worked to perfection. When Obaysch saw the man, he charged and the zookeeper sprinted into the hippo's enclosure heading straight for the ladder that was positioned in place, enabling him to quickly skedaddle up and over the walls of the enclosure with Obaysch hot on his heels. The cage door was slammed behind the hippo and the unique plan was able to check the box for "mission accomplished".

Now let's get back to that breeding proposition we broached earlier. The hope that Obaysch and Adhela would produce offspring suffered an initial setback when their first baby died at two days old, and a second calf died the following year. The third time was the charm however when Adhela gave birth to a female on November 5, 1872. Because that date is the British holiday of Guy Fawkes Day the name of Guy Fawkes was given to the baby even though it was a female. Guy Fawkes would go on to live a long full life, bringing joy to London Zoo visitors until her death in 1908.

 # 3) GLORIA, from DreamWorks' *Madagascar* ~ "Hey guys, I was thinking… when we get back, I just might sign up for the breeding program," Gloria says on one occasion, "I think we all reach a point in our lives when we want to meet somebody, you know, settle down. Have a relationship." This quote serves to illustrate Gloria's somewhat quirky take on life. While the "settle down" sentiment is certainly understandable, the premise of that perfect partner likely looming at the breeding program is probably not the most romantic notion we've heard out there.

Gloria is one of the four primary protagonists who appear throughout the three-film *Madagascar* franchise. They all start at the Central Park Zoo in the 2005 opener with Gloria being amongst the animals thinking a departure from the zoo would not be a good idea, but of course as things work out the entourage ends up escaping initially to Madagascar and subsequently to multiple other stops around the globe.

 # 2) THE COCAINE HIPPOS ~ This is truly one of our most bizarre stories and just to make sure the blame falls on the appropriate parties, it was not the hippos that did the cocaine, it was the owner of their hippo ancestors. So now, take a step back, relax and allow us to connect the dots on this Colombian cartel craziness.

About four decades ago Pablo Escobar emerged in the mid-1980's as one of the most powerful men in the world with his Medellin drug cartel dominating a lucrative Colombian cocaine trade. For reasons that were not drug related, but rather just to flaunt his wealth, Escobar imported four hippos to serve as an interesting attraction for visitors to his personal compound.

While the hippos thrived in captivity, when Escobar died in a 1993 shootout, the animals were abandoned on the drug lord's estate. As the property deteriorated the hippos were left to fend for themselves with somewhat surprising results. For an animal that is endangered in its natural habitat of Africa, one might assume that they would not fare so well on a different continent where they had never lived in the wild.

But not so fast. These newly freed South American hippos headed for the beach where the surf was up and the sex was great. They filled the nearby rivers and, with no natural predators, began reproducing at a surprising rate.

How surprising? Right now, the count is estimated at about 130 and it is projected that the population could increase to 400 by 2030.

So while that may seem good news to the "Save the Hippo" hype, there are additional issues to consider. Some local towns have become used to seeing hippos casually roaming their streets totally complicating the job of the local pooper scooper. They have also become involved in an increasing number of automobile accidents.

A final environmental concern is that the level of hippo feces in the rivers has had a negative effect on the habitat of manatees (huge aquatic mammals) and capybaras (world's largest rodents). Here's our thought on who should bear the greatest culpability in this Colombian conundrum. Of all the drug-addled decisions made in this mess, who was the Colombian authority who decided **not** to take the four hippos that Escobar left upon his death and put them in a zoo?

Ironically, CNN and *The Guardian* both ran news stories on the "cocaine hippos" on March 30, 2023 which offered the following updates. CNN reported that the Colombian government had plans to relocate 70 of the hippos at a cost of $3.5 million. *The Guardian* cited a study that estimated the hippos here would number 1,400 by 2034, an even higher projection than the one cited earlier in this component. That's a lotta hungry hungry hippos!

 # 1) FIONA ~ We've got a real-life loveable story here! It begins on January 24, 2017, when a baby hippopotamus is born at the Cincinnati Zoo. Anytime a zoo witnesses the birth of a baby hippo it has to be somewhat of a story, but the tale of Fiona turns into an international event. Why, you ask? Well for multiple reasons which we're here to share.

For starters, she is the first hippo born at the Cincinnati Zoo in 75 years. She is also the first ever to be seen in the womb via use of an ultrasound and the staff names her Fiona because her ears look like the character in the *Shrek* movie. But the aspect of her birth that really kickstarts the story is that Fiona comes into the world six weeks prematurely initiating a massive medical effort to assure her survival.

Fiona tips the scales at 29 pounds, which probably seems like a fairly hefty weight for a baby. But of course it's all relative. The birthing stats for hippos show that newborns can weigh up to 120 pounds, but it's probably more important to look at the other end of the spectrum. Prior to this, the lowest recorded weight of a hippopotamus born in a zoo had been 55 pounds, so in terms of preparing a plan for this preemie the medical team is clearly sailing in uncharted waters.

The Cincinnati Children's Hospital is called in to contribute their expertise to the process. Another first occurs when Fiona's mother Bibi is milked in order to bottle feed the baby who is unable to stand. February 5th becomes a red-letter day when Fiona takes her first steps and we'll continue the timeline with a few more milestones.

On May 31st she is introduced to the media for the first time, all 375 pounds of her! From that point on the zoo posts daily updates and Fiona's story begins to ascend to meteoric status. In August *The Fiona Show* debuts on Facebook with the star weighing in at 450 pounds. *The New York Times* dubs the phenomenon *Fionamania*.

When her first birthday rolls around in January of 2018, she is tipping the scales at over 650 pounds. Later that year *Saving Fiona*, her "biography" is published in June. According to zoo director Michelle Curley, "Lots of people got engaged next to the window where Fiona was visible. She was in a lot of engagement photos." She even had a huge hippo mural unveiled in downtown Cincinnati. *Fionamania* indeed!

Fiona's birthday has become a citywide celebration in Cincinnati with dozens of businesses offering hippo-related specials and prizes. As of July 2023, Fiona weighed 2,036 pounds and continues to enjoy her celebrity status. If you're looking for a very special holiday gift for that animal lover on your list, one suggestion would be the classic holiday hippo book, *A Very Fiona Christmas*.

Here's our poem regarding the desire to have engagement pictures taken with Fiona...

The favorite choice for a lot of us
In a photo op certain to rank a plus
If logistics aren't proven too much a fuss
Could we pose with a cute hippopotamus?

RHINOCEROSES

When it comes to the rhinoceros there are two types in Africa; you have the black rhino and the white rhino... and they're both gray. So how did this color conundrum come about? It all traces back to the shape of the rhinos' mouths and the Afrikaans language which was the most commonly used language throughout the southern part of the continent during colonial times.
Black & White ~ White rhinos have a wide square lip while black rhinos have a pointed lip. The Afrikaans word for "wide" was "weit" which became the word the Afrikaans language used to designate the wide-lipped rhinos. When the early English explorers arrived, they mistook "weit" for "white" and subsequently the wide-lipped rhinos became known as white rhinos.

Then, essentially by default, the "other" type of rhino became known as black rhinos. So in terms of the two colors in place in the names of African rhinos, they're both based on a misconception and have nothing whatsoever to do with the actual color of the animal.
Black Rhino ~ These animals live primarily in southeast Africa and fortunately they have also enjoyed a bit of a comeback in terms of population. Efforts by the World Wildlife Federation beginning in 1961 targeted the goal of bringing the black rhino back from the brink of extinction. By 1995, the estimated

population of the species reached its low point at about 2,400. Today's tally shows that number exceeding 6,000.

White Rhino ~ While this species of rhino does boast the largest numbers, it is still classified as "near threatened". There are about 16,000 white rhinos living in central and south Africa. In terms of size, the white rhino is the largest species achieving a height of 10 feet, a length of 13 feet, and a weight of 4,500 pounds. That establishes them as the second largest land mammal, behind only the elephant.

While we're breaking down rhino types by continent, let's leave Africa and head for Asia. On that continent there are three types of rhinos, fortunately with more functional names. Those types would be the greater one-horned, the Javan, and the Sumatran.

Greater One-Horned Rhino ~ There's actually somewhat of a success story to be shared on this species. In the year 1900 the total world population of this rhino hovered at around 200. Subsequently, effective protection and management plans by wildlife authorities have resulted in one of the most impressive conservation stories in world history. Currently there are about 4,000 greater one-horned rhinos populating a swath of Asia that starts in eastern Pakistan, sweeps through northern India, southern Nepal & Bhutan, and ends in western Bangladesh.

Javan Rhino ~ One issue in play for every type of rhino on the planet is that they are endangered with the level of endangerment ranging from significant to borderline extinction. Three of the five species (Javan, Sumatran and black) are listed as "critically endangered" by the IUCN, the International Union for Conservation of Nature. We'll get the worst news out of the way first, beginning with the Javan rhino. There are about 75 remaining in the world and they all can be found at the Ujung Kulon National Park on the island of Java in the country of Indonesia.

This World Heritage Site provides protection and around-the-clock-monitoring by the national park staff. So while the human protection is in place, this location is vulnerable to a few natural threats. It is only 30 miles from the active volcano of Krakatoa and, located on the tip of the island, it would be susceptible to a tsunami. Subsequently there are exploratory efforts to start a second sanctuary site, somewhere safer, in Indonesia.

Sumatran Rhino ~ This rhino roll call pretty much reflects the Javan stats just stated. When we began our research for this project there were said to be 75-80 Sumatrans remaining, all found on the Indonesian islands of Sumatra and Borneo. During our writing process, our expert consultant Simon Jones, CEO of the advocacy group Helping Rhinos, provided an update telling us that, "There are now only 34-47 Sumatran rhinos in the wild. Complicating matters for this species is the fact that they are more spread out, with colonies on two separate islands which makes their protection more difficult while also simultaneously limiting breeding options."

The Sumatran Rhino Survival Alliance is spearheading the mission to save the species. Below is an outline of their three-pronged strategy…

* Establishing two new Sumatran Rhino sanctuaries in Indonesia, while also expanding the existing facility in Way Kambas National Park.
* Searching for and rescuing as many rhinos as possible, relocating them to breeding facilities.
* Incorporating the rhinos into a single conservation breeding program with high-quality veterinary and husbandry care.

Palm Oil Controversy ~ Our collegiate zoological guru Lindsey, who actually visited Indonesia as part of her course work, has firsthand awareness of this issue, and thought that this would be the most appropriate spot to drop in her perspective which she states as follows, "Palm oil is one of the world's most commonly used edible vegetable oils and is found all throughout products in your local grocery store including food and beauty products! The demand for palm oil across the world is rapidly causing deforestation to occur in areas like Indonesia and Malaysia, which is putting species like the orangutan at risk."

"As almost everyone reading this book consumes or uses products with palm oil every day, it is important to be informed about products that may produce palm oil in a more sustainable way, and the Palm Oil Scan App by the World Association of Zoos and Aquariums allows you to do just that! You can scan barcodes at the grocery store and the app will give you a rating regarding how sustainable the production of the palm oil used in that product is."

Conservation Status ~ While loss of habitat is a general factor affecting the endangerment of many animal species, the fate of the rhinoceros is further plagued by poaching. There is an element of this which is rather hard to explain because the demand for rhinoceros' horns is fueled by centuries-old social beliefs in some Asian cultures.

These beliefs include the notions that the horns have medicinal powers ranging from curing cancer, to recovering from a hangover, to solving problems with erectile dysfunction. Aforementioned *Helping Rhinos* CEO Simon Jones further clarified this by saying that "the [cancer/hangover/ED storylines] are really a western media myth and not strictly true of the cultural beliefs that drive the demand for the rhino horn. It would be more accurate to say they also believe they can cure the common cold."

All of these beliefs are implicitly false. Rhino horns are made of keratin which is the same material found in your nails and hair. There is no medical magic to be found there which adds to the frustration of the poaching problem.

That being said, the law of supply and demand is what it is and as long as a market exists, there will be opportunistic criminals willing to break the law to make a buck. Furthermore, poachers have become more brutal and sophisticated in their efforts, examples including the use of helicopters and military surveillance equipment to swoop in on a target, kill the animal, and chop off the horns.

All of this has resulted in a somewhat surprising environmentalist counter offensive. There is now a concerted effort to execute a pre-emptive dehorning of rhinos to prevent them from being targeted by the poachers. The animals are sedated to allow veterinarians to safely cut off the horns.

The animals are not hurt; it's basically similar to you cutting your hair or fingernails. And while the resulting look is unnatural, even the most prima donna of the rhinos would probably agree, it's a better look than being dead.

Life & Speed ~ The rhinoceros has a life expectancy of 40 to 45 years in the wild and 50 in captivity. Check out the countdown entry on Fausta below for the overall record in this category. The black rhino is the fastest, able to reach a top running speed of 34 mph providing a 100-YDT of 6 seconds.

They may be big but they are by no means slow! On that note, let's not be slow about getting on to our countdown of 5 Fine Rhinos…

 # 5) ROCKSTEADY, from *Teenage Mutant Ninja Turtles* ~ "I'm going to pop your head like a blueberry," was a threat once uttered by the villainous Rocksteady in the TV series *Teenage Mutant Ninja Turtles* which began in 1987 and has continued in various incarnations ever since. As the age-old adage goes, nothing like a fruit-filled threat to throw a scare into a Ninja Turtle.

In terms of villainy in the *TMNT* franchise, you have Shredder at the top of the pyramid. There are a variety of second tier henchmen who serve him and one of the more notorious pairs would be Bebop and Rocksteady.

For the record, Bebop's species would be identified as a warthog with Rocksteady being his dutiful hippo partner in crime. Rocksteady is a Ukrainian refugee who brings both brains and brawn to the party.

 # 4) GANDA ~ The year was 1515 and an interest was piqued; the Portuguese people were positively primed and pumped up over the impending Lisbon landing of a rhinoceros which the Indian Sultan Muzafar II had sent to their King Manuel. On the long trip from India to Portugal, having been fed only hay and rice as opposed to her regular diet of grass, Ganda was probably grateful to deboard.

Putting time in perspective, you'd have to go back to the height of the Roman Empire to find the last documented presence of rhinos in Europe. There was a rhinoceros present at the opening of the theatre of General Pompey in 55 B.C., and there was also one housed at the Colosseum when it opened in 80 AD. Those had been brought to the city essentially to symbolize the empire having conquered northern Africa.

But a millennium and a half later, with the Rome rhinos relegated to the rear view, the arrival of Ganda was big news. In January of 1515 Ganda departed from Goa, India for what would be a four-month sojourn. With the Suez Canal still centuries away, the ship would sail around the Cape of Good Hope at the southern tip of Africa, arriving in Europe in May of 1515.

While Ganda's arrival in Portugal had been much anticipated, it would turn out to be fairly short lived. The exchange of exotic animals as gifts during that era was not an uncommon practice and King Manuel soon decided he might be able to trade up and gain Portuguese pull with the Papacy. In one of those pesky problems of, "What do you give the Pope who has everything?" Manuel decides that the one thing Pope Leo X probably needs most would be a rhinoceros.

So in December of 1515 Ganda finds herself back on board a boat and heading out for that Mediterranean cruise she had always dreamed about. Unfortunately it would not have the ending she would have hoped for. After a layover in Marseilles at the request of King Francis I, who apparently had always wanted to meet a rhino, the boat departed for Italy.

So, what does a girl who's lotsa fun, and weighs a ton, wear to meet a Pope? How 'bout a flower-laden green velvet collar. Very slimming! But alas, 'twas not to be. Shortly after shipping out, the boat fell victim to a storm and sank, Ganda tragically drowning in the disaster. A sad irony was that if she had not been shackled to the deck there's a good chance she could have swum to shore. According to the International Rhino Foundation, "Her body washed ashore, was recovered, stuffed and ultimately delivered to the Pope." While we're sure Pope Leo would have had fun playing with a live Ganda, the stuffed version would have been much easier to clean up after!

 # 3) DURER'S RHINOCEROS ~ This one is predicated by the story we just shared, and it's strangely intriguing for two different reasons. After the visit of Ganda to Portugal, a German artist named Albrecht Dürer was commissioned to craft a woodcut sketch of the rhinoceros. That term needs a bit of explanation. The woodcut is basically two-dimensional, but with a slight element of depth where the wood has been carved to create the image. There are two intriguing aspects of Dürer's Rhinoceros.

Intrigue #1) Dürer never actually saw the rhinoceros before it set sail and drowned. He did his work based upon a sketch and written description with which he was provided. So the accuracy was a little suspect, as might be anticipated. Dürer's rhino has armor-like plates with rivets covering the body and a small horn on its back. Upon close inspection, other discrepancies can be discerned.

Intrigue #2) Despite the flaws in the image, Dürer's artwork becomes legendary. For the next three centuries, Dürer's depiction becomes the world's defining image of the animal, despite the imperfections. About the artwork it was said that "probably no animal picture has exerted such a profound influence on the arts." It was not until Clara's European tour of the mid-18th century (see #1 below) that more accurate depictions were crafted.

Between the storyline of Ganda's actual life, and the historic significance of the artwork subsequently based upon her, we are going to give her our vote as the most significant animal of the Renaissance.

 # 2) FAUSTA ~ It was 1965 when an eastern black rhino was initially identified in the Ngorongoro Conservation Area in the African country of Tanzania and named Fausta. Established in 1959, Ngorongoro includes vast expanses of forests, savanna woodlands and highland plains.

It also contains the Ngorongoro Crater, the world's largest caldera, which is a cauldron-like hollow that can form after the eruption, and subsequent collapse, of a volcano. The collapse would be due to the chamber that held all the molten lava becoming empty after the eruption, and thus taking away the structural support of the shell of the volcano.

This particular crater was formed over three million years ago and it is thought that before the volcano collapsed, the peak would have been higher than Mt. Kilimanjaro, the highest point on the African continent now. So how big was the crater the collapse created? It's 10 miles long, 12 miles wide and 2,000 feet deep, so big that it has created its own ecosystem which is now the home of a menagerie of animals which, in addition to rhinos, also includes gazelles, hyenas, wildebeests and zebras.

Monitored throughout a long happy life, old age finally began to catch up with Fausta in 2016 when her eyesight was noted to be failing and she was suffering the lingering effects of being attacked by hyenas. At that point she was removed from the wild of the conservation area and lived out her final years in a sanctuary within the site.

When she died of natural causes on December 27, 2019, she had the oldest documented age of any rhinoceros in history, 57 years.

 # 1) CLARA ~ While Fausta's story is better in the sense that she was able to live most of her life in the wild, Clara nudges her out for the #1 spot in the poll because in terms of fame and notoriety she honestly has to be given the edge. Clara was a superstar and here's her story.

Let's set the Wayback Machine with the following coordinates… Year: 1738, Location: the colony of Dutch India. After being orphaned when Indian hunters killed her mother, Clara was adopted by the director of the East India Company. In 1741 Clara was transported back to the Dutch port of Rotterdam where she would begin a 17-year tour as one of the most popular attractions on the continent of Europe.

With Captain Douwe Van der Meer serving essentially as Clara's agent and constant companion, the show began with Clara being put on display to adoring crowds in the Netherlands. Appearances followed in Antwerp and Brussels, Belgium in 1743 and Hamburg, Germany in 1744. Those exhibitions proved so successful that Van der Meer decided to make a full-fledged European tour with Clara as his primary attraction.

To that end, he built an eight-horse-drawn wooden carriage to transport his rhinoceros around the continent. Armed with a solid supply of special fish oil to keep Clara's skin soft, the tour began in earnest in 1746. The carriage went to Berlin where Clara was greeted by Prussia's King Frederick II in April. The next royal encounter occurred in Vienna in November with the rulers of the Holy Roman Empire, Emperor Francis I and Empress Maria-Theresa. And the route of royalty was not over.

The tour would go on to include stops in modern day Germany, Poland, Switzerland, France, Italy, Austria, Lithuania, the Czech Republic, Denmark, and England. The British Isles would be the last stop on her tour as she died there, at the age of 20, in 1758. It was a long and illustrious tour and they never ran out of fish oil for Clara's skin.

We'll wax poetical and finish with a bit of whimsy about a rhino story with an unexpected happy ending.

You're sinking in quicksand that's bottomless
In a dead-for-sure scene most preposterous
Facing atrocity
What are the odds you'd be
Pulled ashore by one friendly rhinoceros?

ELEPHANTS

African or Asian? ~ It's all in the ears; that's the rather unique trick you can employ to tell which continent the elephant you're looking at comes from. Elephants only live in the wild on two continents and there are only three surviving species, so they are fairly easy to sort out in that regard. Those three species would be African Savanna, African Forest and Asian elephants.

The ears of the two African species are considerably larger than the Asian's and there's also a shape differential in place which comes with a conveniently easy pneumonic device. The African ears are shaped like the continent of Africa and the Asian ears are shaped like the subcontinent of India. In layman's terms, if you'd rather not hold a map up to their ears for the sake of comparison, think of it this way…

Large "U" shape = Africa
Small "V" shape = Asia

One final differentiation would be that the African elephants have a trunk with two "fingers" at the tip, while Asian elephants have trunks with just one "finger." According to Carol Buckley of Elephant Aid International (EAI), "another distinguishing feature is that the African elephant has a 'sway back' or concave back, while the Asian elephant has a 'high rounded back' or convex back."

Intelligence ~ The fact that elephants are extremely intelligent is made evident on multiple levels. Let's start with the old cliché "An elephant never forgets". There is a basis in fact for this expression which is connected to the structural division of their brains. For the sake of comparison, 5% of the human brain is dedicated to memory while in elephants that percentage goes up to 7%.

In terms of self-awareness, elephants find themselves on a short list of animals who can recognize themselves in a mirror. Also notably included on that list would be primates and dolphins.

That list above would also obviously include humans and we'll close this intelligence thread out with another behavior that is observed in humans and elephants. We are members of only a few species known to exhibit clear expressions of mourning their dead. Burial rites in the elephant world include covering the dead body with branches and vegetation. The herd may also linger at the site of the dead for a period of time, and according to Carol at EAI, they also "caress the bones of family members years after their death."

Life ~ Moving on to a new topic, but continuing the thread of elephant/human comparisons, we rank one–two in life expectancy for land mammals. While that number for humans is in the low 70's, the life expectancy for elephants living in the wild is 80.

Guinness World Records acknowledges the longest living elephant in history to be Chengalloor Dakshayani (1930-2019) who lived to be 88 at the Chenkalloor Mahadeva Temple in India. That being said, there is an elephant named Vatsala at the Panna Tiger Reserve in India, who is an elephant living in the wild. That reserve claims Vatsala to be 105 years old, but since their documentation of her birth does not meet its standards, Guinness has not afforded her official recognition.

Size & Speed ~ In terms of size, African elephants are slightly larger than Asian with the males 10 to 12 feet tall and weighing 13,000 to 15,000 pounds, those numbers for females coming in at about 20% less. They can run 25 mph giving them a 100-YDT of 8.2 seconds.

Conservation Status ~ All species of elephants have suffered significant population decline over the past century with the percentage of decline estimated at 90% for African elephants and 50% for Asian. The Animal Welfare Institute officially labels African elephants as "threatened" with about 400,000 animals remaining and the Asian elephant is "endangered" since 1974, with about 50,000 remaining. Humans are the primary threat to elephants due to two basic causes, poaching due to the illegal ivory trade and loss of habitat.

Beehive Fences ~ We have the following contribution from Liaison Lindsey for this one… "One of my favorite conservation stories is the use of beehive fences to prevent elephant crop raiding and human wildlife conflicts. Locals and conservation agencies will hang beehives along a fence, all connected, so that if an elephant knocks into any part of the fence, it will shake the bees. The elephants have demonstrated being 'scared' of bees, because African bees swarm, and they can sting elephants in sensitive areas like the trunk, mouth, and eyes. So this fence is actually really effective, and it provides the locals a way to make money and food with the honey."

Let's get on with our list of Super 7 Elephants…

 # 7) QUEENIE ~ Unique as a waterskiing elephant in the late 1950's and early 1960's, Queenie toured the country appearing at circuses, state and county fairs, and on TV shows while billed as "The World's Only Water-Skiing Elephant". She was trained to balance herself on a large set of water skis before being tugged around slowly by a powerful motorboat.

Queenie was born in Thailand in 1952 and much of this storyline is certainly reflective of how much times have changed. Here's the Queenie (1952-2011) backstory... in 1953, at the age of 6 months and weighing 250 pounds, she was exported to a pet store in New York City and subsequently sold to an animal trainer named Bill Green in a transaction which was broadcast on the *Today* show.

The Asian elephant was trained by Green and his daughter Liz to perform tricks such as dancing, playing the harmonica, and of course the aforementioned water skiing. Amidst any concerns that Queenie was misused, Liz went on record as saying, "She thoroughly loved skiing. She would put her trunk in the water and get a big scoop of water and spray it all over the place! She loved it. Elephants can swim, and in that particular area, the water wasn't that deep. Even if she did spill over, they can swim. There was no danger."

In terms of her media resumé, in addition to the *Today* spot mentioned above, Queenie also appeared on *The Tonight Show* and on *I've Got a Secret*. In print she was featured in a series of advertisements for Mercury outboard motor boats. After retiring from the entertainment business, she lived out the rest of her life at the Wild Adventures theme park in Valdosta, Georgia.

 # 6) BABAR ~ A takeaway from this one would be that if you are the King of the Elephants, do not cut corners when it comes to hiring the royal mushroom screener. More on that in a minute. Babar was the protagonist in a series of seven children's books written by the French author Jean de Brunhoff between 1931 and 1937.

The storyline begins with the mother of the young elephant Babar being killed by a hunter. Later Babar escapes to the city, learns the secrets of human civilization, and then returns to the jungle to share his knowledge with his people, or perhaps his pachyderms might be more appropriate. When the Elephant King dies from ingesting a poisonous mushroom, the Kingdom Council urges Babar to ascend the throne noting the wisdom and experience he has acquired from living among mankind.

The throne is not always the most comfortable of seats as subsequent stories in the series have King Babar dealing with lionous roars and rhinoceros wars. The franchise spawned a TV series which ran from 1989 to 1991.

 # 5) TAI ~ Step right up and meet the most famous elephant actor of all time! That would be Tai (1968-2021). She was an Asian elephant whose movie career resumé boasts 17 films. The three films considered to be her best performances are *Operation Dumbo Drop* (1995) where she plays the role of Bo Tat; *Larger than*

Life (1996) where she plays Vera; and *Water for Elephants* (2011) where she plays Rosie.

Other significant films include…

* *Annie* (1982)
* *Big Top Pee-wee* (1988)
* *The Jungle Book* (1994)
* *George of the Jungle* (1997)
* Britney Spears' "Circus" video (2008)

Her name came from the fact that she was born in Thailand and she even got to return to her homeland for the filming of *Operation Dumbo Drop*. Filmmakers took significant steps to ensure Tai's well-being during the making of the movie importing all of her food and water, even her bathing water, from the U.S.

The American Humane Association (AHA) rated as "acceptable" her treatment during the making of the film. Any scene depicting Tai in possible danger was staged carefully. In the scene with her snoring, that noise was actually not emitted from the animal but dubbed in later. In another scene where she is shown to be sedated, she is actually just lying down as per her trainers' directions.

 # 4) TANTOR, from *Tarzan* ~ Before Uber arrived in the jungle, when Tarzan needed a lift anywhere the call would go out for his go-to elephant Tantor, who was also very proficient at stomping on things when the need arose. Between the piercingly shrill cry of Tarzan's call and the excellent ears of Tantor, the man and beast always maintained excellent channels of communication.

The original Edgar Rice Burroughs series consists of 24 books written between 1912 and 1966, and dozens of movies made during that same time period, in which Tantor is an umbrella name applied to different elephants. The single elephant in the 1999 Disney movie was a red African forest elephant.

 # 3) HORTON, from Dr. Seuss ~ This elephant is one of the few characters who Dr. Seuss was so fond of that he actually received the lead role in two different books. The first was *Horton Hatches the Egg* (1940) and the second was *Horton Hears a Who* (1954). The characterization is the same with the naïve and kind elephant looking to help others only to be taken advantage of in the process.

In *Horton Hatches the Egg*, the elephant happens upon a lazy bird named Mayzie who has just laid an egg but would rather vacation in Palm Beach than perform the requisite parental duty of sitting on the egg until it hatches. Horton reluctantly agrees to step in for the vacation-bound bird who says…

I'll hurry right back. Why, I'll never be missed...."
"Very well," said the elephant, "since you insist...
You want a vacation. Go fly off and take it.
I'll sit on your egg and I'll try not to break it

So the deal is struck, and while that crazy Mayzie is carefreely packing her bags, Horton does trouble-shoot nest-sitting snags. In other words, what problems should he be thinking about regarding this new assignment he has agreed to take on.

H-m-m-m... the first thing to do," murmured Horton, "Let's see...
The first thing to do is to prop up this tree
And make it much stronger. That has to be done
Before I get on it. I must weigh a ton.

So Horton successfully addresses the construction issues and begins his stint of sitting on the egg, which turns out to be more than he bargained for, but of course didn't we all see that coming!? Summer falls into autumn which wafts into winter but for Mayzie, spring break never ends. Horton, never derelict in his duties, continues to man his station on the egg despite the cold weather setting in. This affords him the opportunity to deliver what may be the signature lines of this Seussian legend.

But Horton kept sitting and said with a sneeze,
"I'll stay on this egg and I won't let it freeze.
I meant what I said and I said what I meant...
an elephant's faithful 100 percent!"

The ending of the story is interesting in that while it is biologically suspect, it does certainly serve as a wonderful example of poetic justice. Mayzie returns and wants to reclaim the egg just as it's about to hatch, but when the shell cracks the hatchling has elephant ears and a trunk, justly rewarding Horton's devoted perseverance.

Moving on to the second Seuss book, *Horton Hears a Who!*, one interesting note is that the good doctor introduced the concept of the town of Whoville, inhabited by miniature Who creatures, well before that concept became iconic in his 1957 book *How the Grinch Stole Christmas*.

In this story Horton is leisurely wallowing in a pond, as elephants are prone to do, when he hears a cry for help emitted from a speck of dust. He places the speck on a sprig of clover for safety. Further investigation by Horton reveals that this small speck of dust is actually a microscopic world in and of itself, named Whoville, which in turn is inhabited by even more microscopic beings called Whos.

Horton hears a Who who's afraid that the dust speck that is his home will blow into the pond thus ending the world of his people. The Who Horton heard is the Mayor and he's eternally grateful to Horton for saving his people from this fate and thankful for Horton's promise to keep them safe.

Problems however ensue when Horton is the only one in his world who can hear the invisible Who, thus causing him to incur the wrath of the animal kingdom surrounding his pond.

Dr. Seuss describes Horton's response to his fellow animals as follows…

"Believe me," said Horton. "I tell you sincerely,
My ears are quite keen and I heard him quite clearly.
I know there's a person down there. And, what's more,
Quite likely there's two. Even three. Even four."

Everyone from the kangaroos, to the monkeys, to the eagles, labels Horton as crazy and vows to take away from him the sprig of clover, which holds his speck of dust, which holds the Whos. Sensing the peril imposed on his Whos, Horton doubles down on his commitment to protect them.

"Should I put this speck down?…" Horton thought with alarm.
"If I do, these small persons may come to great harm.
I can't put it down. And I won't! After all
A person's a person. No matter how small."

That last line essentially serves as the theme for this story, Horton not yet realizing the lengths to which he will have to go to protect the Whos for whom he's assumed responsibility. However, the intolerant ire of the animals elevates to the point where they conspire to have the eagle Valad Vlad-l-koff steal the clover and fly away to hide it. With Horton in hot pursuit, the eagle flies to a hundred-mile-wide clover patch and drops the Who clover inside.

So, how many clovers do you think there would be in a clover patch that was a hundred miles wide? Turns out that the answer just happens to be… roughly three million. They counted you see. Why don't we let Dr. Seuss recount the part of the story where Horton finds the huge clover patch and embarks upon his needle-in-a-haystack hunt for those Whos. His search continued…

Then, on through the afternoon, hour after hour…
Till he found them at last! On the three millionth flower!
"My friends!" cried the elephant. "Tell me! Do tell!
Are you safe? Are you sound? Are you whole? Are you well?"

Actually the Whos are whole, doing quite well indeed, leaving Horton's one need, that the others concede and accept the news, that there really are Whos. Did you notice us rhyming there? Isn't the fun contagious?

To confirm the existence of the Whos, Horton organizes a massive Who holler where everyone in Who-ville unites in simultaneous screaming, finally reaching a clamorous crescendo which is able to make believers of the others in the animal kingdom. We'll sum up the story, in our own poetry, as follows…

When the facts they peruse
And no longer confuse
It's their pride they must lose
And then those kangaroos
They must accept the news
That there really are Whos

 # 2) JUMBO ~ One sure sign that an animal, or a person, or a thing has become ultimately impactful upon society is when the name of that animal, person or thing becomes so famous that it becomes synonymous with the concept it most epitomizes. The ultimate achievement in this regard would be that the proper noun enters the language as a common noun. Such is the case with the most famous elephant of the 19th century, Jumbo.

Let's share such a story and we promise to return to the etymology. Born around Christmas Day, 1860, in the African country of Sudan, Jumbo's mother was killed by hunters. The orphaned elephant was captured by natives, sold to an Italian animal dealer, transferred to the Jardin des Plantes Zoo in Paris, and eventually ended up at the London Zoo in 1865.

That's a lot of traveling for any elephant already, but the biggest trip is still looming on the horizon. Jumbo spends the next 17 years as the pride of the London Zoo, absolutely loved by an adoring British public. What could possibly bring this love affair to an end? How 'bout a boatload of American bucks and the Greatest Show on Earth?

Enter circus entrepreneur P.T. Barnum, the guy responsible for the legendary line, "There's a sucker born every minute." In 1882, Barnum pays the London Zoo $10,000 to buy Jumbo so he can take him back to the states and make a killing at his Barnum and Bailey Circus. Let it be known that this transfer happens amidst a massive public outcry of disapproval in the UK.

Barnum didn't make his millions by miscalculating business opportunities and Jumbo may have been one of his finer financial feats. It took just two weeks of circus ticket sales to recoup the ten grand and it was all money in Barnum's bank after that.

So how big was Jumbo? He tipped the scales at 7 tons, with "tipped" being perhaps not the most operative word around which to wrap a cliché in this case. His height was a subject of some debate with the acknowledged showman Barnum advertising that Jumbo was 13' 1" tall, but photographs, with humans in the picture frame, show the actual height to be closer to 10' 7".

Anyway you size it up, Jumbo's fan appeal was… well, jumbo. And if you look at our calculated use of capitalization in that last sentence, it will bring us back to the etymology piece we previously promised.

Before the circus elephant "Jumbo" came to the states in 1882, the word "jumbo" was **not** a word in the dictionary. It was by the sheer existence and fame of the animal that Jumbo became jumbo. Or, another way of saying it would be that a proper noun came into such common usage that it became a common noun.

Just to throw out some other examples to illustrate the concept in the English language, Jell-O became jello, Kleenex became kleenex, and Band-Aid became band aid. And our closing thought on this would be to run through some expressions where you could ask yourself how many times you've uttered the phrase without realizing that if it weren't for a 19th century elephant you would never be saying, "jumbo shrimp", "jumbo marshmallows", or "jumbo jet".

 # 1) DUMBO, from Disney ~ "Embrace what makes you different," says Timothy Mouse. "Why didn't I think of this before? Your ears! Just look at them, Dumbo! Why, they're perfect wings!" So we know we're heading for a happy landing when the conclusion has Dumbo taking flight. But it does take some work to get there in the 1941 Disney film *Dumbo*.

When this turns into a successful circus-saving act, Dumbo is suddenly endeared to, and embraced by, that circus community which had shunned him. Is there perhaps a Christmas song in this scenario? Do you recognize the concept of a kind character, cursed with a physical abnormality, being ostracized by his community until that abnormality proves of service. Isn't that the same basic storyline for the "Rudoph the Red-Nosed Reindeer" song which would be written just a few years later?

Chapter 5

GRACEFUL MOVES UPON THEIR HOOVES

GIRAFFES

Let's fill our carafe
with the joy of giraffe

If a job description which dictates that you have to stand for almost your entire life and only get to sleep for one hour a night doesn't sound like your cup of tea, then make sure you never apply to be a giraffe. That is the gig they get; they eat, sleep and even give birth while standing up.

Appearance ~ Their legs are so long that their heads actually cannot reach the ground by leaning over. They absorb most of their water from the food they eat, but if they ever do need to drink water directly, they must go through a rather awkward approach where they spread their front legs and kind of kneel so as to get their heads close enough to reach the water.

Size ~ With adult males standing as much as 18 feet tall, giraffes get the nod for being the tallest animal in the world and they can weigh in at just over 4,000 pounds. Then in terms of superlatives, they also have 18-inch prehensile tongues which they can use to grab that high-hanging food that other animals can't reach.

Life & Speed ~ All the world's giraffes living in the wild are found in sub-Saharan Africa with the greatest concentrations living on the grasslands and open woodlands of East Africa. In terms of life expectancy, they can live 25 years in the wild and 30 in captivity. The oldest recorded living giraffe ever was Momo who died in Japan in 2021 at the age of 32. Top speed for these tall guys is 37 mph giving them a 100-YDT of 5.5 seconds.

Fun Facts ~ Here are a couple traits which giraffes share with humans…

* Giraffes have fingerprints, sorta… The dark patches on their bodies are all unique with no two ever being exactly the same.
* Giraffes have a sweet tooth… In zoos, they're often fed bananas, while in the wild, apricots and mangoes are favorites.

And we'll close with Liaison Lindsey's fun facts of… "A giraffe's tongue is 18-20 inches long, and the blue-purple color acts like sunscreen for their tongue as they spend a lot of the day eating trees. They also have sticky saliva that helps protect their tongue from spiky thorns on trees they like to eat like the acacia. Giraffes (actually most mammals excluding a few weird ones) have the same amount of neck vertebrate-seven! Crazy to think we have the same number of bones in our neck that giraffes do!"

Not-So-Fun Facts ~ Regarding the conservational status of giraffes, we're going to defer to Executive Director Stephanie Fennessy of the Giraffe Conservation Foundation who outlined the situation as follows. Note that Stephanie opts to use the alternate plural form of "giraffe" without the "s".

* "We now know that there are 4 distinct species of giraffe and not as previously assumed only one.
* Giraffe are in trouble and are undergoing a silent extinction. There are only about 117,000 giraffe remaining in all of Africa – that means there is **one** giraffe for every **four** African elephants! If you then consider that there are four distinct species, there is a real risk that one or two of these may become extinct." The biggest threats are posed by habitat loss and poaching.

At this point we'll proceed to our countdown of 9 Fine Giraffe Stories…

 # 9) EARLY AMERICAN GIRAFFES ~ This entry is to serve as an intro for the component on Lofty & Patches which logs in at # 3 below and shares the story of the first famous giraffes to come to the U.S. which the pair did in 1938. Ironically that was almost a century after the first documented giraffe of any kind in America.

Getting a giraffe to this continent during that period of time was not an easy task, because even if you were able to complete the capture component, they were tricky to transport. The first documentation of giraffes appearing in American traveling shows can be dated to 1837. In 1872 giraffes made their first appearance in Central Park in New York City and by 1874 Philadelphia had followed suit.

Credit for the first U.S. giraffe born in captivity goes to the Cincinnati Zoo in 1889. And after that, if you're looking to follow the giraffes-in-America storyline thread, feel free to fast forward to our aforementioned Lofty & Patches component below.

 # 8) ZATZ-IT, from Dr. Seuss ~ This is a giraffe creature whose creative conception could only have occurred in the cosmic mind of Dr. Seuss…

We have for you here one that will make you laugh
The Zatz-it which is a new kind of giraffe

In his book *On Beyond Zebra,* Dr. Seuss waxes poetic about some animals whose names begin with letters which come after the letter "Z" in the alphabet, letters to which only Dr. Seuss is privy. One such animal is the Zatz-it and here's his story.

And ZATZ is the letter I use to spell Zatz-it
Whose nose is so high that 'most nobody pats it
And patting his lonely old nose is the least
That a fellow could do for this fine friendly beast

Of course, if you're Dr. Seuss and noticing a situation where a kind, deserving animal needs a pat on the nose which he currently is unable to receive, there's no way you leave this sorrowful situation unresolved. Especially when all it requires to rectify the situation is picking up a pen and drawing a new Seussian invention. We'll let the good doctor take it from here and tell you what he does…

So, to get there and do it, I built an invention:
The Three-Seater Zatz-it Nose-Patting Extension.
If you try to drive one, you'll certainly see
Why most people stop at the Z. But not me!

 # 7) THE CAMELEOPARD ~ The first giraffe known to have set foot on the European continent was one brought back by Julius Caesar in 46 B.C. after his conquest of Egypt. This had been a good year for Caesar and he staged a parade in Rome to impress his subjects with the menagerie of animals he had been able to assemble.

Contemporary records indicate the variety of animals promenading in that parade to have included baboons, Egyptian salukis (greyhounds), flamingos, monkeys, ostriches, panthers, parrots, and of course the very unique giraffe which Romans had never seen before.

They assigned the species the name of "cameleopard" based upon the fact that it combined the long legs of the camel with the spots of the leopard. While in retrospect that may seem a little silly, the Roman name does survive in what is now the giraffe's actual scientific species name, "giraffa camelopardalis".

 # 6) THE MEDICI GIRAFFE ~ In 1487, this giraffe was the most notable to set foot on European soil since Caesar's giraffe, more than 1,500 years earlier. It was given to the Italian Prince Lorenzo de Medici who maintained a menagerie of animals for public viewing in his hometown of Florence.

This gift was from the Sultan of Egypt and qualified as an example whereby African countries during that era would sometimes swap exotic animals for political favors. While Medici did previously have a wooden giraffe in his menagerie, this live one was clearly a step up. Unfortunately the giraffe would only live a couple of months and it would be 350 years before another giraffe would set foot on the continent. See countdown entry #1 below.

 # 5) APRIL & TAJIRI ~ Go ahead and blame the damn internet. April gets the honor of becoming the first giraffe to ever become famous by going viral on YouTube. All she had to do was give birth in front of a live audience that included 1.2 million viewers. No pressure there.

The big day occurred on April 15, 2017 at Animal Adventure Park in Harpursville, New York. That morning park officials announced that April had gone into labor with the calf's hooves protruding from the womb. If you were busy filing your taxes on that fateful day back in 2017 and missed the show, we're here for you with a recap.

April gives birth in a standing position and the actual process of delivery takes about five minutes. The baby drops onto a bed of wood shavings where the mother immediately attends to him by licking and cleaning the calf to get its blood circulating. Within an hour the newborn giraffe is on its feet, standing almost 6 feet tall and weighing 129 pounds.

A "Name the Baby" contest had predetermined the name would be the Swahili word for "hope" which is "Tajiri". The YouTube feed had been sponsored by Toys "R" Us as a promotion for their mascot who was Geoffrey the Giraffe. While an affiliated GoFundMe campaign was a big moneymaker for the park and the Giraffe Conservation Foundation, turns out Toys "R" Us might have been better off conducting the fundraiser for itself.

Only one year later all the giraffes in this story would still be alive, but Toys "R" Us would be dead. Read on…

 # 4) GEOFFREY THE GIRAFFE ~ "I don't wanna grow up, I'm a Toys "R" Us kid." How many of you remember that classic advertising jingle? At this point we're thinking probably most of you, but it's a percentage that's destined to decrease, the franchise having closed its doors in June of 2018. Here's another "do you remember?" question for you.

As you examine the Toys "R" Us name as we have presented it here, do you recall one nuance as the name appeared on the store front that differs from what you just read? We'll give you one sentence to think about it before revealing the answer that… the middle letter "R" actually appeared backwards.

The advertising icon debuted in 1948 going by the name of "Doctor G. Raffe," the good doctor representing the franchise under that moniker until 1965. At that point it was decided that the advertising concept would be more kid-friendly if the doctor title were dropped and the first name fleshed out to something fun like Geoffrey.

 # 3) LOFTY & PATCHES ~ We're got two women and two giraffes that loom large in the legend of Lofty & Patches, the first two giraffes to become famous anywhere in the Americas. They had to survive a hurricane to do so, but more on that later. So now that we've slapped positive IDs on our giraffes, let's lead with our first lady. Here's her story…

Belle Benchley, aka "The Zoo Lady," is hired by the San Diego Zoo in 1925 and is essentially its director from 1927 to 1953. Funny thing about that "director" title. Officially she never has it, what with that "it's-a-man's-world" mentality dominating the era.

Benchley operates under the moniker of "executive secretary" until the year of her retirement when she becomes "managing director". But make no mistake about it, as the men who work under her would have confirmed, addressing her with genuine respect as "Boss Lady"; she is in charge of things during an era when the San Diego operation evolves from a modest menagerie of animals to the status of world class pre-eminence it holds today.

A milestone along that path is Benchley's 1938 decision that her zoo needs a pair of breeding giraffes and, to that end, arrangements are made for the delivery of Lofty & Patches from the country of Uganda in east Africa. The 3,200-mile, 54-day ocean voyage is not a delivery devoid of drama, far from it.

In an era before such storms are officially named, their ship is battered by what comes to be known as "The Great New England Hurricane" causing their giraffe crates to crash into one another with the female Patches' crate tipping over, breaking almost completely apart, and leaving the crew to initially think the giraffe is dead.

While Benchley has taken out a giraffe life insurance policy with Lloyds of London, we're sure Lofty & Patches are hoping that this will be one policy which will not be cashed in. While Patches does survive, all of the giraffes' food, along with a live rhinoceros, are washed overboard. The giraffes' reward for surviving the crashing of their crates is the ship's chef providing them with impromptu pancake breakfasts in lieu of their standard bill of fare which could, at that point, be found floating all over the Atlantic Ocean.

The pancake meal plan persists for three days before the ship makes port in New York City. When the American media picks up on the fact that two giraffes have survived being thrashed by what would turn out to be the second worst Big Apple hurricane in history, (behind only Sandy in 2012,) it is the beginning of a national story that will be followed by over 500 newspapers.

Right now, we'll let the Lynda Rutledge leg of the story kick in. She wrote a 2021 historical fiction novel called *West with Giraffes* which chronicled the transcontinental journey of Lofty & Patches "driven cross-country in little more than a tricked-out pickup truck" with their heads extended out of holes cut in the top of their crates.

Keep in mind, this is pre-interstate America, and one can't help but wonder, not only what the unique visual perspective would have been from the point of view of the giraffes, but also from the pedestrians taking in the passing of what must have seemed a preposterous sight. In one interview, Rutledge said, "I actually had a mental image of a little farm girl sitting at her window beside a road, bored to tears, when suddenly a couple of giraffes whoosh by in a truck." In the throes of the Great Depression, with World War II hovering on the horizon, when the giraffe truck unexpectedly ambles by how could people not be pondering, "Just how crazy has this world become?"

In October of 1938 Lofty & Patches arrive at the zoo in San Diego where they will have nearly 30 years together and produce seven offspring. The names of their children list as mostly typical animal names with one standout exception. As time marches on, so does history, and their calf which is born on June 6, 1946, on the one-year anniversary of the historic event, bears the moniker of "D-Day".

 # 2) MELMAN, from *Madagascar* ~ After escaping from the Central Park Zoo, the animal cast at the core of the first DreamWorks *Madagascar* film (2005) head to Grand Central Station where they enter human bathrooms for the first time. This sets up a very funny line which is funnier yet if we preface it with some characterizations. The rest of Melman's all-star quartet cast consists of Gloria (hippo), Alex (lion) and Marty (zebra). Melman has always been in love with Gloria but never had the courage to express it. With a full name of Melman Mankiewicz III, he is perfectly voiced by David Schwimmer in a self-deprecatingly Jewish schtick, not unlike his Ross character from *Friends*.

Meanwhile, let's return to Melman's first excursion into a human bathroom. After his initial encounter with urinals, he exits the bathroom to share the following observation with the rest of the crew. "Hey! Hey, you guys!" Melman says, "That room has some nifty little sinks we can wash up in, and look! (taking a urinal cake out of his mouth which had been laying on his tongue) Free mints!"

Juxtaposed to his giraffe size, Melman exudes an insecure hypochondriac little-old-man persona characterized by lots of meds and doctor's appointments. When he notices the brown spots on his neck, he immediately assumes he's dying. You get the idea. When they get to Madagascar there's a festive scene where the lemur monkeys are suggestively dancing and while everyone else is enjoying the show, Melman is counting the number of health code violations he's noticing.

 # 1) ZARAFA ~ Eventually we're going to be sharing with you a fabulous 19th century French frenzy encompassing everything from women's hairstyles to wallpaper patterns. But before we hit high society Paris, let's take a jaunt through the jungles of Sudan. As alluded to earlier, diplomatic gifts of exotic animals were fairly commonplace during the 1800's and that will be the premise in place for this story.

In this unique display of diplomacy, we have France's King Charles X on the receiving end of a generous gesture on the part of the Viceroy of Egypt, Muhammad Ali. Let's pick things up in the spring of 1826 with native hunters in Sudan capturing a two-year-old Nubian giraffe, who would come to be named Zarafa, and proceeding in a process that would not be PETA approved. No way, no how, never.

If there is anything in this upcoming storyline that conveys an appropriate level of human compassion in this tale it would be that a Black Sudanese animal caretaker named Atir joins Zarafa at this point and will accompany the giraffe through the rest of her life. And she does have two decades in front of her to spend with Atir. Lots of human/giraffe bonding time.

Zarafa is carried by camel from the capture site to the Nile River. She is then put on board a felucca, a small boat propelled by oars and/or sails. From there it's Khartoum, here we come! Upon reaching Sudan's capital city, there will be a rather nice upgrade in Zarafa's food, accommodations, and means of transportation. Nothing but first class from here on out, baby!

Zarafa is loaded on board a custom-designed barge to traverse the next part of the Nile which will deliver the giraffe to the port city of Alexandria, Egypt on the Mediterranean Sea. Still a growing kid, Zarafa requires vital nourishment and lots of it. To that end her barge is equipped with three cows which provide her with seven gallons of milk every day.

Upon arrival in Alexandria, Zarafa is loaded onboard a seafaring ship set to navigate the Mediterranean. And… we have more special accommodations! A hole is cut into the deck of the ship so that the giraffe can stand in the cargo hold, poking her head and neck through the hole to get some fresh air and enjoy the view.

The voyage from Alexandria to Marseilles takes a little over a month with the ship landing in France on October 31, 1826. If Zarafa is thinking, "Are we there yet, are we there yet?" she will only be getting a qualified, "Yes" at this point. Yes, a giraffe has set foot in France for the very first time ever, but this girl is still a long way from what will be her home. The port city of Marseilles is obviously going to be on the southern coast of France and Zarafa's new digs are going to be in Paris which is still 550 miles away.

So there are lots of logistics coming into play at this point. Consideration is given to sailing the ship around the Iberian Peninsula (Spain and Portugal) and up the Atlantic coast of northwestern France but that is deemed to be too dangerous. Another factor in dismissing that option is that even if the nautical component is successfully negotiated, you're still over 100 miles from Paris at whatever location you land.

The French appoint a naturalist named Etienne Geoffroy Saint-Hilaire to take over at this point, and make the decisions determining what would be the best course of action now that Zarafa is on French soil. He decides that the safest way to proceed is to have the giraffe walk the distance, and with various aspects of preparation needed and winter approaching, that sojourn would take place when the weather warms up the following spring.

So Zarafa winters in Marseilles, every giraffe's dream, and a departure date of May 20, 1827 is set. The 55-year-old Saint-Hilaire is to join the team making the trip. He also orders special shoes and a two-part yellow raincoat designed especially for Zarafa to help keep her comfortable on this final part of her journey.

Setting the stage for this last leg, picture the spectacle of this entourage. Promenading down the street, you've got a 55-year-old scientist, a Black Arab animal groomer (Atir), a giraffe, and the three cows which are continuing to serve as Zarafa's mobile milk machine. Now that's something you don't see every day.

Needless to say, the entourage is a subject of sensational reception at every town through which it passes. A crowd of 30,000 turns out on June 6th when they arrive at Lyon and the 550-mile walk ends up taking a grand total of 41 days. When Zarafa arrives in Paris on July 9, 1827 there are over 100,000 people in her welcoming party, constituting almost 15% of the city's population.

As Zarafa is presented to King Charles X she wows the crowd by nibbling rose petals from the king's hand. She's a charmer indeed, and over 600,000 people line up to visit her new residence at the Jardin des Plantes within the Museum of Natural History and Botanical Garden in Paris.

That particular French museum is one of the world's foremost destinations of its type. Upon her arrival, Zarafa Fever infects France as she becomes a social phenomenon of epic proportions. On July 12th the French paper *La Pandore* reports that, "The giraffe occupies all the public's attention; one talks of nothing else in the circles of the capital."

Women fancy "towering horn" hairstyles. Giraffe themes become the rage in commodities ranging from ceramics to wallpaper to clothing to toys. While related plays and paintings appear, a shade of yellow dubbed "belly of giraffe" becomes the new national color. It is a French frenzy for the ages.

While the degree of sensation eventually subsides, Zarafa will be a public attraction for the next 18 years before she dies at the age of 21 with Atir by her side, a tear in his eye. Immortalized by the taxidermist, Zarafa is still on display in the French Museum of Natural History.

ZEBRAS

If you're a zebra and you've committed a crime don't think for a minute that the fact you have hooves rather than fingerprints is going to help you avoid detection. If those security cameras are on, the truth-be-told of the matter is that your stripe pattern has identified you equally as well as a fingerprint. Overzealous Zebra, your stripes are one-of-a-kind!

In one of our more sagacious segues ever, we will pass on to the zebras that if you do go to prison, those unwelcomed jailhouse risks of being attacked in a compromised prone position will be minimized by the fact that you have the ability to sleep standing up. All it takes is that quick little locking of your knee joints.

Habitat ~ First off, those in the wild are all in Africa, except of course for that ragtag band of California zebras which is a story in and of itself, and we'll get to that later. If you look at the map showing the habitat areas of the zebra it somewhat resembles a "J" drawn onto that map of Africa.

African zebras can be found in a vertical strand running down the eastern side of the continent from Ethiopia southward (the stem of the "J"); then at the bottom of the continent that habitat strand curls horizontally westward through the country of South Africa (the bottom hook of the "J"). In terms of habitat terrain, they prefer woodlands and grasslands and, for the most part, avoid deserts and rainforests.

Species ~ There are three species of zebras on the planet and, ranging from most to least endangered they would be "Grévy", "mountain" and "plains". We'll give you a quick overview of each.

Grévy Zebra ~ The explanation for the name comes at #6 in the upcoming countdown so we'll get to that later. In terms of appearance, Grévy zebras are generally considered to be the most beautiful which, unfortunately for them, made them the most sought after by hunters. Their stripes are thinner and tighter than other zebras and their bellies are white and stripeless. One visually striking aspect of this species is the concentric rump stripes.

These are the largest of the three species standing 5 feet tall and weighing just under a thousand pounds. Their range has receded to just Kenya and Ethiopia, with a population that has decreased from 15,000 to 2,000 in the last 50 years. The International Union for Conservation of Nature (IUCN) officially lists the species as "endangered."

Mountain Zebra ~ There are two main coloring distinctions that will set the mountain zebra apart from the other two species. These are the only zebras that have a single black stripe down the middle of their backs running from the chest to the tail. The other unique stripe pattern for this species is that their leg stripes remain vivid all the way to their feet whereas the leg stripes on the other two fade or disappear before that.

In terms of size, the mountain zebra is the second largest coming in at about 4½ feet in height and weighing around 800 pounds. In terms of their current population, there's a fairly wide range of estimates given by various organization with IUCN putting the number at 9,000 with Defenders of Wildlife offering the much lower figure of 3,000. Either way, it's an optimistic comeback from the 1930's when they were hunted to the verge of extinction with only 100 animals surviving. The IUCN lists the species as "vulnerable".

Plains Zebra ~ This zebra is also known as the common zebra simply because there are more of them and they span the widest area. Here are your two distinguishing trademarks to differentiate them from the other two species. They are the only ones that have belly stripes with the Grévy and mountain zebras both sporting that soft white underbelly look. The other difference is that they have what is called a "shadow stripe" in between the black ones; every other stripe on this species is a faint gray one.

These are the smallest zebras at about 4 feet tall and weighing about 600 pounds. Probably because they're the most numerous and spread out, we've got a range of population estimates here as well. While the IUCN coming in at 500,000 while Defenders of Wildlife establishes the figure at 750,000. The IUCN officially lists the species as "near vulnerable".

Life & Speed ~ In terms of life expectancy, zebras are good for about 25 years in the wild and 40 in captivity. They can hit a top speed of 45 mph giving them a 100-YDT of 4.5 seconds. Closing with a fun fact, zebras have a successful record of cross breeding with zorses and zedonkeys being most prevalent. But there are also other examples such as the one where a stallion zebra is bred with a mare Shetland pony to produce…, you guessed it…, a Zetland pony.

At this point let's move on to our "Super 6 Zebra" countdown.

 # 6) ZEBRAS IN ROME ~ The very first documented appearances of zebras anywhere outside the continent of Africa occurred in Rome during the opening of the Colosseum in 80 AD. During the 211-217 reign of Emperor Caracalla (full name: Marcus Aurelius Antoninus), zebras were noted to be part of the entertainment offered to the public at the Colosseum in Rome. There would be no record of zebras in Europe again until the 19th century, as covered below.

 # 5) DAN ~ As Teddy Roosevelt assumed the presidency at the beginning of the 20th century, America found itself on an optimistic path. The Spanish-American War had been chalked up in the win column, the 100th anniversary of the Louisiana Purchase was being commemorated at the World's Fair in St. Louis, and American engineering expertise was directing the digging of the Panama Canal.

Amidst this America mania how could things possibly get any better for the new president after whom the Teddy Bear would be named? On Thanksgiving Day of 1904, Roosevelt was informed that Menelik II, Emperor of Abyssinia (modern-day Ethiopia), had a very special Christmas present on his way to the American president who he knew to be an avid animal enthusiast.

Teddy must have been a very good boy that year because in addition to his already extensive menagerie of live animals, he would be adding two baboons, two lions, two ostriches and… saving the best for last… one 4-year-old zebra named Dan. What a mess will be left under the tree this year!

 # 4) ON BEYOND ZEBRA, from Dr. Seuss ~ How can we get to the end of the alphabet without a shout-out to the greatest literary master in the history of hysterical wordplay? Our zebra countdown will continue with a fanfare from the awesome and wonderful world of Dr. Seuss.

In his book *On Beyond Zebra*, the good doctor is about to bestow the most wonderful lesson upon an adolescent learner who feels confident that he has mastered the alphabet. The book begins…

Said Conrad Cornelius o'Donald o'Dell,
My very young friend who is learning to spell
"The A is for Ape. And B is for Bear.
The C is for Camel. The H is for Hare.

Right off the bat you can see the verbiage of the Seuss book aligning with ours in the sense that it's all about the animals. And the alphabet and animals can be used to take people to wonderful places. As a matter of fact, it turns out that Dr. Seuss is privy to some magically mysterious letters that actually fall **after** the letter "Z" and, wouldn't you know it, each of these intriguing new letters is the first letter in an equally intriguing new animal that neither you nor

Conrad would have ever been aware of if you'd not read the book. So, we'll let the good doctor tell you what he, Dr. Seuss, did next...

I led him around and I tried hard to show
There are things beyond Z that most people don't know.
I took him past Zebra. As far as I could.
And I think, perhaps, maybe I did him some good...

As the book concludes, Dr. Seuss is exalting in the fact that he certainly seems to have made a believer out of Conrad Cornelius o'Donald o'Dell. About Conrad, Seuss summarizes...

Because, finally, he said:
"This is really great stuff!
And I guess the old alphabet
ISN'T enough!"
Now the letters he uses are something to see!
Most people stop at the Z...
But not HE!

 # 3) GRÉVY'S ZEBRA ~ The 1600+ year European zebra drought would finally come to an end in 1882 when Menelik II, Emperor of Abyssinia (modern-day Ethiopia), gifted a zebra to Jules Grévy, the President of France. (Yes, this is the same Abyssinian emperor who gifted Dan in #5 above.) This story doesn't turn out nearly as nicely as some of the other political gifts of exotic animals we've covered such as Zarafa (giraffe who went to France) or Billy (rhino who went to the U.S.).

The zebra died shortly after arrival but manages to live on in two capacities. It was preserved and is still exhibited in the Museum of Natural History in Paris. The species of zebra which was sent has taken on the name of that French president and is now known as Grévy zebras.

 # 2) MARTY, from *Madagascar* ~ "Alex, look at me. I'm ten years old," Marty says to his best friend Alex the lion. "And I don't even know if I'm black with white stripes or white with black stripes." Talk about your paradoxical dilemma – which way is a zebra to turn. For the record, if it really matters, the scientific take would be that zebras are black animals with white stripes.

As the first of the three movies in DreamWorks *Madagascar* franchise opens, the gang is celebrating Marty's 10th birthday and the stripe thing is not his sole source of consternation. Marty is bothered by the boredom he sees characterizing his life.

"Another year's come and gone and I'm still doing the same old thing," he dejectedly laments, "stand over here, trot over there. Eat some grass. Walk back over here." And when you put it that way, it does sound like there might be some room for improvement in the lives of these creatures collectively congregating at the Central Park Zoo.

So when Marty gets wind of the news that the penguins are planning a breakout it's perhaps not surprising that he is the first of the primary Core Four characters to leave the calm of the zoo in favor of the wild of Madagascar. Let the adventures begin!

Marty is voiced by Chris Rock who absolutely instills a funky soul vibe into the zebra's zany humor. If your DreamWorks film franchise following is more fixated on *Shrek* than *Madagascar*, here's your Chris Rock/Eddie Murphy analogy... What Donkey is to *Shrek*, Marty is to *Madagascar*.

 # 1) THE CALIFORNIA ZEBRAS ~ Okay, you're cruisin' Cali on the Pacific Coast Highway, soakin' up some sun and baskin' in peaceful Pacific breezes when suddenly you're shocked by the roadside sight you're seein' in San Simeon. You ask yourself, "What **am** I seeing here? Could it be a zoo break out?" Nope, there are too many of them.

Second thought... "Did I just drive through the entrance to a California Safari Park and not even realize it?" That would seem unlikely, right? With no recourse left but brutal honesty, you ask yourself the question, "What the hell are all these zebras doin', runnin' alongside my car as I weave my way up Highway One?"

At this point we come to your rescue and reassure you that you are not hallucinating and have not succumbed to the desert heat. You have happened upon a phenomenon known as the California Zebras, and we have a logical explanation we're willing to share with you. Well, it's sorta logical; keep in mind we are in Cali.

This tracks back to William Randolph Hearst who became one of the richest men in the world, making a fortune in the 1890's off the newspaper practice of "yellow journalism" willing to sacrifice ethics and integrity in order to sensationalize and sell papers. He was caricaturized and exposed in Orson Welles' classic 1941 film *Citizen Kane*.

Driven by a desire to flaunt his wealth, the tycoon built his self-absorbent Hearst Castle in San Simeon, an impeccably-furnished 165-room palace surrounded by pools, landscaped gardens, and gorgeous guest houses, on a modest 127-acre plot of land which eventually expanded to a not-so-modest 250,000 acres. Oh, and a few things we forgot to mention were the tennis courts, movie theater, and airfield.

At this point we're sure some of you are waiting for us to connect the stripes on those zebras we promised you, so let's do that. The world's largest private zoo was part of the glitz synonymous with the Hearst Castle. The menagerie was more impressive than most public zoos and, to convey that concept, we're going to opt for an opulent, exhaustive and alphabetical roll call of residents at what was officially the Hearst Garden of Comparative Zoology.

Please call out "here" if you are... an antelope, bear (black or grizzly), bison, camel (one-hump or two), deer (red or sambar), elephant, elk, emu, giraffe, goat, kangaroo, lion, llama, monkey, ostrich, ox, sheep, stork, swan, tiger, wildebeest, yak or, and here's the one we've been waiting for... zebra.

So what the hell happened? Turns out even tycoons are vulnerable to Great Depressions and the zoo closed down in 1937. Most of the remaining animals were sold or donated to other zoos, but Hearst hung on to his zebras. Then that next winter a storm knocked down the enclosure which contained the zebras and at that point they were all out on their own.

Your first thought might be that this would put the zebras in a dangerously vulnerable position, but that was not the case. Because of the similarity in climate and landscape between sub-Saharan Africa and central California, the zebras have not only survived, they've thrived. While the herd that escaped the Hearsts was fairly small, their numbers have increased to 151 as of last count making the California Zebras the largest herd anywhere outside the continent of Africa.

So at this point we are going to turn our black & white keyboard over to the black & white zebras and allow them to assume the first person perspective and tell this tale from their own colorful perspective...

Yes, we lived at Hearst Castle
Which indeed was a hassle
Then the storm of '38
It for sure did seal our fate
Now we zebras all do run
Up and down on Highway One

DEER

Here is what we found to be the most intriguing fun fact in our arsenal of deer research and we'll hand things over to those fun Finns for this one. According to *Smithsonian Magazine*, in Finland they have adopted the policy of painting their reindeer antlers with reflective paint for the purpose of decreasing the number of deer/car collisions. No word on how the reindeer feel about this.

Life ~ The average deer in the wild can expect to live 4-6 years, but if they're lucky enough to avoid danger, the high end of that spectrum would be 8-10 years. They do live longer in captivity with the record being a red deer at the Milwaukee Zoo who lived to be 26 years, 8 months old when it died in 1954. Deer can be found on every continent except Australia and Antarctica.

Size & Speed ~ The largest deer, caribou or reindeer, can weigh up to 400 pounds while an adult white-tailed deer, the most common species found in North America, would be about 150 pounds. In terms of largest antler span, according to Caesar Kleberg Wildlife Research Institute, "We will use 40 inches as our criterion to define an outlier in antler size of mature bucks." At full speed, a mule deer can peak at 40 mph which gives them a 100-YDT of 5.1

seconds but, confirming Santa's decision as a wise one, reindeer max out at 50 mph, yielding a 100-YDT of 4.1 seconds.

Name Game ~ Returning to the reference of the previous paragraph, caribou and reindeer are the same thing, with one subtle distinction. Europeans tend to use the word reindeer across the board, while in North America that same animal is referred to as caribou if it is in the wild and a reindeer if domesticated.

In a few related facts of interest, reindeer are the only species of deer that can be domesticated. And also, reindeer are the only species where the females also grow antlers. Next, we'll fawn over the Favorite 4 Deer in our list.

 # 4) ELLIOT, from *Open Season* ~ Always entertaining, Ashton Kucher voices the mule deer Elliot in the first 2006 installment of Sony Pictures' *Open Season* franchise. He was a spot-on fit for the part with Elliot's character being the embodiment of the persona Kucher exemplifies. In his role as protagonist, Elliot is a quite clever, quick-talking, hyperactive deer who wisecracks his way through the wilds of the woods.

Much of the humor is derived from the storyline where Elliot becomes paired with Boog, who was essentially the pet bear of the female game warden Beth. So Boog is soft and spoiled, while Elliot knows the ways of the woods and endeavors to bestow his expertise upon the new guy. Sample lesson… Elliot imparts, "Okay, Forest 101: These tall stick things are called trees. The big rocks are called mountains and the little rocks are their babies."

Please allow us to include another animal liberation exhilaration epitomizing the era. The Nabisco company changed the packaging of their classic animal crackers so as to not portray the animals as being in barred boxcar cages. As Elliot led his food-foraging friends in search of sustenance, one unavoidable reality was set upon them. "Yes," as Elliot acknowledged regarding animal crackers, "the giraffes taste almost exactly like the elephants."

 # 3) SANTA CLAUS'S REINDEER ~ While there have been alternate takes on the Santa Claus reindeer roster throughout time, far and away the most prevalent version would be the one rendered in Clement Moore's 1823 poem "A Visit from St. Nicholas". But there have been some changes since Moore first penned the poem, so even if you think you know this one inside out, we think we'll probably be able to bring something to the holiday table you haven't already heard before the end of this component.

Circling back to the very beginning, the first documented reference to reindeer pulling Santa's sleigh appears in the 1821 poem "Old Santeclaus with Much Delight". While authorship is not attributed it may have been written by the publisher William Gilley. If you've noted the dates, it's clear that it didn't take Moore long to pick up the reindeer name game and run with it.

It was only two years later when Moore fleshed out the story by establishing the numeration of the reindeer as eight, as well as giving them names. His piece appeared in the *Troy* (NY) *Sentinel* on December 23, 1823. The pertinent portion of the poem read as follows…

> *More rapid than eagles his coursers they came,*
> *And he whistled, and shouted, and call'd them by name:*
> *"Now! Dasher, now! Dancer, now! Prancer, and Vixen,*
> *On! Comet, on! Cupid, on! Dunder and Blixem;*
> *To the top of the porch! to the top of the wall*
> *Now dash away! dash away! dash away all!"*

Other than the fairly minor change of replacing the apostrophe in "call'd" with an "e", the other more noticeable differences are of course the names of the last two reindeer. In terms of etymology, those two names come from the Dutch words for "thunder" and "lightning".

Moore dabbled with those last two names over the years using "Donder" and "Blitzen" for the first time in 1860, by then settling on 7 of the 8 current names. Those were the names Moore would take to his grave.

The final update occurred in 1939 when Robert May wrote the story that first added Rudolph to the roster, a story which we'll cover in entry #1 below. May gave no indication of why he changed "Donder" to "Donner" so it's not known whether that changed inadvertently or if May just thought it sounded better. At any rate, when the "Rudolph the Red-Nosed Reindeer" song came out, all the reindeer names, and their reindeer games, would be carved in stone for all eternity.

 # 2) BAMBI ~ When Walt Disney released his 5th full-length feature *Bambi* in 1942, it would be the last such film the studio would produce in that decade. Because of the fallout from WW II, everything Disney released throughout the remainder of the 1940's would be compilations of shorter films. The next single subject movie would not come along until *Cinderella* in 1950.

At least they paused on a high note. This movie was based upon the 1923 novel *Bambi, a Life in the Woods* by Austrian author Felix Salten. In that book Bambi was a European roe deer, but to Americanize the animal the studio brought in a mule deer, native to California, whose movements were studied by the animators to achieve the greatest degree of realism possible.

Most everyone is familiar with the coming-of-age story where Bambi's mother is killed by a hunter leaving him to be raised by his father. Bambi's pathway to adulthood is enhanced by friends Thumper the rabbit and Flower the skunk. Female deer Faline becomes his best friend and eventual mate.

Of the many accolades accorded the film, one that stands out would be that from the American Film Institute. When members were polled in 2008 to pick the 10 best animated films ever, *Bambi* was voted #3. To save curiosity seekers that immediate trip to Google, we'll share that the poll started with #1 *Snow White* and #2 *Pinocchio*.

1) RUDOLPH THE RED-NOSED REINDEER ~ It's been a while since we blasted off in our Wayback Machine so why don't we fire the old girl up for our salute to Rudolph. We need to set our coordinates for… Time: 1939, Location: Chicago. Robert May is working in the publicity department for the Montgomery Ward department store which has established a holiday tradition of giving out free coloring books to the kids. The store decides it wants to up the ante this Christmas and give away books that are already colored in, while also coming up with a nice new story.

May is given the task of writing a children's Christmas story that the company could turn into that year's holiday giveaway in the form of a softbound comic book-type pamphlet. So as he's sitting at his desk one late autumn day, watching the Lake Michigan fog roll into Chicago, an idea sparks. He has been toying with the concept of a reindeer story and the proverbial light bulb goes on over his head. "Suddenly I had it!" he later exclaimed. "A nose! A bright red nose that would shine through fog like a spotlight."

May then wrote the original version of "Rudolph the Red-Nosed Reindeer" and over 2.4 million copies hit the press that year alone. So the initial success was truly overwhelming and the Rudolph giveaway became an annual Montgomery Ward event. But the initial success subsided and by the late 1940's May found himself seeking ideas to perpetuate the popularity of his reindeer.

As fate would have it, May had a brother-in-law Johnny Marks who was a songwriter and he agreed to turn the Rudolph story into a song. They thought the result had potential and Marks had the connections to pitch the tune to some top-notch talent. They met initial rejections from Perry Como, Dinah Shore and Bing Crosby, but soldiered on.

The right fit finally materialized when they hooked up with "singing cowboy" Gene Autry who had scored a holiday hit in 1948 with "Here Comes Santa Claus" and thought a Christmas follow-up might be a marketable mistletoe move. "Marketable" would prove to be an understatement as the Autry track flew to #1 during the week of Christmas 1949, selling 2.5 million copies.

"Rudolph" would go on to sell 25 million copies and held the position of being the second-best selling song ever through 1980. Energized by this genre of musical success, Marks, who was actually Jewish, went on to write multiple Christmas classics including "Rockin' Around the Christmas Tree", "Silver and Gold", and "A Holly Jolly Christmas".

Animal Planet ranks Rudolph as #26 on its list of "50 Greatest TV Animals".

Ranking deer
Tell you this much
Can't be done
Without Christmas

CHAPTER 6

THERE'S NO SHORT SUPPLY MATES IT'S TIME FOR THE PRIMATES

MONKEYS & APES

No more monkeying around, let's get down to business and lay some groundwork for our paean to the primates. In terms of vernacular, we can start by dividing the entire order of primates, which includes over 500 species, under two umbrella titles... basically you've got "apes", the bigger ones, and "monkeys", the smaller ones. That's a somewhat informal way to word it, but the Japanese Monkey Centre Academic Department served as our fact checkers on this component and they were good with it.

Other distinguishing features include the fact that apes do not have tails, while monkeys do, and apes rely more on their eyesight while monkeys have a stronger sense of smell. Apes have an edge in that, while there is variation among species, apes are generally more intelligent and boast longer lifespans. These last factors no doubt contribute to apes having more intricate social structures.

One sign of this ape intelligence would be that they are among an elite group of animals (also including dolphins, Asian elephants, and Eurasian magpies) that can recognize themselves in a mirror. How do you make this determination?

Scientists place an odorless mark on the ape in a spot where it cannot be seen directly, like the side of the head or the back of the shoulder. When put in front of a mirror, if the ape sees the mark in its reflection and goes to take it off, then clearly the ape has identified itself as the reflection in the mirror. We should note that there is some controversy surrounding the mirror test.

Shifting to the monkey realm, they can be divided into two groups – New World and Old World. New World monkeys live in Central and South America, while the Old World monkeys can be found in Asia and Africa. The biggest difference between the two groups would be that the American monkeys have prehensile tails, ones with the ability to grip which enables them to live in trees, while monkeys in Asia and Africa do not, and subsequently they live primarily on the ground. Remember, apes do not have tails at all.

Conservation Status ~ Liaison Lindsey added that, "It also may be interesting to note how many species are in trouble. From the journal *Science*, it appears that about 60% of primate species are threatened with extinction, and about 75% have declining populations, and with over 500 species, that is a lot of animals at risk."

Life ~ Regarding monkeys, baboons live the longest, 35-40 years, with the average monkey life span in the range of 25-30 years. For apes, both chimpanzees and orangutans can live up to 60 years.

The record life span for an ape is a double bonus enabling us to summon a name with a claim to fame. Foreshadowing #3 in our upcoming countdown, Tarzan's movie co-star Cheetah way-outlived his human sidekick, clearly in cahoots with a fine film agent who left him with a great health plan. His final credits, so to speak, did not roll until 2011 when he died at the Suncoast Primate Sanctuary in Palm Springs, Florida at the age of 79.

The record for a monkey is held by Buenos, a spider monkey who lived to the estimated age of 53 in the Japan Monkey Centre. Buenos died with no film credits, but he did have a story to tell. Our contacts in Japan asked us to insert the word "estimated" in the previous sentence because according to the Japan Monkey Centre Academic Department, "Buenos came to the Centre on September 15, 1961 and died on March 26, 2005. When she arrived at Japan Monkey Centre, she was already "Adult". The veterinarian back then estimated the age by the size and other elements.

The Centre went on to add, "If you think this information is too uncertain to be published, we have other spider monkey, who has arrived to our center on June 27, 1974 from zoo in Canada and she is still alive, so estimated age is over 50. Her name is Obake." We see this contribution from Japan as yet another example of the world rallying to share their stories in this project!

Size ~ The big boy in the primate playground would be the silverback gorilla. They can stand up to 6 ½ feet tall and weigh almost 600 pounds. The male mandrill is the largest monkey, measuring 3 feet long and weighing 100 pounds. On the other end of the primate spectrum would be the pygmy marmoset which measures about 5 inches and weighs about 5 ounces. Rather than eating a banana, this monkey is about the same size as one.

Speed ~ In a hypothetical primate face-off race, turns out the monkey would just edge out the ape with the pata monkey streaking to a speed of 35 mph followed in hot pursuit by the gibbon ape at 34 mph. These times equate to 100-YDTs of 6.0 and 5.8 seconds respectively.

Cover Your Ears ~ We'll close with a final fun fact, although it wouldn't be that fun if the inherent howl were happening within earshot. Howler monkeys are the loudest land animal in the world and can reach sound levels of 180 decibels (dB) – loud enough to cause permanent damage to human eardrums. If you're up for further "howler hijinks" they have extremely long tails, five times as long as their body. Now on to our Top 10 Primates.

 # 10) MONEKE ~ This primate definitely occupies an historical niche. In the medieval story "Reynard the Fox" dating from the second half of the 12th century, the son of Martin the Ape is named Moneke which etymologists generally consider to be the origin of the word "monkey".

 # 9) PLANET OF THE APES ~ Buckle your seat belts as complex sociological issues run amuck in this sci-fi classic. The entire franchise is initially established in 1963 when Frenchman Pierre Boulle who, after being inspired by the human-like facial expressions of the primates at the zoo, writes the novel upon which the first movie was based. *Twilight Zone* creator Rod Serling wrote the screen play and, teaser alert, it has an all-time *Twilight Zone* ending to die for.

In the story, three 20th century astronauts find themselves marooned on a planet where, in terms of intellectual dominance, the apes have managed to leapfrog the humans, who now serve the simians as silent slaves. In this new world which, due to a time-warp phenomenon, is existing centuries in the future from when the astronauts left Earth, the astonished astronauts find themselves subservient to the dominant creatures on this Planet of the Apes.

This franchise spins off into eight more movies and two TV series so the "franchise tag" is aptly applied. Explore that as you're so inclined, but here's the ironic twist that ties up movie #1. The human astronauts and the new planet's ape rulers find themselves together on a sandy beach with a single spike protruding through the sand.

At this point the camera pan reveals that the spike is from the crown of the Statue of Liberty which lays battered and buried in the sand, now only a tortured remnant of mankind's nuclear war which centuries ago had turned Earth into the Planet of the Apes. Cue up the *Twilight Zone* music.

 # 8) MARCEL, from *Friends* ~ The funniest recurring gag during the Marcel era of the sitcom *Friends* had to be how the monkey was able to manipulate the humans into multiple replays of his favorite song. If you've forgotten, or perhaps were not a *Friends* fan, the answer to the question of, "What was Marcel's go-to tune?" The answer would be "The Lion Sleeps Tonight", which began with the vocalization of the sounds "uh-wee-muh-way, uh-wee-muh-way" followed by the opening lines of…

> *In the jungle,*
> *the mighty jungle,*
> *the lion sleeps tonight*

Marcel was a small capuchin monkey who was good for a laugh right off the bat. In his first appearance at Monica's New Year's Eve party, Ross walks into the gala with Marcel sitting on his shoulder setting up the always sarcastic Chandler to deliver the line, "Hey, this monkey's got a Ross on his ass!"

 # 7) RAFIKI, from Disney's *The Lion King* ~ Perhaps no character in the history of animation got more mileage out of simply holding up a baby, but Rafiki certainly did make the most of his moment on Pride Rock. Standing at that summit, he hoists the child towards the heavens with all the animals of the jungle looking up against a majestic backdrop. At that point Rafiki uses the

Swahili language to invoke the "Circle of Life" concept which becomes the movie's mantra.

 # 6) J. FRED MUGGS, from the *Today* show ~ When the sun rose on the morning of January 14, 1952 it brought with it a shiny new nuance to American television viewers in the form of the first morning news show, NBC's *Today* show, which of course is still on the air today, no pun intended. The show was characterized by one of early TV's more memorable gimmicks, a co-host chimp named J. Fred Muggs.

When the show's ratings sagged during the first year, host Dave Garroway was convinced to share his stage with the chimpanzee who could be a bit of a scene stealer and not always in a positive manner. But when the ratings took an upswing and the advertisers started lining up, NBC found that it had painted itself into a corner and J. Fred would remain on the show until his retirement in 1957.

On the plus side, J. Fred could be a real entertainer. He would feign reading the newspaper while the morning news was being delivered. He played the piano with Steve Allen and could mimic Popeye's facial expressions upon command. He was clearly an intelligent animal who eventually mastered over 500 words.

J. Fred was smart enough to have his handlers procure a girlfriend for him who went by the name of Phoebe B. Beebe. Has a nice little ring, doesn't it? He made his initial appearance dressed in a diaper like a baby, but by the end of his run had accumulated a wardrobe of 450 outfits.

J. Fred became a marketing bonanza being featured on a vast array of merchandise and he was a sought-after figure for public appearances across the country. His downside was that he, as wild animals are prone to do, occasionally became too rambunctious and aggressive toward people. How smart was he? Smart enough to figure out that he could misbehave without being disciplined when the red light was on because that meant the show was on the air.

Animal Planet ranks J. Fred as #48 on its list of "50 Greatest TV Animals".

 # 5) KOKO ~ While our simian survey is suffused with superlatives, we'll take this opportunity to award the honor of the most intelligent primate in the parade. That distinction will go to Koko, a western lowland gorilla who lived from 1971-2018 under the supervision of her trainer Francine Patterson. She was born at the San Francisco Zoo and went on to spend most of her life at The Gorilla Foundation in Woodside, California in the Santa Cruz Mountains.

Two parameters often used to calibrate the depth of her mental capacities were that she understood approximately 2,000 English words and had command of about 1,000 gestures of sign language. Those abilities, corroborated by IQ tests administered to Koko where the results averaged around 80, would put her intellect on the level of a typical 3-year-old human.

Truth be told, there were naysayers who questioned the level of language mastery attributed to Koko. Some critics acknowledged that while she did receive significant popular media coverage, the scientific publications were outnumbered by those appearing in the popular press. Regarding that media mania, Koko's resumé did include two appearances as the cover girl on *National Geographic*. A 1978 issue features Koko in front of a mirror taking her own picture, and in 1985 she's shown cuddling her pet kitten.

While we're on the subject, another of Koko's accomplishments was that she took care of five pet cats in her lifetime, all of whom she personally named. The aforementioned 1985 cover shows Koko gently caressing All Ball, and her four subsequent cats which she named Lips, Smoky, Miss Black and Miss Grey. All of her cats were lovingly cared for, much like a baby gorilla would have been.

Want one more astounding example which serves to convey Koko's intellect? She had the ability to observe and comment about language. In one situation she was watching another gorilla attempting to learn sign language, and when that other gorilla successfully replicated the desired signal, Koko gestured "good sign."

Koko's celebrity status could be substantiated by reviewing her guest log at the preserve. Visitors of note included Leonardo DiCaprio, Flea (from rock's Red Hot Chili Peppers), William Shatner, Sting (from the Police), Betty White and Robin Williams.

 # 4) THE FLYING MONKEYS, from *The Wizard of Oz* ~ Attired in their ornate caps and complementing vests, the winged purple monkeys act as servants to the Wicked Witch of the West, carrying out her wishes upon request. While the monkeys in L. Frank Baum's 1900 novel could speak English, those in the 1939 MGM *The Wizard of Oz* movie starring Judy Garland just chatter and screech, although they do clearly comprehend the witch's verbal directions.

And just to refresh your memory, if it's been a while since you last visited Oz, what were those directions? Before departure, the monkeys are instructed to, "Bring me that girl and her dog. Do what you want with the rest of them, but I want that girl alive and unharmed. Now fly! Fly! FLY!". In completing their mission, they do wreak a little havoc by scattering some of the Scarecrow's straw before returning to the Witch's castle with their two primary targets. Their mission accomplished, the flying monkeys are not seen again in the film.

In modern pop culture, the flying monkeys from Oz have certainly attained iconic status. An internet meme search will quickly find the likes of, "Flying monkeys ~ Freakin' people out since 1939," and "Don't make me unleash the flying monkeys."

 # 3) CHEETAH, from *Tarzan* ~ If you're a dude living alone in an African jungle, you need a BFF you can truly trust and for Tarzan, that friend was Cheetah. Tarzan's simian sidekick was (almost) always played by a chimpanzee. But as one would correctly assume in a character role that has spanned the years from 1932-2017, the Cheetah baton has been passed on from primate to primate over the course of the franchise, one which includes over 50 movies and 5 television series.

It all started in 1932 with the film *Tarzan the Ape Man* which starred Johnny Weissmuller and Maureen O'Sullivan as Tarzan and Jane. The first Cheetah was played by a chimpanzee named Jiggs and if you'd like some clarification on our "almost always" wording from above, there have been a total of 19 animals who have played the part and 18 of them have been chimpanzees. The one odd-monkey-out was an orangutan named C.J. who landed the gig in the 1981 movie which starred Miles O'Keeffe and Bo Derek.

The storyline of Jiggs, the original Cheetah, swings on a very long vine. After his film career ended in the mid-1930's he retired to Florida, living at the Suncoast Primate Sanctuary. As previously stated, his film agent clearly left him with a great health plan because he was almost 80 when CNN reported his death on December 28, 2011. Debbie Cobb, the Suncoast spokesperson, identified the chimp's three greatest late-in-life passions as…
* listening to Christian music
* finger painting
* watching football

ironically replicating the typical Sunday schedule of many folks. Well, maybe not the finger painting. One comment we noted on the Suncoast Primate Sanctuary website in the aftermath of Jiggs death was "God bless you, Cheetah. Now you and Tarzan are together again."

 # 2) CURIOUS GEORGE ~ The very first Curious George book, written in 1941 by H.A. and Margret Rey, has the Man with the Yellow Hat going to Africa to capture George and bring him back to America, which is probably politically incorrect on some level by today's standards, but George seemed to suffer no serious psychological consequences from the abduction as the pair went on to become best friends. George's human pal was the only recurring character in the stories.

George's species is tough to pin down as his relative size seems to cast him as a smaller monkey but his character design resembles that of a gorilla or a chimpanzee, sans tail. The resumé of Curious George boasts 87 books, 198 cartoon episodes (beginning in 1979), and a movie (2006).

 # 1) KING KONG ~ While he was only the "Eighth Wonder of the World," the big fella comes in at #1 on our primate countdown. He's got a tall order to fill, but King Kong will be ready, willing and able to climb to the top of the Empire State Building to prove us right. With the original hitting the silver screen in 1933, the 2024 release became the 13th film in the franchise. Here's the story that got things started…

We have Carl Denham leading an American film crew to study Skull Island in the Indian Ocean which is inhabited by an intriguing assortment of oversized animals and dinosaurs. Denham captures King Kong and brings the ape back to New York City in order to exhibit him as the aforementioned Eighth Wonder of the World.

The Big Apple proves to be a difficult adjustment for the ape, but he does develop a fondness for one particular female, poignantly played by Fay Wray. Unfortunately, Kong allows his hormones to get the best of him as he carries the horrified heroine to the top of the Empire State Building. At this point the authorities see no available options other than to call in the heavy artillery. Atop the building and taking heavy fire while being buzzed by biplanes, Kong cradles a flailing Fay Wray in his hand before gently setting her down on a skyscraper ledge after receiving his fatal blow.

As the rescuers narrow in on our heroine, King Kong's abductor from Skull Island, Carl Denham, succinctly summarizes the situation by saying, "It wasn't the aeroplanes; it was beauty killed the beast." Right, Carl, or maybe it was you for bringing him to New York City in the first place.

SECTION TWO
EVERYTHING'S BETTER, DOWN WHERE IT'S WETTER

CHAPTER 7

IT'S TO THE BEACH WE HEAD WITH OUR FAVORITE PINNIPED

SEALS & SEA LIONS

The species umbrella opening over our animals in this semi-aquatic component is the pinniped. That would be Latin for "fin-footed". And while that phrase may sound a bit like an insult someone has dealt in your direction, if you're a seal, sea lion or walrus, you're going to just have to live with it. Of course, an inside joke would be the one where the sea lion turns to the seal and says, "Well, at least my fin can rotate!" More on that later.

One of our expert guest contributors on this component was the Seal Conservancy and their president Dr. Jane Reldan who led by saying that, "Your information about seals looks great. We appreciate your good work and thank you for supporting the seals!" Many casual observers might be hard pressed to differentiate between a seal and a sea lion so we thought we'd begin with the Seal Conservancy summary.

Size ~ Easily the most noticeable difference is that sea lions are bigger and much louder. The average weight of a male harbor seal is about 300 pounds and they are about 6 feet long, while a male California sea lion weighs on average 700-800 pounds and is 7-8 feet long.

"However," according to Kim Raum-Suryan, Coordinator of the Pinniped Entanglement Group (PEG), "California sea lions look pretty puny compared to Steller (or northern) sea lions, which are the largest members of the 'eared' sea lion family. Steller sea lion females weigh up to 800 pounds and are up to 9.5 feet long, and males can get up to 2,500 pounds and a length of 11 feet."

Appearance ~ Seals lack external ears – they have a tiny ear hole on each side of their head – while sea lions have small flaps for outer ears.

Seals have short, hairy, webbed front flippers with claws; while sea lions have long, hairless, skin-covered front flippers without claws.

On land, sea lions' hind flippers can rotate, enabling them to essentially walk on all four flippers. Seals on the other hand use their stationery but powerful hind flippers to propel themselves along the ground in a bouncing manner called galumphing.

Seals have spotted coats in a variety of colors ranging through the following spectrum: white/silver/gray/black/dark brown. Sea lions are brown, ranging through a spectrum from a light golden brown to a dark chocolate brown.

Sound ~ You may not know when you are near a haul-out (resting site) of some species of seals, such as harbor seals, as they are often pretty quiet. But you **will** know if you are near sea lions, even from a mile away. And you can even tell different sea lions apart by their vocalizations. For example, California sea lions sound like they are barking but Steller sea lions sound more like a roar. With that knowledge at your disposal, the next time you find yourself approaching an area with sea lions, you might try closing your eyes and trying to determine what species is out there based upon what they sound like. Just a thought.

Life ~ Life expectancy of seals is about 20-30 years in the wild, more in captivity; for sea lions its 15-25 in the wild, and also more in captivity. Duke was the sea lion who lived the longest, making it to almost 32 years old at the Cincinnati Zoo in 2019; Skinny is currently holding the record for seals, still enjoying life at the Oregon Coast Aquarium at the age of 48.

Speed ~ In terms of speed, seals top out at 25 mph and for sea lions it's 30, giving them 100-yard swim times of 8.2 and 6.8 seconds respectively.

WALRUSES

When you conjure up visual images of walruses and penguins in their natural habitat, you might have a tendency to see them in the same icy snowy environment. It turns out, however, that walruses and penguins get to share no quality time together whatsoever. The only scenario where these two species would ever make eye contact would be in a zoo. While penguins reside in the Southern Hemisphere, walruses are strictly Northern Hemisphere inhabitants.

Size ~ There are basically two types, the Atlantic walrus living in northern Canada, Greenland and Europe and the Pacific walrus living in northern Russia and Alaska. You won't have much trouble recognizing the animal if you see one as they can be almost 12 feet long and weigh 2500 pounds. Their most distinguishable physical characteristics would be their wrinkled brown skin and long tusks. Both male and female walruses have tusks; males measuring up to 39 inches and females 31 inches.

The primary function of the tusks is actually to dig into the ice and snow to help haul their heavy bodies out of the water. They're also used during walrus infighting (usually having to do with mating) and defense against predators, although walruses actually do not have many of those. A polar bear or a killer whale may take a shot at a young or injured walrus, but their imposing size discourages most attacks.

Life & Speed ~ Their life expectancy comes in at 30-40 years, slightly longer in captivity. The longevity record holder is the walrus Slowpoke who reached 44 at SeaWorld Orlando in 2023. While they are capable of a four-flipper walrus run on land, they are much quicker in the water, reaching a top speed of 21.7 mph, which calculates to a 100-yard swim time of 9.4 seconds.

Kim, our connection from PEG, felt it would be great if we could add a small section about threats to pinnipeds that could link to their website, so at this point we'll hand the mic back to Kim who shared that… "One of the greatest threats to pinnipeds worldwide is entanglement in fishing gear and marine debris. There are a lot of dedicated people around the world working to prevent [these two threats]. Check out the Pinniped Entanglement Group website to learn more about a global collaboration of pinniped scientists and responders. [and Urgent Request] Please remember to 'Lose the Loop' - please cut any [plastic] loop before discarding properly in the trash. Thank you!"

Next let's dive into our countdown of 5 Fine Pinnipeds…

 # 5) TORY ~ As sea lion animal actors go, things could not have broken much better for Tory. Born in California in 1984, he was at the perfect age and level of training to score the title role in the 1994 film *Andre*. The one irony of the casting was that while Tory was a sea lion, he played the part of a seal in the movie.

In terms of animal acting, it certainly constitutes a rarely rivaled range. Stay tuned for our stellar story on the real-life Andre coming up below.

 # 4) ESMERALDA ~ This sea lion appears in the live-action 1954 Disney film *20,000 Leagues Under the Sea*. In a move we don't usually make, we are going to default to a website called *theGreatDisneyMovieRide* for their take on this one.

Their exuberance is contagious as they describe the sea lion scene as follows… "Cut to the captain's dining table. A sea lion (!!!) plops in, barking happily. Her name's Esmeralda and the captain feeds her some table scraps for being so darn cute. She even gives some sea lion smooches and I'm in love. I want a sea lion."

 # 3) THE BEATLES' WALRUS ~ In the mid-to-late 1960's the Beatles taunted music fans with a series of clues in song lyrics and on album covers that suggested Paul McCartney had died in a tragic car crash and been replaced by a lookalike. You didn't think your generation invented conspiracy theories, did you?

The ruse was actually very well executed with the clues being subtle enough to be dismissed with at least an element of plausible deniability. And to this day all the Beatles, living and dead, have stuck to the story and denied there was any conscious effort to perpetuate the "Paul Is Dead" hoax.

So that entire tale is fodder for another book, but the one thread we will share with you here is about the walrus who was a centerpiece for some of the clues. Keep in mind that other clues had already dropped by the time the walrus appears so you're picking this up in midstream, so to speak.

Let's go back to November of 1967 when the Beatles released their *Magical Mystery Tour* album. This album features one major "Paul Is Dead" clue which actually takes two albums to come to fruition. On the cover, each of the Beatles is attired in an animal costume and from the picture it's impossible to tell who is who.

The animal in the forefront is a black walrus, with outstretched arms, who is kneeling in front of three white animals, a chicken, a rabbit, and a hippo. In Scandinavian mythology, a black walrus was a symbol of death so right off the bat, there's your potential for the next clue.

There was a booklet, however, which accompanied the album and included some pictures of the costumed Beatles performing in the *Magical Mystery Tour* film. In the pictures the walrus was playing the piano which would typically be John Lennon's role. Therefore, these character assignments would initially seem to defuse this of any potential value in furthering the "Paul Is Dead" theory. According to the imagery contained in the booklet, the symbolically dead black walrus was John, not Paul.

However, let's fast forward one record to the *White Album*. The song "Glass Onion" on that album contains one of the more glaring examples of how any attempt by the Beatles to deny the fact that this was an intentional effort on their part is difficult to take seriously. In "Glass Onion" John Lennon sings, "And here's another clue for you all, the walrus was Paul."

So in terms of pop culture walrus references, here's one that certainly has some mystique and ties in the biggest band in rock 'n roll history. And here's another clue for you all… up next in our countdown we have…

 # 2) FREYA ~ Named after the Norse goddess of love and beauty, Freya gets our nod for the most famous real-life walrus by virtue of the international sensation that was created when Norwegian authorities shot and killed her on August 13, 2022. The stated government reason was that the decision was made "on an overall assessment of the continued threat to human safety."

How 'bout we rewind and pick up the story from the beginning. Perhaps as early as 2019, Freya sightings are reported off the coasts of the U.K., Denmark, Germany and the Netherlands. That Netherlands visit occurs in October of 2021, the first reported in that country in 23 years, walrus habitat generally being found several hundred miles further north in the Arctic.

The working theory on why Freya has strayed so far from home becomes climate change. Because the Arctic ice which walruses have always lived upon is receding, increased competition for food is forcing the animals to venture further away from their natural habitat.

Fast forward to the summer of 2022 and Freya has found her way to the harbor in Oslo, Norway where she begins to cause problems on multiple levels. Walruses have a natural need to occasionally get out of the water which, under normal circumstances, would be achieved by their climbing onto the ice or a rock. But in the iceless, rock-free Oslo harbor, this need is most readily fulfilled by the walrus hauling herself onto boats which are subsequently damaged or sunk due to the weight.

Another issue is that people are flocking to the harbor to take in the sight. Because walruses typically do not show aggression toward humans, people are able to approach the animal within touching distance. And while they are generally gentle animals, you're still talking about a one-ton creature creating some dangerous situations.

It was the hope of Norwegian authorities that Freya would tire of the attention and move on of her own volition. But when that doesn't happen, and the crowds continue, the Norwegian Directorate of Fisheries comes to the decision that Freya would have to be put down. On August 13, 2022, a team of four officers shot and killed the walrus.

As might be expected, people came down passionately on both sides of the decision. Here is the official statement from the head of the Norwegian WWF. "This is Norway in a nutshell," he said, "too often we kill the animals we don't like or can't cope with. They should have been more patient."

 # 1) ANDRE ~ The morning of May 16, 1961 starts like most any other spring morning for Rockport, Maine harbor master Harry Goodridge. That is until he discovers an injured baby seal trapped in a fisherman's net. He brings the seal home and along with his daughter Toni, they undertake efforts to nurse the seal back to health, even though the veterinarian who is consulted doesn't feel there's much hope.

Well, for the Goodridges, if there's a will, there's a way. They name the seal Andre, and Toni assures him that if he can pull through she will be his BFF. When initial nursing attempts fail, the figurative light bulb goes on over Harry's head.

He decides to build an artificial mother seal suit and, just in case you find yourself in need of doing the same, we will share with you here his supply list…
* wetsuit material
* bucket
* two feeding bottles

At this point we'll move to the "some-assembly-required" phase of the project and allow you to conjecture the rest on your own. Obviously this works or we'd be totally breaking our momentum with the saddest story ever. So what happens next? Actually the details are duly documented through multiple media sources which we'll timeline as follows…

* 1975 book ~ *A Seal Called Andre: The Two Worlds of a Maine Harbor Seal* written by Goodridge himself.
* 1994 movie ~ titled simply *Andre*.
* 2014 PBS documentary ~ *The Seal Who Came Home*.

Here's our up-to-date summary of the whole shebang. Andre and the Goodridges develop an inseparable bond, with Andre living in the Rockport harbor as a virtual pet of the family. And not just any pet, Andre is a pet in training being taught an array of tricks which includes…

* shooting basketballs through a hoop
* jumping through a suspended tire
* towing a boat while playing dead
* blowing a horn
* dancing "The Twist"

Connecting the timeline dots, we'll point out that "The Twist" is the dance craze of the era, thanks to musical artists such as Chubby Checker and the Beatles. The stage for Andre's performances is what Goodridge called a "floating tent". Later, upon his death, that structure would become a shrine of sorts for the seal.

Toni even takes Andre to school for Show & Tell, with the permission of her teacher and the help from her father. Andre's performances become a go-to summer attraction in Rockport drawing tens of thousands of visitors to take in what becomes daily shows. It's like, "Oh, my God, a seal star is born." The next thing you know there are network TV appearances and Andre has become a national celebrity.

So what could go wrong? A bit of an Andre backlash develops whereby local fishermen blame seals in general and Andre in particular for compromising their catch. There are also accusations of Andre wreaking havoc with their boats. The degree to which these issues can be substantiated is suspect, but there certainly is a jealousy issue with the notoriety that Andre has singlehandedly secured.

The height of the blowback occurs when a Maine gubernatorial candidate, Joseph Brennan, complains to the Associated Press that the attention accorded the Goodridge/Andre phenomenon had gotten out of hand. This results in a "blowback-to-the-blowback" scenario where the public outcry results in Brennan releasing a formal apology, "I consider Andre a supporter," Brennan said. "And I found out that if you don't give Andre his just priority, it will come home to get you."

During the height of the controversy, Goodridge does acquiesce to a compromise scenario whereby he takes Andre to an aquarium in Boston for the winters. So in 1973 when he is 12 years old, Andre begins spending November through March at the aquarium. Every April, Goodridge travels down to have Andre released into the Atlantic and somehow the seal intuitively knows to return to the Rockport harbor. The timeframe varies between three and six days, but the seal returns home for the summer every year until he dies.

So that sets up our sunset. In his later years Andre had been diagnosed with cataracts and when he made his final return sojourn to Rockport in 1986 the vet said that he had made that trip almost blind, in virtual darkness. Andre would die in July of that year after losing a fight with another seal. His body was found eight miles from home, identifying scars confirming Andre's passing.

As mentioned earlier, his floating-tent structure was left intact in the harbor as a memorial to Andre but as the pen began to fall into disrepair, it was eventually dismantled. There is, however, a permanent statue still in place as a tribute to the seal that spent 25 summers in Rockport replacing the town's previous anonymity with popular acclaim. "Many seals may live longer," eulogized Goodridge, "but few live as full a life as Andre."

Chapter 8

SALUTING OUR FAVES FROM BENEATH THE WAVES

FISH

So we're starting to write this fishy introduction, which was approved by the Oceanic Preservation Society, and looking for a fun fact to lead with when we come across this story about how intelligent fish are with the example given as evidence being the fact that they can use tools. The "use tools" descriptor is all we initially have, so after we fight off that visual image of a sunfish holding a hammer in its mouth while pounding in a nail during the construction of that sundeck he's building in order to catch some rays, we decide to rachet up our research regimen a notch.

After Googling tool-wielding fish, we are rewarded by the results with our first revelation being that in such tool-use instances, the fish doesn't wield the tool, it actually wields the target of the tool. Our favorite example was the tuskfish which can use a rock as a tool to open a clam shell. So from Google to YouTube we go because as clam lovers ourselves, this is something we really feel we need to see.

If you're also curious, join us on YouTube, go to "Tuskfish breaking clam" and check out this fish as it first blows the cover off the sea floor sanctuary where the clam is hiding, grabs the clam in its mouth, and swims to a nearby bed of coral. If clams could see this, it would certainly not be a sight to savor. The tuskfish aligns itself perpendicular to a solid stretch of coral and then the most striking aspect of what happens next is the realization that these fish are able to generate some serious upper-body torque.

After setting up with the clam in its mouth 2–3 inches away from the rock, the fish jerks its head violently smashing the clam into the rock. After multiple such smashes, you notice a small hole opening up on one edge of the shell. The end is now near. Upon the next rock smash, the shell breaks open and the fish slurps that juicy clam meat right out of the half shell, no butter needed.

Size ~ Moving on to some analytics, once they've eaten, how big do fish grow? Keeping in mind that we're excluding sharks which have bitten off their own component in the book, the largest fish on record was a black marlin which was caught in Peru in 1955 weighing 1,560 pounds. The longest fish is the giant oarfish which is an eel-like creature that can grow up to 30 feet in length. On the other end of the spectrum, the smallest fish is a variety of the minnow which lives in waters off of Indonesia, maturing at a length of just 0.4 inches.

Life~ In terms of lifespan, the Washington Department of Fish and Wildlife has documented a rougheye rockfish that lived to the age of 205. These guys swim in waters 500–1,500 feet deep off the coasts of Japan and the western U.S.
Speed ~ Next let's check out the speed gauge. The fastest swimmers in the fish world are the marlin and the swordfish which can crank it up to 80 mph. Applying this to our 100-yard-dash barometer, this would equate to a swim time of 2.6 seconds.
Sexcapades ~ So now, what say we close with some sex? Let's pay a surprise visit to your nearest colony of emperor angelfish, the "emperor" moniker being derived from the fact that a single male lives together with a cluster of up to five females. Obviously that's a lifestyle that could take a toll, so what happens when the male dies?

If you haven't been shocked by anything we've shared so far, maybe we'll get you with this one. Upon the death of the emperor, one of the females transitions into a male and assumes the throne, so to speak.

Let's follow that gender bender and get our fix of 6 Fun Fish…

 # 6) MUDDY MUDSKIPPER, from *Ren & Stimpy* ~ In this component, brace yourself for the news that may well have been the crime of the 20th century. We'll get to that in the next paragraph but to bring you into the loop, Muddy Mudskipper was a character in Nickelodeon's *The Ren & Stimpy Show* which ran from 1991-1995. The name, for the record, was modeled after that of classic cartoon character Woody Woodpecker.

So now, getting back to that crime of the century… how 'bout the one where the fish walks out of the water onto land and insanely kidnaps the Pope before tying him to a barrel of TNT, only to be thwarted by the superhero Powdered Toast Man?!

Just a day in the life of Muddy Mudskipper, that rare breed of fish that can literally walk onto the land and breathe air. Oh, and just to up the ante on the level of craziness purveyed by the previous paragraph… what if we had the role of the Pope voiced by Frank Zappa; we're sure this sacred scenario had always been a popular papal fantasy!

 # 5) CLEO, from Disney's *Pinocchio* ~ Cleo is the pet goldfish of the puppet maker Geppetto in the 1940 Disney film *Pinocchio*. As such, she witnesses the creation of the puppet and in the naming process she conveys her disfavor with the moniker of "Pinocchio". Although overruled, she maintains her loyal, affectionate and obedient personality. She never speaks, but conveys her communicative efforts through facial expressions and body language.

Cleo faces adversity such as being held captive inside the belly of Monstro the Whale, surviving that ordeal to witness the fulfillment of Pinocchio's dream to become a real boy. But her emotional zenith comes in the finale when she gets to share a celebratory through-the-fishbowl-glass kiss with Figaro the Cat, the resulting kitty lip prints on the fishbowl being a small price to pay.

 # 4) THE FISH, from *The Cat in the Hat* ~ You can remember it like it was yesterday, can't you? Conrad and Sally are stuck home alone on a cold rainy day which seems destined for dreadful boredom. True, they do have a talking fish, but he has a tendency of being somewhat of a stick-in-the-mud.

But then that knock on the door which leads to an unexpected encounter with The Cat in the Hat who brings a new perspective to the dreary day saying,

"I know it is wet
And the sun is not sunny.
But we can have
Lots of good fun that is funny!"

Well, this would be one of those examples which seems teeming with potential but alas, one must always beware of those unseen perils possibly lurking below the surface. Upon gaining entry to the abode, the cat proceeds to run amuck totally trashing the house with his antics. Things escalate when the family's pet goldfish becomes embroiled in the proceedings. The fish is uncomfortable when the cat lofts his fish bowl up in the air, balanced on top of an umbrella, but when the cat ups the ante by performing the balancing act while standing on top of a ball, we find the fish in freak-out mode...

"Put me down!" said the fish.
"This is no fun at all!
Put me down!" said the fish.
"I do NOT wish to fall!"

Chaos subsequently ensues, but when the kids' mother's return is imminent, the Cat in the Hat employs his magical powers to clean up the house in a jiffy, popping out the back door just as mom is coming through the front.

 # 3) FLOUNDER, from Disney's *The Little Mermaid* ~ On the rating scale of best friends, Flounder rates a 10 out of 10, while on the rating scale of risktakers, not so much. In Disney's 1989 film *The Little Mermaid*, Ariel is all about exploring the unknown, often luring Flounder into adventures he would have otherwise avoided.

Let's Disney-define one word that has connotations in this film above and beyond what you would find in the dictionary, which denotes a "guppy" as being "a young fish". In the vernacular of Ariel, a "guppy" would be "someone who is naïve, timid, easily surprised, and likes to play it safe." Use that definition to put the following conversation in the context which essentially defines their unique relationship...

(as they're about to explore the sunken ship...)
Ariel: Flounder, you're such a guppy.
Flounder: I'm **not** a guppy! This is great – I mean, I really love this. Excitement, adventure, danger lurking around every corner – Yay!

 # 2) CHARLIE THE TUNA ~ You cannot help but admire the tenacity of this tuna. Over six decades of rejection and Charlie is still coming back for more. He presents as a tastefully hip and cultured "cool cat", so what's the scoop behind the rejection? It's really all just a misunderstanding. As the announcer is oft compelled to inform Charlie, "StarKist doesn't want tuna with **good taste**, they want tuna that **tastes good**."

Charlie the Tuna was spawned by StarKist in 1961 as a jazzy blue and white beatnik-type tuna who stood on two fins, with a red beret on his head along with a pair of thick black glasses. The hipster spoke in a New York City accent which combined Brooklyn bravado with Broadway class. It was never made exactly clear why he would want to end up in some kid's sandwich, but the template of the commercials was always essentially the same.

Charlie would endeavor in one way or another to convey to StarKist that he had good taste. Example efforts would have him playing classical music, setting a fancy dinner table, or reading from a revered author. A written message would then descend on a fishhook, essentially serving as a letter of rejection, that always read, "Sorry, Charlie". At that point, the aforementioned finale would be reiterated that, "StarKist doesn't want tuna with **good taste**, they want tuna that **tastes good**."

Animal Planet ranks Charlie the Tuna #31 on its list of "50 Greatest TV Animals".

 # 1) NEMO & DORY, from the Disney Pixar films ~ "I suffer from short term memory loss, it runs in my family. At least I think it does." Thus epitomizes the most prevalent running gag punctuating *Finding Nemo* (2003) and its sequel *Finding Dory* (2016). The forgetfulness is played to the humorous hilt behind the talented voice acting of Ellen DeGeneres as Dory. Whenever facing difficult challenges in life, Dory falls back upon her catch phrase of… "Just keep swimming!"

SHARKS

dun dun… dun dun…. dun dun dun dun dunnnnnnnnnnnnn!

Just when you thought it was safe to go back in the water…

(foreboding mood music and advertising slogan tagline from the 1975 movie thriller *Jaws*.)

Take a look at the following list and your assignment is to guess what these things all have in common…

* taking a selfie
* getting struck by lightning
* falling out of bed
* getting stung by a bee

If you didn't deduce the answer based on the chapter title, here it is… you are more likely to die doing any of those things than from being killed by a shark, which for the record is a type of fish. So while exhibiting proper caution at the beach is always sound advice, everything is probably going to be just fine. Another factor playing to your advantage is that sharks actually don't like the taste of humans; attacks on people usually occur when sharks mistake them for seals or some other prey.

Life~ If you were to make the statement that sharks have been around forever, it actually would not be that much of an exaggeration. Amongst several facts confirmed by Samantha Lee Hansen, one of the directors at the Shark & Marine Research Institute in South Africa, would be that sharks have been swimming the oceans for about 450 million years. They saw the dinosaurs come and they saw the dinosaurs go. Another amazing way to look at it is that there were sharks on the planet before there were trees.

And once they're here, sharks can stick around for a long time. A species called the Greenland shark can live over 400 years. Here's another strange-way-to-look-at-it shark stat... a Greenland shark that saw the Pilgrims dock the Mayflower at Plymouth Rock in 1620 could still be out there swimming off the coast of Massachusetts today.

Size~ So how big do those bad boys get? We noted some discrepancies in researching this so we defaulted to a *USA Today* article which cited the whale shark as being the largest, coming in at over 60 feet long and weighing 20 tons. On the other end of the spectrum the dwarf lantern shark is only 7 inches long and weighs just a few ounces.

Speed ~ In some other shark superlatives the mako is the fastest, able to hit speeds of over 45 mph. This would equate to a 100-yard-swim time of 4.5 seconds.

End Notes ~ The great white can jump the highest, able to launch 10 feet into the air, and is generally considered to be the most savage hunter. But for sheer savagery, we may have to give the shark award to the unborn babies in some species which practice, for lack of a better term, in-the-womb cannibalism. The strongest babies will eat the weakest while still in the womb in order to assure that they are actually born.

On that mouth-watering note, let's proceed to the countdown of our Sharp 6 Sharks...

 # 6) JABBERJAW ~ The cartoon shark that we find circling at the top of our list would be Jabberjaw, who rode the wave of cartoon fame in the mid-1970's. Here's a premise you can't help but love half a century later. Jabberjaw is the drummer in a rock band called the Neptunes, whose speech is patterned after Curly Howard, from *The Three Stooges*. The starring shark is surrounded by a human core of bandmates.

Between their live performances, Jabberjaw and the kids solve crime mysteries, drumming up remembrances of the Scooby-Doo gang. This plotline resemblance was not missed by Swedish musicians Pain who proffered the following lyrics in their 2001 tribute song "Running Underwater (Jabberjaw)".

> *"Me and my friends get no respect,*
> *What does Scooby do that we neglect?*
> *We be puttin' all our foes in check,*
> *but me and my friends get no respect!"*

Okay, and full disclosure acknowledged, there's also a little Rodney Dangerfield shout-out embedded in those lyrics. But, as opposed to Scooby-Doo, there were no subtle drug references swimming to the surface in Jabberjaw!

 # 5) LAND SHARK, from *Saturday Night Live* ~ When the Steven Spielberg movie *Jaws* was released in 1975, it was the summer blockbuster of the season, but it was actually a bit more than that. In addition to selling a boatload of movie tickets, the movie embedded the shark theme into the American psyche to a degree which has rarely been replicated.

There was a proliferation of pop culture parodies and of the many manifestations none were more manic than *Saturday Night Live*'s "Land Shark" skits. The fall of 1975 was *SNL*'s debut season and the Land Shark was certainly in the mix of what made the series such an unexpected runaway hit.

In this skit an unsuspecting woman would be lounging at home before hearing a knock on the door. Unbeknownst to her, the knock would be coming from Chevy Chase dressed in a giant open-mouthed shark costume and speaking hesitantly in a muffled voice.

Upon inquiring who was there, the woman would receive a series of random bogus attempts to convince her to grant access to her unknown visitor. Included among the farcical responses as to who was there would be answers such as "repairman", "package delivery", "door-to-door salesman", etc. Eventually, through some comic twist, the victim would be tricked into opening the door whereby she would be immediately engorged in the mouth of the giant Land Shark.

The three original female *SNL* cast members (Gilda Radner, Jane Curtin, Larraine Newman) alternated playing the victim, and guest hosts, like Candice Bergen and Lily Tomlin were also occasionally consumed.

As the seasons progressed, many clever variations were conceived and the skit nailed down a nice niche in *SNL* history. The Land Shark made his last appearance in 2015 on the 40th anniversary special when Tina Fey, Amy Poehler and Jane Curtin are tri-hosting "Weekend Update". When a doorbell surprisingly rings Curtin, who had been around for the original reign of terror, knows the danger all too well, and cautions the newbies about opening the door. But Fey impetuously ignores the veteran, enabling the Land Shark to eat his final victim, to date that is. We have a sneaking feeling that at some point we just might be hearing that thumping music again!

 # 4) BABY SHARK ~ If you hate the concept of songs sticking in the back of your mind forever, please drop what you're reading and step away from the book right now. Assuming, perhaps falsely, that you're still reading along, "Baby Shark" has become the song that in recent years has managed to simultaneously emerge as the tune that, while it is the most repetitive and beloved by young children, has become the most hated by parents and babysitters. Worst news yet... "Baby Shark" now has its own series on Nickelodeon!

Rather than sing the song, or hum the lyrics, we'll allow you to fall into that trap on your own if you choose to do so. Instead, we'll share a Facebook conversation thread which will serve to convey the depth of passion prompted by "Baby Shark".

The thread originally began with the prompt...

Question: Does anyone know how to get the "Baby Shark" song out of your head? Asking for my sanity.
Answers:
* Nope, when it's there it stays there.
* It's just like herpes. Once you're exposed to it, you can never truly get rid of it and it always comes back to haunt you at the worst times.
* It's a tool of the devil. You'd have to sell your soul to get rid of it.
* You've got a better chance of getting the white off of rice.
* Tempted to Google the song and listen to it but... afraid of the consequences...

So there's your choice. Your sanity or your child. Choose wisely.

 # 3) SHREDDER ~ This great white shark became the most famous, as well as most photographed ever, as the highlight of the Caribbean island Guadalupe Shark Tours from 1900-1911. He originally received his name when he bit through and shredded the anchor line to one of the boats during an early tour, but things took an upswing after that incident.

Shredder seemed to take a liking to the tour group visits after that point. He was known for playing to the audience, for lack of a better term, and would follow the boats for days. While he never showed signs of aggression, he also showed no signs of caution, repeatedly approaching within close proximity of the boat, charismatically affording fabulous photo ops.

 # 2) LEFT SHARK ~ Recounting the most memorable moments in Super Bowl halftime show history... well, we've got Prince dancing in the "Purple Rain" (2007), Janet Jackson's "Nipple-gate" (2004), and Rhianna's "I'm having a baby" announcement (2023). But perhaps nothing went more viral than the performance of Left Shark during Katy Perry's 2015 show.

It happened during the performance of "Teenage Dream" with Perry immersed amidst a stage backdrop of surfboards, dancing beach balls, and at the key point in question, flanked by two supersized costumed dancing sharks. Left Shark was so designated by his appearance to the left side of Perry, as you were facing the screen.

At about the 3-minute mark, Left Shark seemed to lose sync with the rest of the team and go rogue with his own impromptu dance moves. Ah, the pleasures and perils of live TV! People could not climb onboard the internet joyride fast enough. Snoop Dogg tweeted, "If you were wondering, that was me inside the Shark costume!!" Alas, a confession.

There was one other celebrity Left Shark shout-out we wanted to share; Meredith Vieira invoked the incident in her 2015 speech to the graduating class at Boston University. The key words are excerpted below where she urged students **not** to…

"… strive for somebody else's notion of perfection. Remember last Super Bowl, when the Patriots won? You may be thinking of Tom Brady's deflated balls right now, but I'm thinking of Katy Perry's halftime performance. She was on stage dancing with two sharks. The shark on the right knew every dance move and performed perfectly. But it was the left shark, the one who went rogue and danced to his own crazy beat, who stole the show. So don't ever be a conformist for convenience's sake. Or as Mark Twain put it, 'Whenever you find yourself on the side of the majority, it's time to pause and reflect.' Be the left shark."

 # 1) THE JAWS SHARK ~ As we previously addressed in our entry for *SNL*'s "Land Shark", the cultural phenomenon that accompanied the release of the 1975 movie thriller *Jaws* was a generational tsunami. This would be one of those movies that would help define the career of director Steven Spielberg who masterfully told the tale of the man-eating great white shark who sets its sights on the fictional beach resort town of Amity Island.

But this book is about the animal, not the film, so let's direct our focus there. Spielberg went to that era's guru of special effects using large fake animals, one Bob Mattey who had created the giant squid for the *20,000 Leagues Under the Sea* movie. Mattey was directed to create three 25-foot air pressure-powered prop sharks each of which weighed 3 tons.

If right now your brain is begging the question, "Why would you need three?" we have a pragmatically interesting answer for you. Each of them was open on one full side so the inner mechanics could be accessed and manipulated. Think about it… you need some shots looking at the shark from the top, the right, and the left, so the staging necessary for any given shoot would dictate which fake shark got the starring gig.

If you didn't live it, it's almost hard to accurately explain what a cultural phenomenon the 1975 *Jaws* movie became during that era. It was suddenly incumbent upon any responsible parent to implement the safety precautions necessary to deal with the threat. The catch phrase of the movie was, "Just when you thought it was safe to go back in the water." Here's our satirical summary of this topical parental paradox…

It was '75 when your daughter
Did see Jaws with those tickets you bought her
But after the movie you fought her
Over lessons you thought you had taught her
About not heading into the water
To wind up a lamb to the slaughter

DOLPHINS & WHALES

We have a classification discussion at hand in this chapter which can definitely be confusing and throughout this book we have prided ourselves on concerted efforts to explain scientific concepts in layman's terms. It goes back to our guiding principle of wanting to write a book that is entertaining, informative and humorous while purposefully not intended to be a science text book.

That being said, a parallel goal has been to never sacrifice scientific accuracy for the sake of making a story funnier or more interesting. We've said that this is a book of humor for scientists and a book of science for humorists.

The waters get a little bit murky on this one, so our strategy is to start with the simplest overview and then proceed to delineate some of the dicey details. Simply put, a dolphin is a type of whale. Another way of wording it would be to say that all dolphins are whales, but not all whales are dolphins.

Just to throw a little science at you, if you picture the family tree-type diagram descending it would look like this…

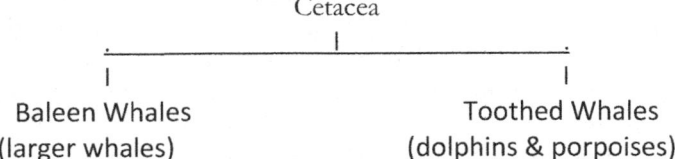

Baleen whales are the big boys, the really huge ones, which would include blue, gray, and humpback whales. Toothed whales would include dolphins, porpoises and orcas. In reviewing our material Andy Rogan of Ocean Alliance pointed out that in connecting the dots on this, it would be accurate to say that, "The sperm whale is a tricky one [in our 'no teeth=large, with teeth=small' formula above] because it is a toothed whale, but they are also huge."

As per Liaison Lindsey's suggestion, how 'bout we explain how the "baleen" component essentially takes the place of teeth. A whale's baleen plates facilitate its filter-feeding process. To feed, a baleen whale opens its mouth widely and takes in dense schools of small prey together with large volumes of water. The whale then partly shuts its mouth and presses its tongue against its upper jaw, forcing the water to pass out sideways through the baleen, thus sifting out the prey, which it then swallows.

Orcas, aka killer whales, fall into the "toothed" category but because they are big like whales, and because our go-to term for them is "killer whales", we have followed what aligns with people's intuitive sense and included the killer whales in the whale countdown. Think of it this way... for the purposes of our upcoming countdowns, if they are over 25 feet long, they're a whale. Smaller than that, they're a dolphin or a porpoise.

Dolphin or Porpoise ~ Next, we'll take a look at how to tell the difference between dolphins and porpoises. To tell these two cetaceans apart, first look at the head. Dolphins typically have a bulbous head and often a clearly-defined "beak," or long nose that sticks out from their face. Porpoises, on the other hand, usually have a rounder face without the pronounced beak.

If you can't get a good look at the head, take a peek at the fin. Dolphins have curved dorsal fins, whereas porpoises have dorsal fins that are more triangular in shape. This is one of the quickest ways to tell them apart, especially if you spot one while out on the water and can't get a look at the whole animal.

If you are able to see the entire animal, you can tell the two apart by their size and shape. Dolphins tend to have a sleeker, more streamlined body shape than porpoises. Dolphins are also longer, averaging about six to 12 feet in length, while porpoises only reach a maximum of seven feet.

Size ~ Since we're obviously only going to be able to do this one time in the entire book, please allow us to cue up a little drum roll and introduce you to... the absolute largest animal on the planet, the Antarctic blue whale weighing in at a whopping 400,000 pounds and stretching up to 100 feet in length.

If you wanted to hypothetically picture the largest set of balancing scales in the world and you put an Antarctic blue whale on one side, you would need 33 elephants on the other side to balance things out. Moving on to dolphins, the orca would be your heaviest coming in at around 9,000 pounds and growing to about 25 feet in length. A bottlenose dolphin would weigh around 1,000 pounds and a porpoise would be 200 pounds.

Life ~ In most cases these life expectancies would be estimates with the upper end for blue whales coming in at 90 years and fin whales at a little more than that. But exceeding both of these could be the bowhead whale which lives in icy Arctic waters and comes in as the longest living mammal of all.

Because of their remote habitat, tracking these animals is a difficult task but we have one specific historical event which can offer some documentable numbers. In 2007 a bowhead whale which was killed by Eskimos was found to be carrying the tip of an old harpoon in its neck. That particular harpoon point could be traced to an 1880 manufacture date, so you can do the math on that one. Scientific analysis ranges from 150 to 200 years as to how long a bowhead could live.

Dolphins are one of the few animals whose life expectancy is longer in the wild than in captivity. As we've seen throughout most of this book, usually the protection provided by captivity will extend life expectancy, but the stress and restriction of being deprived of their natural surroundings has the opposite effect upon dolphins.

An orca named Granny was thought to be 65-80 years old when last seen off the coast of Washington state in 2016. A bottlenose dolphin named Nicklo was 67 years old when last seen in Florida's Sarasota Bay in 2017. Their life expectancy in captivity is less than 30 years.

Speed ~ Now it's time to take our Cetaceas to the racetrack and top speeds for these guys are all fairly consistent as you might suspect. For top recorded speeds we show the following numbers in mph… whales (25), dolphins (35), and porpoises (34) which has them able to swim a hundred yards in the following times… whales (8.2 seconds), dolphins (5.5 sec.), and porpoises (5.9 sec.)

Conservation Status ~ While the Cetacea population flourishes in many of our planet's waters, there are some striking examples of pending extinction. The most alarming example would probably be the vaquita porpoises. According to the Porpoise Conservation Society, "The vaquita is a small porpoise found only in the northern Gulf of California (Sea of Cortez) in Mexico. Fewer than 20 of these animals remain, making the vaquita the most endangered marine mammal in the world."

The Maui dolphin is also a great concern. Todd Sain Sr. from *Our Breathing Planet* confirmed for us that they "currently estimate the entire population of this marvelous species to number fewer than 50 individuals," going on to say, "the magnificent Maui Dolphin has only one known range of habitation, the waters off the west coast of North Island, New Zealand."

The International Fund for Animal Welfare brings attention to the plight of the North Atlantic right whale pointing out that it "is one of the most critically endangered animals in the world, with fewer than 340 individuals remaining in the population, of which only 70 are reproductive females. Since 2017, a staggering 98 right whales have died or been seriously injured in U.S. and Canadian waters."

Next let's dive down to our Dolphin Quartet Countdown…

 # 4) MOKO ~ If you happened to spend your summer of 2008 on the east coast of New Zealand's North Island, you might recall hearing conservation officer Malcolm Smith describe a bizarre event which took place by saying, "I don't speak whale and I don't speak dolphin, but there was obviously something that went on." If you happened to **not** spend that summer in New Zealand, we'd be happy to fill you in on what you missed.

Moko was a bottlenose dolphin who made himself a prominent fixture on the local shores that summer, swinging by on a fairly regular basis to splash and play with the beachgoers. So while that unfettered friendliness was uniquely noteworthy, that alone would not warrant *Animal Kingdom* countdown status. We need a story, right? Well, here it is…

One day in March, a local beach walker comes upon a pair of pygmy sperm whales, a mother and daughter, trapped between a sandbar and a beach. Smith assembles a rescue team which attempts for 90 minutes to get the whales back into the swim of things. But no luck. Thought is given to killing the animals in order to end their suffering.

Then, as if the "Dolphin Rescue Signal" has been flashed into the sky just as surely as the "Bat Signal" had been flashed in a *Batman* episode, Moko comes swimming in to the rescue. The dolphin approaches the whales and in whatever kind of cosmic cross-species communications Moko can muster, she is able to coax the whales into the water, leading them through a narrow channel back out to the sea.

 # 3) KEVIN HART'S DOLPHIN ~ In 2022 we published a book *called Blacks Facts ~ An Ultimate Primer to the Historical and the Hysterical* which happened to include a hilarious Kevin Hart dolphin story. This is one that makes the countdown just because the story is so funny, not because of the significance of the dolphin involved.

In Hart's stand-up comedy routine, he has a bit where he talks about different animals he's afraid of. The best one is the dolphin story and that's the one we're sharing with you right here. The shtick goes as follows…

I don't like dolphins; I'm scared of dolphins. Me and my wife, we was in Maui, right. She say, "Come on, baby, we should go swim with the dolphins."

I'm like "Nah, I told ya how I feel about the dolphins."

She goes, "Stop bein' a bitch and let's just do it."

[I say,] "Don't call me no bitch, Bitch. Man, whatever." We go and they got these dolphins in this tank; it's like eight dolphins in this tank, right? When I get there, I see this old lady on the back of a dolphin and see this little boy. [I say,] "You know what babe, I might just be overreactin'; get the camera, take some pictures of me on the back of the dolphin."

I was hyped, right? I get in the water, I'm on the back of the dolphin, and the instructor, he's like, "As soon as you grab the dolphin's fin, dolphin gonna start takin' you around. So whenever you're ready, grab its fin."

Then I say, "Alright, cool." Soon as I grab my dolphin's fin, my dolphin went straight to the bottom of the tank. So because I was scared I didn't let go, I held on like, you know, when you're scared you start to mentally create sh*t in your own mind, I was like, "I've got a racist dolphin. He don't like Black people."

So I let go, I get to the top and I'm so scared I start snappin' on the instructor as soon as I see him. I'm like, "Nobody saw f***in' dolphin #8 missing? You all didn't notice I was gone 30 seconds? He tried to kill me, he tried to kill me!" I was mad, I was so f***n' scared. [I say,] "Y'all saw the old lady and the boy but nobody saw the Black f***in' swirl missin'? Nobody noted that the Black guy wasn't goin' around? You all didn't notice that?"

He's like, "Calm down man, calm down. It's 3 feet deep. Just stand up."

 # 2) DOLPHIN TALE ~ Cool true story here and one that we're sure many folks have not heard. The 2011 Warner Bros. drama film *Dolphin Tale* was based upon events that transpired in 2005 and it definitely tugged at some heartstrings. The movie featured some big names including Morgan Freeman, Harry Connick Jr., Ashley Judd and Kris Kristofferson and grossed $100 million.

The story centers around Sawyer Nelson a young adolescent boy who is on his way to summer school one day when he comes upon a fisherman coming to the aid of an injured dolphin who had become entangled in a crab trap. An immediate bond is developed between Sawyer and the dolphin, and when the dolphin is taken to Clearwater Marine Aquarium for treatment, Sawyer finds a way to sneak in and visit his newfound friend.

The head of the aquarium is one Dr. Clay Haskett (Connick Jr.) whose daughter names the dolphin Winter, perpetuating a sequence of successful dolphin rescue efforts for earlier animals who had been named Summer and Autumn. As Sawyer's involvement with Winter comes to light and intensifies, his mother Lorraine (Judd) and Dr. Haskett debate the extent to which this unique relationship should be allowed to develop.

But with the undeniable connection clearly benefitting both boy and dolphin, a joint decision is made. The verdict comes down that volunteer work at the aquarium, about which Sawyer is passionate, would provide a more valuable hands-on learning experience than summer school. Sawyer subsequently turns in his school books for a wet suit and the Clearwater Marine Aquarium has a new staffer.

Meanwhile, let's return to the story about Winter's rehab. After her injured tail is amputated, the dolphin adapts to the lack of the body part that dolphins primarily use to propel themselves by employing a fishlike side-to-side motion. While this proves a short-term success, Dr. Haskett realizes it is causing spine damage that would eventually become life threatening.

A coalescence of causes occurs when Sawyer visits an injured cousin needing a prosthetic limb at a local veterans' medical center and approaches the director Dr. Cameron McCarthy (Freeman) asking if he could make a prosthetic tail for Winter. McCarthy accepts the challenge and work is under way.

Suffice it to say there remain some obstacles to be faced, as well as some ebb and flow in the fate of the boy, the dolphin, and the aquarium, and at this point we would direct you to the book or the movie if you would like to enjoy the fleshed-out version of this compellingly heartfelt story.

#1) FLIPPER ~ Flipper did his first fishing on the big screen in the self-titled 1963 film. This spawned a 1964 sequel and then the hit TV series which would run on NBC from 1964-1967. The Miami Seaquarium where the TV series was filmed still runs *The Flipper Show* on a daily basis in honor of their former star. Animal Planet ranks Flipper as #3 on its list of "50 Greatest TV Animals".

In researching this book there have been a handful of occasions where our childhood memories have been swallowed up like delectably delicious fish being dined upon by a dolphin. Flipper flabbergasted us with one such scenario. Certainly a charm of the show was the dolphin's interactions with his human companions to whom he often "talked", conveying a wide range of emotions.

So if you delve into who did the "voice" of Flipper guess what you find? Not only was it not Flipper, it wasn't even a dolphin! When Flipper was conversing with family and friends, we were actually hearing the voice of a freakin' kookaburra bird! So much for those childhood memories.

Next, foreshadowing what Monstro is going to do below, we'll blast the rest of this dolphin and whale component through our blow holes and splash into the waves with 6 Wonderful Whales…

Now as the dolphin splashing curtails
Let's move on to our tales of the whales

WHALES

 # 6) HUMPHREY THE HUMPBACK WHALE ~ This whale had his 15 minutes of fame and it happened on two separate occasions! He became a major public interest news story by swimming inland and prompting significant human efforts to come to his rescue. And while the short-bout-of-fame concept implied by the "15 minutes…" expression is applicable in this case, we should point out that his first "15 minutes" actually lasted about three weeks. The drama all goes down while the 40-foot humpback whale is on his annual migration from Alaska to Mexico.

The adventure gets underway on October 10, 1985 when, about halfway through his trip, Humphrey takes a wrong turn. Whether it's just curiosity or a faulty GPS, Humphrey takes a left into San Francisco Bay. As he spends a couple days taking in the sights around the Golden Gate Bridge, the Bay Area media is all abuzz and bestow upon him that "Humphrey" moniker by which he will always be known.

With everyone assuming that the novelty will soon end abruptly with Humphrey heading west, back to the Pacific, the wayward whale springs a surprise, wending his way through the Carquinez Strait to the Sacramento River where he heads east. Obviously the saltwater whale in a freshwater river is not a natural fit and with people thinking, and hoping, that he'll turn around on his own, Humphrey proceeds to swim a full 69 miles up the river to Rio Vista where the water becomes too shallow for him to proceed.

So with the situation at a standstill, various plans are floated to get things headed back in the right direction. Plan A is to play orca killer whale noises hoping it will scare Humphrey and send him back toward the ocean, but turns out Humphrey ain't afraid of no orca and stays put.

Plan B is to form a human "sound net" which at least provides some slapstick humor in the logistics of the attempt. They assemble an armada of people on boats and floats, arm them with steel pipes, cowbells and an array of the most annoying noisemakers known to man, and right on cue the entire "orchestra" begins a performance of perhaps the most calamitous concert ever. Undaunted, Humphrey enjoys the show and patiently waits for the encore.

As we put our irreverent spin on the situation, in real life things are beginning to get tense. Humphrey is starting to show signs of stress, appearing listless and having his black skin lightened to gray. The possibility that he could die right there in Rio Vista is a culmination to the story none of the natives are wanting to become a part of their legacy.

Following the cliché of "third time's the charm", a team of biologists collaborate on Plan C. This involves playing the sound of humpback whales feeding in the waters of Mexico. When Humphrey hears the sounds of his friends at a Mexican dinner party, he is immediately ready to belly up to the raw fish bar. Humphrey happily follows the boat back down the river, under the Golden Gate Bridge and out to the Pacific where he hangs a left and heads to Mexico on November 4th.

Humphrey makes a second visit to the Bay Area in 1990 where he makes things a little easier for his hosts by hanging by the coast. But it would not be like Humphrey to totally forego the drama. At one point he becomes beached on a San Francisco Bay mudflat requiring the collaborative extrication efforts of the U.S. Coast Guard and The Marine Mammal Center in Sausalito to send Humphrey on his way.

 # 5) MONSTRO, from Disney's *Pinocchio* ~ "This Monstro, I've heard of him!" said Jiminy Cricket. "He's a whale of a whale! Why, he swallows whole ships alive!" Never let it be said that Walt Disney had not mastered the art of foreshadowing. And if the monstrous whale was capable of swallowing a whole ship... a man, a boy, a cat, and a goldfish in a bowl should be child's play, right?

Pinocchio was a unique film in the annals of Disney in that it did not have one major antagonist, but rather has that bad-guy role transition through four different villains over the course of the film. All of those details are best left for another book, but we will set up this segment by identifying Monstro as the fourth and final antagonist.

In terms of character design, Monstro is a "whale combo" having the skin color, underbelly and size of a blue whale but the teeth and body shape of a sperm whale. We'll pick up our story with the Blue Fairy aiding Pinocchio and Jiminy's quest for Geppetto by informing them that the puppeteer and the pets, Figaro and Cleo, have all been swallowed by Monstro. Despite Jiminy's aforementioned warning, Pinocchio perseveres in his pursuit only to find himself also inside the belly of the whale.

The prisoners' plan goes pyrotechnic with Pinocchio's idea to start a fire which manages to illicit a sneeze from Monstro ejecting the captives and leading to the frenetic finale. While the five protagonists (add Jiminy Cricket to the core four from inside the whale) are safely reunited to have the Blue Fairy turn Pinocchio into a real boy, Monstro's fate is left intentionally vague. Is he still out there... ? Maybe someday we'll have a whale of an answer.

 # 4) KEIKO, from *Free Willy* ~ This orca's story begins with his birth in 1976 in the Atlantic Ocean waters near Iceland. He was captured in 1979 and sold to the Icelandic Aquarium where he stayed until 1982 when he was purchased by Marineland in Ontario, Canada. Keiko started his performing career at that facility where, in addition to being small for his age, he began experiencing health issues.

Keiko did not enjoy the benefits of a stable youth with his next move being to Reino Aventura Amusement Park in Mexico City in 1985. Here he became a popular attraction settling into his entertainment role and of course the life-changing event for Keiko was his selection to play the title character in the 1993 film *Free Willy*.

In the story a troubled boy named Jesse is cleaning the Northwest Adventure Park as part of his probation when an unconventional bond is established between the boy and a captive orca performer at the park. Through the course of the series Jesse and Keiko collaborate to combat corruption in various forms including hunters, poachers, oil disasters and corporate greed.

The success of *Free Willy* spawns a franchise that would go on to include three more movies and a TV series. We will note at this point that the first movie was the only one in which Keiko performed, his part being replaced by an animatronic double in all subsequent productions.

 # 3) JONAH AND THE WHALE, from the Bible ~ If you liked the Monstro component at #5 above, you're going to absolutely love this one. The only thing better than your everyday man-in-the-belly-of-the-whale story would be to up the ante with a little religious scandal. If your go-to take on the Jonah story was that he must have been one of God's favorite characters for surviving that whale watch, you might need to update your analysis.

This story starts with God asking Jonah if he will go preach to the people of Nineveh because they are particularly wicked. But because Jonah hates Ninevah he decides to take off rather than preach. Which prompts two questions...

1) Jonah, why such a wuss, man? Your universally-respected boss gives you a straightforward assignment... man-up and do your job.
2) and rather than do the job, you take off... Jonah, it's God... are you really thinking he's not going to find you?

So, hindsight being an irreversible 20/20, Jonah finds himself trying to escape on a boat bound for Tarshish but, no spoiler alert needed here, God spots him on the deck and sends a great storm. His shipmates, realizing that

Jonah is the target, throw him overboard with their decision being validated by the fact that as soon as Jonah cannonballs into the drink, the damn storm stops.

At this point, if you're Jonah, you have to be thinking, "This is probably not going to end well." And you would be right. God, always adept at revenge, sends a whale to swallow Jonah whole. Of course, there's nothing like spending a few dark days in the belly of a whale to give a man pause to reflect upon a few of the decisions he's made.

Although it may seem a little self-serving at this point, Jonah repents and prays to God for forgiveness. Apparently it takes some time for God to think this over because Jonah spends three days in the holy penalty box before God has the whale vomit Jonah onto the beach near Nineveh, sunscreen not included.

At this point, feeling like God has pretty much painted him into a corner, Jonah preaches to the Ninevites and converts them. Further conflict ensues, but this is a book about animals rather than religion so please refer to the book of Jonah for the epilogue.

> *When those whales swallow people alive*
> *One would think, funeral plans, they would thrive*
> *When the whales ingest people*
> *You'd suspect that it's lethal*
> *But Geppetto and Jonah survive*

 # 2) SHAMU ~ We've got a whale of a story for you here and it's been brewing for about 60 years now. As of January 2024, there were three SeaWorld Parks in operation in the United States which served as the homes for eighteen orca whales. Those locations (along with the number of whales at each site) were San Diego (8), Orlando (5) and San Antonio (5). These parks have been the subject of more than their fair share of controversy over the years, a topic which we'll tackle today.

Let's go back and recap the story. The original SeaWorld opens on March 21, 1964 on a 21-acre complex located along the shore of San Diego's Mission Bay. The timing of television happens to play positively into their hands when NBC debuts its hit series *Flipper* that year, making dolphins somewhat of a national sensation. With multiple dolphins and sea lions as attractions, the park draws almost half a million visitors.

It would be 1965 when the first orca (killer whale), named Shamu is brought to SeaWorld and the marketing strategy employed by the park is absolutely effective. Profits are actively reinvested, the facility expands into a marine zoological park complemented by an increasing array of amusement park rides and other family attractions. Within four years, SeaWorld has surpassed its chief rival Marineland in annual attendance.

But there is a seamy side to this story that SeaWorld seeks to suppress. Not mentioned in the park flyers that families pick up for free is the sordid story of how Shamu signed on to become part of Team SeaWorld. Self-described "marine cowboy" Ted Griffin led a team which shot Shamu's mother with a harpoon and killed her as the two-year-old Shamu looked on. The young whale was then captured and later sold to SeaWorld.

Shamu was only the third orca to be taken into captivity, and the first healthy one to be taken intentionally. The previous two were rescues of compromised animals. So there you essentially have the groundwork of the debate that has accompanied the SeaWorld saga ever since. Shamu was retired after she attacked a trainer in 1971 and died just four months later. The Shamu name has been copyrighted and used as a stage name with subsequent whales at SeaWorld.

Over the past several decades the debate has raged on regarding the harmful effects of keeping orcas in captivity. Organizations including the Whale and Dolphin Conservation Society and World Animal Protection have advocated for the termination of captivity for both whales and dolphins.

In 2010 PETA and rock group Mötley Crüe's Tommy Lee (ex of Pamela Anderson) tried to push the envelope sending SeaWorld a letter addressing their confinement of the orcas, along with their captive breeding program referring to their male orca Tilikum (more on him later) as the "chief sperm bank" of SeaWorld, then adding that they "hope it doesn't take another tragic death for SeaWorld to realize it shouldn't frustrate these smart animals by keeping them [confined] in tanks."

The previous quote broaches the topic of deaths that have occurred in connection with SeaWorld. There have been four of them, with three involving Tilikum, all of which are addressed in the 2013 documentary film *Blackfish*. This CNN Films documentary was an exposé on the entire SeaWorld scenario, detailing everything from the mistreatment of the animals and the consequences they suffered to the human fatalities that occurred.

Blackfish managed to become somewhat of a turning point in this story, although SeaWorld has always tried to minimize the impact the film had on events which have transpired in the aftermath. That being said, changes in the past decade include the fact that the orcas no longer perform "tricks" and there are no humans in the water with the whales during the performances.

Also, as of 2016, SeaWorld has discontinued its breeding program. That program had been put in place to remove the concept of capturing the whales in the wild, as the first Shamu was. This means that the current population of orcas at the three parks will be the last to live there.

In terms of those previously popular performances, the last theatrical show in San Diego took place in 2017, with the Orlando and San Antonio parks subsequently following suit. So there are no more people riding on whaleback, divers being launched into the air from the tip of the whales' snouts, or people in the front rows being splashed by whales' tails.

With those options no longer on the table, what does the current show consist of? Nowadays visitors are offered a family friendly 30-minute educational presentation about the daily lives and habits of the orcas.

Amidst declining profits, investors sued SeaWorld alleging that the park had fraudulently downplayed the negative effect that the *Blackfish* documentary had on park attendance. SeaWorld settled the suit for $65 million.

 # 1) MOBY DICK ~ There are only a few novels in the annals of literary history where the plot is so powerfully timeless that an idiom enters the English language based solely upon the events of that novel. But such is the case with Herman Melville's 1851 novel *Moby Dick* which features Captain Ahab at the helm of the whaling ship *Pequod*.

Captain Ahab is by no means your traditional whaler; he is a man on a monomaniacal mission which has nothing to do with commerce, and everything to do with revenge. Ahab is not seeking whales; he is seeking one specific albino whale, namely Moby Dick, a white whale to whom he has lost a leg during a previous encounter.

The idiomatic expression of a "white whale" denotes a situation when a person becomes so obsessed with a particular object or goal that the obsession ultimately leads to that person's demise. The person allows the white whale to define and dominate their life so much that they compromise their health and/or safety, despite having little or no chance of success.

In the storyline Captain Ahab is so obsessed with killing the white whale that he ends up allowing the whale to take his life.

CHAPTER 9

CRUSTACEAN ELATION DOWN-UNDER SENSATION

The animal classification of crustacean is derived from the Latin word meaning "to have a crust or shell". Common characteristics of these creatures are that they all have an exoskeleton which they molt during the growth process. Liaison Lindsey's spin on this was to explain, "that an exoskeleton is an external skeleton, so they only have this body being structurally supported from the outside. It would be like our clothes making our shape, and without clothes we would not be able to take shape."

Our guest experts for the next three chapters will be Education Specialist Teagan Smith and her team at the Oklahoma Aquarium (hereafter referred to as OkAq). The first of their contributions came at this point when they added that, "Crustaceans never stop growing!" This concept is known as "indeterminate growth" referring to species whereby growth occurs throughout the life of an organism. Most crustaceans are marine animals with prominent examples including shrimp, crabs, lobsters, crayfish and barnacles.

SHRIMP

In our self-declared crustacean elation, we're going to start small and work our way up. Shrimp fun facts include that, depending on what type of shrimp you are, your life expectancy could range from one to seven years. Perhaps surprisingly, shrimp can swim faster going backward than forward, and their name can be a bit of a misnomer. Regarding size, OkAq identified the Idiomysis shrimp as the smallest at "around 3 to 5 mm" which would be between 0.1-0.2 inches, but the tiger shrimp can grow to be more than a foot! Shrimp can swim at 5.1 mph so they could navigate 100 yards of water in 40.1 seconds.

CRABS

The size spectrum for crabs ranges from half an inch (pea crab) to 12 feet (Japanese spider crab). With their 10 legs they usually scurry sideways and, in terms of life expectancy, their range is quite diverse. Smaller crabs live 3-4 years, but that giant Japanese guy we mentioned above could last for almost 100 years. The ghost crab, the fastest, can swim at 10 mph so they could cover 100 yards in 20.5 seconds.

LOBSTERS

Next, strap on your bib for lobster-fest where we'll start with the stats, then close with a story we found a bit startling. The largest lobsters can grow to be 4 feet long and the heaviest one ever caught weighed 44 pounds. In terms of life expectancy, they could join the crabs in the old crustaceans' home, some living to the age of 100. Lobsters can swim at 11 mph so they could cover that 100-yard swim in 18.6 seconds.

Here's our "Who'da thought it?" Going back to colonial times, lobster was considered a food for paupers and prisoners, referred to as "the poor man's chicken". The lobster population was drastically higher then and, especially during storms, mass quantities of them would wash up on the beach. So part of it was supply and demand but it is still hard to imagine a world where Red Lobster would be giving their stuff away while Chick-fil-A would be charging top dollar.

Here's the countdown of our Fab 4 Crustaceans.

 # 4) LARRY THE LOBSTER, from *SpongeBob SquarePants* ~ As the lifeguard at the Goo Lagoon, Bikini Bottom's popular beach, Larry the Lobster shares the following philosophical banter with his co-star SpongeBob SquarePants as he is about to temporarily turn over his lifeguard whistle to SpongeBob who has offered to serve a substitution stint high atop the lifeguard chair.

"You know, SpongeBob, the babes and the big chair are great," says Larry, "but the best part is knowing that you're the only thing standing between these good people and a watery grave. That's what it's all about." We'll tell you how this one turns out in a minute.

And of course this all ties in with the bizarre absurdity of the show's appeal which is that the setting is underwater yet the characters speak, eat, drink, and play as if they are landlubbers. The lifeguard thread is however perhaps the jewel of the juxtaposition, with these folks at the bottom of the ocean making excursions to the beach where they have a lifeguard to keep them from drowning, despite the fact they are already underwater. Love it!

At any rate, how does that substitute lifeguard gig go for SpongeBob? Not well, we're thinking. Returning to our opening quote of this segment, after Larry tells SpongeBob that he is the only thing standing between the beach patrons and death, here's how the conversation finishes up.

Larry: Their lives are in your hands now, 'cause I have a date with the tanning booth. So long.
SpongeBob: But... I can't swim. If only I had known that being a lifeguard meant guarding their lives, I would never have said yes.

 # 3) JACQUES, from Disney Pixar's *Finding Nemo* ~ How's this for a resumé... born in the fish tank of the president of France, he's then gifted to the prime minister of Australia, before ending up in the Aussie fish tank of Dr. Sherman, a dentist. Here the cleaner shrimp, Jacques, is in charge of decontaminating new fish entering the tank and then coordinating the initiation rite of passing through the Ring of Fire in the tank's ceramic volcano which is called Mount Wannahockaloogie (pronounced Wanna-hock-a-loogie).

Such is the life path of Jacques in the 2003 Disney Pixar film *Finding Nemo*. He is one of seven marine animals who comprise the "tank gang" in the dentist's office aquarium before Nemo joins them to spend much of his time in the movie.

First off, depending on the level of your marine biology background, you may or may not need to be told that a cleaner shrimp is actually a thing. They are a type of crustacean which forms a mutually symbiotic relationship with fish whereby they clean the unwanted parasites off the fish which serve as the food for the cleaner shrimp. Everybody wins! Well… everybody but the parasites.

 # 2) MR. KRABS, from *SpongeBob SquarePants* ~ Eugene Harold Krabs plays the Ebenezer Scrooge role as the penny-pinching owner of the Krusty Krab restaurant, the finest eatery in the underground town of Bikini Bottom, on the 4th longest-running animated series in history, *SpongeBob SquarePants*.

Playing the equivalent of the Bob Cratchit role were loyal employees SpongeBob (fry cook) and Squidward Tentacles (cashier). We'll close with one classic quote that epitomizes the curmudgeonly condescension of Mr. Krabs. In a misguided attempt to instill enthusiasm in his staff, he once proffered the pessimism that, "What doesn't kill you the first time around, usually succeeds in the second attempt."

 # 1) SEBASTIAN, from Disney's *The Little Mermaid* ~ "Everything's better, down where it's wetter, under the sea." So sings Sebastian in one of his two songs in the 1989 movie where his reggae-calypso style earned the red crab **two** Oscar Award nominations for Best Original Song. In addition to the aforementioned "Under the Sea", he also got the nod for "Kiss the Girl", the song he uses to urge Eric to kiss the now-human Ariel before the time deadline expires for her to have her voice returned.

Through the course of the film, Sebastian's original role as being Ariel's supervisor/guardian morphs somewhat magically into being her advocate/friend. And when it comes time for the marriage of Ariel and Eric, you can bet your red claws that Sebastian is gonna be there. His retirement goal… to lay out on the beach, "Getting a tan and sipping a tuna colada."

Chapter 10

GETTING TO KNOW THE CEPHALO

The species of Cephalo (pronounced Sehf´-uh-low) includes several marine mollusks, the most notable of which would be octopuses and squids. Let's start by sharing the etymology that cephalo means "head foot" in Greek, a term employed to identify this type of animal which has multiple tentacles or legs extending out from their heads.

OCTOPUSES

The octopus etymology would be that in Greek "okto" means eight (think octagon), identifying the octopus as a sea creature with 8 arms. They have 3 hearts pumping blue blood through their bodies which have the ability to regenerate. If some predator lops off a leg, that appendage will grow right back. Because the only hard part of their body is a beak, the octopus is extremely flexible and capable of squeezing into, and through, surprisingly small spaces like empty jars and coconut shells, as well as any small openings.

With the octopus, you get not only brawn, but also brains. They actually have the most developed brain and nervous system of any of the oceans' invertebrates. Check out the videos on YouTube where an octopus, when approached by a predator, picks up a coconut shell from the ocean floor, then places it over the top of its head to hide; that qualifies as the behavior of using a tool. Also on its mastery-of-tools resumé is the fact that an octopus can open a bottle or twist a jar lid to get at food hidden inside.

Speaking of food, Octopuses eat clams, crabs, shrimp and mollusks. So who eats the octopus? Their predators include large fish, whales, seals and birds. Oh, and there's also man. While octopus is available at seafood specialty markets in the U.S., in certain Asian cultures it is a dietary staple. And unlike that occasional Thanksgiving dilemma in America, if everyone wants a leg… never a problem!

One aspect associated with the octopus that we've yet to cover would be the inking. A defense mechanism they have to their avail is the ability to release clouds of black ink to disturb and distract predators. The ink is mostly made of melanin, the same substance that adds the color to your skin, hair and nails.

The other trick the octopus has up all 8 of its sleeves is the ability to camouflage itself by changing color and shape to blend into the background of any given situation. As was the case with our previous chapter, Educational Specialist Teagan Smith and her team from the Oklahoma Aquarium (OkAq) are serving as our guest experts here and they added the facts that, "Chromatophores are the cells that octopus and other cephalopods have that allow them to change color to mimic their surroundings so efficiently. Octopuses can also change the texture of their skin."

Size ~ Check out this range in size between different species... the Atlantic pygmy octopus only grows to 3 inches across and weighs just over an ounce. The giant Pacific octopus (GPO) can grow to 30 feet and weigh 600 pounds. That big boy could have horror movie written all over him. And not just for people, that octopus even eats sharks after using its powerful arms to crush the shark's spine! OkAq added that, "The average weight for a GPO is around 100 pounds. The 600-pound individual was a major outlier; it is also difficult to find definitive information on that particular finding, i.e. date, location, etc."

Life & Speed ~ The life expectancy of different octopus species ranges from 1 to 5 years. In terms of speed, the GPO is the fastest, able to use their water-expelling power of jet propulsion to reach speeds of 25 mph which enables them to traverse 100 yards of water in 8.2 seconds.

SQUIDS

Next, we'll squeeze on over to our friend Mr. Squid who, not surprisingly, shares several storylines with the octopus. Rather than reinvent the wheel, how 'bout we start with a chart to cover the squid storyline where we could basically say, "Please see above – squids and octopuses have the following trait list in common." About each it can be said that they...

* have eight arms
* live in all parts of the world
* can eject black ink for defense
* have three hearts
* face the same prey and predators
* can change color to camouflage from predators

Here OkAq added that, "In addition to eight arms, squids also have two tentacles. Cephalopod arms and tentacles are differentiated by the placement of suction cups; arms have suction cups throughout the entire length of the arm, tentacles only have suction cups at the ends."

Size ~ In terms of size, the smallest squid is the Thai bobtail squid which measures less than a half inch across and weighs under one tenth of an ounce. On the other side of the coin the "giant" squid can grow to over 40 feet long, and the "colossal" squid can weigh almost 1,100 pounds.

Life & Speed ~ How long do they live? The average life expectancy of most squid species is 1-3 years, while the giant species may roam the ocean depths for as much as five years. In terms of speed, the Humboldt squid is the fastest, maxing out at 15 mph which enables them to traverse 100 yards of water in 13.6 seconds.

Liaison Lindsey ~ By the time our collegiate zoological guru came on board with this project, the first draft of the book had already been written. That timing was perfect because it afforded her the opportunity to read through the entire work and offer her feedback in chosen locations. That being said, she did also serve as our muse inspiring some totally new literary endeavors on our part. Such was the case when, about the cephalos, she said, "People usually freak out when they find out that octopuses and squids have beaks, so maybe talk a little more about that and how cool it is!" Duly inspired, we took her advice and waxed poetic on the following foray into the idiosyncrasies of the cephalos.

> *The octopus and the squid*
> *We can't undo what God did*
> *'Cause when they do get their beak out*
> *Most people just wanna freak out*
> *Then when fickle fate harms*
> *Any one of eight arms*
> *They always do know that*
> *That limb will just grow back*
> *And that blood, colored blue*
> *What are they gonna do?*
> *'Cause just one heart thumping*
> *Won't get that blood pumping*
> *C'mon, use your street smarts*
> *They're gonna need three hearts*

Here's the way our countdown goes, from 3 to 1 with cephalos.

 # 3) STRETCH, from Disney Pixar's *Toy Story* ~ In *Toy Story 3*, Stretch takes the audience on a roller coaster ride (she's good, she's evil, she's good), ironically setting up the franchise's final tribute to her which occurs in *Toy Story 4*. In *TS3*, Stretch is a purple toy octopus (voiced by Whoopi Goldberg) at the Sunnyside Daycare who starts out as a nice girl before being lured into Lotso's evil gang.

On the verge of following Lotso's order to push all the toys into the dumpster, she refuses. This ultimately exposes Lotso's true villainy leading to his downfall. In *Toy Story 4*, during the scene when Buzz and Woody are perusing the carnival, a huge purple octopus ride is shown in the background which serves as the final salute to Stretch. Nice touch.

 # 2) SQUIDWARD TENTACLES, from *SpongeBob SquarePants* ~ "If I had a dollar for every brain you don't have, I'd have one dollar," was the type of putdown for which Squidward Tentacles becomes well known in the Nickelodeon series (1999-present). In general, he is characterized as arrogant, bitter, and short-tempered, constantly annoyed by the disruptive antics of his neighbors.

Squidward lives in a moai (Easter Island head) in between SpongeBob's pineapple house and Patrick Star's rock. Their neighborhood can be found in the thriving underwater city of Bikini Bottom. One unique nuance of the storyline is that while Squidward's distaste for his neighbors is clearly conveyed to the audience, SpongeBob and Patrick remain oblivious to it.

 # 1) URSULA, from Disney's *The Little Mermaid* ~ conveying the notion that one of Disney's greatest villains could maintain a sense of humor, even as her house of cards is about to collapse, Ursula acknowledges that, "I should've known! There's only one thing more potent than my black magic… teenage hormones!" Yep, those'll getcha every time.

Here's the backstory… Ursula, a human-octopus hybrid, was once a member of the royal court of King Triton, the merman ruler of the underwater Kingdom of Atlantica. Banished for her treachery, Ursula erects an evil empire establishing the goal of usurping Triton's throne and empowering herself as the queen of the seas. It all ends in explosions and drama of monstrous proportions with Prince Eric saving the day and killing Ursula.

So while Ursula has cashed in her tentacles and suction cups by the end, she definitely performs impressively along the way, establishing herself as one of the most evil ever. In movie website polls of the "Greatest Disney Villains of All Time" SlashFilm.com ranks her at #2 and GoldDerby.com has her at #4. Rankings that certainly evoke evil envy.

Chapter 11

COMING TO TERMS WITH ECHINODERMS

The species of echinoderms (Uh kih´ nuh dermz) is comprised of invertebrate marine animals that live at all depths of every ocean. The etymology of the word is a Greek/Latin combo... with "echino" meaning spiny in Greek and "derm" meaning skin in Latin.

In addition to their spiny surfaces and marine habitat, their other linking characteristic is that they all have a radial shape such as a star, a ball, or a cylinder. Primary examples would be sea stars, sea urchins, sea cucumbers, sand dollars and sea lilies. Right off the bat we'll address that first item in our list and explain why the animal that you probably grew up calling a starfish, is now known as a sea star. Making a final appearance as our undersea guest experts in this chapter are Teagan Smith and her team at the Oklahoma Aquarium (OkAq) who added at this point the fact that, "All echinoderms have tube feet...pretty cool!"

SEA STARS

Regarding this animal we're going to lead right off by diving into the name game. As stated, we know "starfish" is probably what you grew up with, but there has been a push by marine biologists to encourage the general public to switch from calling this critter a starfish and opt for the more scientifically correct term of sea star. The reason is that starfish are not actually fish so why employ a moniker that perpetuates confusion? Old habits die hard, but we're going to give it a try. Here are the highlights of our sea star story.

One reality that might actually be considered a lowlight is that sea stars have no brain or blood, so they're swimming upstream right from the get go. What do they have working in their favor? They have eyes on the end of their arms and if you cut an arm off, it will grow back in time. So while being hunted, if they can convince their predators to perhaps settle for just an arm appetizer, the sea star can live to swim another day.

What kind of predators are we talking here? Well, that list would include seagulls, lobsters, crabs, larger fish, and other sea stars. Other than the quirky cannibalism, what do sea stars eat? Their diet consists primarily of mollusks whose shells they pry open with what look to be suction cups on their feet. OkAq clarified that, "Their tube may look like suction cups however, they are equipped with adhesive proteins that enable them to stick to things, rather than suction." That sea star diet menu includes clams, mussels and oysters.

Speaking of food, here's a line we promise you won't hear anywhere else in the book. Sea stars eat inside out. What in the world do we mean by that? Okay, brace yourself... When a sea star encounters food, its stomach exits the body through its mouth to digest the food and when the meal has been concluded the stomach is retracted back into the body. No need for a napkin.

Size, Life & Speed ~ Next, let's talk sea star size. On the smaller end of the spectrum we will spotlight the paddle-spined sea star, less than ½ an inch in diameter and at the top end we've got the sunflower sea star which maxes out at 40 inches and can weigh up to 13 pounds. In terms of life span, some sea stars can live for 35 years and while we're tossing some numbers around, the Antarctic Labidiaster annulatus sea star can have as many as 50 arms, making them capable of some serious arm waving. The ability to wave goodbye for a long time comes in handy because they travel at just 0.12 mph, giving them a 100-YDT of 28 minutes, 24 seconds.

SEA URCHINS

Riddle us this, readers. What is found all over the world, shaped like a ball, and comes in an array of beautiful colors? While your list of possible answers might include marbles, hard candy, and billiard balls, we're actually headed in a different direction with this one. In this chapter on Echinoderms, we're going to point to the sea urchin, but while we're extending our appendages, we must be careful not to step on one.

Why would that be? All sea urchins have spiky surfaces which act as a deterrent to predators. And here's a notion even more nefarious, some sea urchins have venomous spikes... Yikes! With a name clearly veiling its evil potential, the venom of the flower urchin contains a substance which can cause convulsions, anaphylactic shock and death in humans. Definitely be careful with this bad boy in your salt water aquarium at home.

Five Times the Fun ~ At this point, you high and mighty humans are probably looking down condescendingly upon the lowly sea urchin. Well, just to help you put your view on the hierarchy of life into perspective, please allow us to share with you one undertaking they can accomplish five times better than you. They only have five teeth, but here's the cool thing; each tooth is muscled by an independent set of jaws.

A sea urchin could literally be eating five different meals at the same time. Next time you're looking at a mouth-watering, multi-course meal, and can't decide where to begin, just hope that in your next life you come back as a sea urchin so you could be diving into everything from the salad to dessert simultaneously.

Size, Life & Speed ~ Sharing some sea urchins stats... their average size is about 4 inches in diameter and the largest ones, the red sea urchin, can achieve a diameter of 7 inches and can live up to 100 years. They travel at just 0.002 mph giving them a 100-YDT of 28 hours and 24 minutes.

SEA CUCUMBERS

As much as you might be into exotic vegetables, this is one cucumber that you're probably not going to want to cut into thin slices and place on top of your salad. Since we've already fixated on the food fetish let's finish that theme, allowing the sea cucumber to eat before it gets eaten.

Dinner Time ~ First, we'll get a visual picture of these guys as it does help explain the dining process. You have a squishy, leathery tubelike creature slithering through the sediment of the ocean floor with a mouth at the front end of the tube and a butt in the rear. The menu for these guys is rather bland; all they actually do is eat the sand.

The mouth serves as an intake valve, ingesting sand and silt from which the sea cucumber filters and extracts any viable nutrients. Process completed, a trail of clean sand is left in the wake of the slow-moving cucumber, making the ocean world a better place for all of its inhabitants.

Size ~ They range from red to brown to yellow in color and most average 6-9 inches in length, but for those who like their cucumbers large, the good news is that some of them grow to be over 6 feet long! So who are the predators that might like to see that 6-foot snack wending its way toward them? The list would include crabs, turtles, fish and even some sharks.

When being pursued, sea cucumbers have some unique defense mechanisms. Initially they shoot out sticky white threads, but let's face it... what self-respecting shark is going to shiver at that shot? Plan B at least shows a level of creativity on the part of the sea cucumber.

They are able to regurgitate non-essential internal organs which they can eventually regenerate, with the apparent strategy being to essentially say, "If you're willing to settle for an appetizer, we could both get out of here alive." Good luck with that one.

Life & Speed ~ If they can avoid getting eaten, a healthy sea cucumber can live for up to 10 years. They travel at 2.1 mph giving them a 100-YDT of 1 minute 37 seconds.

Prepare for our final fun fact to kick you right in the butt. Clearly unable to fend off unwelcome intruders, some small invertebrates will hide in the rectum of the sea cucumber for safety. So if you've heard those rumors about an "almost anything goes" attitude pervading the decadent lifestyle on deep sea ocean floors, this fun fact will probably serve to justify those suppositions. In such situations you just can't count the times you've heard one invertebrate turn to another and jeeringly mock their predators saying, "They'll never think to look for us in here!"

Liaison Lindsey ~ Our too cool zoo guru contributed a delineated species breakdown of the echinoderms we thought worth sharing.

There are over 7000 different types of echinoderms, and they each fall into the five categories of:

* Sea stars (star fish, close to 2000 species)
* Brittle stars (over 2000 species many live deep in the ocean)
* Sea cucumbers (look like a large slug, about 1700 species with a subspecies called sea pigs, estimated that they may account for over 90% of the total biomass of animals on the deep-sea floor)
* Sea urchins (these are the "regular urchins" meaning they have 5-part symmetry), Irregular urchins (they still have the 5-part symmetry, but they have an added bilateral symmetry which means that their symmetry is from the front and the back and also the left and the right, also includes sea biscuits which is a fun name)
* Sea lilies and feather stars (often have more than 5 arms, but some have over 150 arms, they are suspension feeders so they eat drifting particles)

Next we'll cue up our Top 3 Echinoderms countdown…

 # 3) PEACH, from the Disney Pixar film *Finding Nemo* ~ From her vantage point, firmly suction-cupped to the aquarium glass in the dentist's office where she lives, Peach has a perfect view of the x-ray machine monitor and she has been around long enough to know a thing or two about how to read them. On one particular day as she updates her fish friends in the aquarium, her analysis is, "Root canal, and by the looks of those x-rays, it's not gonna be pretty."

Peach is one of seven marine animals who comprise the "tank gang" in the dentist's office aquarium before Nemo joins them to spend much of his time in the 2003 film *Finding Nemo*. She is a reddish-pink sea star, a color which the film's promo info refers to as "ochre", so next time you are describing a deep pink color, feel free to use that one if you're so inclined.

 # 2) KEVIN C. CUCUMBER, from *SpongeBob SquarePants* ~ A special intro provided by SpongeBob himself goes like this… "It's the Jellyspotters, Bikini Bottom's premier jellyfish enthusiast club! Ah! And their leader! The coolest jellyfish enthusiast ever! Kevin the Sea Cucumber!"

Despite SpongeBob being initially enamored of the guy, Kevin is eventually exposed as a treacherous sadistic farce who's only out to embarrass and humiliate SpongeBob. Turns out SpongeBob's ability to spot jellyfish exceeds Kevin's and God does rain down His reward upon the virtuous.

When Kevin is stung by a jellyfish, SpongeBob saves the rest of the Jellyspotters from peril thus revealing Kevin as the farce that he is, leading the Jellyspotters to abandon him as their leader.

 # 1) PATRICK STAR, from *SpongeBob SquarePants* ~ A sample conversation might go like this...

SpongeBob: Patrick, you're a genius!
Patrick: Yeah, I get called that a lot.
SpongeBob: What? A genius?
Patrick: No, Patrick."

This serves as a perfect set-up for Patrick's characterization because he essentially serves as the village idiot in the underwater town of Bikini Beach. And you can add to that resumé overweight, lazy and unemployed. One episode even has Patrick tutoring SpongeBob's nephew in "the art of doing nothing". Probably not an "Uncle of the Year" award awaiting Patrick after this one.

SECTION THREE
WE'LL SWIM AND WALK AND FLY THROUGH THE WATER, LAND AND SKY

CHAPTER 12

AMPHIBIANS IN LOADS
LET'S BRING ON THE FROGS AND TOADS

FROGS & TOADS

Our teaser for this chapter comes from Dr. Kerry Kriger, Founder and Executive Director of Save the Frogs! who wrote about this amphibians component, "It looks good to me and I enjoyed the upbeat style."

Fun Facts ~ Frogs have lots of tricks for survival and here's our favorite, one mastered by the glass frog. These animals like to rest on leaves, but by doing so they become vulnerable to predators. So what do they do? They transfer almost all of their red blood cells to inside their livers making them virtually invisible. This is one trick you should definitely not try at home.

There are some other nuances to this performance that are noteworthy. With the skin translucent at this point, upon close inspection you can see inside the animal and actually watch its heart beat and its stomach digest food.

Another wild one is the wood frog which allows most of its body to be frozen for the winter. Their metabolism slows to a crawl and the water in the cells of their vital organs is replaced with glucose and urea to prevent collapse. They weather the winter in this state and when spring springs, things thaw and the wood frog hits the ground hoppin'.

The frog order boasts one of the most poisonous animal families in the world, Dendrobatidae, the poison dart frogs which are native to the jungle rainforests of Central and South America. Candace Hansen of the Amphibian Survival Alliance (ASA) told us that, "Within this family, the superstar supreme is the species *Phyllobates terribilis,* the Golden Poison Frog, that produces the toxin batrachotoxin." Pound for pound they certainly pack a punch. They're just a couple inches long and weigh less than one ounce, but check this out… the venom contained by one frog is enough to kill 10 humans or 20,000 mice!

Never one to miss out on the fun, Liaison Lindsey adds that, "My favorite frog and toad fact is that when they eat, frogs and toads close their eyes, which push their eyes into their mouth which in turn helps push their food down into their stomach, super gross, but honestly so cool."

Conservation Status ~ Lindsey advises that, "The frog is endangered and declining. Actually most amphibians are, and there is currently an amphibian crisis happening due to the chytrid fungus. Let's add a conservation message here and also talk about how local amphibians are super important, and that most amphibians are ecosystem indicators, suggesting the health of the overall ecosystem they are a part of."

Frog or Toad? ~ Are they the same? Are they different? Allow us to sort it all out for you. Consider "frog" an umbrella title with two underlying categories, frogs and toads; there are frogs that are toads and there are frogs that are not toads. Mark Mandica of the Amphibian Foundation told us that, "One way that we generally explain the difference, is that a toad is a specialized type of frog, similar to a newt being a specialized type of salamander, or sharks being a specialized type of fish."

That being said, there are some clear ways to differentiate frogs and toads. Skin texture would probably be #1 with toads having rough dry bumpy skin as opposed to the smooth sleek skin of a frog. Frogs like water while toads love land, although both require the water for breeding purposes. If you see one on your lawn or driveway and would rather not feel the skin to make the differentiating determination, fall back on an assessment of their movement.

A frog on the lawn or driveway will leap with the large muscular legs in a way that true toads can never accomplish. Toads can crawl (but so can frogs) – Toads, however, with their short, stubby legs, have more of a hopping gait, so a toad will flee with a series of fast, short hops, but a frog will depart with long, gliding leaps. That's why you might find frog legs as an exotic dining option, but toad legs are not going to make it onto the menu.

Size ~ As you might suspect, you can find frogs on every continent except Antarctica and they come in a wide variety of shapes and sizes. On the top end, you've got the Goliath frog in the western African jungles which can weigh seven pounds and grow to 15 inches long, which translates to 2.5 feet with legs extended. On the other end of the spectrum, the jungles of Papua New Guinea, in the Pacific Ocean near Indonesia, are home to the Paedophryne amanuensis mini-frogs. While it's a mouthful to say, these tiny creatures are only about the size of the fingernail on your pinky.

Life ~ In terms of life span, the average would be about 15 years in the wild and 20 years in captivity. The longevity award in the frog world goes to the Maud Island frog which can live 35 years or more, with some toads hopping along even longer. Read on.

On December 3, 2023, the *Hindustan Times* in Melbourne, Australia reported that scientists at Victoria Institute in Wellington, New Zealand were monitoring a Maud Island frog named Wellington who had reached the age of

37. Slightly besting that frog, in terms of life span, was a toad named Georgie who died at the age of 40 at York University in England in 2009.

Speed ~ The Goliath frog is the fastest, able to hit a speed of 10 mph which gives it a 100-YDT of 20.5 seconds. Based upon the frog/toad differentiation explained above, it's no surprise that toads are slower with the swiftest speedster of that sub-species peaking at about 5 mph which doubles that 100-YDT to 41 seconds. The fastest frog swimmers can hit 5 mph.

Regarding frog superlatives, we also thought the longest leap was worthy of acknowledgement and the Guinness record in that category belongs to a South African sharp-nosed frog for making a 17.6-foot leap, 90 times its own body length, at California's 1975 Calaveras County Frog-Jumping Contest.

Love is in the Air ~ How 'bout we close with a little romance? With rare exceptions, frog eggs are fertilized outside the female's body. This fertilization occurs as the eggs are being laid with the male hugging the female around the waist, or under the armpits, in a process called amplexus. This process takes hours as frogs lay thousands of eggs, knowing most won't survive.

Mark, from the Amphibian Foundation, contributed some comedy when he shared that, "There are also lots of other types that you should look up if you want a chuckle, like goofy males with short arms (not long enough to hug the female) will glue themselves to the lady to make sure he stays in the right place to fertilize the eggs." Who knew that super glue could serve as an aphrodisiac!?

What happens after the babies are born was the one topic that Candace and the ASA, felt we should address, saying, "We would suggest including something on one of their most special characteristics, which is the process of metamorphosis, where they transform from an aquatic larvae (tadpoles) to terrestrial mini adults."

If you were impressed by that 17' 6" jumping record we shared earlier, prepare to be blown away by this one. The longest recorded session of amplexus occurred with a pair of Andean toads who remained in the reproductive mode for four months. You certainly have to respect that kind of stamina!

On that note, here's our Sexy 6 Frogs and Toads appropriately beginning with…

 # 6) FROG AND TOAD ~ This was actually the very last countdown addition to the book, hopping into the countdown by virtue of Liaison Lindsey's comment to us that, "Another contender for a spot could be the characters from the children's book series *Frog and Toad*. Super cute and I remember these books as a kid! They have lots of fun adventures, like learning how to fly a kite!"

The series consisted of 4 books, with 5 stories each, written between 1970-1979 by Arnold Lobel. The two main characters were both caring and friendly anthropomorphs, with the taller green-colored Frog being more easy-going, while the stout brown-colored Toad was the more serious of the two. The stories shared life lessons – often humorous and sometimes poignant.

There's an end story you might not have seen coming. Lobel's daughter Adrianne revealed in an interview, "that there's another dimension to the series' sustained popularity. Frog and Toad are both male, and they love each other." Her father was gay and spent much of his life in the closet before coming out.

 # 5) BIBLICAL FROGS, from the Bible ~ The Ancient Egyptians should have known better than to mess around with God but apparently those old Nile-dwellers were a stubborn lot. Just to make sure nothing is lost in the translation, we are going to go directly to God in this next quote which comes from Exodus 7:25 when he tells the Egyptians, "Let my people go, that they may serve me. But if you refuse to let them go, behold, I will plague all your country with frogs. The Nile shall swarm with frogs that shall come up into your house and into your bedroom and on your bed and… into your ovens."

So when the *Cairo Times* was published the next morning, the people were forewarned that, according to God, they would be sleeping and eating with frogs… certainly a plague any way you look at it. But as previously stated, those ancient Egyptians trended toward the stubborn side. They decided to hold on to their Hebrews rather than heed the word of the Lord.

 # 4) MR. TOAD, from *The Wind in the Willows* ~ Mr. Toad is the main character in Kenneth Grahame's 1908 novel *The Wind in the Willows* and was featured in Disney's 1949 film. Finding himself in charge of a diverse animal kingdom, Mr. Toad is rich, rash and arrogant, but also generally jovial, friendly and kind.

His animal entourage likes him and loyally rallies to his support when he finds himself in trouble. He tends toward new-fad obsessions and, when motorcars begin to replace horse-drawn carriages as the primary means of transportation, he is hooked. Unfortunately this leads to one of the worst driving careers ever, a storyline fleshed out by both Grahame and Disney.

 # 3) THE CELEBRATED JUMPING FROG OF CALAVERAS COUNTY ~ This is not only a quite recognizable Mark Twain title, the 1865 short story became Twain's breakthrough work and the first to put him in the national spotlight. The story is about a man named Jim Smiley who lives in Calaveras County, California and has a gambling problem which finds him looking for opportunities to bet on most anything.

Smiley's most compromising vice is his all-consuming propensity to bet on his jumping frog Dan'l Webster. At one point Smiley is so desperate to take a gamble that he temporarily leaves Dan'l with a stranger who stuffs the frog full of lead gunshot. Weighed down as a result of Smiley's compulsive behavior, Dan'l loses his next frog jumping contest and the celebration is over.

There are two sure bets left at this point… Smiley is no longer smiling and PETA clearly did not sign off on this storyline.

 # 2) MICHIGAN J. FROG, from *Looney Tunes* ~ About this character he created, legendary animator Chuck Jones pontificated that, "It's extraordinary that a character that only appeared once, in one cartoon without any other starring character at his side, has such a lasting impact." Highlighted on Jones' resounding resumé of animation accolades would also be Bugs Bunny, Daffy Duck and the Grinch.

Michigan J.'s image is certainly iconic… the bright green frog, with the top hat and cane, high-stepping his way across the stage while he belts out classic pop tunes like "Hello My Ragtime Doll" from the Golden Age of Hollywood. As familiar as that image is to many, the biography of Michigan J. Frog can be fed through the eye of the needle on a pretty thin thread.

In the original run of the Warner Bros. cartoon studio, Michigan J. appears in literally only that one film which would be the short cartoon "One Froggy Evening", a New Year's Eve 1955 release. The storyline has an ordinary construction worker discovering the singing frog and feeling sure he can cash in on the anomaly, only to realize that Michigan J. will only sing for him. It turns into a classic fable about the foible of greed.

At any rate, Michigan J. went into a four-decade hiatus at that point until Warner Bros. decided he would be a good fit as mascot for the new WB cable network they were launching in 1995. When the new network debuted on January 11th, there was a brilliantly conceived set-up to reveal the mystery mascot choice. The scene opens with *Looney Tunes'* two most iconic stars, Bugs Bunny and Daffy Duck, nervously pacing as the drama gradually unfolds on the mascot-reveal, both certain that one of the two of them will be anointed.

Then the camera pans to Chuck Jones at an easel and the zoom-in reveals Jones to be drawing none other than Michigan J. Frog! At that point MJ springs to life, hops onto Jones' shoulder and unleashes a perfectly timed "What's up, Frog?" clearly mimicking Bugs' "What's up, Doc?" line to pour a little salt in the rabbit's wound. Touché.

 # 1) KERMIT THE FROG, from *The Muppet Show* ~ "Someday we'll find it, the rainbow connection, the lovers, the dreamers, and me." So went the lyrics of the only hit song to emerge from the Muppet franchise with "The Rainbow Connection" streaking up the charts in 1979. In 2021 the song was added to the Library of Congress's National Recording Registry.

Jim Henson was the voice and puppeteer for Kermit from his *Muppet Show* debut in 1975 until Henson's death in 1990. Henson's own characterization of Kermit described him as, "kind of easy-going, very likable… sometimes slightly a wiseguy." Henson's biographer Brian Jay Jones wrote that, "The more Jim performed Kermit, the more the two of them seemed to become intertwined… it was becoming harder to tell where the frog ended and Jim began."

In terms of acknowledging accolades, Kermit has so many it's difficult to determine where to start so we've opted to pick three… 1) His balloon has been in every Macy's Thanksgiving Day Parade since 1977… 2) He received a star on the Hollywood Walk of Fame in 2002, and 3) The original Kermit puppet we mentioned above went on permanent display in the Smithsonian in 2013.

While he was always noted for saying, "It's not easy being green," Kermit certainly seemed to make the most of it.

A closing note... *Animal Planet* ranks Kermit as #2 on its list of "50 Greatest TV Animals".

CHAPTER 13

WE'VE GOT LOTS OF TOOTHY TALES WHEN THOSE REPTILES FLASH THEIR SCALES

TURTLES

Okay kids, raise your hand if you know the difference between a turtle and a tortoise. For those whose hands we do not see moving, one way to look at it would be to say that all tortoises are turtles, but not all turtles are tortoises. Which would seem to make sense because, as the more commonly used term might imply, "turtle" is the umbrella that covers the whole category. Feel free to stick your head out of your shell for the full explanation.

So what distinguishes a tortoise? If we were to proffer the most basic distinction it would be that tortoises are terrestrial. With few exceptions, tortoises are walking on the land and cannot swim, as opposed to turtles which are amphibious. There are a few fairly easy-to-recognize visual clues to tell the difference. Tortoises have fat stump-like feet while the other turtles have webbed feet. Tortoise shells are more humped, while the other turtles' shells are more streamlined for the purpose of swimming with less water resistance.

Their diets vary depending on habitat. On the land, turtles eat some plants as well as beetles, snails and worms. In the water, some eat algae but most are carnivores, dining on small fish, squid and jellyfish.

Size ~ In terms of size, turtles can range from 3 inches to 5 feet and, in terms of weight, the smaller ones can weigh as little as a few ounces but on the other end of the spectrum, according to Jana Saure of the Turtle Foundation, "If you count in the leatherback sea turtle (a very impressive animal indeed), they can reach up to 907 kg which equals a little bit less than 1,000 pounds."

In terms of time on the planet, turtles are the oldest reptile group in existence, known to pal around with the dinosaurs 200 million years ago. Their lifespan is also the longest of any reptile and we'll soon be introducing you to the leader in that category!

Speed ~ Probably not surprisingly, the turtles in the water can travel much more quickly than the tortoises on the land. The leatherback turtle can swim at speeds up to 22 mph, enabling it to cover 100 yards in 9.3 seconds. The leopard tortoise is the fastest on land at 0.63 mph which equates to 100-YDT of 5 minutes 24 seconds.

Life ~ Typically, turtles in captivity can live 10-15 years while in the wild some species can live up to 80 years and even more. It is tortoises however that reign superior in this category with some species able to live well over 150 years. Jana from the Turtle Foundation also shared with us that, "There are documents that prove some species have lived in captivity up to 100-250 years." You can read about Jonathan, potentially the all-time record holder for tortoise longevity, at #4 below.

We'll close with a final fun fact and one turtle accomplishment that can never be taken away from them. The first animals to ever orbit the moon were a pair of Russian tortoises who accomplished the feat riding aboard the Soviet's *Zond 5* space ship in 1968.

At this point we will begin the countdown of our Great 8 Turtles.

 # 8) SONNY ~ Let's get things started with a splash! If it can be said that of every animal that ever lived on the planet, you are one of only two to have completed a particular feat, well, that would have to go down as a noteworthy accomplishment. So what lands Sonny in such rarified air? We'll tell that tale next and, teaser alert, don't let that concept of rarified air drift too far away from your brain.

Quirky set of circumstances… you are George Stathakis, a chef in Buffalo, New York, you have a 150-year-old pet tortoise named Sonny, and you come to the conclusion that you and your tortoise need to cement the bond by going over Niagara Falls together in a barrel. This may be the former teachers in us coming out, but right now we want to pose a multiple choice question to our readers. Who do you predict will survive the plunge over the falls?

A) George and Sonny both survive.
B) Sonny survives, George dies.
C) George survives, Sonny dies.
D) George and Sonny both die.

Please lock in your answers right now and read on. Here's what happens…

On July 4, 1930, Buffalo chef George Stathakis straps himself and his pet tortoise Sonny into a 1000-pound wooden barrel which is 10 feet long and 5 feet in diameter. George unfortunately ignores the warning of daredevil advisor Red Hill, Sr. who tells him that his barrel is too big and too heavy.

When George and Sonny go over the falls their barrel survives relatively unscathed, but unfortunately, and probably because of the weight, it becomes the only barrel ever to end up lodged behind the falls. The barrel cannot be retrieved for 18 hours and George does not have that much oxygen. Although he has survived the initial fall, George dies of suffocation.

In a significant side note, apparently you don't live to be a 150-year-old tortoise without having a lot of free time to practice holding your breath. Sonny had obviously gotten very good at this because he survived the ordeal. All of which makes the correct answer to the above multiple choice question land on letter "B".

 # 7) FRANKLIN ~ When your resumé sports the boastful claim that you can "count by twos, and tie your shoes" then obviously your best years are still lying ahead of you and preparing preschool children for those glory years was the purpose of the *Franklin and Friends* franchise. It warrants inclusion in our countdown because they did a fine and family-friendly job at what they were out to do. And they did it in multiple genres over a long period of time.

The franchise spanned the genres of books, TV and movies with the first book written by Paulette Bourgeois in 1986. The TV series originally ran from 1997-2004 generating 78 episodes and there were movies made in 2000, 2001, 2003 and 2006. Finally the TV series was rebooted for a second run from 2010-2012.

Franklin lived with his parents Mr. and Mrs. Turtle and sister Harriet. Episodes dealt with the everyday issues faced by kids with titles such as "Franklin Growing Up Fast" and "Franklin and the Tooth Fairy". Brings back memories of finding that first quarter under your pillow.

 # 6) HARRIET ~ Let's lead with a boast no other living creature on the planet could dare to claim. This turtle was handled by both Charles Darwin (1809-1882) and Steve Irwin (1962-2006)! Darwin came across Harriet on an 1835 research trip to the Galápagos Islands.

He brought Harriet back to England for his studies and she eventually ended up at the Australia Zoo which was founded in 1970 by Steve Irwin's parents, Bob and Lyn. So, by that point, Harriet has achieved the proud age of at least 135 years old.

Moving forward, a young Steve Irwin, while taking care of Harriet, may have hypothetically posed the question, "Which one of us do you think will live longer?" The answer to that potential question would prove intriguing.

The pair would die within three months of each other in 2006, Harriet on June 23 and Steve on September 4. The world felt sorry for Steve's life being cut short at the young age of 44. On the other hand, Harriet's life was certainly a cause for celebration. The mere idea that a single living creature could have, and did, feel the gentle embrace of both Charles Darwin and Steve Irwin, kind of boggles the mind, doesn't it?

 # 5) YERTLE THE TURTLE, from Dr. Seuss ~ Gotta love it when Dr. Seuss uses actual, rather than fictional, animals. Not that we don't absolutely love the Lorax, the Grinch and the Sneetches, but every once in a while it's nice to enjoy a fable featuring an actually existing animal such as the turtle that is Yertle. With cut-in quotes from Dr. Seuss, here's his tale...

The turtles had everything turtles might need.
And they were all happy. Quite happy indeed.

That was the status of the turtles on Sala-ma-Sond island where Yertle the Turtle was king of the pond. And while the islanders were happy, their king was not. Yertle, you see, had arrogant aspirations for expanding his kingdom which he defined as including everything that fell within his view. So the formula for kingdom expansion seemed simple; the higher he could build his throne, the more he could see and hence, the larger his kingdom would become.

If I could sit high, how much greater I'd be!
What a king! I'd be ruler of all that I see!

His modest throne at the beginning of the story consisted of only one rock, and a problem inherent on the island of Sala-ma-Sond was a sad shortage of building supplies. As king, the only asset he had available in mass quantities was turtles, so turtles it would be that Yertle would put to use as the building blocks for the burgeoning throne which would expand his kingdom.

In acknowledging the masterfully poetic magic of Dr. Seuss, we will include each of his rhymes documenting the ascension of Yertle's quest for power. It starts out rather humbly with Yertle's throne increasing from a mere rock to what he could quickly assemble from his turtle subjects immediately at hand...

He made each turtle stand on another one's back
And he piled them all up in a nine-turtle stack.

But while Yertle is enjoying the view of the new things he has added to his kingdom, such as a cat, a cow and a berry bush, problems are developing below. The turtle at the bottom of the stack, whose head everyone must use as a stepping stone to begin their ascension to the top, is beginning to feel the stress. That turtle, named Mack, conveys the following sentiment to his king...

"Your Majesty, please... I don't like to complain,
But down here below, we are feeling great pain."

But Yertle, impervious to Mack's pleas, proceeds to summon even more of his subjects to elevate his throne.

From all over the pond, they came swimming by dozens.
Whole families of turtles, with uncles and cousins.

What kinds of numbers are we talking here?

"My throne shall be higher!" his royal voice thundered,
"So pile up more turtles! I want 'bout two hundred!"

As his teetering tower of turtles grows higher, Yertle's view expands to add birds and bees and butterflies to his kingdom. The added weight of this expansion prompts Mack to proffer the protest that...

"I know, up on top you are seeing great sights,
But down here at the bottom we, too, should have rights."

As evidenced by Yertle's tyrannical abuse of power to this point, he is not a king compelled to care about the commoners. Ignoring those concerns, he ups the ante proclaiming...

"I'll call some more turtles. I'll stack 'em to heaven!
I need 'bout five thousand, six hundred and seven!"

But as is often the case, the greedful lust for power eventually comes with a price. His body bearing the weight of almost six thousand turtles makes its mark on Mack. He lets out an involuntary burp sending a ripple effect up the teetering tower and Yertle's entire throne comes crashing down into the mud, subsequently effecting a realignment of the kingdom in Yertle's view which is described in the following two lines...

And to say the great Yertle, that Marvelous he,
Is King of the Mud. That is all he can see.

And we'll close with Dr. Seuss's own philosophical summary of this situation.

And the turtles, of course... all the turtles are free
As turtles and, maybe, all creatures should be.

 # 4) JONATHAN ~ Talk about having a nice little run on life, this dude reached 192 years old in 2024 and was still blowing out birthday candles. Guinness World Records has validated the tortoise Jonathan as the world's oldest living land animal which is of course a claim that warrants some substantiation.

Let's go back to the egg and we know Jonathan's was laid in about 1832 in the island nation of the Seychelles which is in the Indian Ocean between Africa and India. The Seychelles were a British colony at that time and for whatever reason, in 1882 Jonathan was shipped, along with three other 50-year-old turtles, to the British island of Saint Helena which is located in the Atlantic Ocean between South America and Africa.

So at this point the turtles arriving at Saint Helena are billed to be 50 years old upon delivery, but how do we, or Guinness World Records for that matter, document the age of turtles arriving at a remote island in 1882? Don't worry, we're here for you! First off let's verify Jonathan's species, which is one that won't exactly roll right off your tongue; he's actually an "Aldabrachelys gigantea hololissa". If you find that phrase running repeatedly through your brain for the rest of the day, like a song you can't get out of your head, we will hereby accept full responsibility.

At any rate, the body measurements of this species do not reach full maturity until the age of at least 50 years old. Photographs taken of Jonathan upon his 1882 arrival display dimensions which confirm his age was at least 50 when he got to Saint Helena. So there is your independent corroboration of the Seychelles-stated birth year of 1832. You can do the math from there and extrapolate to the point of establishing 2024 as the year of his 192nd birthday.

 # 3) OOGWAY, from *Kung Fu Panda* ~ You need not be familiar with this franchise to enjoy its pearls of wisdom such as… "You are too concerned with what was and what will be. There's a saying: Yesterday is history, tomorrow is a mystery, but today is a gift. That is why it is called the present." These words are spoken by the overarching sage and spiritual leader Grand Master Oogway, an elderly Galápagos tortoise, to his student and protégé Po launching the *Kung Fu Panda* franchise which began in 2008.

Here is another of our favorite more thought-provoking pearls of Oogway wisdom… "One often meets his destiny on the road he takes to avoid it."

 # 2) THE TORTOISE AND THE HARE, from *Aesop's Fables* ~ Perhaps the most famous of Aesop's Fables, "The Tortoise and the Hare" teaches a lesson which begins when, after being challenged to a race, the overconfident hare surges to an early lead. He then decides to take a nap during which he is passed and subsequently beaten to the finish line by the tortoise. Thus, the moral is established that… slow and steady wins the race.

 # 1) TEENAGE MUTANT NINJA TURTLES ~ Cowabunga, dude! This rowdy expression of excitement and jubilation became a 1990's catch phrase after being popularized by four superheroes with artsy anachronistic names. With monikers surfing centuries, the roster of Italian Renaissance artists would provide Leonardo, Michelangelo, Donatello and Raphael to become the names of the quartet of sewer-dwelling crime fighters battling evil in modern-day New York City.

The TMNT franchise began with a comic book series in 1983 which morphed into a TV series in 1989. To date the Turtles have grossed literally billions of dollars. When their work is all said and done, it becomes time for these superheroes to order up some pizza, become totally radical, and once again caterwaul their catchphrase of "Cowabunga, dude!"

SNAKES

How Long is Long? ~ Ready for a field trip? What say we go to the Show Me State of Missouri and visit the Edge of Hell Haunted House in Kansas City. What will they show us there? Prepare yourself to see the longest snake in captivity!

That honor goes to our girl Medusa, a reticulated python who has been awarded this accolade by Guinness World Records. She measures a whopping 25' 2" and weighs about 350 pounds. A key word in that previous sentence would be "about" because Medusa is subject to sudden weight gains.

No, it's not a female hormone thing; it's her diet. When a girl's standard bill of fare includes live whole hogs, raccoons, and even deer, she can pack on those pounds in a heartbeat… or perhaps "in a mouthful" might be the more appropriate idiom. As the longest snake ever, Guinness states, "the record length is 32' 9.5" for a [reticulated python] shot in Celebes, Indonesia in 1912."

How Heavy? ~ Now that we've broached the subject, we'll carry on with the story of the heaviest snake in captivity. AZ Animals and Guinness both designate the record-holder as being a female Burmese python named Baby who tipped the scales at 403 pounds. She lived from 1979-2006 mostly at the Serpent Safari in Illinois. For the record she was 18' 10" long.

Heavy Venom ~ Venomous snakes are smaller but we'll share the superlatives in their regard. Again, defaulting to Guinness, the heaviest venomous snake was an eastern diamondback rattlesnake that weighed 34 pounds, while the longest was a king cobra which had reached a length of 18' 7" at the London Zoo by 1939. Unfortunately, it was euthanized at the beginning of WW II to avoid endangering the public should the zoo suffer bomb damage which might enable the snake to escape.

Next, let's look for the most venomous snake in the world, regardless of size. That scary accolade goes to the inland taipan snake which is native to Australia. Astute Aussies always opt to steer clear of these guys or perhaps it might be more accurate to say the snakes steer clear of the humans. They are known to strike quickly and one snake carries enough venom to kill a hundred humans but, that being said, they don't strike humans, only their smaller prey.

Our guest expert for this component was Brian Kleinman, owner of the Riverside Reptiles Education Center in Enfield, Connecticut. Regarding this snake Brian pointed out that, "There have been zero deaths attributed to this species. This is because it is found in uninhabitable areas of Australia where people are few and far between, so encounters are rare." He added that inland taipan snakes are known for their lack of aggression towards humans with "shy and placid" being words that appear in descriptions of the snake's disposition.

Life & Speed ~ Depending on species, the average life span of a snake ranges from 20-30 years. The oldest confirmed living age of a snake was a Colombian rainbow boa named Ben who lived 42 years, 6 days. In 1974, the Hattermann family bought Ben at Pet World in Peoria, Illinois and cared for him until his death in 2016.

The question of, "Which snake is the fastest?" provided one of the best examples to validate our approach of seeking out expert information validation rather than relying on more easily accessible internet info. We were all set to list the sidewinder as the fastest before turning our draft over to Brian at the Reptile Center who countered with, "Although this 'fact' seems to be everywhere on the internet, I do not think it's correct. I personally have heard of this before, and to me it seems physically impossible for such a small species of snake. The only scientific article I could find on sidewinder speed clocked them from 0.31 to 2.3 mph." He added that, "The fastest confirmed snake is the Black Mamba at 12 mph." That would give it a 100-YDT of 17 seconds.

How 'bout we slither right away to our countdown of 4 Famous Snakes…

 # 4) MEDUSA'S SNAKES ~ Let's start by lighting you up with this now-mostly-legalized riddle-pun. Q: What does Medusa and marijuana have in common? A: They both can get you stoned. Medusa was the most famous of the three Gorgon sisters who were a terrifying triumvirate of wicked women with mouths that could spit poison, a gaze that turned humans to stone, and a head that grew snakes for hair.

It was a persona of Greek mythology that certainly would not present well on a modern-day dating app. Medusa could have wreaked havoc indefinitely were it not for the fact that the goddess Athena had it in for her. It had been Athena's curse that had turned the beautiful maiden into Medusa in the first place and as if that wasn't enough, it is Athena that crafts the plan that kills her.

It's the mortal Perseus who **executes** said plan, pun intended. Stealthily approaching Medusa in her sleep, Perseus walks backward, guiding himself with the use of a mirror which acts as a safety net should Medusa wake up during his approach. Perseus successfully navigates the bedroom of Medusa and beheads the sleeping villainess. The decapitated trophy is given to Athena who incorporates the image onto her shield, having it become one of her permanent symbols.

We'll close with the story behind a favorite single-panel comic from *Dan Piraro's Bizarro Comics*. The image depicts a priest and an exasperated bald woman sitting at a table with drinks. The caption reads, "Ill-fated blind date: St. Patrick and Medusa" with a voice bubble from St. Patrick simply saying, "Sorry". Get it?

 # 3) KAA, from *The Jungle Book* ~ This Indian python is the original creation of British author Rudyard Kipling who first used the character in his 1894 anthology *The Jungle Book*. In Kipling's version Kaa acts as a friend and mentor of Mowgli, the human "man-cub" main character of the entire franchise. Kipling casts Kaa as virtually a father figure to the boy.

When Disney assumed control of the franchise in the 1960's, the character of Kaa underwent the most significant character transition, essentially shifting from benevolence to the dark side. The reason for this was that Walt himself felt that the audience would struggle with the snake serving as a protagonist. For the record, Disney's extensive film history features only three protagonist snakes, all of whom slithered the Earth after Walt had left it.

 # 2) CLEOPATRA'S ASP ~ Here's one of history's most classic snake stories ever. We begin with Cleopatra ascending the throne as Queen of Egypt in 51 B.C., beginning the reign of one of the most fascinating women in the history of the world. Her love life boasts a most impressive dance card which includes dalliances with some of the world's most powerful men of the first century B.C.

That list features Roman romances with both Julius Caesar and Marc Antony. When the battle for power in the Roman Empire sends Antony south, retreating to Egypt, he commits suicide leaving Cleo with options that are sketchy at best.

When she learns that the conquering Romans plan to take her back and parade her through the streets of Rome as a symbol of their conquest of Egypt, she decides to follow Antony's example and check out. So here's Hollywood's take on what happens…

Cleopatra releases a poisonous Egyptian asp in her chamber and the audience watches the slithering reptile approach the ill-fated Queen to deliver the deadly bite. The only question is how and where, with different movies offering various takes on the details.

If you go to the classic 1963 Elizabeth Taylor movie version... beware of the basket of figs, there's a scaly surprise slithering under the surface. No wonder snakes get such a bad rap.

It was Caesar's hand she would first grasp
With Marc Antony make her last gasp
She would opt out of Rome and
Decide to stay home and
Succumb to the bite of an asp

 # 1) THE GARDEN OF EDEN SERPENT, from the Bible ~ After setting up Adam and Eve with some divine digs in the Garden of Eden, there's really only one clause in the lease to which the tenants must strictly adhere. Pointing out the Garden's most impressive piece of landscaping, God identifies it to the couple as "the Tree of Knowledge of Good and Evil." Pretty impressive title for a tree, right?

So in caring for their new tree, the aforementioned clause of consequential concern would be simply, "Don't eat the fruit." But as we all know, the devil is always in the details when it comes to these lease agreements. When you make it down to the fine print, the punishment for fruit eating is that, "In the day that thou eatest thereof thou shalt surely die." (Genesis 2:17)

Sounds a little harsh, but what are they going to do? Look for another realtor? So, if Adam and Eve had avoided temptation they could have blissfully lived in the Garden of Eden forever, but that wouldn't have made for much of a story and we all know what happens next.

At this point please allow us to introduce you to the next character in our story, the Serpent. This dude is evil incarnate and he's got a line for everything. The Serpent convinces the couple to violate that clause in their lease promising, "Then your eyes shall be opened, and ye shall be as gods." (Genesis 3:5)

Well, who wouldn't want to be a god? And those apples just look so tempting, so Adam and Eve decide to partake. As they engage in this blatant violation, wouldn't you know it, God just happens to be walking in the Garden. Talk about your bad timing! As stated in Genesis 3:8, "The man and his wife heard the sound of the Lord God as he was walking in the Garden in the cool of the day." Can anyone say, "Busted!"

So Adam and Eve get kicked out of the Garden which of course is not an end to their problems. Next come Cain and Abel and, with absolutely no parenting books to fall back upon, this one doesn't end well either. But if it's any consolation, things turn out even worse for the Serpent. The punishment for his fruitful offense is that God issues the eternal edict, "You will *crawl* on your *belly* and you will eat dust all the days of your life." (Genesis 3:14) Hopefully you weren't waiting around for a happy ending on this one.

ALLIGATORS & CROCODILES

Remember from our childhood the mantra, "See you later, alligator; after a while crocodile." Well, let's forget the "see-you-laters" and the "after-a-whiles" before we charge right into the swamp to get down with the gators and go crazy with the crocs.

Croc or Gator? ~ Okay, there's a giant lizard-like creature crawling toward you on short legs, with a large dark scaly body and a huge powerful tail wagging back and forth. Is it an alligator or a crocodile? Either way, you're probably going to want to get the hell out of there, but wouldn't you like to know just what you're running from? Well, that's what we're here for.

This was the way we had originally written our intro for this component before we were resoundingly admonished by Dr. Marisa Tellez, Executive Director and Founder of Crocodile Research Coalition, an organization based in the Central American country of Belize. Dr. Tellez informed us that, "The CRC promotes co-existence with crocodilians, being careful with words and phrases to ensure we do not instill fear subconsciously." Most crocodiles are not out to get people and, as a matter of fact, "Out of the 28 crocodilian species in the world, only 3 are deemed dangerous to humans; the rest are quite shy and timid."

From a visual perspective, the easiest way you can tell the difference between a croc and an alligator is when their mouths are closed. If you can see the teeth from the upper **and** lower snout, that's a croc. If you can only see the teeth from the upper snout and it looks like it has an overbite, that's an alligator.

Color would be another visual cue. Alligators are darker, ranging from a dark green to a dark gray while crocodiles are usually lighter shades of green, gray or brown. That being said, Dr. Tellez added that, "Some crocodilians have a dark shade like an alligator as well; they can change their color hue depending on their environment."

Size ~ If you happen to have your tape measure with you, you could take advantage of the size distinctions. Alligators are smaller than crocodiles with an average adult length of 12 feet vs. 16 feet. Going to superlatives, our largest recorded alligator was 15' 9" and the heaviest weighed 1,380 pounds. The equivalent crocodile numbers are 20' 3" and 2,370 pounds.

Geography ~ Switching from visual to geographic clues, the only place in the world where you could find both alligators and crocodiles in the wild, on the same fieldtrip, would be if you paid a visit to the Florida Everglades. Venturing out from there, the alligator has a much narrower range of habitat.

The American alligator can be found across a swath of the southeastern U.S. that curls from Texas around to North Carolina. The only other alligator species in the world is the Chinese alligator which can be found on the IUCN's endangered species list in "extremely endangered" numbers estimated at 68-86 animals in a small band along the Yangtze River in China.

If the U.S. and China ever went to war, a wise strategy on our part would be to suggest that each country send out its alligator population for a reptile-to-reptile confrontation. Throwing the odds in our favor would be that in this hypothetical battle we would have them outnumbered one million to under a hundred. One caveat to the stated numerical advantage would be that, as Dr. Tellez points out, "The Chinese alligator is critically endangered in the wild but there are over 15,000 in captivity in rearing centers in China."

Conservation Status ~ Contrary to the fate of the Chinese alligator, the American alligator provides one of the more successful conservation stories of our era. After the Endangered Species Preservation Act of 1966, the U.S. alligator population had dropped so low it received immediate protection in 1967. The environmental support produced significant results, the animal came off the endangered list in 1987, and today there are over a million of them.

The world habitat map for the crocodile checks more locale boxes than the alligator, but is also plagued by multiple endangered species issues. You can find crocodiles on every continent except Europe and Antarctica. But the IUCN lists five crocodile species as "critically endangered" which we'll share in the list below.

* Cuban (native to Cuba)
* Orinoco (Venezuela and Columbia)
* Philippine (the Philippines)
* Siamese (southeast Asia)
* Slender-Snouted (central and western Africa)

Life ~ Continuing the trend that the crocs have been, in general, besting the gators, let's take a look at life expectancy. For alligators the "in the wild/in captivity" numbers are 50/80 years; while for crocodiles those numbers would be 70/100. Both the alligator and the crocodile who lived the longest are covered in our countdown below.

Speed ~ Of course, they slow down when they get older, but at their fastest, which would be while they are swimming, "alligator/crocodile" speeds max out at 35/22 mph, which would enable them to traverse 100 yards in 5.8/9.3 seconds.

How 'bout we close this game the same way we started it with the, "is it croc or gator?" question. If you see the reptile crawling toward you and there are dinosaurs in the background, are you able to identify your adversary? Nope, alligators and crocodiles both roamed the planet in the mixed company of dinosaurs.

Crocs and gators do align, for our Countdown List of 9…

 # 9) LEAVE IT TO BEAVER GATOR ~ Let's kick into our countdown with this historical moment in TV history. Of the many accolades attributed to the alligator, certainly one of the most unique would be its involvement in the first toilet to ever appear on TV.

It is the hit 1950's sitcom *Leave It to Beaver* which first floats the bowl on this one. You might suspect that the toilet's first appearance on a TV show would have been a casual in-the-background-while-the-kids-are-brushing-their-teeth moment. But alas, 'twas not to be.

Wally and the Beaver used a comic book ad to order an actual Florida alligator. Of course the prevailing premise of that show was that the kids' miscalculations consistently managed to create comic calamities. The boys initially expected to receive the full-grown alligator seen in the picture in the comic book. Imagine their surprise when they receive a shoebox size package with a live baby alligator.

The original plan had been to keep the alligator in their bathtub. Deeming that abode too big for a baby, they opt for Plan B which is to allow the baby gator to take up residence in the tank of their toilet. So the toilet's first TV gig is to serve as an aquarium. Won't parents Ward and June be surprised?!

 # 8) SATURN ~ Did you hear the story about Hitler's pet alligator? Probably a bit of Berlin urban legend at play here, at least as far as the word "pet" goes. What we do know is that Saturn was a resident of the Berlin Zoo until the end of WW II and Hitler was known to have visited that zoo. So, at the very least, Saturn and Hitler probably made eye contact at some point, unless Saturn chose to turn his head away.

Right now Saturn is alive and living at the Moscow Zoo, a scenario which warrants some connecting of the dots. WW II ended with Berlin in shambles, zoo included, and all the Nazi officials that survived were looking for the quickest way out to Argentina.

Of the Allied forces involved in the mop-up activities, the alligator somehow came under the auspices of the British Army who gifted Saturn to the Russians (remember they were on our side during WW II) because the logistics would have been more practical to get the gator to Moscow than to London.

Thought to have been born around 1937, Saturn shows up as just a tad younger than Muju, who you'll meet just below, in the #4 slot. He remains one of the most popular attractions at the Moscow Zoo and while he's not officially recognized as the oldest alligator in the world, there is still one designation to which Saturn can take sole claim. He is the only still-living creature on the planet to have had contact with Hitler.

 # 7) BEN ALI GATOR, from Disney's *Fantasia* ~ We're going to award the esteemed accolade of Greatest Alligator Dancer ever to this guy. Ben Ali Gator flaunts his masculine bravado in the "Dance of the Hours" segment from Walt

Disney's 1940 masterpiece *Fantasia*. Through his masterful moves, he is able to reel in his romantic choice, a conquest which is confirmed when Ben Ali Gator and Hyacinth Hippo share a dance, and then a departure, in the segment's grand finale.

 # 6) HENRY ~ There were 122 candles on the cake at the December 2022 birthday party of Henry the crocodile when the festivities took place at the Crocworld Conservation Centre in Scottburgh, KwaZulu-Natal, South Africa. After taking care of those candles, Henry was able to celebrate his ongoing status as the oldest living crocodile on the planet.

Let's circle back, way back, to the beginning and see how the early stages of the story of Henry do not necessarily forebode a long lifetime. At the beginning of the 20th century, as a young croc in the southeast African nation of Botswana, Henry picks up the pesky problem of eating people.

Hoping to put an end to this unwanted activity, the Botswana natives hire an elephant hunter named Sir Henry to kill the croc. He is able to capture the animal and, for reasons unspecified, the death sentence is commuted to life in captivity. Henry, the crocodile (now named after the hunter), certainly breathes a sigh of relief at this point but, even at his most optimistic, we're sure Henry is not thinking that he's just managed to tack another 120 years onto his life.

In addition to the cake and party, Henry has quite a cushy Crocworld life of leisure. He's fathered over 700 baby crocs and is currently housed with a harem of a half dozen lady crocodiles. We'd have to call these accommodations not too shabby for a kid who wouldn't have been there in the first place had he not developed a sweet tooth for Botswana natives.

 # 5) WALLY GATOR ~ It was 1962 when Hanna-Barbera introduced this Cajun character to the world on *The Wally Gator Show*. Having previously been "the swingin' alligator of the swamp" according to the very cool theme song, Wally is struggling to adapt to his new life and home at the city zoo where he finds himself under the constant and dutiful watch of zookeeper Mr. Twiddle.

Most storylines involve Wally's constant attempts to escape the zoo and explore outside life and, truth be told, zoo security is shockingly lax as Wally seems to have more trouble staying in the zoo than getting out.

 # 4) MUJU ~ Living at the historic Belgrade Zoo since 1937, the alligator Muju (pronounced Moo´-ya) has certainly seen some history in his time. Because of its crossroads location, Belgrade, Yugoslavia was one of the few cities bombed by both the Axis and Allied powers during WW II. Then there was the Communist takeover in 1945, the breakup of Yugoslavia in the early 1990's with Belgrade becoming part of Serbia, and finally the NATO bombing of Serbia in 1999.

Muju is one of two alligators competing for the recognition of being the oldest alligator ever. These calculations can be a bit tricky with the one sliver of uncertainty in Muju's case being the question of how old the alligator was when it arrived in Belgrade in 1937. The zoo itself published information regarding Muju's 87th birthday celebration which occurred in June of 2023, establishing 1936 as the year of birth which would make sense in aligning with the 1937 arrival.

So what is life like for Muju these days? He remains a popular attraction at the zoo and maintains a significant social media presence with many followers on multiple platforms. He's still a hardy eater with his meaty diet consisting of beef, birds, horse meat, rabbits, and skinned rats. (Side thought: That job of rat skinner cannot be one of the more sought-after assignments at the Belgrade Zoo!)

So now returning to that aforementioned oldest alligator competition, Guinness World Records has designated Muju as the record holder since 2007. But that seems to be in contradiction with our next countdown companion Marta. Here's her story…

 # 3) MARTA ~ Are you ready to meet a legendary heartbreaker with a movie star line in her resumé and 93 candles on her most recent fish-flavored birthday cake? We hope so, because we have Marta cued up and ready to celebrate. At this point, please let us defer to some of the information provided on the birthday party announcement from Marta's Płock Zoo in Poland.

According to the zoo… "Alligator Marta hatched in 1930 in the now defunct Reptile Jungle Garden in Slidell, Louisiana (USA). She arrived in Płock on August 19, 1960. Since then, Marta has been fulfilling herself as a star of our zoo, and even tried her hand at the silver screen. In the summer of 1970, she played the role of crocodile Herman in Andrzej Kondratiuk's film *Hydro-Puzzle*. Marta is not only the favorite of Płock residents and employees of the Płock Zoo, but also the oldest animal in European zoos."

The film *Hydro-Puzzle* was a superhero crime comedy set in Warsaw, Poland which was perfect for Marta in that it enabled her to flash her extensive range in acting. She not only had to cross genders to play the male character Herman, she also had to cross species to play a crocodile. Certainly a legendary performance.

Moving on to that "heartbreaker" status to which we earlier alluded, there were multiple Marta mating attempts, but she proved to be a mistress with no interest. According to Płock Zoo spokesperson Magdalena Kowalkowska, "There were several attempts to set Marta up with other male alligators, but without success. She didn't like any of them. In the end, we accepted that Marta preferred to lead a single life."

As Marta settles into her senior years, she does so on a diet much less diverse than that of Muju, which we saw above. Marta usually dines on beef and freshwater fish, which at her 93rd birthday party was supplemented with a special seafood cake. Humans attending the party feasted on cake cooked in the shape of an alligator.

Kowalkowska summed up the event by saying, "Marta is unique. She is a record holder in terms of life expectancy, so we celebrate her every birthday with fanfare and we will do so, as long as she's with us." So the one question in the wind as we close this segment is that the Płock Zoo does seem to have solid documentation of Marta's timeline leaving the question unanswered as to why Guinness does not recognize her life as being the longest.

In her last email to us, Kowalkowska wrote, "We are currently trying to enter the Guinness Book of Records."

 # 2) TICK-TOCK, from Disney's *Peter Pan* ~ "I suppose it's like the ticking crocodile, isn't it? Time is chasing after all of us." – J.M. Barrie, author of *Peter Pan*. When Barrie wrote his book in 1904, the concept of the ticking crocodile, having achieved that status by swallowing an alarm clock, was an invention all his own. But his novel and the Disney studio's subsequent embrace of the franchise, beginning with the 1953 film *Peter Pan*, have elevated Tick-Tock to legendary croc status.

An early encounter where Tick-Tock is able to chomp off the hand of antagonist Captain Hook, not only explains how the evil one-handed Captain got his nickname, it also sets up Captain Hook to decry his fate. "That cursed beast liked the taste of me so well," laments Hook, "he's followed me ever since, licking his chops for the rest of me."

A climactic final walking-the-plank sword fight scene ensues between Pan and Hook with Tick-Tock ticking hungrily in the water. When Pan prevails and hurls Hook into the drink, the subsequently stirring sunset scene is set. As Hook scurries and scrambles to swim for survival, we see Tick-Tock once again in hot pursuit of his pirate prey.

 # 1) MR. FRESHIE ~ Okay, so you're a crocodile taking a casual swim in the river one day when you notice a human in the distance who seems to be purposefully approaching you. As the man nears, you notice this is not just any human, this is Steve Irwin the Crocodile Hunter and he wants to wrestle. How's your day going so far?

So while this turn of events may not seem like a best case scenario for a crocodile, ironically it actually serves to save Mr. Freshie's life. How can that be? Turns out this crocodile has been shot twice by hunters leaving him severely injured and blind in his left eye.

After securing the animal, Irwin has him transferred to the Sunshine Coast Zoo in Queensland, Australia where Mr. Freshie receives critically needed medical attention. After recovering from his injuries, the crocodile settles into the facility that he will call home for the rest of his life.

At that time, scientists determine his age to be about 100 years old. Just to put this in some kind of historical perspective, when Mr. Freshie was born, the Civil War had been over for just five years and Thomas Edison was hard at work on the new invention he was going to call the phonograph.

The crocodile would live the last 40 years of his life at Sunshine Coast dying peacefully in 2010. Doing the math, Mr. Freshie lived to be about 140 years old establishing the record for the oldest crocodile ever.

Since the Crocodile Hunter has crept into the story anyway, we'll close this chapter with one of the hottest humor tips in our *Animal Kingdom*. Ever wonder what might happen if Steve were visiting the ESPN studio and the University of Florida's Gator mascot happened to step out of the elevator. We give you our gator guarantee that you'll thank us after visiting YouTube to see "Steve Irwin Wrestling Gators Mascot".

DINOSAURS

When we first decided to embark upon this project we shared the comment, "The dinosaur component should be really fun." Well, we're glad to finally arrive in the Mesozoic Period and begin by confirming the fact that our instincts were exactly correct. There is a fascination and mystique with dinosaurs that many find captivating.

Early Misconceptions ~ So when did all this fun begin? The first documented discovery of a dinosaur bone was made in 1677 by Robert Plot. He was the director of Ashmolean Museum in Oxford, England and he described the discovery in his book *Natural History of Oxford-shire*. While the fossil itself has been lost, Plot's intricate drawing allows later scientists to confirm his find but Plot, himself, identified the bone as belonging to a "human giant".

That was the approach taken for the next 150 years where humans attributed any discovered dinosaur fossils to giants or other random fairy tale creatures or beasts. It wasn't until the 1820's that scientists began to zero in on the theory that the collective group of dinosaur bones that had been assembled constituted a distinct species of reptile that no longer existed.

Accepting Extinction ~ Actually the concept of animals becoming extinct was new to science. Thomas Jefferson, who was certainly one of the smartest men in the world, held firm to the belief that none of God's creatures could ever die out. To that end, he had specifically directed Lewis and Clark to be on the lookout for woolly mammoths as they embarked upon their two-year exploration of the Louisiana Purchase in 1802. He was just sure that there had to be some wandering around out west somewhere.

It would be in 1842 that English naturalist Richard Owen first coined the term that would stick as the overall name for this newly identified animal. That was the first year that the word "dinosaur" saw the printed page with Owen deriving it as a portmanteau of the Greek words "deinos" and "sauros"... English translation... fearfully great lizard.

Geologically Speaking ~ For the most part we have avoided the use of geological time periods in this book because, as previously stated, our goal was to have this book be scientifically accurate, but not be a science book per se.

This is the one time in the book where we are going to cross that line with the goal of making more clear some of the dinosaur interconnectivity we want to share. Some of the most famous dinosaur species that you had fighting each other with your plastic dinosaur toys as a child never actually fought because they were never on the planet at the same time.

The geological era that encompasses the entire existence of the dinosaur would be the Mesozoic Period, which means "middle life" and ran from 252 to 66 million years ago. The Mesozoic Period was comprised of three smaller geological eras which break down as follows...

*Triassic Period ~ 252 to 201 million years ago
*Jurassic Period ~ 201 to 145 million years ago
*Cretaceous Period ~ 145 to 66 million years ago

The Cretaceous Period ended with a bang which also ended the run of the dinosaurs on the planet. The accepted scientific theory as to why dinosaurs became extinct is that it was the result of a massive 6-mile-wide meteor which is known to have crashed near the Yucatan Peninsula in Mexico. The subsequent climate change took out not only the dinosaurs, but also 75-80% of all life on Earth. (Note: We opted to capitalize all species for consistency.)

Fighting On ~ So the different species of dinosaurs did not all roam the Earth together at the same time. One of our favorite dinosaur fights to stage as kids was between the Tyrannosaurus Rex and the Stegosaurus. While the T. Rex was menacing with its powerful jaws, the Stegosaurus had those super cool plates running down the middle of its back and that bad-ass spiked tail which it wielded like a medieval flail.

So now that we've brought the pre-fight hype to a fever pitch, step back and don't get blown away by the air as we let it all out of the tire. The Stegosaurus thrived during the late Jurassic Period while the T. Rex did not make its debut until the late Cretaceous Period. The last Stegosaurus checked out millions of years before the first T. Rex even appeared.

While it's always hard to wrap your brain around time periods spanning millions of years, we'll close with a statistic that easily puts one thing in perspective. The total time that dinosaurs roamed the planet was about 185 million years, while humans have walked the Earth for 2.5 million years. Suffice it to say that if we break their record, you and I will be missing the celebration.

Sizing Things Up ~ Let's seize upon some superlatives. The tallest dinosaur was the Brachiosaurus which stood almost 40 feet high, while the award for longest and the heaviest goes to the Argentinosaurus at 130 feet, 220,000 pounds. For the flying dinosaurs, the Quetzalcoatlus boasted a wingspan of 40 feet. Our final stat in the "How Big Is Big" category would be that the largest dinosaur eggs were 20 inches in circumference. The omelet chef is sure gonna want some advance warning on this one!

Shifting gears to look at the most diminutive examples, the smallest dinosaur egg ever found was 1.2 inches in diameter and weighed 2.6 ounces. The smallest adult dinosaur was the Microraptor which was about 2½ feet long, weighed 2-4 pounds, and had a feathered wingspan of about 3 feet. It was thought that they could attain flight for short distances.

This just in… After we had already composed this component, we came across a publication from The Natural History Museum which said, "An international team, including scientists affiliated with NHM, discovered the skull of a tiny dinosaur trapped in 99-million-year-old amber from Myanmar. It was about the size of a bee hummingbird, making it the smallest dinosaur discovered yet. The findings were published in [our museum's magazine]."

Here's a final thought on size, that to many is probably a surprise… if you were to stand face-to-face with every dinosaur that ever existed, in order to make eye contact you would be looking down more often than you would be looking up. In terms of percentages, the majority were shorter than humans.

Life ~ If you're wondering how scientists could broach this topic when the species is extinct, dinosaur bones had growth rings which could be used to determine age. Some of the more common species averaged about 30 years with Raptors coming in at 32 and the T. Rex at 28. On the long end of the spectrum, the Sauropod could live 70-80 years.

Speed ~ The fastest runner in the dinosaur races was the Ornithomimus which scientists estimate could reach a speed of 43.5 mph giving it a 100-YDT of 4.7 seconds. Let's sprint into our countdown of Half a Dozen Dinos…

 # 6) THE LAND BEFORE TIME ~ We definitely extend kudos to this franchise in the category of prolific moviemaking. The original 1988 theatrical film spawned 13 direct-to-video sequels and Cartoon Network's 2007-08 TV series.

That first film stood out for a few reasons, in addition to the fact that it was the only one to play in theaters. It was directed by Don Bluth and produced by Steven Spielberg and George Lucas and it was the only one that was **not** a musical. Spielberg, Lucas and Bluth all have no involvement in any of the sequels, thus establishing the 1988 film as superior within the franchise.

That one has a Bambi-esque beginning with a Tyrannosaurus Rex killing the mother of the main character Littlefoot (an Apatosaurus, the big ones with the long necks). Littlefoot is subsequently joined in a multi-species ensemble of young dinos with Cera (a Triceratops, the ones with three horns); Spike (a Stegosaurus, the ones with the spiked tail and row of plates down their back); Ducky (a Saurolophus, the ones with the horn-like headcrest); and Petrie (a Pterodactyl, the bird-like ones with wings).

Aided by heavenly assistance from the spirit of Bigfoot's mother, the quintet embarks upon a quest for the Great Valley where their salvation awaits. Along the way they will be learning life lessons about loyalty, friendship and survival. Perhaps if they'd known that the studio had 13 sequels instore for them upon reaching that Great Valley, the dinosaur entourage might have taken a little more time on their trek to stop and smell the roses.

 # 5) GERTIE THE DINOSAUR ~ We soundly agree with the February 28, 1914 issue of *The New York Evening Journal* which called Gertie "the greatest act in the history of motion picture cartoonists." Especially for a piece of work over a hundred years old, this one is truly intriguing. Gertie, the work of cartoonist and animator Winsor McCay, is generally considered to be the first cartoon **character** ever. This girl sure does ooze personality and charisma.

Walt Disney was also a huge fan and protégé. He often referenced McCay in the animation history segments on his TV show. Also, the shore of Echo Lake in the Disney Hollywood Studios Park at Disney World is home to a giant recreation of Gertie which houses an ice cream stand.

Just to confirm that we and Walt are not the only ones perceiving this Gertie girl as timeless, the 1994 book *The 50 Greatest Cartoons of All Time* compiled the results of a comprehensive polling of people in the field of animation and "Gertie the Dinosaur" landed at #6 in that poll!

 # 4) REX, from Disney Pixar's *Toy Story* ~ Not that you're likely to be afforded the opportunity in real life, but if you ever find yourself face-to-face with a Tyrannosaurus Rex, here's our best piece of advice. Don't mock him out about having short arms; they **hate** that! And that was one of several personal insecurities felt by Rex, dinosaur star of the Disney/Pixar *Toy Story* franchise (1995-present), who suffers from the inferiority complex that he is not scary enough.

Clearly the concept of juxtaposition was the gist of the characterization calculations on this bad boy. You have perhaps the most notoriously terrifying animal in existence, so in order to play upon that, you give him the personality of a meek, insecure, angst-riddled pacifist peacemonger, whose go-to line is, "I don't like confrontations!"

 # 3) DINO, from *The Flintstones* ~ In terms of Flintstones pets, one casting perk that Dino could celebrate would be that he received much more screen time than the pet cat, Baby Puss. Despite the fact that he had the body of a dinosaur, and was alternately referred to as a "snorkasaurus" and a "dogasaurus," Dino was essentially the Flintstones' pet pooch in the 1960-1966 TV series, and the dozens of other subsequent manifestations of the franchise that followed.

The fact that Dino held a special spot in the family was made evident right out of the gate. When those opening credits roll, we see Fred rushing home from work. Once home, Wilma comes running out to the car with Pebbles, followed by Dino at full gallop, and finally we see Baby Puss sprinting to join the party. Then they zip next door to pick up the Rubbles with their baby Bamm Bamm. Next, it's off to the drive-in where Dino pops his head through the roof of the car, placing the kids on his head for the best possible view.

Dino proves to be a devoted, loyal and loving pet. One running gag in the series is when patriarch Fred comes home from work, Dino is so overcome with excitement he knocks him down on his back, climbs aboard, and starts smothering his owner with kisses. Fred puts up mild resistance, but generally succumbs to the barrage of tongue lashings.

2) BARNEY ~ If you're in the preschool age range, here are some words you could live by…

> *Barney comes to play with us*
> *Whenever we may need him*
> *Barney can be your friend too*
> *If you just make-believe him*

The purple dinosaur dominated the little kiddie airwaves on PBS from 1992-2010, not bad for a costumed prehistoric reptile, no matter what color you are. Barney and his assistants used song and dance to hug their way through lovable lessons like learning to count, mastering your ABC's, and brushing up on the often tricky and ever-changing social standards of the preschool world.

1) JURASSIC PARK/JURASSIC WORLD ~ "Your scientists were just so preoccupied with whether or not they could, they didn't stop to think if they should." This might be the quote that looms central to the *Jurassic* franchise and in providing an overview, we are going to mention three individual characters for the purpose of keeping this component concise and user friendly.

From the outset of the first film in 1993, you had the older gray-haired Dr. Alan Grant (Sam Neil) who was the guy in charge of the operation, and the younger pair of level-headed scientists, Dr. Ellie Sattler (Laura Dern) and Dr. Ian Malcolm (Jeff Goldblum). Our lead-off quote was Malcolm expressing his concerns to Grant.

It was Michael Crichton's 1990 novel about the creation of a theme park of cloned dinosaurs that first postulated the possibilities of what might go wrong. This would spawn the franchise that would grow to include two movie trilogies, so six feature films altogether, as well as various spin-off projects. The groundbreaking animatronics and computer-generated imagery certainly served to rejuvenate worldwide interest in dinosaurs and paleontology.

Assuming a dinosaur isn't knocking at your door right now interrupting the flow of this chapter, we'll close with one final financial fun fact. The *Jurassic Park* franchise is one of the highest grossing of all time having earned over $6 billion dollars. And not a single one of those dollars is extinct.

CHAPTER 14

NEVER AT A LOSS FOR WORDS WITH THE CHICKENS, DUCKS & BIRDS

CHICKENS

Chicken questions ignite powder keg!
Corn flakes now?, chicken wing?, want a leg?
Hey diddle diddle
Is that Chicken Little?
Chicken first?, was it that?, or the egg?

You'll have to make your own decisions on those menu choices above but, as promised in our book's intro, if you've been wondering about that chicken/egg conundrum, your question will be answered by the end of this chapter.

We have an egg carton full of charming chicken fun facts for you to read and when Global Animal Welfare Specialist Liam Hodgson of The Humane League reviewed this he said, "What you have here so far looks great and it really made my day reading it this morning!" So let's crack this thing open...

On that topic of fun facts, turns out chickens can see better than you can; they can see shades of color undetectable to the human eye. It has to do with seeing ultra-violet light rays and the explanation that clicked best with us was that they can see color shades that people would only see under a black light.

There are a few different aspects of their intelligence that stand out. They can recognize people and other chickens and are able to remember over a hundred different faces. They also have a vocabulary of over 30 different sounds addressing concepts ranging from food to danger to mating.

At this point Liaison Lindsey commented, "There are estimated to be around 500 different breeds of chickens, some of which are very funky looking, for a good kick look up a polish chicken!"

Chickens descended from the red jungle fowl, a species which still exists in the wild in Southeast Asia, the only continent to harbor wild chickens. If you're thinking that you've heard of prairie chickens roaming wild in the midwestern U.S., that layman's term is a misnomer, as the type of bird to which it refers is actually a grouse.

As smart as they are in some regards, it's a good thing for us that they can't organize because with a global population of 33 billion, there are more than 4 times the number of chickens on the planet as there are people. An idiom that is only a cliché for humans is an actuality for chickens. They can literally sleep with one eye open.

Life ~ Wild chickens have a life span of 5-7 years while chickens in captivity, assuming they are not harvested for food, could expect to live 15 years. According to Guinness World Records the chicken who lived the longest life was a red quill muffed American game hen named Muffy. She died in 2012 at the age of 23 years and 152 days.

Size & Speed ~ Due to breeding improvements, chickens have gradually increased in size with average birds now standing over 2 feet tall and weighing over 5 pounds. Record-setting roosters have hit a full 15 pounds. In terms of speed, domestic chickens can run 9 mph while those in the wild can hit 20 mph with predators in hot pursuit. Those convert to 100-YDT's of 22.7 seconds and 10.2 seconds, respectively.

Closing with a few final fun facts… you can tell what color eggs a chicken will lay by checking out their earlobes. White lobes = white eggs, red lobes = brown eggs and, by the way, the colors are equally nutritious. Meanwhile, we promised you an answer to that whole, "Which came first, the chicken or the egg?" conundrum and you know we'd never let you down.

If you'd like to crack this one open for the last time, we've got *National Geographic* on the line to provide you with the final answer once and for all. According to them… "Reptiles were laying eggs thousands of years before chickens appeared. The first chicken came from an egg laid by a reptilian-type bird that was not quite a chicken. Therefore, the egg came first." Now, if we could only figure out why the chicken crossed the road, we could have all our boxes checked.

Next up find the picks, for our Final 4 Chicks…

 # 4) CORNELIUS ~ Here's a rooster who may not have that enormous name recognition, but visual recognition… now that's another story. We're betting that there's not a reader in our audience who has not sat face-to-face with this bird at the breakfast table because, you see, Cornelius is the mascot and box coverboy for Kellogg's Corn Flakes.

Can't you all picture the green body, yellow beak, and red comb and wattle (that funky-looking thing that dangles from beneath a rooster's chin). After Kellogg's introduced the cereal in 1906 the company went with a simple farm girl on the cover for six decades, but after enjoying 1950's marketing success with other cartoon mascots, like Tony the Tiger (Frosted Flakes) and Snap, Crackle & Pop (Rice Krispies), the decision was made to create a mascot for Corn Flakes with Cornelius Rooster making his debut in 1957.

The gag used in the beginning years was that Cornelius, or Corny for short, found himself unable to muster a crow before downing that first bowl of Corn Flakes. But upon consumption thereof, Corny was cackling cock-a-doodle-doo till the cows came home! Recent years have seen him mostly silent, but let's face it… with a profile like this guy's got, who needs to say a word?

 # 3) CHICKEN LITTLE ~ The earliest versions of this story date back 2500 years and the first printed versions appeared in Denmark (1823) and the U.S. (1840). Upon feeling an acorn fall upon her head, Chicken Little initiates mass hysteria by proclaiming that the sky is falling. This of course never happens with the moral of the story being that by perpetuating rumors based upon unsubstantiated facts, Chicken Little finds herself in Trouble Big, learning the hard way about the perils of faulty danger assessment. In Disney's 2005 feature-length film treatment of the tale, the star character underwent a gender transformation and was portrayed as a male.

 # 2) FOGHORN LEGHORN, from *Looney Tunes* ~ "Gal reminds me of the highway between Fort Worth and Dallas – no curves." Such was the crude and somewhat unrefined humor of *Looney Tunes* star Foghorn Leghorn. The heavyset human-sized rooster debuted in the 1946 cartoon "Walky Talky Hawky" and would go on to appear in 29 short films from 1946-1964.

His character was based upon Senator Claghorn who was a blustery and bombastic Southern politician from a popular 1940's radio show. Some of Claghorn's speech nuances became Foghorn catch phrases such as, "That's a joke, son!" and a repetitive, "I say, I say, I say" before strongly making a point. Foghorn's signature song was "Camptown Races" to which he would modestly sing the verses, before belting out the "Doo Dah's" in the chorus.

Foghorn's ribald outgoing style was engagingly funny and, unlike most of the other *Looney Tunes* cast, he was equally good at playing both the victor and the victim. And that's not a joke, son.

 # 1) SAN DIEGO CHICKEN ~ *Miami Herald* sports writer Bob Rubin once praised the San Diego Chicken as being the most gifted physical comic since Curly, Larry, and Moe (The Three Stooges). Let's face it; physical comedy acclaim does not reach much higher than this. And before we check out this chicken, please allow us to throw out the following disclaimer.

For the most part we have avoided sports mascots, but here is one of the few instances where an exception is clearly warranted. The Chicken was the first, the most famous, and while this last point could be debated, arguably the best costumed mascot of all time.

It was 1974 when Ted Giannoulas first started roaming the stands of the San Diego Padres ballpark in his chicken costume. The basic shtick began with the Chicken responding to the prompt of, "Lay one on me," by squatting and pretending to lay an egg which would turn out to be a promotional item of some kind to be given to the fan.

It is at this point that, counter to the realities of biology, the Chicken truly takes flight. In a manner never before seen in professional sports, the mascot manages to mime, joke, and connect with players, umpires, and fans. It's the ultimate win–win. Well, the Padres weren't actually winning that many games on the field, but the ticket turnstiles were spinning.

San Diego's attendance, which had been the lowest in the league, actually doubled. The Chicken's schedule expanded to concerts, community events, and NBA games. Our favorite quote we came across was from Jack Murphy, a San Diego sports reporter, who described the Chicken as an "embryonic Charlie Chaplin in chicken feathers."

DUCKS

Duck Birth ~ Ducks don't just get quacked up. For the record, their first communications occur when they're still chillin' inside their unhatched egg shells. The purpose of this sibling shout-out is to synchronize simultaneous hatching, or at least get it as close as possible.

A critical component of their early survival strategy is to avoid predators by sticking together as a group while they swim or walk behind Mom and, to that end, the teamwork starts early. It's not duck, duck, goose... it's duck, duck, duck.

Duck Mirth ~ Upon achieving adulthood, males and females can easily be distinguished by physical appearance. The hens are drab in color which serves to camouflage them from potential predators while not compromising their mating possibilities because in the world of duck-dating dynamics, the female gets to choose her partner. And it is true for most birds that the females have less exciting colors, even for peacocks! That classic beautifully-colored image of a peacock, the one that first comes to everyone's mind, is a male!

The competing males are called drakes, a term which does resonate with a bit of a dashing debonair. And, during mating season for some species, the brightly feathered drakes perform detailed dancing displays to entice the female judges to make them the drake of choice. Certainly a much more rewarding prize than anything offered on *Dancing with the Stars*!

Size & Life ~ Size and life expectancy vary by species with adults weighing 2-4 pounds and measuring about two feet in length. Life expectancy in the wild ranges from 5-10 years while under the safest circumstances in captivity, ducks can live over 15 years. Guinness World Records recognizes the oldest living ducks to be a pair of real outliers owned by Gladys Blackbeard in South Africa. They reached the age of 49 in 1966!

Speed ~ Maximum speed in unaided flight is about 50 mph, but with a strong tail wind during a long migration flight, they are capable of exceeding that speed for hours at a time. A 55-mph speed would enable them to fly 100 yards in 3.7 seconds. Next our countdown deluxe, with 6 Super Ducks...

 # 6) THE MIGRATION DUCKS ~ Illumination Studio's 2023 film *Migration* features a duck family transitioning from New England through New York to Jamaica with lots of fun and "Lindsey Life Lessons" along the way. Lindsey's favorite line...

Jamaican macaw Delroy (about evil chef): He'll make you into duck a l'orange.
Daughter duck Gwen: What's "duck a l'orange?"
Pigeon pal Chump: It's you with "l'orange" on top.

 # 5) SCROOGE McDUCK ~ (from *Mickey's Christmas Carol*, about his old partner Jacob Marley…) "He was a good one. He robbed from the widows and swindled the poor. In his will he left me enough money to pay for his tombstone, and I had him buried at sea." Because, right down to the name, this character had been based upon Ebenezer Scrooge from Charles Dickens' *A Christmas Carol*, when Disney undertook its *Mickey's Christmas Carol* project, the casting of Scrooge as Scrooge was clearly a no-brainer.

Boastful of his status as the richest duck in the world, Scrooge occasionally immerses himself in avarice by literally swimming through the gold coins in his money vault. As was Dickens' goal, Scrooge McDuck is greed personified, a trait which is personally witnessed by his family who you will be meeting next.

 # 4) HUEY, DEWIE, AND LOUIE ~ "They were real little hellions; they thought they could get away with anything." Those were the words of Carl Barks who was the man behind the creation of the triplets who are cast as Donald Duck's nephews. They first came to animated life on the silver screen on Tax Day, April 15, 1938. We mention the Tax Day reference not because it would have been of much significance to the young kids, but it probably was to their aforementioned penny-pinching grand uncle Scrooge McDuck.

The "hellion" descriptor applied by Barks was an apt one. This was a calculated effort on the part of the studio as the trio was created as a catalyst to spark the fire of their "Unca Donald's" hair-trigger temper. Their mischievous shenanigans provided the impetus for Donald's requisite ranting and raving.

Finishing with some nephew logistics… Their mother was Donald's sister Della and in the original 27 theatrical cartoons from 1938-1967 their personalities were quite similar. They could be differentiated by the color of their caps and shirts with the equation being Huey=red, Dewie=blue, Louie=green. When they were rebooted in the 1996 series *Quack Pack* they had aged a few years and were teenagers with distinct personalities following the equation of Huey=group leader, Dewie=computer whiz, Louie=sports nut.

 # 3) THE AFLAC DUCK ~ This is not a "We-like-him" #3; this is a "You-can't-get-away-from-him" #3. The omnipresent advertising icon was conceived in 1999 when, charged with creating an ad campaign for Aflac Insurance, the ad man responsible was walking through Central Park and couldn't help noticing how the ducks' quacks sounded like the product he was seeking to promote. Since the commercials are still running a quarter century later, the assumption must be that while they can be grating, they must be leaving an impression.

The Aflac Duck has compiled an impressive resumé of co-stars including athletes like Yogi Berra & Yao Ming, coaches like Lou Saban & Mike Krzyzewski and cartoon characters like Bugs Bunny & Rudolph the Red-Nosed

Reindeer. His most famous voice artist was Gilbert Gottfried who was fired in 2011 for tweeting insensitive jokes after 3,000 people had died in Japan's tsunami.

Just how insensitive does one have to be in order to get fired from being a duck? Well, a sampling of Gottfried's postings included… "Japan is really advanced. They don't go to the beach. The beach comes to them," and another read, "Japan called me; they said, 'Maybe those jokes are a hit in the U.S., but over here, they're all sinking.'" Definitely not funny enough to lose a job over.

 # 2) DAFFY DUCK, from *Looney Tunes* ~ Accounting for the lisp and the quirky somewhat sloppy speaking nuances, "Youuu're deththpicable!" is the spelling that we're landing on for Daffy Duck's most memorable exclamation. It was a defamation of character experienced by many amongst Daffy's adversaries. And that roster ran rampant with Daffy's legacy of *Looney Tunes* logging in at a total of 130, behind only Bugs Bunny's 167 and Porky Pig's 153.

Daffy was bombastic, impetuous, petulant and the perfect foil for Bugs Bunny. Their series of hunting cartoons during the 1950's were mutually symbiotic bouts of comic genius. One classic scene has the duel between "Duck Season" and "Rabbit Season" signs leaving Elmer Fudd befuddled and Daffy lamenting, "Go on! Shoot me again! I enjoy it! I love the smell of burnt feathers and gunpowder and cordite!"

Daffy Duck was ranked #14 in the article acknowledging "*TV Guide*'s 50 Greatest Cartoon Characters of All Time".

 # 1) DONALD DUCK ~ "One of the greatest satisfactions in our work here at the studio is the warm, cozy relationship that exists within our cartoon family. Mickey, Pluto, Goofy, and the whole gang have always been a lot of fun to work with. But like many large families, we have a problem child. You're right, it's Donald Duck." Those were the words of "papa" Walt Disney describing his troublesome "son" Donald.

Sometimes referred to simply as "The Duck", Donald was prone to tumultuous temper tantrums and fiery fits of frustration when things did not go his way. Some considered him unlucky but his misfortunes were usually due more to the fact that karma is a king who often rules that there is indeed a price to be paid for pomposity. As the words read below Donald's plaque at the Walt Disney Family Museum in San Francisco, "Like a Western hero, Mickey is straightforward, good-natured, and modest. Donald is greedy, conceited, sneaky, and hot-tempered."

That being said, Disney animators often gravitated toward Donald because with his character came the freedom to explore edgier emotional nuances that would not fall within the realm of nice guy characters like Mickey Mouse and Goofy. That may be the explanation for why, in the rankings of most films by Disney characters, Donald ranks #1 with 190 appearances beginning with "The Wise Little Hen" in 1934.

All of those appearances have led to an accolade-laden legacy which includes an Academy Award, a star on the Hollywood Walk of Fame, and a footprint at Grauman's Chinese Theatre. We'll close with one of Donald's more introspective quotes... *"Don't get confused between my personality and my attitude... my personality is who I am, and my attitude depends on who you are."*

BIRDS

*Next let's flash our way with words,
And wax poetic on the birds*

When your typical audience is asked what three things come to mind when it comes to birds, the leading answers are that they... lay eggs, have feathers, can fly. Let's bat those three abilities around for a quick introductory activity to our bird component. Second Chance Bird & Reptile Rescue Owner Barb Vagg commented that, "You did a fantastic job on your research on birds, everything looks wonderful" so on that note, let's take flight.

All birds lay eggs but, for the record, several other animals do as well. All birds also have feathers, but as opposed to the egg thing, they **are** the only living feathered animal. We do, however offer that fact with a caveat. Some species of dinosaurs did also have feathers back in the day.

On the topic of flying, several species of birds cannot, ranging from ostriches to penguins. And regarding those penguins, they can't fly but they are the only bird that can swim underwater. And while focusing on the non-flyers why don't we close with the kiwi conundrum. Native to New Zealand, they firmly lead the no-fly list as the only bird with no wings whatsoever. Flying... don't even think about it.

Size ~ Birds show quite a range when it comes to the concept of size. On the high end of the spectrum would be the ostrich, which can stand 9 feet tall and weigh 300 pounds. Conversely, the bee hummingbird, which is endemic to Cuba, comes in as the smallest bird in the world weighing just 1.6 grams or 0.056 ounces. They are just over 2 inches long and the wording of the species name alludes to the fact that they are actually about the size of a bee. When it comes to egg extremes, not surprisingly, it's the superlative birds mentioned above who establish the parameters. Ostrich eggs are about the size of a cantaloupe while bee hummingbird eggs are the size of a small pea.

Life ~ Because the species of birds are so varied, their life expectancies follow suit. For your average bird, say your red red robin that's bob-bob-bobbin' along the sidewalk in front of your house, it would be about 6 years. A candidate for the longest living bird ever is the Australian sulphur-crested cockatoo Cocky Bennett whose unverified dates of birth and death cross three separate centuries, spanning from 1796-1916 which would have put Cocky at 120 years old. The blue and gold macaw, Charlie, who was born around 1910 is still living at the Heathfield Nurseries in England at 114 years old. This macaw was supposedly taught to swear at the Nazis by Winston Churchill who was his owner during WW II.

Speed ~ We'd like to cue up a little drum roll heading into this one as we are to reveal the highest speed in the entire book to be achieved by an animal moving under its own power. We have the Audubon Society specifying that, when it is diving, the peregrine falcon can reach a mind-numbing speed of 186 mph which would give it a 100-yard-flight time of 1.1 seconds.

Lindsey Fun Facts ~ We hope you've been enjoying the comments from our college-kid collaborator because we've got lotsa Lindsey coming at you right now. When it came to the aforementioned falcon, she shared the side story that, "Some of our modern-day airplanes and fighter jets have designs that resemble that of a falcon. Due to their adaptations, like their wing shape, falcons are incredibly fast flyers," as mentioned above.

Regarding this bird Lindsey added, "Falcons have a baffle bone inside their nose that helps them not get lightheaded when diving or flying so fast! It is a spiral shaped bone which slows down the air coming into their nose! If they didn't have that it would be like us trying to breathe with our head out the car window!"

Shifting our analysis to the category of level flight, the spine-tailed swift (aptly-named) can hit 105 mph, which would enable it to traverse 100 yards in 1.9 seconds. For those birds who hit the ground running, the speediest would be the ostrich at 43 mph giving it a 100-YDT of 4.8 seconds.

We'll close with a medley of memorable bird banter with a little something for everybody. In ancient Greece the late-breaking results of Olympic game competitions were conveyed from Athens to the various outlying city-states by pigeon. In a great example of using one skill to overcome the lack of another, owls cannot move their eyes at all, but they make up for it with neck flexibility.

Lindsey adds that, "Owls can turn their head 270 degrees, which would be enough to look back over their other shoulder. Some fun reasons for that include: Their eyes are shaped like lightbulbs, and we are seeing the small end of the lightbulb when we look at the bird. Their eyes take up so much room in their skull, that they touch each other and touch the back of their head, which leaves little room for two things: brain and muscle attachment. Though owls don't have a comparatively large brain, they are incredible primitive hunters, and are very good at their job with a family of barn owls killing around 4,000 prey items over a year!"

"So saying someone is as wise as an owl, may not be the best compliment. In regard to muscle attachment, owls actually cannot move their eyes while keeping their head still, which is why they have the extra mobility in their neck to see around them! Another biological adaptation that allows them to turn their head this far is that they have two times the amount of neck vertebrae that most mammals have! That's right, owls have more neck bones than a giraffe!"

The hummingbird boasts the heartbeat record of the animal kingdom able to hit rates of 1,260 beats-per-minute. Makes your heart flutter just to hear that, doesn't it? And finally, the commonly used expression "to eat like a bird", describing a light-eating person, is really a misnomer. There are several species of birds that actually consume twice their weight in food on a daily basis.

Now let's fly away to our countdown of 11 Heavenly Birds...

 # 11) TO KILL A MOCKINGBIRD ~ As an author, Harper Lee was a one-hit wonder whose mockingbird symbolized an "innocent victim" motif whereby she masterfully threaded the themes of mystery, sexuality, and racism through the eye of a single needle.

 # 10) TOUCAN SAM ~ He doesn't look like he's sixty years old, does he? Yes, the cereal advertising icon has certainly aged well since assuming the role of mascot for Kellogg's Froot Loops in 1963. If your choices in the cereal aisle have not brought him home recently, be advised that there is a slimmer, sleeker Sam still reciting his original directions to, "Follow your nose! It always knows, the flavor of fruit, wherever it grows."

 # 9) HENERY HAWK, from *Looney Tunes* ~ The humorous premise which the original Henery Hawk Warner Bros. cartoons were based upon from 1942-1961 would be this. Henery is a diminutive chicken hawk who, despite his hostile temperament and New York City-accented tough-guy bravado, is plagued by an ironic sense of naïveté. He knows that chicken hawks are supposed to hunt chickens, but he is not sure what a chicken looks like.

So your typical storyline has Henery on the hunt and encountering primary nemesis Foghorn Leghorn who, while he is a chicken, would rather avoid the annoyance of Henery's pursuit and, to that end, takes advantage of the young chicken hawk's aforementioned naïveté. Foghorn convinces Henery that Barnyard Dawg (the other regular in this trio) is actually a chicken.

At this point, physical comedy runs rampant as Foghorn and Dawg continue to redirect Henery's hunting focus in the other's direction, with hilarity inevitably ensuing.

 # 8) WOODSTOCK, from *Peanuts* ~ We considered starting with a quote but we knew it would come out as nothing but chicken scratch. You see, that's pretty much all Woodstock could muster in his voice bubbles when he debuted in the Charles Schulz' classic comic strip *Peanuts* in 1966. The then-nameless bird's vocabulary did expand to the point where he could emote symbols such as "?", "!", or "Z"s to indicate sleep.

Within the next few years, as the bird became a permanent fixture, a name was needed and Schulz took a topical approach. The 1969 Woodstock Music Festival had been a generational event and the iconic poster featured a small bird standing on the neck of a guitar. The image clicked for Schulz and Woodstock had a name. Peace out.

 # 7) THE GOOSE THAT LAID THE GOLDEN EGG, from *Aesop's Fables* ~ This is certainly one of the most tried and true of Aesop's Fables, and there is an expanded version of the title which has become cliché in the English language. But first, the fable…

There is a married couple of heretofore modest farmers, of simple means, who are suddenly blessed with the situation that every day one of their hens lays a golden egg. The couple exalts in their blessing. Now you, or we, might be of a mind that given such circumstances the logical course of action would be to relax, kick back, and allow the fruits of our blessing to accumulate.

But of course, no couple becomes immortalized in a fable by playing it smart. The farm couple assumes that the hen must have a huge hold of gold stored in her gut. Rather than patiently wait to have the gold bestowed upon them on a gradual basis, they decide to kill the hen in order to extract all of the gold immediately.

But upon sacrificing the hen, they open her up to find the inside of the bird to be no different than any other. Thus, the moral of the fable boils down to greed. Because they lacked the patience to accept their blessing gradually, rather than receive it all at once, they ended up losing everything.

The cliché to which we alluded earlier would be to expand the title into the expression of "killing the goose that laid the golden egg" to refer to any short-sighted decision which sacrifices long-term benefits in the fruitless pursuit of immediate gratification.

 # 6) WOODY WOODPECKER ~ After his 1940 debut, this high-strung bird would go on to star in 203 cartoons before the Walter Lantz Studio closed in 1972. Woody's aggressive persona made him particularly popular during WW II when his image was frequently featured as a military mascot on planes and buildings.

As the Walter Lantz Studio rolled over into Universal/Paramount, Woody Woodpecker ascended to flagship status. Just like Mickey Mouse is to Disney, and Bugs Bunny is to Warner Bros., Woody Woodpecker now serves as Universal Studio's official mascot. Stop by and say hi next time you're in Orlando.

Animal Planet ranks Woody #21 on its list of "50 Greatest TV Animals".

 # 5) EDGAR ALLEN POE'S RAVEN ~ Let's start by establishing the setting. It's a dark and dreary December evening with our narrator sitting by a dying fire lamenting the death of his beloved and recently departed Lenore. In Poe's poem "The Raven," his grief is interrupted by a staccato sound which he eventually discerns to be a raven tapping at his window. When he goes to the window the raven flies in and assumes a perch on top of his parlor bust of goddess Pallas Athena. Because who doesn't have one of those in their living room, right?

At any rate, Athena was the Greek goddess of wisdom and the black raven has always had connotations of death. So your roadmap to the symbolism that

Poe is postulating is that it's time for our bereaved narrator to have a conversation about death with the deity of wisdom.

By alighting on the head of the goddess, the raven essentially assumes her voice. The raven is limited to a one-word vocabulary and since Poe has a penchant for getting a bit wordy, we will offer our long-story-short transcription of the conversation…

Poe: What's your name?
Raven: Nevermore.
Poe: Are you going to fly out of my life?
Raven: Nevermore.
Poe: Am I ever going to get over losing Lenore?
Raven: Nevermore.
Poe: Will I be reunited with Lenore in Heaven?
Raven: Nevermore.

Picking up on the theme in place here, and hypothesizing upon the advice we would have given the narrator if we could have gone back in time, if only he could have thought to reword his questions so that "No" was the answer he was looking for, perhaps he could have extracted an answer better suited to his hopes, but alas, 'twas not to be.

If you look at the progression of the four "nevermore" responses received by the narrator above, you could accurately describe the transition of the narrator's emotional state as escalating from contemplative to despondent to enraged to insane. General literary rule of thumb… if you're hoping for a happy ending you should probably take a hard pass on Poe.

We Smiths, on the other hand, are much better at that happy ending gig and we've even got an uplifting and lasting legacy for both Poe and his raven. It was in their honor that, when Baltimore was granted its newest NFL franchise in 1996, a fan vote with 33,288 respondents resulted in the "Ravens" being established as the team mascot in honor of the city's most famous writer and his most recognized work.

If you'd rather not see us sell out with that happy horsesh*t ending, we can certainly spin things back the other way for those of your ilk. Imagine you are a writer of Poe's stature. Betrayed by your Baltimore buzz, they find you dying in the gutter of drunken debauchery and rabies at the age of 40. At this point has not your sacrifice for the city attained the level that maybe coughing up a sports team nickname for you might not be too much to ask?

 # 4) THE ROAD RUNNER, from *Looney Tunes* ~ Do you know what an aphorism is? The definition would be… a terse, concise and memorable expression conveying a general truth or principle. Chuck Jones, the creator of the Wile E. Coyote and Road Runner cartoons, has himself personally invoked an aphorism from Spanish-American philosopher George Santayana to define the essence of this franchise and its fanaticism.

As we researched this project, we came across a second Santayana saying that we feel serves as the ultimate complement in forming a one-two punch of perfect Road Runner/Coyote commentaries. So right now let's defer to Santayana and lead with the Smiths', followed by the Jones', choice of aphorisms defining these characters...

* Those who cannot remember the past are condemned to repeat it.
* Fanaticism consists of redoubling your efforts when you have forgotten your aim.

Perhaps the most notorious cartoon chase tandem ever, it began in 1949 with the Coyote embarking upon a series of inspired attempts to catch and assumedly eat the Road Runner. The humor was derived from the complex absurdity of the gizmos and contraptions employed by the Coyote in the ambitious pursuit of his prey.

A running gag was the Coyote's unflagging loyalty to the Acme company, which was the mail-order outfit that supplied him with the never-ending arsenal of weaponry used to launch his assaults on the Road Runner. One example of such would be the Acme Jet-Propelled Pogo Stick. Right from the get-go, it's easy to see how this one has disaster written all over it.

Other recipes for disaster from the company included Acme Giant Rubber Bands, Acme Invisible Paint, Acme Dehydrated Boulders and, always a favorite, the Acme Rocket Powered Roller Skates. The challenge for the production team was to devise uniquely comical manners in which the contraptions would backfire.

And backfire they did. In terms of the suffering endured by a single character, the Road Runner certainly put the Coyote into the conversation as to who was the most ill-fated cartoon character of all time. Between falls off of cliffs, boulders crushing him, and explosions gone awry, the poor Coyote died multiple times in every outing. But of course, even after being burnt to a crisp, he would be back all fresh and new for the next scene. Ah, the beauty of animation!

 # 3) MOTHER GOOSE ~ Let's take a gander at the fictional matriarch of a collection of English nursery rhymes. Our story starts in France in the 1620's when the name "Mere l'Oye" first appears in French literature with the English translation being "Mother Goose". Later, a 1650 French publication called *La Muse Historique* refers to a written tale as being "like a Mother Goose story," thereby establishing the premise that at this point in time the expression had fallen into common usage.

The debut of the moniker in the English language dates back to the early 1700's when Frenchmen Charles Perrault's story compilation was translated into English as *Tales of My Mother Goose*. Later that century, a subsequent collection of similar tales was released under the title *Mother Goose's Melody* which served to cement the name as the matriarch of children's stories.

So while we're sure the name rings true, we're also thinking many of our mature readers may be asking yourselves, What exactly were the Mother Goose stories? "Little Red Riding Hood"— No. "Cinderella"— No. "Snow White" – No. So to finally put some "Yes" in this address, please allow us to offer up our montage of Mother Goose gold…

Jacks could be wild with "Jack and Jill", "Jack Be Nimble", and "Little Jack Horner". For the love of Pete, we've got "Peter Piper" and "Peter, Peter, Pumpkin Eater". You could "Sing a Song of Sixpence" to "Three Blind Mice" or make a "Ring Around the Rosie" while you "Rock-a-Bye Baby".

Heading to the farm and the females, "Little Bo Peep" lost her sheep while "Mary Had a Little Lamb". Also, "There Was an Old Woman Who Lived in a Shoe", and "Birds of a Feather" love "The Itsy Bitsy Spider", no matter whoever sits down beside her.

And if "Humpty Dumpty" can't get it right, sing "Hey Diddle Diddle", "Starlight Starbright".

 # 2) TWEETY, from *Looney Tunes* ~ "I Tawt I Taw a Puddy Tat… I Did, I Did, I Did Taw a Puddy Tat!" Exemplifying Tweety's speech impediment, this signature line was often used to indicate the arrival of his primary nemesis Sylvester, the cat. That being said, there are some character design aspects of Tweety's tale that predate Sylvester.

In his initial 1942 appearance Tweety was a baby bird, born in the wild, and to that end he had a light pink flesh-like color such as you might see on a baby bird before it gets feathers. After a few films in this visual representation, the censors viewed as problematic the fact that "he looked naked" and Warner Bros. was given the ultimatum to change his color or put clothes on him. So there's your story on how Tweety came to be yellow. Tweety went on to star in 46 films in his *Looney Tunes* "Golden Age" career between 1942 and 1964. Sylvester made his adversarial debut in 1947.

 # 1) BIG BIRD, from *Sesame Street* ~ Since his debut on *Sesame Street* in 1969, Big Bird has certainly been a kid fave, and often an adult one as well. After all, how many 8' 2" costumed birds can sing, dance, skate, swim and ride a unicycle?

Originally, creator Jim Henson was going to play the character, but when it was determined that Henson could not walk like a bird, the role was relinquished. Henson was probably busy working on that upcoming Muppet project anyway.

One of Big Bird's early accomplishments was singing the entire alphabet as one long word. Try that next time you've got a free moment. He was such a breakthrough hit that within his first year, Big Bird had made appearances on *Hollywood Squares* and *The Ed Sullivan Show*. Apparently 1970 was the Year of the Bird; he had the name and achieved the fame.

Animal Planet ranks Big Bird #16 on its list of "50 Greatest TV Animals".

SECTION FOUR
FINAL ROUND UP, SEARCH THE ANNALS
CLOSING STORIES STARRING MAMMALS

CHAPTER 15

HERE'S THE PART WHERE WE REGALE YA WITH OUR STORIES FROM AUSTRALIA

KANGAROOS

There's a certain sense of wonder, 'bout these creatures from down under. Ready for a quick kangaroo quirk… they don't have a reverse gear. It's true; because of their large tail and long feet, kangaroos cannot hop or walk backwards. Australia actually used that nuance to their symbolic advantage by placing a kangaroo prominently on the country's coat of arms to represent the concept that it is a nation which is always moving forward.

Speed ~ When the kangaroo itself is moving forward, it does so in impressive style. In terms of hopping ability, their longest leaps can cover a span of 25 feet while attaining a height of as much as 6 feet off the ground. They are the only large animal that moves by hopping.

As our kangaroo expert, we called in Bronwyn Macreadie from the Healesville Sanctuary in Australia who provided the information that, "All kangaroo species can do an average hopping speed of 31 mph with the Red Kangaroo males being clocked at top speeds of 40-43 mph." That top end speed equates to a 100-YDT of 4.8 seconds.

Size ~ In terms of superlatives here, the red kangaroo is right back in the running, along with the eastern grey. With both these species, the males' top weight ranges from 176-198 pounds and they can stand 6 feet 6 inches tall. Females are smaller in both weight and height. Kangaroos are the largest marsupials, a class of animal whose most unique identifying feature is that they all carry their young in pouches.

Life ~ "Average life expectancy in the wild is 10-12 years," Bronwyn told us, "and in captivity 15 years." The kangaroo who achieved the longest life was Patty, a Matschie's tree kangaroo who lived for 27 years and 5 months at Zoo Miami, passing away in January 2016.

Conservation Status ~ Speaking of the tree kangaroo, it is the most endangered of the extant marsupials. They can only be found in northeastern Australia and the island of New Guinea where the status of the 15 species ranges from "near-threatened" to "critically endangered" on the IUCN red list.

They're also the least known of the kangaroo species. Be honest now… how many of you knew that there were three-foot long mini-kangaroos climbing around in trees, that arboreal ability enhanced by some of the most threatening-looking claws you could ever imagine. Even the Aussies are sometimes unaware… Liaison Lindsey shared the story that, "one of my friends who lived in Australia didn't even know they existed."

TASMANIAN DEVIL

Upon seeing this name, the first image that pops into many people's heads is that of the Warner Bros. cartoon character spinning like a cyclone while devouring everything in his path. So how close is that cartoon Taz image to the actual animal? Well, Samantha Fox from Save the Tasmanian Devil Program told us that, "In the 15 years that I have worked in the field with devils I have never seen them do the 'spinning thing'. It's certainly not something that wild devils do, so that might be special Taz behaviour ☺."

Behavioural Analysis ~ That being said, while Samantha is totally correct regarding her work "in the field with devils," Dean Reid, the Operations Manager of the environmental group Aussie Ark, did offer one caveat regarding an explanation for the evolution of the spinning behavior saying about the first British visitors that, "this came from when they first saw devils in captivity in Tasmania, they used to keep them in very small enclosures so the devil actually ran around in circles." So in terms of the devil spinning like the cartoon character, we can check that box and move on to the question of power. There are a few ways to put their power in perspective and we'll start by acknowledging that they have the world's strongest bite for any animal their size. They can bite through bones, wooden fences, and metal cages.

Now let's move on to the "devouring everything in his path" line. When Tasmanian devils eat, there's little need for a doggy bag; leftovers are not a major factor when the devils dine. Samantha Fox put the consumption rate of their prey at about 80% saying, "They will eat the majority of an animal including fur and feet, but even their jaws won't go through a wallaby skull or the thigh bone of a kangaroo."

Name Game ~ Next let's tackle the story of how the animal got its name. When the British first arrived, they heard the creature before they saw it, so in terms of visualizing what they may have encountered all they had to work with was the ungodly, bloodcurdling howls and shrieks emanating from the depths of the brush. The noises were so demonic that the Europeans started to call the creatures Tasmanian devils and the name stuck. Dean from Aussie Ark added that, "Also when the sunlight catches their ears, they turn bright red, so when their little ears stick out of the grass, they glow bright red and look like devil horns."

Conservation Status ~ Tasmanian devils were added to the endangered species list in 2008, with a few factors in the flow. First of all, the animals are not native to mainland Australia, they're endemic to the island of Tasmania which is the small one off the southeastern coast. They were actually on the mainland of Australia until 3,000 years ago but died out due to the predatory pursuit of humans and dingoes, so their habitat is quite limited to begin with, and it has been compromised by population growth and more deaths due to being hit by vehicles.

Actually, allow us to put an asterisk by our "endemic" in the previous paragraph. In 2020, an initiative was undertaken to reintroduce the Tasmanian devil to the Australian mainland. A total of 26 devils were relocated to the Barrington Tops National Park, just north of Sydney. We'll keep you posted.

The fact that Tasmanian devils became restricted to the one island initially may have been a positive because with fewer humans and no dingoes, it became a safe haven which was more protected from predators. That being said, the negative outcome of their narrow habitat is that the species has become dangerously inbred with immune systems not recognizing some diseases.

Their biggest problem has been the development of DFTD or devil facial tumor disease which has taken the lives of 350,000 devils since it first appeared in the late-1990's. This is a form of transferable cancer that causes tumors to develop on the devils' faces which eventually compromises their ability to eat, subsequently causing starvation. Despite this dire news, by 2020 the disease had stabilized bringing optimism that the devil can avoid extinction.

Size & Speed ~ So when they do eat, how big do the devils get? As the world's largest carnivorous marsupial, they stand about 12 inches tall, 30 inches long and weigh almost 30 pounds. Regarding speed, in short bursts they can reach up to 16 mph which, if they could sustain it, would equate to a 100-YDT of 12.8 seconds.

Life ~ In terms of life expectancy, they can live up to 7 years in the wild and 9 in captivity. The longest documented life of a Tasmanian devil was achieved by Candice, a she-devil who reached that ripe old age of 9 with Dean at the Aussie Ark.

PLATYPUSES

The egg is the theme of the monotreme. The only modern monotremes include the platypus and four types of echidnas. The platypus lives only in

Australia. Echidnas (which look a bit like porcupines but have fixed spines rather than loose quills) include three types of long-beaked echidna found in Papua New Guinea and the short-beaked echidna found in both PNG and Australia.

Monotremes are truly unique animals in that they are warm-blooded, fur-clad mammals who also happen to lay eggs and lack teats. Instead, milk is secreted onto fur through the female's belly pores to feed the babies. The concept of laying soft-shelled eggs is basically a reptilian trait that has strangely carried over to just these mammals.

Unique Appearance ~ Focusing on the platypus if you were to come across the expanded name of "duck-billed platypus", not to worry, it's the same animal. The platypus, truth be told, is one of the strangest looking animals on the planet and we will defer to comedian Robin Williams' take on that topic in just a bit. Our short version, just to keep you in the loop, would be to refer to it as a Mother Nature combo platter where this critter has a bill like a duck, a body like an otter, webbed feet like some bird species and a flat tail like a beaver.

But you best not make fun of a platypus because the males have venomous spurs on each of their hind legs. All in all, they really are quite the package! Melody Serena of the Australian Platypus Conservancy (APC) has also offered the following elaboration on the bill of a platypus telling us that it, "superficially looks ducklike but is actually nothing like a duck's bill, as it's covered by soft skin and is pliable around the edges."

Right now we'll offer another testament to the perplexing platypus. Upon settling Australia in 1788, when the British first came upon the platypus their scientists seriously thought it was some type of hoax, somehow created by piecing together parts of other animals.

Perpetuating this platypus party, we are going to next hand over the mic to WWF Australia as we found so funny their take on this next topic regarding how the animal appears to glow under black light, which is a type of UV light.

WWF Australia wrote that, "No one knows why, but when these small brown creatures are put under UV lights, they, as well as some other animals, give off a biofluorescent green-blue glow. Which **is** strange, but even stranger are the people who keep putting them under UV lights."

When the Australian Platypus Conservancy was reviewing our work two additional "fun facts" were suggested and when they come from a colleague with a name as beautifully poetic as Melody Serena, there's no way we're not singing, "Yes!" So here we go...

"The platypus engages in more REM sleep than any other known adult mammal – typically 8 hours per day. It's not known if a platypus actually dreams during REM sleep but the bill and head twitch vigorously and the eyes (though remaining closed) move about rapidly, implying that it does."

"Platypus fur is incredibly dense, with an undercoat that contains up to 900 hairs per square millimeter of skin (about the size of a small pin head). This traps a layer of air next to the skin when a platypus dives, so most of its surface actually stays dry in the water."

Size & Speed ~ An adult male platypus is up to two feet long and weighs about 4-5 pounds, while there is an extinct platypus species believed to have been over four feet long. Another unusual feature of the platypus is that it swims using only its front legs to paddle, while the back legs basically trail behind and serve as rudders. The APC puts their typical point-to-point swimming speed as 1 mph when travelling upstream or 1.5 mph when travelling downstream.

Life~ The average life expectancy of a platypus is about 8 years. The APC had some late-breaking news for us on the upper end of platypus life expectancy. Melody told us, "By coincidence, I'm currently writing a paper about platypus life span – it's now known that a platypus can survive up to the age of at least 23.9 years in the wild and even a few years older in a zoo."

Conservation Status ~ The national conservation status of the platypus is "near threatened". While they are holding their own in most areas, their overall population has declined due to loss of habitat, development of dams and irrigated cropland, and a drying climate.

We'll close with Robin Williams' stand up take on the uniqueness of the platypus which, with apologies to the theologians out there, is based upon the premise that God was a partier. Williams hypothesized that, "If God drinks, don't ya think God gets stoned once in a while? I think so; look at a platypus. I think God's up there goin', "Let's take a beaver, and let's put on a duck's bill. [pretending to take a drag on an imaginary joint.] Hey, I'm God; what are you gonna do? Okay… he's a mammal, but he lays eggs. [then in a takedown of history's most famous evolutionist] Hey Darwin, [flipping him off] take this."

WOMBATS

If we were to try and verbally create an image in your head as to what a wombat looks like, we might say they look like a large gopher or a giant hamster. Wombats are herbivorous and usually don't endanger humans unless they feel threatened. Bronwyn Macreadie, our friend from Australia who served as our kangaroo expert earlier in the chapter, is making a return appearance here, flashing her wisdom as our wombat woman.

Size ~ "The average wombat is approximately 33-45 inches long," Bronwyn told us, "and weighs up to 80 pounds."

The largest wombat on record was a big fella named Pat who resided at the Ballarat Wildlife Park in Victoria, Australia. Nicknamed "Fat Pat from Ballarat", he tipped the scales at a whopping 88 pounds!

Life ~ While we are on the subject of superlatives, Pat was also acknowledged as being the longest living wombat when he died at the age of 32 years in 2017 far surpassing the average life expectancies of 15 years in the wild and 20 in captivity. That record however was surpassed by Wain, a wombat living in the Satsukiyama Zoo in Japan who reached the age of 34 in 2024.

Speed ~ Regarding speed, they are faster than you might think. "They can sprint up to 25 mph but they cannot keep this up over a long distance," Bronwyn said, "it is generally to try and get themselves back to the relative safety of their burrow." If they were able to sustain their top speed it would calculate to a 100-YDT of 8.2 seconds.

Conservation Status ~ There are only three species of wombats and they are all endemic to Australia. The bare-nosed and southern hairy-nosed wombats are fairly prevalent and have "least concern" status on the IUCN red list. The northern hairy-nosed wombat, however, is "critically endangered" with only about 90 remaining in the wild, all in the northeastern Australian state of Queensland.

Before we kick off this Aussie countdown, we need to issue the following warning… in the millions of words that we've written, we have never before employed the Australian expression of "fat-arsed" and in all likelihood we can't see ourselves ever using it again, but as you'll see momentarily these irreverent Aussie's left us no choice!

Of course, the most intriguing question this challenge poses is how in the world is the expression "fat-arsed" going to come up within the context of a chapter on Australia? Trust us, you're gonna wanna stick around for this one.

Without further ado
Next we'll cue up for you
Choices that we contrive
As our Aussie Top 5

 # 5) PERRY THE PLATYPUS, from *Phineas and Ferb* ~ "In your letters, you described your nemesis as a 'suave, semi-aquatic personification of unstoppable dynamic fury.'" – Dr. Gevaarlijk to Heinz Doofenshmirtz, referring to Perry. The entire concept of how Perry the Platypus, aka Agent P, is incorporated into the 2009-2015 Disney TV series is quite intriguing.

When the kids Phineas and Ferb first choose Perry at the pet store, the choice is based upon the fact that his blank stare creates the impression that he is looking at both of them at the same time. The show's slick schtick is that the kids never realize that Perry has a secret identity and perceive him only as a dull and docile domestic pet about whom Phineas says, "He's a platypus, they don't do much." Oh, if they only knew!

So in every episode, Perry emerges from his placid pet persona to star in a sub-plot that manages to somehow overlap with the adventures Phineas and Ferb are pursuing. More on that in a minute, but first let's refocus on Perry's secret agent gig. He is a member of the OWCA, an animal espionage agency where the letters stand for Organization Without a Cool Acronym. Love it!

Perry's nemesis is the twisted Dr. Heinz Doofenshmirtz who is hell-bent on taking over the tri-state area. More underplayed humor here; while most evil scientists would be wanting the world, Heinz is willing to settle for a mere chunk of New York, New Jersey and Connecticut. To this end he continuously comes up with complicated contraptions to accomplish the conquest, but alas, Perry never fails to foil the plot leaving Doofenshmirtz to recite his mantra of, "Curse you, Perry the Platypus!"

So while all of that's good, there is another double layer of the plotline that adds to the intrigue of the show. In the process of dooming the Doofenshmirtz deal, Perry also somehow manages to accidentally destroy the episode's summer scheme upon which Phineas and Ferb have been feverishly working.

Always oblivious to the actual cause, the generally laissez-faire attitude of Phineas and Ferb inevitably allows them to take the setback in stride and start over again next episode. That being said, the boys' super-anal sister Candace knows that there has to be some type of connection, and it drives her absolutely crazy that she can't figure it out.

For the record, Perry's character was made a platypus because of the animal's striking appearance and lack of public knowledge about the creature, which allowed the writers to be more creative in how the species was depicted.

 # 4) HIPPITY HOPPER, from *Looney Tunes* ~ After debuting in "Hop, Look and Listen" in 1948, Hippity Hopper would go on to star in 14 theatrical Warner Bros. cartoons before his last appearance in 1964. The template for the films was quite formulaic with Hippity Hopper being a baby kangaroo who the bumbling Sylvester the cat would mistake for a giant mouse. Hippity was occasionally seen in the pouch of his mother Gracie.

More often than not, Sylvester Jr. would appear with his dad turning the adventure into a father-son lesson on how a cat catches a mouse. Subsequently when Hippity would proceed to punch, kick, gouge and spin Sylvester into submission, it would serve not only as a defeat, but also a paternal embarrassment, leaving Sylvester Jr. to lament, "Oh, the shame of it all."

#3) FATSO THE FAT-ARSED WOMBAT ~ If you love any story where the irreverent, rebellious, underground rises up against the establishment, and uses the establishment's rules to beat them at their own game, then buckle up for this joy ride. This story from The Land Down Under is truly over the top.

The "underground" in our story takes the form of two men in the entertainment field who take on the stage personas of Roy Slaven and HG Nelson (real names John Doyle and Greig Pickhaver). Let's pick things up in the year 2000 with the pair hosting a sports/comedy show on Australian TV called *The Dream with Roy and HG*.

The setting is doubly significant because Australia is hosting the Summer Olympics that year which is central to the story. Roy and HG saw the games as a motherlode of comedic fodder for their TV show. Some examples would include overdubbing footage of obscure events with their own humorous takes, creating some silly names for standard moves in men's gymnastics, and spontaneously making up bizarre background bio info on competing athletes.

They also looked for opportunities to do some feather ruffling during interviews. Our favorite was one they did with U.S. swimmer Gary Hall Jr. who had been busted in 1998, having tested positive for marijuana. Hall, a member of the relay team, resorted to rock 'n roll metaphor in predicting they would smash Australia like guitars.

As Roy was interviewing Hall about this prognostication, he could not resist the urge to go sideways with a question of only marginal relevance regarding comparisons between the U.S. and Australia. Had the opportunity presented itself, Roy queried, for the American hipster to contrast the quality of the Aussies' wacky weed to that of his native land? They had perfected the ploy of pushing the envelope just far enough to be edgy but not obnoxious.

Okay, now that our set-up work is done, let's move on to the main course. In the work-up to the Olympics, while planning the comedic content of their TV show, one brainstorming session resulted in a lightning flash of sheer brilliance. Why not create their own Olympic mascot and put it out there to compete with the official ones which had been established as Syd (a platypus), Millie (an echidna), and Olly (a kookaburra)?

"These mascots have given us the sh*ts forever," bemoaned Roy. "None of them are any good. They're obviously constructed usually by some sort of marketing backroom ... [but] we understood what Australia wants."

"What we wanted to invent was a mascot that was not for sale, that somehow represented the higher Olympic ideals – or the ideals the Olympics once pretended to have," HG added. "The only instruction was that he had to have a huge arse." Always good to have at least one creatively ethical standard upon which you are unwilling to compromise.

Wherever the games are held, part of the tradition of Olympic mascots is that the animals chosen are indigenous to the home country and, to that end, Roy and HG opted for a wombat to be named Fatso. Sydney cartoonist Paul Newell came onboard to create the comic design which rendered a 3-dimensional character whose appearance was whimsically ebullient and adorned with the requisite rear end. He was nicknamed the "battlers' prince" with "battlers" being Australian slang for working class.

Fatso the Fat-Arsed Wombat had become a reality who began making regular appearances on *The Dream with Roy and HG*, as well as at the games themselves. Originally there were only two physical versions of Fatso in circulation, one at the TV station and one at the athletes' village. The mascot was an immediate hit with the Australian athletes, several of whom carried him onto the Olympic platform while receiving their medals.

At this point the Australian Olympic Committee (AOC) officials were beginning to bristle with this upstart wombat upstaging the official mascots which of course was the dream-come-true scenario for Roy and HG who could not have drawn this thing up any better. Behind-the-scenes efforts were made to encourage the athletes to distance themselves from Fatso but it was too late.

People had fallen in love with that fat arse, and Fatso was trending on a global basis creating a scenario whereby any efforts by the AOC to squelch the wombat were being perceived in the vein of an arrogantly domineering Big Brother stomping on the freedom of the Little Guy. Any resistance by the ruthless authorities was gold to be mined by the underground rebels.

"We enjoyed it, because we knew they were squirming," Roy exalted, "and we were deflating the pomposity of those who held it most dear." As the groundswell continued, athletes not even competing in these Olympics, like Billie Jean King and Carl Lewis, were lining up for their photo ops with Fatso the Fat-Arsed Wombat.

We'll close with *The Dream with Roy and HG* show's salute to Fatso where Roy summed it all up by saying, "The whole world sees him as a mascot that does celebrate humanity. The little guy that stands for all that's good and decent about the Games. It's about people, against all hardship, overcoming hardship, and pressing on with their lives. Sure, they mightn't get gold or silver or bronze every time, but they put in! [they try hard] He's the battlers' prince!"

 # 2) KANGA & ROO, from *Winnie the Pooh* ~ "A Mother holds your heart forever," would be the kind of line that epitomizes the warm mother-son relationship of Kanga and Roo in the Winnie the Pooh franchise. As the only female in the primary cast, Kanga is slotted into a maternal housewife-type role becoming somewhat of a mother to all the other characters.

As such, she is often left at home in their treehouse, which is literally a house in a tree, while the others are out on their miscellaneous adventures. Kanga is particularly tight with Tigger who shows his respect by refraining from bouncing her like he does the other characters. Along with Eeyore, she presents as the most mature and intelligent.

 # 1) THE TASMANIAN DEVIL, from *Looney Tunes* ~ When Taz, as he is often called for short, made his theatrical debut in "Devil May Hare" (1954) the new character was driven by Warner Bros. desire to create a new and different adversary for Bugs Bunny. When you've conquered everything from spell-casting witches to the Abominable Snowman that's not necessarily an easy task.

In scouring the planet for possibilities, the decision was made that the perfect combination of real-life ferocity and never-been-done-before character innovation was embodied in the Land Down Under where the Tasmanian devil grunts and growls. Those attributes were added to the studio's new whirling dervish "Devil" who would spin like a cyclone, roar like an airplane, and ravenously gorge himself upon literally everything in sight whether the items constituting his menu be animal, vegetable or mineral.

One thing that surprises people, especially because of the character's popularity, is that Taz only appeared in 5 cartoons during the original run of the Warner Bros. animation studio. He experienced a dramatic surge of popularity in the 1990's, headlining his own TV series *Taz-Mania* from 1991-1995 and continues to be one of the studio's most marketable characters.

Chapter 16

Writing Options Blossom with the Gopher, Skunk & Possum

GOPHERS

Well, the lowdown on these guys is that they can be very destructive diggers, a depiction to be confirmed by one particularly iconic movie character in our countdown below. Their sharp claws and teeth are employed to excavate elaborate underground tunnel networks which can become a nightmare for property owners, even if that property may be a golf course, a not-so-subtle hint regarding the aforementioned movie reference.

One of their more distinctive body features is their fur-lined cheek pouches, used to store and transport food, which is why the animals are sometimes referred to as pocket gophers. Returning to their veracity at excavation, another unique body quirk of the gopher is that their lips actually close behind their front four incisors so as to keep dirt from getting inside their mouths during digging.

The "pocket" component of the moniker is derived from the fact that they have pouches on the outside of their mouths to collect and store food. (Squirrel and chipmunk food pouches are on the inside of their mouths.) Gopher pouches can be turned inside out for emptying and cleaning.

The worldwide habitat of gophers is restricted to North and Central America. In the U.S. they can be found in the western and midwestern part of the country, as well as a smaller pocket in the southeastern states of Alabama, Georgia and Florida.

Size, Life & Speed ~ Gophers can weigh up to 2 pounds and grow to 12 inches in length. Their average lifespan in the wild is 2-3 years, while in captivity they can live up to 6 years. At top speed, gophers can motor at about 16 mph giving them a 100-YTD of 12.8 seconds.

Let's get go, go, going off to see our Top 3 Gophers…

 # 3) GO GO GOPHERS ~ This 1966-1969 TV series depicted an Old West scenario where Colonel Kit Coyote was charged with winning the west for the good old U.S. of A. On paper, it shouldn't have been that hard. For crying out loud, the Army had managed to whittle the Gopher Gulch Indian tribe down to just two remaining members.

In an era when you weren't required to say "Native Americans" to be politically correct, those two remaining Indians, Chief Running Board and Ruffled Feathers put up a hell of a fight. Throughout the series run they would never succumb, those Indian gophers outfoxing the U.S. Cavalry at every turn!

Ironically it would provide one of the rare opportunities during that decade when the Indians prevailed over the white man in American media.

 # 2) THE GOPHER, from *Caddyshack* ~ Fueled by drugs and alcohol, and living in the maintenance shed, greenskeeper Carl Spackler, played by Bill Murray, assesses his gopher adversary, acknowledging that he is tasked with the varmint's elimination. The humor results from the fact that the greenskeeper's passionate pursuit of the gopher is characterized by a total disregard for property and/or human life. As the credits roll in *Caddyshack*, we see the golf course reduced to smoldering ruins, while the gopher pops up doing the victory dance to the tune of the movie's theme song, "I'm Alright" by Kenny Loggins.

 # 1) PUNXSUTAWNEY PHIL ~ Revealed here are the words from the original "Groundhog Day Poem" that got this whole thing started.

I wonder if spring is on the way.
I'll go and check the weather today.
If I see my shadow between eleven and noon,
I then will know that I'm out too soon.

The Punxsutawney, Pennsylvania tradition, which has managed to establish itself as the "official" one, began in 1887, and the ritual goes like this. Every year, on the morning of February 2nd, Phil is roused and driven two miles to a wooded hill known as Gobbler's Knob where his handlers help him assume his prediction perch on top of a tree stump.

Everyone pretty much knows the drill at this point. If Phil sees his shadow, he spooks and heads back down to his burrow to wait out 6 more weeks of winter. If no shadow is seen, you put those winter coats away because you're looking for an early spring.

SKUNKS

You can smell it from a mile away; that's the range given for how far the malodorous scent of skunk stink can waft under the right, or perhaps more appropriately assessed, the wrong conditions. If you're looking for a silver lining here, perhaps the good news would be that most of us only experience the awful aroma when we drive by it, as opposed to a direct hit.

For the record, a skunk will first attempt alternate forms of intimidation if it feels threatened, preferring to growl, hiss, stomp the ground, and shake its tail. But if those actions prove to no avail, they will revert to the dreaded spray mode with deadly accuracy up to about 10 feet.

If you, or the more likely scenario your pet, fall victim to a skunk attack, forget the old wives' tale regarding the tomato juice remedy. It won't do a damn bit of good except for temporarily masking the smell. So in the unfortunate circumstance that you get skunked, what do you do?

Expert # 1 ~ We went right to the top for you on this one and consulted Kat Wysocki, the head of Pet Skunk Advocates & Rescue. Kat's advice is, "First, we always recommend using equal parts Dawn dish soap, peroxide and baking soda to remove skunk spray. The key is to not get wet first. We use this mixture because skunk spray is very oily."

Kat went on to add, "There are actually 12 different species of skunks; 5 of which we have here in North America." Living primarily in the Western Hemisphere, the skunk's habitat ranges from southern Canada all the way to the bottom tip of South America. The only Eastern Hemisphere-dwelling exception is the stink badger which can be found in Indonesia, Malaysia, and the Philippines.

In our canvassing of the animal world, Kat was definitely one of the more memorable contributors on a personal level. Regarding skunks she shared with us that, "Pet skunks actually prefer to sleep with each other for the most part. But, I have a ramp next to my bed so right now I have 4 skunks sleeping with me. No wonder I'm single! LOL. Anyway, pet skunks can be very loving and sweet if treated properly. They can be solitary pets but that makes it difficult to introduce new pets in the future."

Expert # 2 ~ Our continuous college collaborator, Liaison Lindsey, added that, "Skunks also do not have an endless supply of spray, so they really only use it when needed because they do not want to run out! It could be important to mention, as with any pet, to do your research, because it is also illegal in many states to own a pet skunk!" Additional note: If they do temporarily run out of spray, the replenishment process takes 6-8 days.

Size, Life & Speed ~ Depending on species, skunks range in length from 2-3 feet and the heaviest, the hog-nosed skunk, can weigh up to 18 pounds. Life expectancy is 3-4 years in the wild and up to 15 years in captivity. They can reach a top speed of about 10 mph which translates to a 100-YDT of 20.5 seconds.

In a countdown quickie, here are our Top 2 Spots…

 # 2) FLOWER, from Disney's *Bambi* ~ "Oh, that's alright," says Flower, "he can call me a flower if he wants to. I don't mind." Those are the first words spoken by the baby skunk when she is discovered hiding in a flower bed by the fawn Bambi in the classic 1942 Disney feature. Of course, it's an ironic name for a skunk which is just the point. Like when in their 2016 film *Zootopia*, Disney names the sloth… Flash.

From a personality perspective Flower is friendly, sweet and unassuming, always remaining a faithful friend to both Bambi and Thumper. Despite his vow to never become "twitterpated", meaning to never fall in love, Flower becomes the first of the triumvirate to find a mate. Eventually he and Petunia have three children who they name Bambi, Buttercup and Primrose.

 # 1) PEPÉ LE PEW, from *Looney Tunes* ~ "Permit me to introduce myself; I am your new lover." Flaunting his French accent, Pepé would speak those words with a suave (over)confidence epitomizing the narcissism that characterized the Warner Bros. skunk during the Golden Age of Hollywood animation.

The template in place for most of Pepé's perils portrayed the amorous skunk in romantic pursuit of a female character who came to be known as Penelope Pussycat. The cat would somehow inadvertently get a white stripe down her back, for example by brushing against a freshly painted fence, which would convince Pepé that she was actually a skunk. The confusion would quickly kick Pepe's hormones into high gear.

Pepé's pursuit of passion would be rejected by a retreating Penelope, offended by his putrid odor, aggressive demeanor, or both. There was also some bothersome biology in the equation regarding the stigma of cat/skunk relationships. A running gag in this series was that while Penelope would be frantically fleeing, Pepé would be just leisurely hopping after her, but somehow never fall far behind in his pursuit.

Pepé Le Pew starred in 17 Golden Age cartoons between 1945-1962, as well as several Warner Bros. projects after that, like the first *Space Jam* movie. That being said, Pepé has suffered from a recent downturn in his career for which he holds Harvey Weinstein personally responsible. In the aftermath of the #MeToo movement, Pepé was deleted from the second *Space Jam* movie because of his aggressive behavior toward women. Just one of those quirky examples of art imitating life.

We'll close with two more relevant quotes, one about Pepé and one by him. Regarding the *Pirates of the Caribbean* franchise, Johnny Depp said, "I imagined *Pirates of the Caribbean's* Captain Jack Sparrow as a blend of Keith Richards and Pepé Le Pew." And our closing thought is one by our #1 himself who once commented that, "The game of love is never called on account of darkness." Certainly words to live by.

OPOSSUMS

The behavioral quirk for which opossums are most known is the playing dead gimmick, so what say we bring in the drama coach to take on this one as the curtain rises on this next component. While the ruse is indeed effectively employed by these animals, there is an element of the operation that makes the term a bit of a misnomer.

The word "playing" implies the opossum is pretending or acting which is actually not the case. This response on the part of the animal is an involuntary one which is prompted by stress. A good analogy would probably be the concept of a human fainting; it's not a conscious decision, it just happens.

So what exactly does this look like? When feeling threatened the opossum will fall to its side, stiffen its body, close its eyes and, for the kicker, emit a putrid odor. It is an effective survival technique because while the stench serves as a deterrent, many predators also prefer live prey. So the stiff and stinky stage antic doubly detracts.

The opossum's habitat is strictly in the Americas, ranging from southern Canada, through the U.S., Mexico and Central America, and as far south as the Amazon River basin in South America. They are the only marsupial native to the Western Hemisphere.

Size, Life & Speed ~ Opossums can weigh up to 12 pounds and grow to be 3 feet long including their hairless tail which is prehensile, meaning they can use their tail to grasp tree limbs as they move and climb. Opossums have comparatively low life expectancies, living 2 years in the wild and only 4 years in captivity. They are also relatively slow, peeking out at 4 mph, which gives them a 100-YDT of 51.1 seconds.

Finally a note on the question of opossum vs. possum? The correct scientific name for the animal is "opossum" so in formal writing you should go with the "o" but with that being said, in common English usage "possum" has become standard and acceptable. And from this point on, we're goin' with it.

There's laughs galore, with our Possums Top 4…

 # 4) OTEY THE SWAMP POSSUM ~ "Arkansas Travelers Introduce Nightmare Hillbilly Possum Mascot" was the headline of a 2014 story on the SBNation (Sports Blog) website. It certainly made for one of the more memorable mascot launches in minor league baseball history leaving fans mired in the possum muck of a "love him or hate him – can't help but debate him" dilemma.

For the record, the Arkansas Travelers (Little Rock locals call them the "Travs") are the AA Texas League affiliate of MLB's Seattle Mariners. And they did have an actual basis for the concept. There is a virtual herd of possums living under the bleachers at the team's Dickey–Stephens Park surviving off the discarded food and slurping up the spilled beer and beverages. And there has never been any effort to eradicate them because they don't hurt anybody and, well, they also clean up the spilled food and beer, while receiving no pay and never calling in sick.

The major beef with Otey is that he perpetuates a hillbilly stereotype which some in the state would like to lose. Websites hosting commentary on the mascot have the pro-Otey people commenting that he's cute and the kids like him. It is the no-Otey folks however, who have landed the most humorous haymakers. Here's a sampling…

* Looks like the Chuck E. Cheese guy fell on hard times.
* Our state took 4 steps back with this fiasco.
* How are we ever going to overcome the hillbilly image with this?
* If you wanted to stereotype Arkansas, a toothless meth head would be less offensive.

And for those looking to kick the habit, perhaps there's some inspiration lurking below at #3…

 # 3) OPIE THE DRUG-FREE POSSUM ~ It was a New Year's Eve tradition that began with the best of intentions in rural Clay County, North Carolina in 1990. As one might suspect, local residents are not of the ilk typically inclined to travel to New York City to see the glass ball drop, so local legend Clay Logan conceives and concocts the Clay County Possum Drop.

If you have a bad feeling about this one already, stick around and we'll confirm your suspicions. Here's how it happens… As the midnight hour approaches every year, a live possum, housed in a glass box, is gradually lowered to the ground in sync with the Times Square Ball Drop. There are similarities and differences between the parallel events.

Similarities… Audiences in both New York and North Carolina find themselves aglow amidst the fireworks, cheers, and countdown chants. Differences… if nature calls, in North Carolina you can just walk into the woods and pee. In New York, people wear diapers in order to not give up their prime positions in the pandemonium.

So in this paradox of political correctness vs. hillbilly hootenannies, PETA initiated a series of actions which successfully brought the Possum Drop to an end in 2019. When we called the Clay County Office to ask for comment in regard to this book, we were offered the reassurance that, "No possum was ever actually dropped during the process."

Thus completes one component of this story, but if you've been paying attention, you may have noticed that we have not yet even introduced Opie the Drug-Free Possum who is the headliner of this component. For a younger audience which may not know the North Carolina nuances needed to connect all the dots on this story, one of the all-time classic TV sitcoms, *The Andy Griffith Show*, was set in rural North Carolina with a young Ronny Howard playing Opie Taylor.

So as the Possum Drop looks to establish itself as an attractive annual family festivity, the combination of two concepts seems to take on a mutually symbiotic appeal. As the Possum Drop planners ponder their potential family appeal, they're thinking, "Mascots are good and drugs are bad." Hard to argue with that.

Subsequently, these two ideas merge into the creation of a costumed human mascot called Opie the Drug-Free Possum who is made available for photoshoots with the kids throughout the duration of the Possum Drop. Would you not love to travel back in time and experience this event at least once?

While the connection between Opie the Drug-Free Possum and the Possum Drop remains a bit vague, we are on board with at least one analysis. That photo op would certainly have had more potential than the one with Opie the Drug-Addicted Possum.

 # 2) HEIDI THE CROSS-EYED POSSUM ~ Sticking with that backwoods North Carolina theme, it all started in May of 2008 when a litter of possums was born there, which included sisters Heidi and Naira. Discovered orphaned, the pair was taken to a wild animal sanctuary where they were nursed back to health.

While the woods-to-sanctuary move may not have been that out of the ordinary, the next one is a bit surprising. The two sisters find themselves the unwitting winners of an all-expenses-paid family vacation for two to Denmark where they are introduced to divine new digs at the Copenhagen Zoo.

If this prompts the question, "Why would Denmark go to these lengths?" flash back to our intro where we noted that possums are only native to the Americas. If you're operating a zoo on any of the other continents, you are going to have to cross the ocean to get one.

Upon reaching Europe, animal trades between zoos on that continent would not be uncommon leading to Heidi and Naira being swapped out to the Leipzig Zoo in Germany. In 2010 it is noticed and noted that Heidi is distinctly cross-eyed. This leads to a feature article in Germany's tabloid magazine *Bild* and the world goes wild, hooked on Heidi, as the pantheon of the planet's possums.

If you haven't already done it, put the book down for a minute and Google this image; Heidi is absolutely adorable! If you think we might possibly be putting you on, check with the 300,000 people who began to follow her on Facebook!

Potentially paving the pathway for future possums to follow, Heidi books a gig on *Jimmy Kimmel Live!* With the Academy Awards approaching, and obviously feeling that opossum Oscar opinions are opportune, Kimmel has Heidi predict the winners. She nails all but one. All hail Heidi!

 # 1) POGO POSSUM, from the comic strip *Pogo* ~ For a respectable span of 27 years from 1948-1975, under the creative prowess of Walt Kelly, Pogo Possum ruled the world, or at least the Okefenokee Swamp, over which he reigned in Georgia. There was a laid-back, no-nonsense charm to the ambiance which permeated the strip.

Pogo himself was an everyman. Characterized as humble, approachable and philosophical, the multitude of other anthropomorphic animals who populated the swamp consistently came to Pogo for needs ranging from companionship to counsel to countenance. Reverting to that philosophical element we alluded to above, the strip managed to interject a thread of political and social satire that truly set it apart.

Walt Kelly may have summed it up best in a 1969 *TV Guide* interview when he painted a picture of Pogo as, "the reasonable, patient, softhearted, naïve, friendly person we all think we are." One of the most enduring elements of the Pogo legacy occurred just a few years before his retirement when he became the poster boy for the newly established environmental initiative of Earth Day.

We are actually going to have to take you back to the War of 1812 for the setup on this one when, after winning the Battle of Lake Erie, Naval Commander Oliver Perry declared, "We have met the enemy and they are ours." Over a century and a half later, on April 22, 1970 when 20 million people attended inaugural events for the first Earth Day, Walt Kelly would retool the quote for the poster used in launching that initial event in 1970.

The image featured Pogo Possum standing amidst a patch of litter-strewn land about to attempt a clean-up. The caption read, "We have met the enemy and he is us." It effectively made the point that people were responsible for the pollution problem and only people could solve it. A lasting legacy was left.

CHAPTER 17

HERE'S SOME TALES IN A FLURRY 'BOUT SOME CRITTERS SOFT & FURRY

RABBITS

We have another Name Game at play here and we'll lead with an introductory statement which is both factual and one that brings into play the three primary name variables. Bugs **Bunny** was a **rabbit** who made his debut in "The Wild **Hare**" in 1940. More fun facts… A "jackrabbit" is really a hare, and a "swamp hare" is really a rabbit. So what kind of rabbit hole are we sending you down with all of this? How 'bout we sort it out.

Let's start with "rabbit" and "hare" because those two are easy. They are two distinct animal species differentiated most notably by the fact that hares are generally larger, and also have longer ears and hind legs. Rabbits are born with no fur and their eyes closed. Hares are born fully furred with their eyes open. The term "bunny" is more subjective because it has no scientific meaning. A somewhat common interpretation might be to say a bunny is a younger rabbit, e.g. bunny is to rabbit as puppy is to dog.

There are however a few problems with that analogy. A puppy is, by definition, a juvenile dog while the same cannot be said about the word bunny. Our coming countdown will bear this out; the aforementioned Bugs is now in his 80's while the Easter Bunny has been hoppin' down that trail for centuries. And what about that cottontail… well, he would be a rabbit.

Our final clarification on this conundrum would be to add that while all hares are wild, rabbits may be wild or domestic. Most wild rabbits fall into the species of "cottontails", but there are actually five species of wild rabbits that are not cottontails. So, navigating the bunny trail on this one can be a little tricky but we're hoping we've simplified it as much as possible.

Beth Woolbright, Board Member and Educator for the House Rabbit Society (HRS) told us that, "Domestic rabbits should be spayed and neutered, which is important because they can have double the number of litters in a year as wild rabbits. Experience around the world tells us that domestic rabbits are also often the third most common animal surrendered to shelters. Euthanasia statistics can be so abysmal that many municipal shelters refuse to keep any rabbit statistics, lumping them under small animals. So it is way better to adopt than purchase a rabbit."

Size ~ These animals can be found on every continent except Antarctica and the variation in size can be significant. At the low end of the spectrum the adult wild pygmy rabbit can weigh less than a pound while domestic Flemish Giant rabbits can weigh over 20 pounds. So as to not contradict ourselves, please allow us to clarify our "hares are larger" comment and qualify that by saying that while hares are generally taller, they are also more streamlined with the heaviest rabbits weighing more than the heaviest hares. The largest documented Flemish Giant rabbit weighed 49 pounds and was 4.3 feet long!

Life & Speed ~ In terms of lifespan, rabbits can live up to 9 years in the wild and 14 years in captivity, while the equivalent number of years for hares would be 4 and 12 respectively. The oldest rabbit ever recorded was an Australian rabbit named Flopsy, who lived to be 18 years, 10 months, and 3 weeks old. In terms of speed, wild rabbits max out at 30 mph while hares can hit 45 mph which puts their 100-YDT's at 6.8 and 4.5 seconds respectively.

Beth from HRS closed our correspondence by sharing that, "There are so many misconceptions about rabbits. And they are smart and clever to boot! Living with a rabbit roommate is like living with a three-year-old child for their first four or five years; then they slow down a bit and turn into 40-year-olds overnight. Physically they are considered elderbuns at six, but they can stay young a long time after that."

Combining the rabbits and hares, let's hop into the list of our Top 9…

 # 9) ROGER RABBIT ~ This character will always hold a sacred position in the Animation Hall of Fame because he was the centerpiece of the only movie ever to celebrate the joint efforts of Disney, Warner Bros., Stephen Spielberg, MGM, and every studio from the Golden Era of Hollywood Animation.

The historical background of this coalescence would warrant its own book, but suffice it to say that the 1988 film *Who Framed Roger Rabbit* (the "?" is intentionally missing) will go down in history as the only opportunity ever to see studio icons Mickey Mouse and Bugs Bunny sharing the same screen. Oh, and there's also that dynamic duo dalliance of Donald Duck and Daffy Duck.

The massive melding of historical aspects of animation is symbolized in Roger's character design which was based upon the confluence of the following character components…

Basic rabbit form… Bugs Bunny
Gloves, red pants with buttons, and no shirt…Mickey Mouse
Baggy pants… Goofy
Blue bow tie and red overalls… Pinocchio
Round head and a red nose… Sylvester
Cheeks extending pronouncedly to the sides… Wile E. Coyote
Tuft of red hair… Droopy the Dog
Eyes popping out of his head… Tex Avery

From a personality perspective, Roger is zany and hyperactive (typical Tex Avery toon); he can be naïve and subject to the whims of those looking to take advantage of him; but he is also endearingly friendly and kind-hearted, and devoutly devoted to his wife Jessica.

Extreme sight gags abound whenever Roger partakes of alcohol. Varied effects are featured... head spins, eyes pop, babbles incoherently, and whistles like a teapot, all while his whole body is spinning. To steal a line from *When Harry Met Sally*, if you saw him out at a bar and the waiter approached to ask what you'd like, you'd probably say, "I'll have what he's having!"

 # 8) THE TRIX RABBIT ~ "Silly Rabbit, Trix are for kids!" was the strong admonishment heard by the defeated character who perpetually sought to coerce the fruit-flavored cereal from the children in the General Mills ad campaign. The floppy-eared white rabbit debuted in 1959 and has remained a Trix treasure ever since.

Marketing mayhem being what it is, there have been occasions where advertising campaigns led to public participation votes which enabled the Trix rabbit to partake. Upon those rare occasions, he is given his own go-to line. When the kids resort to their mantra of "Silly Rabbit, Trix are for kids!" the rabbit's retort is, "And sometimes for tricky rabbits!" Certainly a well-deserved rabbit reward.

 # 7) THE TORTOISE AND THE HARE, from *Aesop's Fables* ~ You know how this one goes. The arrogant Hare taunts the humble tortoise with put-downs about his lack of speed. Annoyed by his haughty attitude, the Tortoise challenges the Hare to a race in which he feels his obvious disadvantage can be countered by a dogged determination.

As the race starts, the Hare, not surprisingly, rushes to an enormous early advantage and becomes so overconfident he decides to take a nap, resting up to celebrate his victory. Of course the Hare oversleeps and is passed by the Tortoise who crawls slowly but steadily away to the victory which establishes Aesop's moral to this fable.

There are a couple ways you can word this... "the weakest opponent should never be underestimated" or "slow and steady wins the race."

 # 6) THE WHITE RABBIT, from *Alice in Wonderland* ~ This quirky rabbit's most memorable lines might be the ones he speaks immediately upon his entry in the 1951 Disney film which are, "I'm late! I'm late! For a very important date! No time to say hello, goodbye! I'm late! I'm late! I'm late!" His late arrival is referring to the Mad Tea Party which is being hosted by the March Hare.

When he staggers into the Mad Tea Party concerned about his watch, it becomes a perfect setup for the March Hare and the Mad Hatter to embark upon a raving repair of the watch which is exactly two days slow. So as logic kicks in, and you analyze the phrase "exactly two days slow," the bottom line would be that the watch is spot-on accurate.

After Lewis Carroll wrote the original novel in 1865, and Disney released the classic movie in 1951, "White Rabbit" took on an additional identity in the late 1960's counterculture when Jefferson Airplane released their hit song "White Rabbit" in 1967. It was during that mind-altering era when obvious parallels were conveyed regarding "Alice in Wonderland" and the use of psychedelic drugs.

 # 5) PETER RABBIT ~ We're going to lead off by doing some rabbit unraveling for you on a topic that can be a little tricky. Our question... What's the deal with Peter Rabbit and Peter Cottontail? Same character? Same book? Same rabbit hole? And the answer to all three questions is the same "sometimes". We found fortuitous the fact that our countdown placed these two Peters in such perfect proximity to each other so as to take a chronological approach to our explanation.

Beatrix Potter wrote *The Tale of Peter Rabbit* in 1902, which was the first of her six Peter Rabbit collections, the last of which came out in 1912. Peter lives with his mother and his three younger sisters, Cottontail (but not Peter Cottontail), Flopsy and Mopsy. The anthropomorphic family lives in a rabbit hole which is furnished like a human house with all the accoutrements.

Peter Rabbit has the distinction of being the first fictional character to be made into a stuffed animal and to date, Potter's *Peter Rabbit* has sold over 250 million copies. The fact that Potter had a licensing copyright on her character will make the circumstances we describe next even more surprising.

 # 4) PETER COTTONTAIL ~ In 1910 Thornton Burgess begins to write his series of books for young readers which is called *Old Mother West Wind*. The Burgess tales lure young readers to the whimsical world of the Green Forest where one could find the Purple Mountains and the Smiling Pool. Oh, and also a character called Peter Rabbit.

We're not sure what the copyright infringement issues potentially at play were with Burgess somewhat commandeering the name of a character that Potter created, and was actually still writing about at the time, but no legal actions ever occurred. Burgess would continue to write stories about Peter Rabbit until his retirement in 1960.

There was, however, a brief period of time beginning in 1914 when Burgess came to the conclusion that "Peter Rabbit" was less inspiring than the alternative choice of "Peter Cottontail", which did seem to add a jolt of jazziness. That being said, after a fleeting flirtation with the "Peter Cottontail" moniker, Burgess reverted to "Peter Rabbit" which he used for the duration.

So now, with "Peter Cottontail" retired by Thornton Burgess in 1914, we need to fast forward through a 35-year hiatus for the resurrection. In 1949 a pair of songwriters, Steve Nelson and Jack Rollins, pen a soon-to-be-classic holiday tune called "Here Comes Peter Cottontail". And you know what he's doin'. Go ahead and sing the next few lines, he's "… hoppin' down the bunny trail. Hippity hoppity Easter's on its way."

Singing cowboy Gene Autry was recruited to record the song, not particularly surprising since he already had the Christmas classic "Rudolph the Red-Nosed Reindeer" under his holiday hit belt. Under Autry's artistic acuity,

"Peter Cottontail" hopped to #3 on the *Billboard* country chart and #8 on the *Billboard* Hot 100 in the spring of 1950.

 # 3) THUMPER, from Disney's *Bambi* ~ "Eating greens is a special treat, it makes long ears and great big feet," Thumper once mused, "but it sure is awful stuff to eat! I made that last part up myself." So there you have a dietary analysis from arguably the cutest character in Disney's classic 1942 film *Bambi*. The name is derived from the fact that the rabbit has a habit of thumping his left hind foot. For the record, in real life, rabbits thump their feet when they are frightened, angry, or annoyed, but in Thumper's case the habit seems to be borne more of nervous energy.

Thumper actually had more of an impact on the film than one might suspect of a supporting character. Early in the production there was a concern that the film might be taking on too somber of a tone, what with Bambi's mother dying and all. The decision was made to elevate the importance of Thumper because of the positive youthful exuberance he brought to the film. The classic scene where Thumper teaches an awkward Bambi to ice skate would qualify as an example of this.

 # 2) BUGS BUNNY, from *Looney Tunes* ~ "I know this defies the law of gravity," Bugs Bunny once said, "but I never studied law!" What he did study was animation and comedy and perhaps no character combined the two better than Bugs. At least that's the opinion that *TV Guide* came to when the magazine's article on the "50 Greatest Cartoon Characters of All Time" perched the "wascally wabbit" atop that poll at #1.

Bugs first hit the silver screen in prototype form in the 1938 cartoon "Porky's Hare Hunt" before making what is considered his "official" debut, with a design and Brooklyn accent voice similar to the modern version, in 1940's "A Wild Hare". His persona provided the template for cooler-than-cool, flippantly unflappable, never nonplussed, and (almost) always one step ahead of the adversary.

Bugs has kept busy in the years since, starring in 167 short films during the Golden Age of Hollywood Animation (1940-1964). Guinness World Records designates Bugs as having appeared in more overall films than any other cartoon character with this designation combining short cartoons, TV specials, and full-length movies.

Another Guinness poll collectively combines and ranks the number of film appearances by actual people, as well as animated characters, and Bugs comes in at #9 in this one. In 1985 his celebrity was cemented in the sidewalk when he was awarded his own star on the Hollywood Walk of Fame.

We'll close with the first words exchanged between two true American icons, LeBron James and Bugs Bunny, in the 2021 film *Space Jam 2: A New Legacy*. Upon first seeing the superstar rabbit…

Lebron: Bugs Bunny? Who! Bugs! I can't believe… Bring it in, man.
Bugs: Hey, you're that famous basketball guy. Come on, aren't you LeBron James?
Lebron: Bugs Bunny knows who I am?
Bugs: Of course. I may live in a hole in the ground, but we still get TNT.

 # 1) THE EASTER BUNNY ~ As God-fearing Christians, we felt that if God so loved the world, his only begotten Son would sacrifice his life so that we should not perish, but be blessed with everlasting life, we kinda owed Him this one. Make that #1. We hereby bestow regal rabbit reverence to this beloved bunny.

So how and when did this rabbit start hoppin' down the bunny trail? While we're in our mode to bestow, we're going to give credit to the Germans for this one. The first reference to the Easter Bunny actually occurs in a 1682 essay by Georg Franck von Franckenau titled "De Ovis Paschalibus" in German, which translates to "About Easter Eggs" in English. While we're on the subject of translations, the essay refers to the "Oschter Haws" which would mean "Easter Hare" in English.

The key passage in the essay would be translated as "these eggs are called rabbit eggs because of the myth told to fool simple people and children that the Easter Hare is going around laying eggs and hiding them in the herb gardens. So the children look for them, even more enthusiastically, to the delight of smiling adults." So while the 1682 essay is the first time we see this concept in print, from the context it is clear that the tradition has been in place for some time.

A History Channel documentary on Easter symbols and traditions reports that the Easter Bunny's first appearances in America occurred in the culture of the German immigrants who settled in what became known as the Pennsylvania Dutch area of that state. So for the purpose of avoiding potential misnomers, allow us to explain the "Dutch" in that cultural name.

It is actually based upon the Germans who came to Pennsylvania from their homeland which they actually call "Deutschland". So the people there are not descendants of the Dutch, which brings us to a final geography note that we've always found quirky.

What's up with this three-names-for-the-same-place deal? We're talking about a European country that goes by two different names. Is it Holland, or is it the Netherlands? And if you are from there, your demonym is that you are Dutch. Perhaps the Easter Bunny will leave the answer to this conundrum in your basket next year.

SQUIRRELS

As we let the suspense build regarding where Rocky the Flying Squirrel will land in our countdown, we'll start out with the fact that "flying" squirrels is a bit of a misnomer. They actually glide using the flaps of skin between their arms and legs and in some cases between their legs and tail! How far can they go in a single launch? The outside range would be about 300 feet and we have for you here an easy-to-picture visual. If a flying squirrel were to take off from the top of a football field goal post, he could make it to the opposite end zone!

Size ~ Moving on to size, there's a greater range than you may have expected. The African pygmy squirrel lives up to its name measuring in at a mere 5 inches. On the other end of the spectrum the red and white giant flying squirrel of China and the Indian giant squirrel both grow to more than 3 feet long.

Life ~ On a worldwide basis, squirrels are probably the most prolific, not to mention fun-to-watch, backyard wildlife mammal species. When you see that cute eastern gray squirrel in your backyard, its average life expectancy is about six years, but they can live up to 12 years in captivity. The record for oldest documented life goes to an eastern gray squirrel who reached the age of 23 years, 6 months at the Racine Zoo in Wisconsin, arriving on June 14, 1949 and then racing around Racine until January 2, 1973.

Speed ~ Even the squirrels that don't fly can hang some significant air time, with their jumping ability maxing out at about 20 feet. And they're also pretty quick with their feet on the ground as the quickest squirrels are able to hit speeds of 20 mph. So with our 100-YDT comparison chart, the squirrel would clock in at 10.2 seconds.

That being said, we would have to get them to violate their instincts for that straight-line-dash event. When they take off to avoid a predator they employ a zigzag pattern, an excellent strategy if you're trying to escape a hawk which does not have the ability to change directions that quickly while in flight. Of course if you're trying to cross a busy road, that strategy can become a bit suspect.

We'll close with a finale you can sink your teeth into, so to speak. Squirrels' teeth never stop growing. Actually we need to say their **front** teeth never stop growing as pointed out by our resident squirrel expert John L. Koprowski, the Dean of the Haub School of Environment & Natural Resources at the University of Wyoming. "Their cheek teeth actually don't grow throughout life and are how we can age animals," clarified John, "old squirrels have very worn molars." Double thanks to John for connecting us with Liaison Lindsey.

They're genetically engineered so that the process of gnawing wears those front teeth down exactly enough to equal the new growth. And those teeth are tough. Squirrels actually shut down the New York stock market for periods of time in 1987 and 1994 by gnawing through power lines!

As the closing bell rings, let's get to our Super 7 Squirrels.

 # 7) MUNGO ~ The death occurred in 1772. And even though that was now more than 250 years ago, the pain is still real. Back in the day, Benjamin Franklin mourned the loss and the fact that he was moved to write such an elegant eulogy enables us to share the grief to this very day.

Mungo was an eastern gray squirrel and his death was not pretty. Details are sketchy as to whether the squirrel escaped out of the house or the dog,

Ranger, somehow snuck in. All we know for sure is that the dog was able to catch the squirrel and rip it into furry gray pieces. Bad Ranger!

The victim was owned by a friend of Franklin's, hence Ben was inspired to put quill to paper, and pen the proper memorial to Mungo. Franklin's eulogy included the acknowledgement that, "Few squirrels were better accomplished, for he had a good education, had traveled far, and seen much of the world." Then pinpointing the specific cause of death, he dramatically added, "Thou art fallen by the fangs of wanton, cruel Ranger!" Again, bad Ranger!

As a finishing touch, Franklin even went so far as to write a poem to serve as the epitaph on Mungo's tombstone. Before we share the poem we need to also share the fact that "skugg" was an alternate 18th century word for a squirrel. The rhyme went...

Here Skugg ~ Lies snug ~ As a bug ~ In a rug

Could a squirrel ask for anything more? That being said, we would be remiss if we did not report the fact that this scenario would not have been as uncommon as a 21st century reader might presume. Perhaps surprisingly, in the 18th and 19th centuries squirrels were fairly common American house pets.

Going back to colonial days, before there were any rules and regs regarding the concept, and before folks had homes full of fragile items and electrical cords, keeping wild animals as pets was much more common. And far and away, the most popular such pet was the squirrel.

We found an 1851 book by Jane Loudon titled *Domestic Pets: Their Habits and Management* which had some interesting thoughts on the topic. First off, it's notable that after covering the compulsory components on cats, dogs, fish and birds, when she proceeds to tackle the less mundane topics, her chapter on squirrels is actually longer than her chapter on rabbits.

We'll share a couple of our favorite quotes. Loudon describes the squirrel as a "beautiful little creature, very agile and graceful in its movements," and she also says that squirrels "may be taught to jump from one hand to the other to search for a hidden nut, and it soon knows its name, and the persons who feed it."

And we hope that Mungo, may he rest in peace, somehow knows that before Benjamin Franklin contributed to the writing of the Declaration of Independence and the United States Constitution, he honed his literary skills writing the eulogy of Mungo the squirrel.

 # 6) SECRET SQUIRREL ~ When the James Bond movie franchise debuted in 1963, divine destiny dictated that of course parodies would follow spanning the TV genres of sitcoms to dramas to cartoons. The first cartoon copying the James Bond motif was *Secret Squirrel* which debuted in 1965. The James Bond motif was played to perfection. Goldfinger be damned, Secret Squirrel's most menacing adversary was archnemesis Yellow Pinky.

 # 5) SANDY CHEEKS, from *SpongeBob SquarePants* ~ One of the more unique characters in the animated series, Sandy Cheeks is an eastern gray squirrel who has been cruising the ocean floor at Bikini Bottom since the show's inception in 1999. The only main character to be traditionally land borne, Sandy would be the one you'd see always wearing a helmeted diving suit to provide that direct feed of oxygen needed to survive.

 # 4) TWIGGY ~ It was the devasting 1978 hurricane David that first put the wind into the sails of this story. When Deltona, Florida couple Chuck and Lou Ann Best rescued a baby squirrel after the storm, they named it Twiggy and initially the squirrel made a habit of sitting on their shoulders even when they would go into their pool.

At that point Chuck Best got his best idea ever. Utilizing Twiggy's balancing ability, he initially taught her to be tugged around the pool on a block of Styrofoam, actually an easier balancing act than being walked around on a person's shoulder. At this point you can probably envision the learning curve… the blocks of Styrofoam were gradually decreased in size and shape to form a small set of water skis.

Things were looking good at that point, but the Bests needed one last nuance to launch this squirrel into the spotlight. After Twiggy had become comfortable with being tugged around the pool by humans, the people were replaced by Chuck's daughter's remote-controlled boat.

At that point it was showtime and the launching point was in 1979 when the act earned accolades on the NBC reality show *Real People*. The Best family has kept the show on the road ever since with a series of Twiggy descendants performing right through the present day.

Over four decades and 9 squirrels later, Twiggy has compiled a resumé which includes two *Frat Pack* movies, namely *Dodgeball: A True Underdog Story* and *Anchorman: The Legend of Ron Burgundy*. In a calculated attempt to display diversity, she also hit the water in the music video for Brad Paisley's "River Bank".

 # 3) TOMMY TUCKER ~ He was an author, a model, a salesman, an inspiration to the armed forces during WW II and he was an eastern gray squirrel. Are we nuts? Nope, nuttin' wrong with us, except for the fact that at this point we probably owe you a story, and here it is…

In 1942, Zaidee and Mark Bullis adopted Tommy Tucker after his mother had died and the baby squirrel had fallen from a tree. When first found, Tommy's eyes were not even open and the couple gradually nursed him back to health. So certainly the reason why the squirrel was so docile and tame was that it essentially had never experienced anything other than human care.

Seizing upon this, Zaidee Bullis took to her love of sewing and began making outfits for him. In 1943, Tommy began his public performing career with a tour of elementary schools where students were entertained by his docile demeanor and winning wardrobe. With the country in the throes of WW II, it was not surprising that Zaidee incorporated a patriotic theme into Tommy's attire.

It was the patriotic piece of the puzzle that led to the next nuance of Tommy's tale. The U.S. Treasury Department partnered with the Bullis family to make the sale of war bonds a centerpiece to the squirrel's tour and the idea totally took off. Tommy Tucker gained national notoriety to the point where in 1944 he was the feature for a *Life* magazine cover story and photo gallery.

When his tour started, Tommy had 30 outfits and by the end he had a hundred. The squirrel was nothing if not photogenic, especially with all of that adorable attire at his disposal. Now for the record, it should be noted that even though Tommy was a male, his costumes always consisted of dresses. There was no gender bias behind this approach, actually just an application of pragmatism. That big bushy beautiful tail precluded the possibility of pants.

As Tommy's popularity with the civilian population grew, the military also hopped on board to thank him for his support of the cause. After a joint radio "interview" was staged with President Franklin Roosevelt, soldiers in Europe began carrying his picture into battle with them and Tommy found his squirrel mailbox full of letters.

Here's one sample documented in his "autobiography" *The True Story of Tommy Tucker*. "We carry your picture with us when we fly," wrote airplane gunner Sgt. Morris A. Goodrich. "And when we look at your picture, we realize the wonderful work you are doing for us and it gives us much more confidence, so we can do the job we have to do." A little squirrely, but we love it.

 # 2) SUGAR BUSH ~ Publishing this book in the 2020's, we feel a contemporary obligation to honor the squirrel who has most managed to master the era of the internet. The most famous cyberspace squirrel is certainly Sugar Bush. Rescued by Kelly Foxton as a baby from her nest in a fallen tree, the eastern gray squirrel is now livin' the good life in Boca Raton, Florida.

What are the circumstances that would lead to such a favorable Floridian follow up from a fall? Sugar Bush was rescued by a "gnawtrepeneur" whose internet savvy led to "International Superstar" status as "The World's Most Photographed Squirrel". If you're wondering what warrants these accolades, check out these stats that Kelly has compiled. The Sugar Bush phenomenon boasts the following numbers …

video set ups with multiple cameras for filming … 1
state of the art sound studios for recording "vocals" … 1
elaborate sound stages in her posh home studio … 7
outfits with matching hats & accessories … over 4,000
modeling photographs for which she's posed … 6,000
stage props she has for photo ops … tens of thousands
number of her pins posted on Pinterest … 150,000

As news anchor of Squirrel News Network, SNN, she has covered bad news, like the obituaries of former presidents and good news, like the announcement of Sugar Bush's own run for the presidency. In addition to the videos she's posted, Sugar Bush is a media marketing frenzy. Merchandise available through her website includes books, cards, calendars, glossy photos, stuffed animals and that's just for starters.

The website is truly worth checking out as the photo gallery is a total trip, with pictures of Sugar Bush dressed in costumes ranging from Fidel Castro to Albert Einstein to Forest Gump, or "Forest Stump" as the picture is labeled for reasons which become obvious when you see it.

We'll close with colossal kudos for Kelly! She took a small animal rescue and turned it into a business behemoth making Sugar Bush a star along the way. We have to say that if we were a baby squirrel about to fall out of a tree, we would certainly hope to be taking the plunge in proximity to her yard! You can access all this squirrel girl fun at SugarBushSquirrel.com.

How 'bout we close with Sugar Bush's own personal tribute to this book...

As literally "The most photographed squirrel in the world" I am honored to bestow my blessing and endorsement upon the Smiths' tribute to the Animal Kingdom. Of course I was most fascinated with the Squirrel component of the book and I salute my fellow squirrels who join me in the countdown.
Sugar Bush Squirrel

 # 1) ROCKY THE FLYING SQUIRREL ~ Rocket J. Squirrel, as the name would read on his birth certificate, was brought to life in 1959 on the *Rocky and Bullwinkle Show*. What did the "J" stand for? It was actually a gesture of self-acknowledgement on the part of the show's creator, comic genius Jay Ward. Just to flesh out his resumé a bit, Ward was also the man behind other bits of 1960's magic which included George of the Jungle, Dudley Do-Right and Mr. Peabody & Sherman.

Rocky's partner and sidekick was Bullwinkle Moose whose compromised intellect inevitably put the pressure on Rocky to do most of the thinking. In that role of being the brains and logic of the operation, Rocky was often cast in the position of playing straight man to Bullwinkle who provided the lion's share of the series' humor.

Their most common adversaries in the serialized adventures were those two Russian no-good-niks Boris Badenov and Natasha Fatale. This evil duo operated under the supervision of a Nazi-style commander known as Fearless Leader. Keep in mind that this series debuted at the height of the Cold War and less than 15 years after WW II ended. Combining the Commies and the Nazis in an adversarial alliance certainly produced a topical tandem of terror.

Taking flight with this final paragraph, Rocky's airborne abilities were able to take him to great heights such as the platform from which he did his high dive in the opening credits. He could even fly from city to city in a matter of seconds if circumstances warranted.

Animal Planet ranks Rocky & Bullwinkle as #15 on its list of "50 Greatest TV Animals".

CHIPMUNKS

With this chapter we're finally going to supply the answer to a Storyline Sampler scenario we shared back in the first chapter when we asked what might connect the four actresses Kaley Cuoco, Christina Applegate, Anna Faris, and Amy Poehler. We'll get to that in our countdown but first let's check out our chipmunk chit chat chart.

The habitat range for these guys is rather quirky. If you look at one of those world maps that color in the area where a specific animal lives, the chipmunk highlights most all of North America and the northern area of Russia that borders the Arctic. If you're looking at a chipmunk in the Southern Hemisphere, you've just walked by a "Welcome to the Zoo" sign.

There are 25 species of chipmunks and 24 are native to only North America. The one outlier in the equation is the Siberian chipmunk which is the one that manages to color in that map of northern Russia. While most humans wouldn't head there, unless they were exiled, these chipmunks seem to enjoy calling the place home.

Size, Life & Speed ~ In terms of size, we'll go with the symmetry of eight ounces and eight inches, including the tail, for a full-grown chipmunk. For life expectancy, it averages 2-3 years in the wild, with the record landing at 9 years for a chipmunk at the London Zoo. As cute as they are, chipmunks are not recommended as pets. Full speed, they can hit 21 mph providing them with a 100-YDT of 9.7 seconds.

Next, we'll fill your cheek pouches with our Top 3 Chipmunk countdown.

 # 3) THE CHIPETTES ~ At this point, the cat is probably out of the bag on our trivia question with which we led off this chapter. Kaley Cuoco, Christina Applegate, Anna Faris, and Amy Poehler all were voice artists for the Chipettes! How's that for lining up some quality vocal talent?! We promise to circle back to the topic, but first let's chip away at the Chipette story.

They were a spinoff within the *Alvin & the Chipmunks* franchise, still upcoming in the countdown, so we need to share a little on that to set the table. That male trio of Chipmunks launched in 1958 and they spent their first 25 years with very little female companionship.

When the animated *Chipmunks* series rebooted in 1983, the decision was made to spice things up by adding a trio of female companions. Brittany, Jeanette and Eleanor, who would be known as the Chipettes, were each paired up with one of the original Chipmunks in terms of personality, as well as romantic relationships on some level.

The success of the new TV series was such that it spawned no less than 8 subsequent Chipmunk movies in the 1990's and early 2000's. As the budgets went up so did the talent level; it would be during this era that Cuoco, Applegate, Faris, and Poehler all realized their dreams of becoming a Chipette.

 # 2) CHIP 'N DALE, from Disney ~ "We're just a couple of crazy rascals out to have some fun!" That was their game plan and they certainly carried through on the execution. When they made their debut in the 1942 cartoon "Private Pluto", Chip 'n Dale were essentially two versions of the same chipmunk; their character designs were identical and they spoke and acted the same.

During their original run of eighteen short films between 1943 and 1956 the format was fleshed out quickly whereby the personalities were differentiated with Chip being the more intelligent and level-headed leader of the pair with Dale, by contrast, playing the goofy carefree sidekick whose offbeat antics often created the problems the pair had to deal with.

Physically, Chip was given a tuft of hair and a gap between his two front teeth (which doesn't always show depending on the angle). But the other difference is really the go-to ID tool. Dale has a red nose while Chip's nose is black. So the mnemonic device is to remember the one whose nose looks like a chocolate chip is Chip.

After a decades-long hiatus, Disney reintroduced the pair in 1989 with their own series *Chip 'n Dale's Rescue Rangers* where the boys were cast as private detectives with their own agency fighting crime. In 2022 Disney released a new *Rescue Rangers* movie using the advertising phrase, "It's not a reboot. It's a comeback."

 # 1) ALVIN AND THE CHIPMUNKS ~ "We **are** talking chipmunks, Dave. We can get ourselves out of a cat carrier. Not really even that hard to do." That is the cynically sardonic response Simon gives to the Chipmunks' owner and manager David Seville when he expresses surprise over the fact that they have managed to escape from the cat carrier cage in which he had tried to confine them. Here's some background…

The Chipmunks were created by Ross Bagdasarian who produced a song in which he recorded his normal voice, harmonized it with high-pitched speeded-up versions of his voice, and released a song called "Witch Doctor" which went to #1 in April of 1958. Looking to build upon that success, he embellished the concept by labeling the high-pitched voices as "chipmunks" and turning them into a virtual band.

The follow-up recording would be a breakthrough event in media history. With the holiday season approaching, "The Chipmunk Song (Christmas Don't Be Late)" was released in November of 1958. The song went to #1 on the *Billboard* Hot 100, a feat that has not been accomplished by another Christmas song since then. Furthermore, it clung to the #1 position for 4 weeks! They would go on to place 8 songs in the Top 40, 14 songs in the Hot 100 and, believe it or not, release over 50 albums!

Some might consider this one of our tightest choices in terms of a #1/#2 borderline call. For any of you questioning how we could drop the Disney darlings Chip 'n Dale below this rag tag band of chipmunks, here's our rationale. To review the C&D resumé, they had 18 short cartoons, one TV series (that lasted one season), and one full-length movie. To be fair, you could throw in some comic books and cameo appearances.

The Chipmunks had no short cartoons because they didn't begin their careers until 1958 when most of the major studios were in the process of closing down their short cartoon animation operations. So, small concession on that note, but the Chipmunks had three different TV series (that lasted a total of 14 seasons) and 8 full-length movies. Edge to Alvin & crew.

Alvin, the middle brother, was the egocentric leader, attention seeker, and all-around clown. Theodore was youngest, very innocent, kind and benign. Simon was the oldest, wisest, and wittiest; as verified by our opening quote. The manager/pet owner of the Chipmunks was Dave Seville, played by creator Ross Bagdasarian. He did his best to keep his crew under control, but it was always an uphill battle.

MICE

Let's start out by busting a couple mainstream mouse myths while creating a new tongue twister at the same time. Try saying "mainstream mouse myths" 5 times fast without stumbling. So which myths are we musing? We are challenging the cheese choice and questioning the "quiet as a mouse quip".

If you've ever had them digging, clawing or nesting in a wall or attic space you know they don't go out of their way to keep quiet. And regarding the cheese thing, they actually prefer grains and seeds. Since they'll eat even garbage, if need be, to survive, they would eat most cheese products but particularly pungent cheeses they would actually avoid.

Life ~ Their life expectancy is usually 3-4 years in the lab, but less in the wild with lots of predators out there. The year 2023 saw the crowning of a new longevity king of the mouse kingdom when Guinness World Records documented that Patrick Stewart (named after the actor), a Pacific pocket mouse living at the San Diego Zoo Safari Park had achieved an age of 9½ years.

Size & Speed ~ No surprise on the size as we've all seen them… 3 inches and about an ounce. Top speed is about 8 mph, yielding a 100-YDT of 25.6 seconds.

Next, we'll get the running wheel spinning with our Great 8 Mice…

 # 8) MIGHTY MOUSE ~ Animator Paul Terry operated a studio known as Terrytoons from 1929-1973 with the flagship character flying high as Mighty Mouse. His classic pose had him in flight in his red and yellow suit, with red cape trailing behind him. His right fist would be thrust into the air with his left arm cocked beside his body.

The theme song was a memorable one featuring a powerful operatic tenor. A new generation of fans was introduced to the character through comedian Andy's Kaufman's regular skit, often on *Saturday Night Live*, where he would lip sync and act out the melodramatic theme song which started out with...

> *Mister Trouble never comes around,*
> *When he hears this mighty sound!*
> *"Here I come to save the day!"*
> *That means that Mighty Mouse is on the way!*

Animal Planet ranks Mighty Mouse #32 on its list of "50 Greatest TV Animals".

 # 7) ALGERNON ~ "Who's to say that my light is better than your darkness?" That is one of the precariously probing questions proffered by Daniel Keyes in his 1966 novel *Flowers for Algernon* which was turned into the Academy Award winning film *Charly*. The movie chooses to change the spelling of the main character's first name who, in the book, is Charlie Gordon, a mentally challenged 32-year-old man who undergoes a transformational surgery to boost his intelligence.

The book benefits from a unique stylistic approach whereby the story is told in the form of a series of journal entries by Charlie. In the beginning we find out that the experimental intelligence-enhancing surgery has been tested on Algernon, a laboratory mouse, and shown extremely encouraging results. Algernon's ability to navigate mazes and perform tasks for rewards reveals exponential growth.

This paves the way for the human testing to move forward with Charlie's intellectual status rendering him as the designated choice to become the first human involved with the project. The fact that the initial results mirror Algernon's success is evident, not only by Charlie's descriptions of what is happening around him, but also by the enhanced level of writing ability displayed in his journal entries.

So there's an initial surge of excitement which is tamped down by a doctor's warning that, "The more intelligent you become, the more problems you'll have." This prophecy proves accurate on a few levels. As Charlie's IQ approaches genius level, a rift develops between his intellect and his social skills.

While the operation is able to make Charlie smarter, it is not able to counter the void created by the lack of social experiences which would typically be commensurate with the level of intelligence he now possesses. It factors into the equation as a strange variable that could never have been anticipated, or corrected, by the surgery.

Furthermore, as Charlie reflects back upon some of the events that have shaped his life through the prism of intellectual perspective he now possesses, he becomes aware of the flaws and mistreatments that characterized some of his relationships and friendships. As these struggles complicate the progress he has achieved, the ultimate irony blows up in a climactic explosion.

Charlie's brilliant research enables him to detect the fatal flaw in the medical procedure he and Algernon have undergone. All of the improvements they have experienced are only temporary and destined to diminish. Because Algernon had undergone the procedure earlier, his skills begin to regress first, serving to confirm Charlie's suspicions.

It all becomes so bittersweet at that point. Charlie's love for Algernon is reflective of that which any human might have for a pet, but in this case it's so much more. In this pantheon of paradox, Charlie while still at the top of his game, sees his fate foreshadowed in Algernon's regression. The shattering blow of experiencing the loss of a beloved pet while simultaneously coming to grips with his own impending plight creates the heartrending crescendo that enables the story to achieve Academy Award status.

Algernon's loss of ability to control his behavior is followed by problems with coordination and then memory loss. He dies "after suffering protracted symptoms of a widespread neurological collapse." It's a despondent death leaving so many unanswered questions about life. And also about happiness and intelligence and the interconnectivity between those components.

Ultimately, the level to which a man can achieve happiness is an end product that functions independently from that man's intelligence. It's a lesson that no one should ever forget. Remember that, and we'll close with Charlie's final journal entry which, the bell curve having been completed, is written on the same intellectual level as the first entry... "P.S. please if you get a chanse put some flowrs on Algernons grave in the bak yard."

 # 6) PINKY AND THE BRAIN ~ "Gee Brain, what do you want to do tonight?"

"The same thing we do every night, Pinky, try to take over the world!" – Pinky and the Brain, at the culmination of each episode's intro.

These attempts to take over the world began in 1993 when *Pinky and the Brain* first appeared as a component within the Stephen Spielberg/Warner Bros. *Animaniacs* TV series. The series stood out immediately with humor that appealed to both adults and children and its popularity led it to spin off into its own series from 1995-1998. It was also a part of the 2020 *Animaniacs* reboot.

In terms of characterization, Brain, as the name would imply, is a brilliantly scheming yet diabolical mastermind. Pinky, on the other hand, sports an intellectually challenged naiveté, but he's blessed with a warm, genial upbeat personality and a comic flair characterized by his ability to deliver preposterous punchlines laughingly launched out of leftfield.

The series' funniest recurring gag came every episode when circumstances would lead Brain to the realization that an opportunity had been presented for the pair to take over the world. The lightbulb would go on over Brain's head and he would look at Pinky and say, "Are you pondering what I'm pondering?"

Pinky would respond in the affirmative but then, with his brain operating on a level way below Brain's brain, Pinky would proceed to proffer an analysis of what Brain might be pondering that would **often** be hilarious and **always** be something totally preposterous. Right now, we're going to offer you our reader the bonus of a countdown within a countdown. Here are our Top 7 Pinky answers to Brain's question of, "Are you pondering what I'm pondering?"

They all begin with, "I think so, Brain, but...

7 ... if they called them "Sad Meals", kids wouldn't buy them!
6 ... if Jimmy cracks corn and no one cares, why does he keep doing it?
5 ... calling it a pu-pu platter? Uh, what were they thinking?
4 ... can the Gummi Worms really live in peace with the Marshmallow Chicks?
3 ... (and while we're on the subject of peace...) if we give peas a chance, won't the lima beans feel left out?
2 ... but this time **you** put the trousers on the chimp.
1 ... but isn't the seashore the worst place to be selling seashells?

And closing with one final quote to allow Brain to put it all into perspective... "This is the Earth. And this is Pinky. You can tell the difference quite easily. One is a lump of inert matter hurtling blindly through the void. The other... is the Earth."

 # 5) THREE BLIND MICE ~ Unfortunately, nursery rhyme life goes from bad to worse for this trio of visually impaired rodents. If you're looking for a silver lining in this sad saga, perhaps it would be the learning of a rule to live by. Long-story-short, if you're blind you should never run after the farmer's wife – that bitch is bad news. How bad? Well, here's what happened when the mice chased her...

They all ran after the farmer's wife,
Who cut off their tails with a carving knife.
Did you ever see such a sight in your life?

While you're pondering an answer to that one, we'll make a sweet segue to sheer speed...

 # 4) SPEEDY GONZALES, from *Looney Tunes* ~ While billed as "The Fastest Mouse in all Mexico", Speedy Gonzales sped across the silver screen in 46 theatrical Warner Bros. cartoons from 1953-1968. In addition to being a speedster, he was heroic, quick-witted, and generally genial, except to his two primary adversaries who were Sylvester the cat (who he referred to as "El Gringo Pussygato") and Daffy Duck ("El Loco Duck"). Speedy spoke with a heavy Mexican accent which led to an interesting storyline when the era of political correctness kicked in.

In 1999 the Cartoon Network, which had the broadcast rights to the Warners cartoons at that time, decided to ban the Speedy films from their rotation because of ethnic stereotyping. Then a funny thing happened; faster than Speedy could zip across the desert, Mexican Americans, led by the League of United Latin American Citizens, began a campaign to bring back the mouse.

Ethic stereotypes notwithstanding, the majority of Mexicans remained enamored of Speedy Gonzales. The Cartoon Network subsequently brought the mouse back in 2002, *The Speedy Gonzales Show* is now a staple of Mexican cable TV, and when Mexico's most popular kids' station signs off the air for the night, the broadcast signal goes to a still shot of Speedy Gonzales playing the guitar, along with the words "Buenas Noches" (Good Night).

We'll close with our favorite quote regarding the Mexicans' attitude on this subject. In 2021 columnist Gustavo Arellano wrote, "I love Speedy so much, I keep a large painting of him in my home office. His kind smile and brown skin takes me back to my childhood – and reminds me of where we as Mexicans exist today."

 # 3) CHUCK E. CHEESE ~ Before all the hullabaloo about transgender became a topic of such media attention, this guy performed perhaps the even more difficult transition of trans-species. After spending the first 15 years of his life as a rat, Chuck E. Cheese underwent the transformation of becoming a mouse. Cosmetic surgery details to follow.

The children's family entertainment center and restaurant chain of Chuck E. Cheese was founded in 1977. After beginning in San Jose, California, the groundbreaking concept of combining kids' games, entertainment, and food under the same roof took off and the franchise spread quickly throughout the country. There almost 600 currently open, in 47 states and 17 foreign countries.

The original owner, Nolan Bushnell, ordered a coyote costume for his planned venture of Coyote Pizza and received a giant rat costume instead. Talk about going with the flow; rather than returning the costume, Bushnell changed the name of the restaurant to Rick Rat's Pizza. Cooler heads prevailed, however, with the decision to nix "Rick Rat's" as the restaurant moniker, choose Chuck E. Cheese as the new name, but still keep the costume. So Chuck E. spent his formative years as a rat.

After the wave of initial success, and a full 15 years into the business operation, the decision was made in 1992 to go with a hipper, more kid-friendly version of the mascot. It was at this point that Chuck E. went through the aforementioned trans-species metamorphosis. He was slimmed down to reflect a more health-conscious persona and he also received a facial makeover with the goal of creating a more genial look. His eyes got bigger, his snout became shorter and more rounded, and these facial features were placed upon a broader cheek structure.

And there you have the details of how you might go from being a rat, to being a mouse, all the while maintaining that the motto for your house is that it's a place "where a kid can be a kid."

 # 2) JERRY, from *Tom & Jerry* ~ After his debut in the 1940 MGM film "Puss Gets the Boot" Jerry would proceed to celebrate one of the most prolific and successful careers in cat cartoon history. The cat and mouse team of Tom &

Jerry appeared in more films and won more Academy Awards than any other cartoon character(s) ever.

During the Golden Age of Animation, MGM's William Hanna and Joseph Barbera were charged with directing the studio's Tom & Jerry cartoons, thus establishing the formula whereby a tenacious Tom was never deterred from his ravenous pursuit of Jerry despite his long-running series of violent defeats. During their original run, from 1940 to 1958 when MGM closed their animation studio, Hanna and Barbera won seven Oscars, the most ever for a team of directors as well as a team of characters.

Animal Planet ranks Tom & Jerry as #41 on its list of "50 Greatest TV Animals".

 # 1) MICKEY MOUSE ~ *"When people laugh at Mickey Mouse, it's because he's so human; and that is the secret of his popularity. I only hope that we don't lose sight of one thing – that it was all started by a mouse."* – Walt Disney. The second half of that quote has probably become the most signature line from the creator of the character who has become the iconic symbol of the largest media conglomerate in the world today. Mickey's the mouse that built the house.

In the initial phases of this mouse story, we have a couple comments and quotes that come together in a quirkily comic coalescence. The name Walt had originally chosen for the new mouse was Mortimer, but that was rejected when his wife Lillian felt it was kind of creepy. Now we're thinking that a comment Lillian might have found even creepier was the one where Walt said, "I love Mickey Mouse more than any woman I have ever known." Not going to sell a lot of Valentine's cards with that sentiment.

The November 18, 1928 debut of an 8-minute cartoon called "Steamboat Willie" proved to be a double landmark event. It was the first Mickey Mouse short as well as the first cartoon with sound. And the steamboat landed just in the nick of time. "Born of necessity," Walt would say of Mickey, "the little fellow literally freed us of immediate worry. He provided the means for expanding."

The characterizations of Mickey Mouse and Walt Disney can certainly be intertwined as alter egos. This concept was epitomized in the beginning by the fact that Walt Disney provided Mickey's original voice. They both began as sympathetic underdogs, prospering through plucky perseverance toward an ultimate destiny whereby both achieve a status anointing them as the kings, reigning over their respective realms.

And regarding Mickey, the premise of this book is to cover the most famous animals, actual and fictional, in the history of the world. That being said, if you could somehow conduct a worldwide poll ranging from every icy igloo in frozen Alaska to every humble shanty in equatorial Africa to arrive at a #1 choice for the most recognizable animal image ever, how could you land anywhere but Mickey Mouse?

CHAPTER 18

HERE COME STORIES FULL OF CHARM FOR OLD McDONALD ON HIS FARM

PIGS

We're sure many of you have frequently fretted over the fact that pigs don't get enough respect. Well, let it be known that we are here to put that pigsty purgatory in proper perspective. With this component we will no longer wallow in the mud; no-no, that's not our style… we are going to deep dive into the murky muck and emerge in a positively pristine posture for our piggy porcine salute. By the way, Duane Hebblethwaite from Savannah Pig Rescue in Upstate New York served as our pundit of the pigs for this component.

Please tag along while we scour the genres of television, movies and literature while surveying our "Great 8" of the most famous pigs in the history of the world. Idiomatically speaking, please don't be **pig-headed,** but join us while we get **high on the hog** and **go hog wild, when pigs fly**. Let's start by putting the poo-poo on some perpetual pig putdowns.

Popular Piggy Putdowns ~ Next time someone tells you that "You're sweatin' like a pig" or "Your room looks like a pigsty," just smile and say, "Thank you very much." Regarding putdown #1, pigs actually don't sweat at all, so there; and assessing putdown #2, contrary to the common perception, pigs are actually quite clean, as animals go.

We know that we're bursting a lot of your bubbles here, so please don't take this personally, but if you had your own pig, it would probably be smarter than that dog of yours. Look it up if you don't believe us. One of the world's smartest animals, they can use tools, play video games and learn tricks.

Pigs are also great communicators. They have over 20 distinctive grunts and squeals to convey their thoughts about issues ranging from hunger to fear to romance. Mother pigs even sing to their babies while nursing.

Pet Piggies ~ Pigs and people… we're all in this together. Pigs are easily domesticated, with China being #1 on the list and the U.S. being #2 in terms of countries with the most pet pigs. They are very social animals who can develop extremely close relationships with human beings, and you won't have to wait long for the evidence… just wait till you read below about the pig parties that went on in the home of actor George Clooney!

Size ~ If you are a pig who lives in the wild we've got good news and bad news for you. You're going to be much sleeker than a domestic pig, but you're not going to live as long. The average wild pig weighs a couple hundred pounds which is going to sound totally anorexic compared to this next stat.

The largest pig ever recorded was Big Bill, who was raised in Martin, Tennessee and reached a weight of 2,552 pounds as documented in Guinness World Records. He was 5 feet tall and 9 feet long. Whether he thrived on the attention or not, Big Bill's huge stature established him as a prominent fixture on the country fair circuit and he died on a train enroute to the Chicago World's Fair in 1933. For the record, he was only 3 years old at the time and his belly was dragging on the ground, which certainly may have contributed to the premature death.

Big Bill's breed was a "Poland China" pig and on the other end of the spectrum, the smallest breed of pig is a "Göettingen" minipig which weighs about 75 pounds at maturity. We're thinking that when we make the move to a pet pig, we're gonna lean toward the Göettingen. That Big Bill litter box had to be an absolute mess!

Life ~ The life expectancy of a domestic pig is more than twice that of a pig in the wild. Domestic pet pigs can expect 10-15 years while feral pigs are looking at 4-8. The record life span for a pig was attained by Baby Jane who lived on a farm in Mundelein, Illinois and died on September 10, 2021 at the age of 23 years, 7 months and 9 days.

Speed ~ In this department the wild pigs boast a slight edge. While the domestics can hit a top speed of 11 mph, wild pigs can crank it up to 15 mph. These speeds provide 100-YDT times of 18.6 seconds for the domestics and 13.6 for the wild pigs.

Next let's speed on to the countdown of our Great 8 Pigs…

 # 8) MAX ~ Max was the pet pig of actor George Clooney who enjoyed Hollywood pet pig perks such as flying on John Travolta's private jet and frequently hobnobbing on Clooney's movie sites. The Vietnamese potbellied pig died in 2006 at the age of 18.

How much did Clooney love Max? Max made frequent appearances on tabloid television shows where Clooney described their relationship as practically inseparable and shared that the two slept in the same bed. In 1998, when a model he was dating named Celine Balitran told Clooney that it was either the pig or her, Celine was soon saying, "Sayonara".

 # 7) WILBUR, from *Charlotte's Web* ~ When we started this project one of Deb's first comments was, "I can't do animal movies; I always end up crying." Case in point… Whether you opt for the classic 1973 Hanna-Barbera animated production of this one, or the 2003 Universal Studios live-action movie, keep that old Kleenex box handy. Author E.B. White's 1952 novel is pretty much guaranteed to bring a tear to your eye.

Quick plot review if it's been some time since you pulled your book off the shelf, or cued up the video… the starring pig, Wilbur, is the runt of his litter when he is born on the Arable family farm and destined for slaughter. Daughter Fern Arable (played by Dakota Fanning in the movie) pleads for Wilbur's life and is allowed to keep the pig as a pet.

But when Wilbur gets older, much to Fern's regret, he is sent to the Zuckerman farm where he is slated to become dinner at some point in the not-too-distant future. In the Zuckerman barn Wilbur is befriended by the spider Charlotte who uses calculated messages spun in her webs to facilitate Wilbur's survival. What sparks Deb's tears? While attending a family fair, Charlotte is taken ill and knowing her death is imminent, provides Wilbur with an egg sac to take back home in order to repopulate the barn with spiders. Such is the circle of life.

 # 6) THE LORD OF THE FLIES ~ If you read the William Golding novel *Lord of the Flies* as an assignment in high school, or on your own as an adult, you know it's a novel that can't help but leave a lasting impression. Your thumbnail plot summary would be that it's about a group of British schoolboys who are marooned on a tropical island after a plane crash. During their struggle for survival a battle between good and evil emerges which essentially serves to reveal the dark side of humanity.

The "Lord of the Flies" is literally a pig's head which has been impaled upon a stake in the jungle and left as an offering to the beast which the boys believe to be inhabiting the island. A generous selfless boy named Simon emerges as the Christ figure in the story. Seeking to save the lives of the other boys, he ultimately sacrifices his own life in the process.

As fate would have it, the pig has been impaled near the spot where Simon goes to meditate and when he sees the head it triggers an epileptic seizure during which Simon hallucinates a conversation between himself and the pig. Simon dubs the pig's head "Lord of the Flies" because by the time he sees it, the insects swarming the head are "black and iridescent green and without number."

When it comes to novels assigned in high school, they don't make you read them unless they're seething with symbolism, so let's go there next. "Lord of the Flies" translates into Beelzebub in Greek which means the Devil. The pig had been a pregnant female and the savagery with which the boys had slaughtered her was indicative of the evil which was emerging from within them during their ongoing struggle for survival.

During Simon's conversation with the pig's head it says, "What are you doing out here all alone? Aren't you afraid of me? There isn't anyone to help you. Only me. And I'm the Beast." The interpretation of this would be to say that the actual danger to the boys on the island is not an imaginary beast that never even actually exists. The true danger is the evil which exists within the boys themselves, a danger which is symbolized by the *Lord of the Flies*.

Sorry we had to get all heavy on you here, but Tim taught this book to his high school students for decades and sometimes he just has to let it all out.

 # 5) PORKY PIG, from *Looney Tunes* ~ After making his *Looney Tunes* debut in 1935's "I Haven't Got a Hat", Porky Pig would establish himself as the first famous pig in entertainment history as well as the longest continuing Warner Bros. cartoon character. Bugs Bunny and Daffy Duck did not make their debuts until a few years later. His most unique character quirk was his stutter which came to be the signature end piece for most all the Warner Bros. cartoons when, after the credits, Porky would pop through the target logo and say, "Th-, th-, th-, that's all folks!"

From a personality perspective he was not as brash as some of his cartoon co-stars, often playing the faithful friend and straight man. That was why he was the perfect choice to star in the first "blooper" in animation history. Here's the scurrilous scoop on that one…

In the late 1930's the Warner Bros. studio embarked upon a project to compile their first set of movie bloopers and outtakes that would provide an entertaining package in and of themselves. When the animation department was approached with this then-novel concept, the somewhat obvious realization was that they didn't have any outtakes because if something goes wrong in the animation process, it would never make it to film.

That being said, the WB animation department wanted to be represented in this new project so they decided to create their own blooper. Here's what they did.

They created one Porky Pig moment that truly stands the test of time and you can access it on YouTube under "Porky Pig Cusses Blooper". It's one of the more scandalously surprising 10 seconds of film you'll ever find. At his workbench, Porky accidently hits his thumb with a hammer and seems on the verge of profanity when he shouts, "Son of a bi-, bi-, bi-, bi-…; Son of a bi-, bi-, bi-, bi-…; Son of a bi-, bi-, bi-, bi-…; Son of a Gun." Then Porky looks directly at the camera and says, "I bet you thought I was gonna say 'Son of a Bitch', didn't you?"

Porky's "good guy" persona is the reason why he's the perfect character for this sketch. The level of humor is elevated because the outburst is more out of character for Porky Pig than it would have been for say Bugs Bunny or Daffy Duck.

 # 4) PUMBAA, from Disney's *The Lion King* ~ If you're inclined to sack us on this one by playing the warthog card, you can just keep that one in your hand. Warthogs are part of the overall pig family so Pumbaa has permission to participate, even though he becomes angry at the hyenas when they toss their, "Who's the pig?" taunt at him.

If your Disney dossier is a little outdated, when *The Lion King* broke box office records in 1994 as the biggest animated movie ever, Simba, the lion lead character, had two primary supporting actors. They were a meerkat named Timon and a warthog named Pumbaa. As singers, Timon and Pumbaa could claim credit for vocalizing what would become the catchphrase of the year, namely "Hakuna Matata", meaning "No worries" which, in a double-karma linguistic event, became a catchphrase in and of itself.

While certainly a character of comedic value, Pumbaa was also a fierce warrior who would go to great lengths to protect his friends. Completing the name game, Pumbaa means "foolish" or "silly" in Swahili and in the *Timon and Pumbaa* TV series which ran from 1995-1999, it was revealed that his last name was Smith, which we Smiths didn't think was very silly at all.

 # 3) THE THREE LITTLE PIGS ~ The earliest printed version of this fable dates back to the 1840's where it is cited as a tale that has been shared for generations, with no specific author credited. In the 1930's a series of Disney cartoons sparked a resurgence of popularity with the American public. The original film in the series, 1933's "The Three Little Pigs" featured one of the year's biggest musical hits, namely "Who's Afraid of the Big Bad Wolf". By the way, you need to repeat "big bad wolf" three times at the end of the lyrics to achieve the desired effect.

Meanwhile, the integrity of building standards will never again be ignored as an issue. While the three pigs may have slipped something by the zoning board back in the day, by modern standards, that straw house… bad idea.

 # 2) PIGLET, from *Winnie the Pooh* ~ The two most important years for this character were 1926 and 1961 and the two most important family names were Milne and Disney. Originally A. A. Milne based the character upon a stuffed animal in the collection of his son Christopher Robin Milne. The senior Milne published the first in his series of *Winnie the Pooh* books in 1926.

When Disney bought the rights to the Pooh franchise in 1961, Piglet would enjoy a new character design and extremely heightened popularity. The Milne family was reluctant to sell the rights, knowing that it was Disney's intention to modernize all of what is now referred to as the "Classic Pooh" character designs to the images most people are currently familiar with.

From a personality perspective, Piglet is a timid flower-loving character with a bit of an inferiority complex, but he is always affable, loyal and kind-hearted. He is the second smallest character in the series, measuring just slightly taller than Roo, the baby kangaroo.

Piglet and Pooh have a special relationship as revealed in the following exchange… "We'll be Friends Forever, won't we, Pooh?" asks Piglet. "Even longer," Pooh answers.

 # 1) MISS PIGGY, from *The Muppet Show* ~ For a small-town female pig whose father died when she was young and who was not treated well by her mother, things turned out pretty well for Miss Piggy in *The Muppet Show*. According to her original voice artist Frank Oz, "She had to enter beauty contests to survive, as many single women do. She has a lot of vulnerability which she has to hide, because of her need to be a superstar."

While the fans certainly enjoyed her carefully calculated use of karate and the fluid frequency with which she could spin a French phrase, it was the curious complexity of the romantic relationship between Piggy and Kermit the Frog which was always center stage in the Muppet storyline. Kermit's skittish skepticism to embrace the relationship only served to intensify the persistence of Piggy's pursuit of her perceived prize, her precious Kermie.

Audiences embraced her temperamental diva superstar personality and Miss Piggy's popularity actually surpassed that of her beloved Kermit as she sold more books and merchandise. All of which leaves us at the point where we can't sign off on this segment without saluting the man who was the genius behind the Muppets, namely creator and producer, Jim Henson who led the Muppets through an impressive run of 120 TV episodes and 8 movies, after the series debuted in 1976.

Returning to the superstar status we alluded to above, we'll share the results of polls from both sides of the Atlantic. In a U.S. *TV Guide* poll, Miss Piggy was ranked #23 in its list of "50 Greatest TV Stars of All Time", and in a U.K. *Channel 4* poll, Miss Piggy was ranked #29 in its list of "100 Greatest TV Characters". Piggy, you're perfection.

CATTLE

We're going to start with a couple cattle fun facts, before we get down to some brass tacks, but not to worry, we've saved some frivolity for the finale.

* The first cow arrived in North America on board a British ship docking at the Jamestown colony in 1611.
* Cows love music. Next time you find yourself carrying a boombox by a cow pasture, jump the fence, point your music machine at the cattle, and watch how many friends will come to join you. If you're at all skeptical of this you can confirm our credibility without having to actually scale that pasture fence as we alluded to in the previous sentence.

The concept has achieved its-own-genre status on YouTube, and our choice for the one that can be milked for the most laughs would be "Grazing Cows Rush to Listen to Accordion Music". This player lures a crowd from 100 feet away with our favorite part being when the herd huddles against the fence jockeying for front row positions like kids at a concert.

Size ~ At the top end of the cattle size spectrum is the Chianina breed which can stand 6 feet tall, 6.5 feet long and weigh 3,500 pounds. According to the *Beef2Live* website, a bull named Donetto holds the world record for the heaviest ever, tipping the scales at 3,840 pounds at the 1955 Arezzo show in Italy.

Life ~ The natural lifespan of cattle who do not become part of the food chain would fall in the range of 15-20 years. The record holder in this category is one

Big Bertha who will be blessed with her own countdown appearance below. Teaser... she will more than double the natural life expectancy.

Speed ~ When seen ambling around the barnyard, cattle usually move at only a couple miles per hour, but that can be deceiving. When escaping potential danger, they can get up to 25 mph which gives them a 100-YDT of 8.2 seconds.

Let's close with those final fun facts we promised. The concept of cows and the milk they provide us has undergone such a drastic change over time that we are often remiss in forgetting the way things used to be. Only a century ago, if people traveling wanted to be assured of having milk they had to bring their own cows with them. It used to take a single person an entire hour to milk six cows by hand, while now modern machinery can milk 100 cows in an hour! As we head into our Fun 5 Cows countdown...

Get psyched to meet the cow that'll
Top our list of favorite cattle

 # 5) CLARABELLE COW, from Disney ~ Because she appeared alongside Mickey Mouse in many of the early Disney films, Clarabelle Cow has earned an esteemed spot in animation history. Truth be told, her debut in the 1927 film "Trolley Troubles" actually pre-dates Mickey's first appearance by a year. So this is a cow that's been around the block. Beginning with *Mickey's Christmas Carol* in 1983, Clarabelle has been brought back in many retrospective Disney projects.

 # 4) BABE, THE BLUE OX ~ The bigger-than-life tales of Paul Bunyan are a conglomeration of stories with their origins in the spoken word tradition of North American lumberjacks. They came to print for the first time in a 1916 collection written by William B. Laughead and various versions have been written by multiple authors since then.

The commonality amongst the tall tales was that they were all based upon exaggerations of such epic proportions so as to render as absurd any possibility that they could be even remotely based upon the truth. That being said, with hyperbole running rampant, the tellers of the tales were free to have some fun.

No better place to start than with the story of how Paul Bunyan came to adopt the Babe. The blizzard winds were howling one stormy day during the Winter of the Blue Snow when Paul heard a little blue bleat emerge from beneath the snow. Upon closer inspection, he found the baby ox who was fighting to get his head above snow level. Paul took him home, dried him out, and when the ox remained blue-stained he got his name.

So how big does Babe grow to push the legend along? The ox is so big that 42 axe handles can fit between his eyes, the lumber camp laundryman uses his antler rack to hang out the clothes to dry, and it takes a flock of crows one whole day to fly from the tip of one antler to the tip of the other. Wait, there's more...

When Babe gets an itch, he rubs against a mountain to scratch it because if he tries to rub against a tree, the tree inevitably comes crashing down. Twisted mountain roads Babe can straighten simply by tugging on the asphalt. Once while pulling a heavy water tank, it springs a small leak which trickles water that flows down to the Gulf of Mexico forming the Mississippi River. Get the gist?

 # 3) FERDINAND THE BULL, from Disney ~ This character proves to be a paradox as a large muscular bull who would rather smell flowers than fight in the bull ring in the 1936 book *The Story of Ferdinand* by Munro Leaf. Disney turned the story into a much-loved 1938 cartoon called "Ferdinand the Bull". The film captured the Academy Award for animation that year.

 # 2) ELSIE THE COW ~ "Whee! Come see me getting milked on a merry-go-round," certainly makes for one of the more titillating teasers in advertising history, doesn't it!? Those were the words that comprised Elsie the Cow's invite to swing by the 1939 World's Fair in New York City to pay her a visit. Many took her up on the offer and it's just a small part of Elsie's sweet saga. Here's the scoop…

And that "scoop" lead-in is apropos as ice cream was one of the products Elsie promoted upon becoming the advertising icon for the Borden Dairy Company in 1936. Elsie had that all-American appeal and by 1939 she had been named #1 in the Annual Advertising Awards.

As she hits #1, the aforementioned World's Fair starts up with a theme of "The World of Tomorrow" and the Borden exhibit features a futuristic farm where multiple cows are on a rotating platform being advanced to milking stations (thus explaining the merry-go-round alluded to in the opening quote). The Borden exhibit guides are given directions to log in the topics of the questions fair visitors are asking, with the subject matter breaking down as follows…

20% – questions about the milking machine
20% – questions about the bathroom location
60% – questions about which cow was Elsie

As the Borden brass assesses this situation on the fly, a somewhat paradoxical reality sets in that had not been previously anticipated. In order to maximize the PR value that has been created with their surprise "star" cow, they need to pick one of the cows they have on hand at the exhibit and designate her to be the "official" Elsie.

What ensues had to have been a somewhat comical scenario whereby the Borden brass executes a spontaneous assessment of the bovine options on site at the fair, and makes a determination of which cow seems blessed with the most charismatic personality. The exact winning behavior driving the decision is not specified, but a Jersey cow named "You'll Do, Lobelia" is anointed as Elsie. She's a 7-year-old who had been born in Brookfield, Mass. in 1932.

So how significant does the transition to a real live Elsie become? Turns out that the demand for her is so great that Borden opts for an approach where there is an "Elsie East" and an "Elsie West". While "You'll Do, Lobelia" is covering the east coast engagements, there are Elsie impersonators covering the west coast gigs. Thus, the answer to the oft-asked question would be that Elsie impersonators actually preceded Elvis impersonators.

So while Borden profits soar, the company's house of cards finally crumbles when one newspaper picks up on wire service stories which, upon connecting the dots, reveal that Elsie is apparently appearing simultaneously in South Carolina and southern California. That exposé leads to an irate parent backlash bemoaning the fact that their kids have been crushed by the Elsie revelation. First Santa, then Elsie… who knew what dominoes could fall next? The Easter Bunny and the Tooth Fairy are both allegedly seen updating their passports.

But Elsie does survive the backlash and there are new milestones to be achieved. Who would have anticipated that there would be romance hovering on the horizon for Borden's bovine babe? In 1940 she marries husband Elmer, whose name might not immediately click in your head, but if we were to attach it to the Borden's product of Elmer's Glue, that perhaps might resonate more resoundingly.

When television became a part of mainstream America during the 1950's, Borden's marketing crossed over into that medium and, for the first time, Elsie became an animated cow character. Multiple accolades have followed. In a 2000 poll conducted by MarketingDive.com, Elsie was voted one of the ten most outstanding marketing mascots of all time and she continues to appear as the official mascot for the 22,000-member Dairy Farmers of America.

 # 1) BIG BERTHA ~ Any animal who receives recognition from Guinness World Records is going to make our radar, but when Guinness acknowledges you as #1 in two different categories then, when your agent reaches out, we become inclined to elevate you to countdown status. Such is the case with Big Bertha who spent her finest days grazing at a farm in Kerry County, Ireland.

Before even getting to the records, we feel obligated to acknowledge the incredibly unique dates of birth and death over which Bertha obviously had no control. For starters, this cow is born in Ireland, on St. Patrick's Day, 1945 and then proceeds to live till New Year's Eve 1993. Could there possibly be a better lifespan scenario that could assure people would be partying just as hard on the day you were born as they were on the day you died?

While those coincidences certainly warrant recognition, let's finish with the superlatives. Guinness World Records acknowledges her having given birth to 39 calves as being the all-time high. Furthermore, her lifespan of 48 years, 9 months is also recognized by Guinness as the world record. If you would like a final cherry on top, Big Bertha helped raise $75,000 for various charities during her lifetime.

HORSES

We thought we'd saddle up some horse humor for the intro to this component, compliments of *Equine Wellness Magazine* and a posting on their website regarding Bizarre Horse Laws. Turns out there's some on the books where the word "bizarre" may not even do it justice. Here's a sampling…

* The fine for riding an "ugly" horse in Wilbur, Washington is $300! ~ Our question here is who gets to judge this beauty contest? Is there a panel on call ready to render a verdict at any given time?

* In Guernee, Illinois it is illegal for women weighing more than 200 pounds to ride a horse wearing shorts. ~ To whom exactly is the perception of protection being awarded here? Is it the overweight woman, the overloaded horse, or the viewing public in general? Furthermore, what about logistics… is every police car in town equipped with a set of scales and every police officer empowered, should circumstances warrant, to approach a potential offender and say, "Excuse me, Miss, I'm going to have to ask you to hop down from that horse and hop aboard these scales please."

* Finally, we'll close with a misworded ordinance from Wolf Point, Montana: "No horse shall be allowed in public without its owner wearing a halter." ~ As the magazine points out, the humor in this one is actually derived from faulty sentence structure. We're assuming the intended goal was to require that, "No horse wearing a halter should be allowed in public without its owner." But, as worded, the ordinance is implying that the owner must be wearing the halter.

So doesn't the meaning as stated above conjure up some humorous consequences? The streets of Wolf Point would have a changing booth on every block with an adjacent vending booth selling halters. Anyone breaking the law would be required to hitch their horse, pick a halter from the assortment available, and re-dress in the changing booth before going on with their day.

Size ~ The average size for a horse is about 6 feet tall and around 2,000 pounds, with significant variations according to species. Here are some superlatives to share with you from Guinness World Records. The tallest documented height and weight for a horse was that of a Shire named Sampson, whose name was later changed to Mammoth for reasons that we are about to make clear.

Sampson, born in Bedfordshire, England in 1846, was bred by Thomas Cleaver and stood 7' 2½" tall and weighed 3,360 pounds. On the other end of the spectrum the smallest breed of horses is the Falabella which grows to a little less than 3 feet and about 100 pounds. The record for longest tail goes to JJS Summer Breeze which was measured at 12' 6" in 2007.

Life & Speed ~ The average domestic horse has a life expectancy of 25-30 years while wild horses average about 15. For the record, the honor of longest life span for a horse goes to Old Billy who lived in Woolston, Cheshire, England from 1760-1822, checking out at the age of 62. An average speed for a galloping horse comes in at 27 mph while, according to *Horse & Rider,* the fastest recorded time for a sprinting quarter horse is 55 mph yielding a 100-YDT of 3.7 seconds.

Then & Now ~ Horses have been around for about 55 million years with their earliest ancestors roaming the planet in miniature form, only about the size of a Labrador retriever. They were actually the first animal domesticated by man, an achievement which occurred about 6,000 years ago.

Horses were originally indigenous to five continents, all but Australia and Antarctica, and these circumstances led to one significant modern-day ramification. The introduction of horses to Australia was initiated in 1788 when the British arrived. Because the long trip was not easy for an animal, only the hardiest horses survived, the gene pool was subsequently stacked, and Australian horses are noted for their strength and endurance.

Let's saddle up again, ridin' in our Horse Top 10…

 # 10) CITATION ~ Born at Calumet Farm in Lexington, Kentucky on April 11, 1945, this beautiful bay colt would go on to win 32 of his 45 races. He peaked at just the right time by horse racing standards, winning 19 of his 20 starts during his three-year-old season which included winning the Triple Crown in that year of 1948.

Just to throw an element of mystery into the mix, just before the Kentucky Derby, Citation's regular jockey went on a fishing trip and was never seen alive again. That bit of fate put Eddie Arcaro in the saddle and the rest, as they say, is history. Arcaro described Citation as "the greatest horse I ever rode," and our "poll of polls" ranks Citation as the third greatest race horse in history.

So, please allow us a moment to explain this poll of polls concept we've just invoked here. In researching the horse racing thread of this component, we wanted to make sure our rankings aligned with the authorities and to that end we took four respected polls and averaged them together to determine a consensus set of rankings which we have used. The four polls we employed were *BloodHorse.com*, *HorseyHooves.com*, *Lines.com* and *HorseRacingSense.com*.

 # 9) MAGIC THE MINIATURE MARE ~ "All of the horses from Gentle Carousel Miniature Therapy Horses in Florida are heroes," said owner/trainer Jorge Garcia-Bengochea, "but therapy horse Magic is our best-known little hero." This accolade sets up one of the most magical stories in our book.

In early 2010 the horse therapy organization sent their blue-eyed miniature mare Magic to visit an assisted-living facility patient who had not spoken during the three years she had been at the facility. Upon seeing Magic, the patient said, "Isn't she beautiful?" Talk about your magic moments, pun intended.

Nurses and doctors were literally brought to tears and, best part of the story, the patient continued to speak from that point forward. The AARP honored Magic with its "Most Heroic Pet" award in 2010 and *Time* magazine honored her as one of the "Ten Most Courageous Animals in History".

So there's the most captivating story from this horse therapy organization, but it's truly just the cherry on top. The organization continues to visit over 35,000 adults and children every year.

 # 8) BOJACK HORSEMAN ~ "I'm responsible for my own happiness? I can't even be responsible for my own breakfast!" That line epitomizes the plight of the title character in one of the most outlandishly unorthodox, yet accolade-laden, TV shows ever. If you've seen it, you'll know what we're talking about, and if you haven't, you'll need some explanation.

To set the table, BoJack Horseman is an adult-oriented, black comedy, animated series (Netflix 2014-2020) which is set in Hollywoo, and that is not a typo. BoJack himself had stolen the "D" from the iconic HOLLYWOOD sign in order to impress a girl. This LA scene is populated by a quirky combination of humans and anthropomorphic animals, BoJack himself being a horse.

He is a washed up 1990's sitcom star who is hoping a 2010's comeback can be achieved on the heels of his autobiography. But things are complicated when you're a pill-popping alcoholic struggling with your addictions, cynicism and self-loathing while still managing to come off as caring and insightful to those around you. It is the manner in which the show somehow manages to straddle that thin line between love and hate, joy and despair, triumph and tragedy, which encapsulates its brilliance.

Let's sample a snippet which manages to extricate humor from horror. Here's BoJack's explanation to a friend of just how badly he does not want the friend to release his musical rock opera. "How can I put this," he explains, "imagine if the Holocaust happened every four years like the Olympics. I would rather THAT happen than your rock opera."

So how 'bout those awards and accolades we promised? Here's a partial list...

* Four Critics' Choice Television Awards for Best Animated Series
* Three Annie Awards
* Two Writers Guild of America Awards
* IndieWire... "one of the greatest animated TV series in history."
* GQ... "one of the best shows of the decade."

Let's close with some more cynical black humor highlights. Our first one is predicated upon familiarity with the old drinking adage, "Beer before liquor, never sicker; liquor before beer, never fear." Playing upon that, BoJack offers the following alcohol and drug advice to a friend...

> "There's that old saying: Liquor before beer, never fear, don't do heroin." Other examples include...

> "Closure is a made-up thing by Steven Spielberg to sell movie tickets."
> "I drove, but I moved my arm a bunch so the Fitbit counted the miles."
> "When you look at someone through rose-colored glasses, all the red flags just look like flags."

 # 7) SILVER ~ "Hi-yo, Silver! Away!" were the directions often commanded by the Lone Ranger when it was time for him and his valiant horse to head out in hot pursuit of the bad guys. Our hero was a Texas Ranger who, along with his Native American sidekick Tonto, fought crime across three mediums. The radio show aired from 1933-1955, the ABC TV series ran from 1949-1957 and there were five theatrical films, released in 1938, 1939, 1956, 1981 and 2013.

Here are the details on how the Lone Ranger and Silver became a team. The Lone Ranger and Tonto are in pursuit of the villainous Butch Cavendish who fires at our hero and kills his horse. Continuing their chase, they come across a fight between a buffalo and a horse and subsequently kill the buffalo in order to save the horse's life.

A bond is formed as they nurse the horse back to health and Tonto comments that when the horse's coat glistens in the sun, it takes on a silver-white color. Upon his recovery, the horse is returned to the wild but chooses to return to the Ranger who, at this point, now has a new horse with a new name. Several different white horses played the part in various productions.

 # 6) THE CLYDESDALES ~ Okay, you're the son and grandson of the owner of the largest brewing company in the country and 13 years of Prohibition have just come to an end. What do the younger Busch boys do for the family patriarch August Adolphus Busch? "Hey, Pops," the boys say, "how would you like a six-horse hitch of the finest fanciest equestrian team on the planet to commemorate the end of this dreadful era?"

That's the story of how the Clydesdales horses began their symbolic representation of Budweiser beer. Shortly thereafter, the team was expanded to eight horses, and eventually the operation also expanded to include three separate teams. The concept of the Dalmatian mascot was introduced in 1950 and since then each team of Clydesdales travels with one Dalmatian.

Ready for some Clydesdale fun facts? How 'bout diet and size. On a per-day basis, each horse can consume 25 quarts of whole grains, 60 pounds of hay and 30 gallons of water. In terms of size, they stand 6 feet tall, weigh about 2,000 pounds and wear horseshoes that measure 20 inches long from one end to the other.

They make hundreds of appearances every year perpetuating their enduring legacy as the proud symbol of the Anheuser Busch Brewery.

 # 5) SECRETARIAT ~ Born in Caroline County, Virginia on March 30, 1970 this chestnut colt would go on to win 16 of his 21 starts in a career that lasted from 1972-1973. In winning the triple crown in 1973, Secretariat set record times in the Kentucky Derby, Preakness, and Belmont Stakes which, amazingly, all still stand today!

The second week of June 1973 turned out to a banner milestone for Secretariat when the horse became the first person or animal to simultaneously appear on the covers of *Time, Newsweek* and *Sports Illustrated*. Other accolades include induction into the U.S. Racing Hall of Fame (1974) and The Kentucky Athletic Hall of Fame (2007). Disney even honored Secretariat with his own eponymous movie in 2010 which starred John Malkovich and Diane Lane.

We still have another race horse remaining in our countdown and one question which may be coming to mind at this point would be, "If Secretariat holds the record times for all three Triple Crown events, how could he not be #1?" Trust us for now and we'll share the full explanation when we get to Man o' War coming up soon.

 # 4) MISTER ED ~ Here's our favorite example of the wordplay available when your lead character is a talking horse, as was the case on the *Mister Ed* sitcom which aired on CBS from 1961-1966. In one episode Ed gets home rather late one night, walks across the barn to check the clock in his stall, and assesses his dilemma by saying, "Midnight… It's too early to hit the hay and too late to eat it."

Parts of the Mister Ed concept were hard to explain. We're sure some of our readers who never saw the show are pondering the premise, while wondering how a series of such suspect plot possibilities could flourish and thrive for six years. That being said, there's a whole generation out there that cannot hear the name Wilbur spoken without hearing Mister Ed's signature, "Wil-*burrrr!*" warbling in their ears.

That was the way Ed would summon his owner when finding himself in a predicament, a scenario which managed to manifest itself every week. Wilbur Post was a genial and loving, if somewhat discombobulated, owner who often found himself playing the role of disciplinarian in light of Ed's rapscallion escapades. These ranged from making phone calls fulfilling various whims to returning home in the morning, hungover and still wearing his party hat after a night on the town.

Ed was played by the same horse throughout the entire series, an American Saddlebred/part-Arabian white palomino whose name was Bamboo Harvester. Wilbur was played by Alan Young who had a bit of an everyman quality about him which the producer said made him seem like the kind of guy a horse would talk to. Perfect.

Animal Planet ranks Mr. Ed as #4 on its list of "50 Greatest TV Animals".

 # 3) TRIGGER ~ He was a golden palomino who had about 100 tricks in his arsenal, and not only did he routinely walk up multiple flights of hospital stairs to visit sick children, when he was on solid ground he could walk 50 feet on his hind legs. Those are just some of the credentials that earn Trigger the nod as our highest rated Hollywood horse. Other talents included the fact that Trigger was housebroken, could sign his name with an "X" and could lay down for a nap and cover himself with a blanket.

Here's the backstory… when Roy Rogers needs to pick a horse for his first leading role which would be in the 1938 movie *Under Western Stars*, we're not sure exactly how the interview process goes down, but given the choice of five horses, Rogers chooses Golden Cloud and one of the greatest man/horse relationships of all time is initiated. The horse, which Rogers renames Trigger, will be his costar for the next two decades until Trigger's retirement in 1957. This collaboration covers over 80 movies and 100 episodes of *The Roy Rogers Show* which runs on NBC from 1951-1957.

Although Trigger died in 1965, he managed to live on as many of the great ones do. Trigger's body was mounted and preserved, prepared for display at the Roy Rogers Museum. Subsequently a 24-foot fiberglass replica of Trigger was created for the museum which caught the attention of the Denver Broncos NFL football team.

If your nickname is the Broncos, what better way to symbolize your team than having the most famous bronco in Hollywood history perched in the most visible point of your Mile High Stadium, right atop the scoreboard. So the Broncos go to Rogers and get permission to replicate the Trigger statue in a slightly larger version so as to be able to honor the iconic horse as well as to be able to say, "We have the biggest Trigger in the world!"

Certainly a boast that many would have liked to have claimed, but few have been able to deliver upon. Animal Planet ranks Silver as #12 on its list of "50 Greatest TV Animals".

 # 2) THE TROJAN HORSE ~ Okay, we're going to have to hop into the Wayback Machine for what is certainly one of the most fascinating horse stories ever. Let's set the Wayback coordinates with the following settings… Time: around 1090 B.C., Location: the ancient city of Troy which was in the modern-day country of Turkey.

Helen is the most beautiful woman in the world and sought after by the kings of all the great Greek city-states. A competition is held for her hand in which King Menelaus of Sparta prevails. In order to vie in the marital contest, each suitor is required to pledge assistance in her retrieval should she ever be abducted or taken away.

Following through on that note, the Trojan prince Paris is able to seduce Helen, an event which obviously casts serious aspersions upon the Spartan security forces. Supposedly, Paris is given a divine assist by the goddess Aphrodite but, let's face it, when you're the head of Sparta Security and the best excuse you have to throw against the wall is that "Aphrodite made me do it," your days may be numbered. Before Menelaus can yell, "Flag on the play!" Paris has whisked Helen away and the couple is sailing on a romantic cruise back to Troy.

Bound by their oath, all of the Greek kings unite in a mission to reclaim the beautiful Helen, thereby earning her the nickname of "the face that launched a thousand ships". You probably know the gist of what happens from here. The Greeks are tough, but Troy has that damn wall around the city which enables the hometown defenders to hold the intruders at bay for ten years.

Our story concludes with the most outstanding example of trickery in the ancient era. The Greeks pretend to give up and start to sail home, leaving behind a huge wooden Trojan Horse as a token of their resignation. The jubilant Trojans roll the horse inside the walls of the city and celebrate with a night of drunken debauchery.

With the Trojans compromised, the Greek soldiers hidden inside the wooden horse sneak out and open the city gates allowing the entire Greek army (who had only pretended to sail away) to enter the city. Troy is burned to the ground, Paris is slain, and Helen is reunited with Menelaus. Apparently able to sell Menelaus on the aforementioned premise that "Aphrodite made me do it," Helen and her original husband live happily ever after.

And talk about a topical cliché with legs, over 3,000 years later people are still saying, "Beware of Greeks bearing gifts."

 # 1) MAN O' WAR ~ Born at Nursery Stud in Lexington, Kentucky on March 29, 1917, this impetuous fiery red chestnut colt was destined to go down as the greatest race horse ever. One caveat to that status was that he did not win the Kentucky Derby, but only because his owner skipped the race feeling that it was an unsafe distance for colts.

Man o' War won 20 of 21 starts in his 1919-1920 career and the one loss comes with an asterisk. That narrow loss occurred at Saratoga Race Course, to a horse that was aptly named Upset, and while the details remain sketchy, there was certainly something off at the beginning of the race. We'll defer to the *Equus* magazine account of what happened. That authoritative source said…

"Reports vary – some say that Man o' War was facing the wrong way when the starter raised the tape – but by all accounts, he left the post near the rear of the field of seven. As the frontrunners vied for the lead, Man o' War found his stride and began to pass horses all along the backstretch."

We promised above to explain why that, despite owning the record times at all three Triple Crown events, Secretariat is the consensus #2 race horse and Man o' War is the consensus #1. Here's the scoop… Jockeys weighed more in the 1920's so Man o' War carried a heavier load. Significant improvements in track surfaces occurred over time, meaning that Secretariat ran on superior surfaces. And finally, assessing the horses' level of competitiveness, Secretariat won 77% of his races while Man o' War won 95% of his.

We'll close by putting two cherries on the top of Man o' War's legendary story. Exemplifying his sheer dominance, he once won a race by a world record 100 lengths. In 1920 the *New York Times* voted him co-athlete of the year, an honor he shared with Babe Ruth.

Chapter 19

IT'S RAINING CATS AND DOGS

CATS

*Ending up this book begats
lots of stories with those cats*

Regarding which animal was going to lead this final chapter, we must acknowledge that considerable pressure was applied to us by our favorite furry feline, Chynna Cat Sunflower Smith, who made it crystal clear that the administration of her morning snuggles and kisses were sure to be cut back considerably if cats were not the first critters to be crowned in this animal kingdom chapter conclusion.

First we'll regale you with Chynna's Super 7 sensational cat quotes…

* The phrase "domestic cat" is an oxymoron.
  – author/TV commentator George Will
* There are two means of refuge from the miseries of life: music and cats.
  – philosopher Albert Schweitzer
* You cannot look at a sleeping cat and feel tense.
  – TV personality Jane Pauley
* One cat just leads to another. – author Ernest Hemingway
* No matter how much cats fight, there always seem to be plenty of kittens.
  – President Abraham Lincoln
* In ancient times cats were worshipped as gods; they have not forgotten this.
  – author Terry Pratchett
* Cats rule the world. – Garfield creator Jim Davis

First, we'll share some cats stats as we have done in every intro.
Size ~ Let's do average and then superlatives… the common housecat is about 10 inches tall and 18 inches long without the tail, weighing in at 10-12 pounds. In the superlative category, according to Guinness World Records…

The longest cat was Mymains Stewart Gilligan (aka Stewie to his friends), a Maine Coon who measured 48.5 inches in 2010. If you're looking at that number and having an "Oh, my God, no way" moment, please allow us to word it in an alternate fashion to confirm our figure. The cat was just over 4 feet long!

The record for heaviest cat goes to an Australian behemoth named Himmy who tipped the scales at 46.8 pounds when he died at the age of 10 in 1986. While Stewie is susceptible to being surpassed in the record book, Himmy will forever be heralded as the heaviest because Guinness retired that category to prevent overfeeding.

Life ~ In terms of longevity, the record is owned by a cat from Austin, Texas named Creme Puff who cavorted for over 38 years from August 3, 1967 to August 6, 2005. A couple notes regarding the dates of Creme Puff's passing...

As you can see, she was able to tack on 3 days after reaching her 38th birthday but alas, she missed the 2005 celebration of International Cat Day, which falls on August 8, by a mere 48 hours. It wasn't the same without her. The average life expectancy of a cat is 12-15 years.

Speed ~ Cats can hit an impressive top speed of 30 mph, a speed which certainly inspires fear in the minds of mice everywhere, as well as providing them with a 100-YDT of 6.8 seconds.

So, without further ado, we'll now share with you, our Top 10 Cat countdown...

 # 10) LUCKY, Annie Edson Taylor's cat ~ This cat certainly had one of the more interesting storylines in feline lore. Here's the history... We need to go about 120 years back in time for this one and revisit the history of people going over Niagara Falls in a barrel. The long-story-short summary of this concept would be that since 1903, when Annie Edson Taylor became the first to do so, 18 daredevils have attempted this fearful feat and 11 have survived.

Please allow us to share this analytical aspect of the Niagara Falls plunge before cutting to the cat who is the star of this component. Of the hundreds of humans who have gone over Niagara Falls you can pretty much divide them into three categories.

* Daredevils who intentionally took the plunge
* People who accidently fell and were swept over
* Suicidal people who were choosing to die

So now as we extrapolate this, we will add a fourth category of living non-human creatures who took the plunge over Niagara Falls. This category will be "Pets who were sent over the falls by their owners" and there are just two members of this elite club, a cat and a turtle. The latter tale was told back in the Turtles chapter. Meanwhile here's the scoop on the cat...

The first person to go over Niagara Falls in a barrel was a 63-year-old retired school teacher named Annie Edson Taylor. Because no one had ever attempted this before, her efforts were not closely monitored but here's what she did after building her barrel. In order to test her device to determine if it were possible for a living being to survive the plunge, Annie decided to conduct a trial run and send her cat, Lucky, over the falls two days before she planned to go over herself. The question we're sure Lucky asked at the time was, "Where's PETA when you need 'em?"

So the bottom line on this adventure was that Lucky survived, prompting Annie to replicate the feat and also survive. While history exalts Annie Edson Taylor as being the first person to go over Niagara Falls in a barrel, as well as the first to survive, history should always acknowledge that the first living mammal to accomplish the feat was Lucky the cat. She's probably on the list of the most appropriate names in feline history. Lucky, indeed.

 # 9) FELICETTE THE SPACE CAT ~ Channeling *Star Trek*, this feline bravely went where no cat had gone before. On October 18, 1963 Felicette became not only the first, but the only cat to ever be launched into outer space, doing so as part of the French space program in order to assess the effects of space flight on animals. Cue up the Tom Jones hit "What's up, Pussycat?"

Turns out being a space cat in France comes with some perks and some penalties. On the plus side, they erect a statue of you at the International Space Museum in Strasbourg, France. Countering the glee attached with the statue status would be the buzzkill that two months after you get back they will kill you in order to examine your brain. How's that for gratitude?

 # 8) ORANGEY ~ At #8 in our countdown, we have for you the hands-down top cat in terms of real-life appearances on TV shows and movies. That distinction would go to a male tabby cat whose name described his appearance. It would be Orangey, full name Orangey Minerva, who was a protégé of the famous animal trainer Frank Inn.

Orangey lived from 1950-1967 and his career spanned virtually his entire life; here's his story. He wins his first animal Oscar Award for his title role in the 1951 film *Rhubarb*. For the record, the animal Oscar, which is no longer awarded, was officially called the PATSY Award standing for Picture Animal Top Star of the Year.

Orangey's resumé lists literally dozens of movies and TV appearances so we're going to focus on just the most well-known ones to convey the ubiquitous range of this cat. Orangey's movie credits also include *The Incredible Shrinking Man* (1957), *The Diary of Anne Frank* (1959), and the one for which Orangey wins his second animal Oscar, his most famous movie role, playing Audrey Hepburn's pet cat in *Breakfast at Tiffany's* (1961).

TV credits include *The Beverly Hillbillies*, *Mission Impossible*, *My Favorite Martian*, *Shirley Temple Storybook*, *Alfred Hitchcock Presents*, *The Dick Van Dyke Show* and *Batman*. The *Dick Van Dyke* gig stands out as Orangey has a recurring role as Mr. Henderson, the pet cat of Sally Rogers (played by Rose Marie). Sally is single in the show and hence has the time to develop a deep relationship with her cat. Recurring storylines joke about Sally and the cat's dating lives. Sample gag... While the cat's sitting on Sally's lap on the couch, he meows a request to be let out. Saying, "You too, huh?" she carries him to the door, opens it and as the cat slides out Sally entices him with the request, "Come back for breakfast, I've got lox."

Orangey saves the ultimate cat role for his grand finale. What is his last act? He stars in back-to-back *Batman* episodes during the 1967 season where his leading lady is none other than Eartha Kitt as Catwoman!

 # 7) FELIX THE CAT ~ Created in 1919 by studio owner Pat Sullivan and animator Otto Messmer, Felix the Cat would go on to achieve some lofty accolades early in his career. During the 1920's he emerged as the most popular cartoon character of the silent era, and the first cartoon character to become famous in his own right. The black cat with the huge white eyes and giant grin was featured in an array of merchandise including toys, games and figurines. He also scored his own comic strip.

But when Disney featured Mickey Mouse in the first sound cartoon, 1928's "Steamboat Willie", the typical animal scenario was reversed and the mouse would eat the cat. While the innovational force, creative Messmer, urged a transition to sound, the financial force, cheapskate Sullivan, resisted change until it was too late, driving the studio into bankruptcy and Felix into hibernation by 1932.

After taking a couple decades off, Felix was resurrected for television in 1953 by Joe Oriolo. Redesigned with a longer sleeker look, Felix returned with one significant new gimmick. In most every episode Felix was able to avail himself of the "Magic Bag of Tricks" which he now had at his beck and call. On *TV Guide*'s "50 Greatest Cartoon Characters of All Time", Felix reached a respectable ranking of #28 and Animal Planet ranks him as #46 on its list of "50 Greatest TV Animals".

 # 6) TOM, from *Tom & Jerry* ~ Half of the most famous cat and mouse team in animation history, much of Tom's background story was shared in Jerry's component in the Mice chapter. We did, however, save a few notable nuances to generate Tom's component here with the Cats.

While usually serving as venomously violent adversaries, there were a handful of episodes where you could feel the love. Creators Bill Hanna and Joe Barbera sometimes used the phrase "the best of enemies" to describe the relationship between Tom & Jerry. There were a few episodes where each saved the other's life, and there were also a few where they collaborated on joint efforts, for example to save a child who had wandered away from home. Check out the YouTube video "Tom & Jerry / Top 10 Best Friends Moments".

But what about that violence which pervaded the majority of their episodes? While Tom could take things to the extreme, with weapons including axes, explosives, firearms, poison, and traps, Jerry's reciprocations often upped the ante. Tom's various plights included having body parts closed into a hot waffle iron, having his entire body sliced in half, being turned into feline fireworks, electrocution, and decapitation. All in a day's work!

That being said, Tom never missed his cue for the next scene. As the great ones know, the show must go on.

 # 5) THE CAT IN THE HAT, from Dr. Seuss ~ It all started with the dire forecast that "The sun did not shine; it was too wet to play. So we sat in the house, all that cold, cold, wet day." If you need a quick plot refresher, here's our long-story-short.

On one rainy day, the Cat shows up at the house of a brother and sister while Mom is not at home. Assisted by his cohorts, Thing One and Thing Two, the kids and their fish watch with an initial amusement that evolves into shock and awe as the Cat and his accomplices totally trash the house. The brother's assessment of the situation is that "This mess is so big and so deep and so tall, we cannot pick it up. There is no way at all!"

Then, when all seems lost with Mom's return imminent, the Cat produces a magical method to whip everything back into shape just in time.

 # 4) SYLVESTER, from *Looney Tunes* ~ Making his debut in 1945, Sylvester would go on to star in 103 cartoons during the Golden Age of Animation. In terms of prolific performances, that places him at #4 on the *Looney Tunes* list, behind only Bugs Bunny, Daffy Duck and Porky Pig. Sylvester appeared as a black & white tuxedo cat who spoke with a lisp.

His most frequent co-star was the yellow canary Tweety, with the most common plot line being Sylvester's never-ending, yet always futile, efforts to capture and eat the bird. Tweety was occasionally aided and abetted by his sometimes-owner Granny who was known to wield one mean rolling pin. Sylvester also sometimes sparred with Speedy Gonzales, the Mexican mouse who always lived up to his first name.

Another alternate storyline involved the pairing of Sylvester with his son, Sylvester Jr., with the father cast in the role of teaching his son how to catch mice. These lessons never ended well because the "mouse" joining the cast for these episodes was Hippity Hopper, who was actually a baby kangaroo that Sylvester would misidentify as a giant mouse.

None of the *Looney Tunes* characters ever took home more Academy Awards than Sylvester with the feline fetching the Oscar on three occasions, namely "Tweetie Pie" (1947), "Speedy Gonzales" (1955), and finally "Birds Anonymous" (1957). Well done, Sylvester!

 # 3) CHESHIRE CAT, from Disney's *Alice in Wonderland* ~ There is that iconically engaging grin which mischievously stretches from ear-to-ear on this pink and purple feline who appears, and disappears, throughout the classic 1952 Disney film. So how 'bout we break out that big smile and acknowledge that in a Wonderland filled with crazed characters, the Cheshire Cat is perhaps the most enigmatic.

Adorned with that perma-smile, and floating in and out of the film as some tempestuous type of pseudo guide for Alice, he is at times endearing, and at times infuriating. At one moment the Cheshire Cat is providing kind sympathetic advice to Alice and the next he is employing shenanigans which lead to the Queen of Hearts' command of, "Off with her head!"

Much of the appeal of the Cheshire Cat stems from his creative philosophical twisted takes on life with examples being, "I am not crazy; my reality is just different from yours." and "If you don't know where you are going, any road can take you there." When Alice awakens from her Wonderland dream, the Cheshire Cat conundrum is certain to rank at the top of her list of otherworldly phenomena.

 # 2) GARFIELD ~ For a cat who has laziness noted as one of his primary characteristics, Garfield sure does cover a lot of bases. He's in comic strips and on *The New York Times* "Best Sellers" list. He's had his own TV series, multiple TV specials and five movies. Garfield can also be found in board games, video games and toys of all varieties.

All this has been accomplished on a steady diet of lasagna and an established track record of getting nothing done on Mondays, a day which he disdains. The cynically egotistical orange tabby cat made his debut appearance in a June 1978 comic strip.

Jim Davis of Muncie, Indiana is the creator of Garfield, and Muncie serves as the setting for the Garfield franchise storyline. His co-stars are owner Jon Arbuckle and Jon's pet dog Odie. The Garfield comic strip is syndicated in over 2,500 newspapers holding the Guinness World Record in that category. Here are our Fab 5 Garfield quotes...

* Eat every meal as though it were your last.
* When the lasagna content in my blood gets low, I get mean.
* Diet is "die" with a "t."
* If people were meant to pop out of bed, we'd all sleep in toasters.
* Love me, feed me, never leave me.

#1) PUSS IN BOOTS ~ Riding the wave of a crest of fame that stretches from 1550's fairy tales to 2022 movie releases, Puss in Boots has captured the #1 slot in our kitty countdown. Let's rewind this all the way back to the beginning and take you to Italy where Giovanni Francesco Straparola published his collection of fairy tales from 1550–1553 which included the first version of Puss in Boots.

In that first story the cat uses guile and trickery to attain not only wealth and power, he also manages to score a princess's hand in marriage for his low-born and poverty-stricken master. The story gained even more historical traction when French fairy tale writer Charles Perrault published his version in his 1697 anthology.

Of course, in the modern day, Puss in Boots has been skyrocketed into the spotlight by DreamWorks' *Shrek* movie franchise. Inspired by swashbucklers like Zorro and Indiana Jones, Puss in Boots made his movie debut in 2004's *Shrek 2* where he becomes an able-bodied assistant to the title character. Voiced by Antonio Banderas, Puss in Boots also appears in *Shrek the Third* (2007) and *Shrek Forever After* (2010).

At that point DreamWorks had become so enamored with the character that they began spinning him off into his own movies. His origins were explored in *Puss in Boots* in 2011 and 2022 saw the release of *Puss in Boots: The Last Wish*. He also crafted a career in television with the Netflix series *The Adventures of Puss in Boots* which ran from 2015–2018.

Closing with some comedy, here is Puss in Boots' modest assessment of his love-making prowess. "Through the years I have been known by many names. Diablo Gato, The Furry Lover, Frisky Two Times and Ginger Hit Man. But to most I am Puss in Boots, outlaw!"

Cat Tale ~ Serving as a segue between these last two components, we will next offer up one of our favorite stand-up comedy routines delivered by animal lover Paula Poundstone. Part of her standard routine is a self-deprecating bit where she acknowledges her stint in alcohol rehab, while connecting the dots between the drinks, the dogs and the cats. About this process, Paula poignantly pontificates…

"I was in a 30-day program… for 180 days. About three weeks before I went into rehab I got really drunk one day and went into a pet store and bought a dog. Which would not have been that big of a deal except for we had nine cats at the time.

Believe me, the cats were hiding the alcohol after that. I believe that's when the tough love began. We now have 10 cats and a big stupid dog, a bearded dragon lizard, a bunny and one ant left from my ant farm.

I am gonna be honest with you people, I've been drunk in that pet store before. and I don't wanna play the victim here, but I believe they knew… and I believe they took advantage. Does anybody else's pet store have a wine section?"

DOGS

Throughout time, dogs have maintained the moniker of man's best friend and most faithful companion so right now, with no bones of contention, it's time for us to issue our doghouse diplomas of distinction. These degrees will be dealt out in various fields of accomplishment ranging from stardom in entertainment, to military service, to contributions in the scientific world.

There's the roster of real-life animals who were trained to flash their skills for, first the silver screen, and then the small screen; we promise a pantheon of popular pet pooches. And moving on to the world of animation, dogs have darn-sure charmed us for decades. We'll take a deep dive, delving into the vaults of Disney where we'll enjoy a taste of that studio's most famous canine stars as well as everybody's favorite spaghetti smooch ever.

Remember that lovable lip-smacking favorite? And we'll find out who was actually behind the wheel of that smoke-filled Mystery Machine van which took us on our psychedelic cruise through the 1970's. A few pages down the road, we'll bring back memories of perhaps the most classic movie of all-time. Who is it that first hears the words, "I've a feeling we're not in Kansas anymore"?

Next we'll share our ten favorite quotes about dogs…

* Dogs' lives are too short. Their only fault, really.
  – author Agnes Sligh Turnbull
* What do dogs do on their day off? Can't just lie around – that's their job.
  – comedian George Carlin
* If you want a friend in Washington, get a dog. – President Harry Truman
* If there are no dogs in heaven, then when I die I want to go where they went. – humorist Will Rogers
* Dogs never bite me. Just humans. – actress Marilyn Monroe
* Happiness is a warm puppy. – cartoonist Charles Schulz
* Don't accept your dog's admiration as conclusive evidence that you are wonderful. – columnist Ann Landers
* Outside of a dog, a book is a man's best friend. Inside of a dog it's too dark to read. – comedian Groucho Marx
* Some of my best leading men have been dogs and horses.
  – actress Elizabeth Taylor
* It's not the size of the dog in the fight, it's the size of the fight in the dog.
  – humorist Mark Twain

Size ~ Next we'll continue with our dog log of superlatives, starting with the largest. According to Guinness World Records the tallest dog ever was a Great Dane named Zeus who passed away in Michigan in 2014. Zeus stood 44 inches tall on all fours and 7'4" on his hind legs. The heaviest dog was an English Mastiff named Zorba who lived in London and weighed 342.8 pounds. On the other end of the spectrum, a chihuahua named Pearl who died in Florida in 2020 stood just 3.59 inches tall and weighed 1.5 pounds.

Life ~ While the life expectancy of dogs varies depending on species, the overall average is about 12 years. The record for longevity goes to a Portuguese pooch named Bobi who died in February 2023 at the age of 31.

Speed ~ The fasted breed of dog is the greyhound and the all-time speed record is held by Australia's Shakey Jakey who topped out at 41.8 mph equating to a 100-YDT of 4.9 seconds. The most successful dog racing career was that of a British greyhound named Ballyregan Bob who won 32 consecutive races, setting speed records at 10 different tracks.

Now unleash yourself for a tour of our virtual doggie dormitory as we begin our countdown of the Top 10 Dogs…

 # 10) MAX, from the Grinch ~ Perhaps no dog in our countdown was dealt a more difficult hand to play than the paradoxical Max from the 1957 Dr. Seuss classic *How the Grinch Stole Christmas*. To make the plotline work, Max must display the expected canine quality of loyalty to his miserable master. How to do that while still managing to maintain a level of likability is the difficult tightrope walking act that Max must master.

In the original 1966 TV special, Max does maintain his loyalty to his owner despite such ignominious humiliations as having a fake reindeer antler strapped around his head. So how does a dog remain loyal to one of the most iconically evil characters in literary history and still manage to come off as a good guy? In the early scenes, Max is compliant with the Grinch's directions as to how the pair will carry out his nefarious plot, but you can tell Max's heart is not really in it.

Max does dutifully follow directions as the Grinch goes about his business of stealing the Who's Christmas. But it is only when the Grinch's heart grows three sizes, upon realizing the true meaning of Christmas, that we see a vitalized and re-energized Max triumphantly leading the sleigh back down the hill before assuming the prized position of sitting next to Cindy Lou Who to enjoy a freshly cut slice of roast beast.

Animal Planet ranks Max as #20 on its list of "50 Greatest TV Animals".

 # 9) 101 DALMATIANS ~ This Disney film features more dogs than any of the studio's other movies and boasts perhaps Disney's most evil villainess. Here's a quick summary... The central characters are the Dalmatian parents, Pongo and Perdita, pets of humans Roger and Anita who are single and looking for love as the story begins. Conveying the calculated sense of caution he is displaying in his romantic pursuit, Roger ominously warns his pet that, "Fools aren't born, Pongo; pretty girls make them in their spare time." As they say, forewarned is forearmed.

Pongo and Perdita facilitate a meeting between Roger and Anita who fall in love and are soon married, with their Dalmatians by their sides. Next there's good news as Perdita gives birth to a litter of 15 puppies, followed by bad news... enter evilly eccentric Cruella de Vil draped in full-flowing fur, trademark cigarette holder in hand. Her fur infatuation is acknowledged with the declaration that, "Oh, yes! I love the smell of near extinction!" she reveals her intention to add a Dalmatian fur coat to her collection.

When Roger and Anita reject her murderously insane offer to buy the puppies, Cruella has them dognapped and the adventure begins. Cross-country escapades ensue which eventually end with the rescue of not only the 15 original puppies, but also 84 more which Cruella had purchased from pet stores. If you're quickly running the math on this one, you'd have to add in the parents to get to your requisite total of 101.

 # 8) TRAKR, the 9-11 German shepherd ~ Ironically emerging as heroes of this American tragedy was Trakr (1994-2009), who was born in the Czech Republic, and his police handler James Symington, who was from Canada. Upon seeing the news of the terrorist attack, Symington grabbed Trakr, left Toronto, and headed to Ground Zero to lend a hand.

While there were over 300 search and rescue dogs whose efforts contributed to the mission, Trakr distinguished himself by being the dog who discovered Genelle Guzman, the final survivor, a woman who had been buried under the rubble for 26 hours. When Trakr detected signs of life, Guzman was still covered by 30 feet of debris.

Trakr was subsequently honored by *Time* magazine as one of its ten most heroic animals of all time. That being said, it should be noted that *Time*'s designation symbolically chose Trakr to recognize all of the dogs that participated in the search and rescue efforts.

Turns out that Trakr's final chapter is a gift that keeps on giving. In 2008, James Symington entered an essay in the BioArts International contest seeking the world's most "clone-worthy dog". Perhaps not surprisingly, Trakr was the chosen one to be the cloned one, and even though Trakr is no longer with us, we are happy to share the news that there are five little Trakrs on the planet who are hopefully being groomed for their own search and rescue missions.

 # 7) LADY AND THE TRAMP ~ This Disney film had a bit of a *Romeo & Juliet* vibe about it with Shakespeare's "star-crossed lovers" from two feuding families being replaced by a romantic couple consisting of Tramp, a straggly street-smart stray mutt as Romeo, and Lady, a pampered and spoiled cocker spaniel as Juliet. Lady is the pet of Jim Dear and Darling, so called because those terms of endearment are the only monikers Lady hears in the couple's conversations around the house.

This 1955 movie had a mostly canine cast which had the humans playing secondary supporting roles. Lady's confidant pals are a Scottish Terrier named Jock and a bloodhound named Trusty, who take an immediate dislike to Tramp because of his scallywag behavior and history of taking advantage of dogs of the feminine persuasion. Tramp's subsistence is seen to be provided by the table scraps he receives from Tony and Joe, the owner and chef from Tony's Italian restaurant.

When Jim Dear and Darling go on vacation, their newborn child and Lady are left under the care of Aunt Sarah who misreads a situation, blames Lady and Tramp for a mishap with the baby, muzzles Lady, and has the dogcatcher take Tramp. A runaway Lady and an escapee Tramp are reunited and begin their adventure together with Tramp promising to show her how to live the good life, "footloose and collar-free".

This segment leads to the movie's most memorable moment when Tony and Joe arrange a romantic candlelight dinner for Lady and Tramp at the Italian restaurant. The spaghetti dinner results in one of the most iconic kisses in all of movie history and we're talking human or animal, live action or animated; it's just one of the all-time best… period.

The whole thing comes neatly gift wrapped with your delightful Disney ending. Lady and Tramp find themselves living comfortably with Jim Dear and

Darling and, best of all, they find themselves the proud parents of a brood of four, three little Ladies and one little Tramp!

 # 6) PAVLOV'S DOGS ~ Let's open up the science book for this entry. The Russian scientist Ivan Pavlov (1849-1936) is famous for his experiments on what he called, "classical conditioning", and while most everyone is familiar with the basic concept, there is one aspect of the storyline that many people have incorrect.

Altogether, Pavlov experimented with 35-40 dogs and, for the record, most of their names are recorded as part of his scientific notes. His favorite was a setter-collie mix he named Druzhok which meant "best friend". Pavlov developed a way to measure the amount his dogs would salivate and his experiments revolved around determining precisely what would prompt the salivation.

When given actual food, of course the dogs would salivate. By having the same technicians feed the dogs, Pavlov was able to determine that once the animals were properly conditioned, they would begin to salivate upon the sight of their technicians entering the room. The next step was to determine if other stimuli could create the same effect as the sight of the technicians.

Here's the part where there seems to be a fairly widespread misconception and right now we'll put you to the test. Pavlov decides to experiment and see if a sound can be substituted as the stimulus to make the dogs salivate, which leads to our question for you... What was the sound used by Pavlov to test this theory? Go ahead and formulate your answer while we share one verse of a song by the band Barenaked Ladies. In their classic tune "Brian Wilson", here is the key verse.

It's a matter of instinct
It's a matter of conditioning
And a matter of fact
You can call me Pavlov's Dog
Ring a bell and I'll salivate
How'd you like that?

So if you remember it the way the Barenaked Ladies and the Smiths remembered it, it was a bell that Pavlov rang to see if the dogs would salivate. Does that match your guess? Well, if it does here's the somewhat surprising truth-be-told tale on this one. Pavlov never used a bell; the noises he used came from a metronome and an organ-like instrument called a harmonium, and of course the dogs did salivate when they connected the sound to receiving food.

 # 5) RIN TIN TIN ~ Our story starts on September 15, 1918 when U.S. Army Corporal Lee Duncan is sent to the French village of Flirey to see if there is a location there which can be used for a landing strip. Recent U.S. bombing had driven the Germans out of the area and also left a sense of uncertainty as to the condition of what was left. Upon his arrival, Corporal Duncan comes across the remains of the German army's kennel facility which had supplied the German shepherd dogs that were used by the German military.

The only living survivors are one starving mother and her five puppies. Duncan brings the animals back to the base, nurses the mother and hence the puppies back to health, and eventually chooses two puppies, one of each gender, to try to sneak back to the U.S. with him after the war. The male he names Rin Tin Tin as that was the name of a good luck charm French children often gave to American soldiers to thank them for their efforts in liberating France from the Germans. In July of 1919 he gets both puppies back to New York, but the female dies before Duncan can make the trip back to his home in California.

Upon returning to Los Angeles, Duncan undertakes an extensive training program with his puppy and begins looking for opportunities to get Rin Tin Tin into silent films. To that end, Rin Tin Tin appears in a dog show where his 12-foot leaping ability catches the eye of an executive from the Warner Bros. studio. Rin Tin Tin subsequently makes his film debut in the 1922 film *The Man from Hell's River* and the dog show is up and running. Between 1922 and 1931 Rin Tin Tin appears in 27 films.

When Rin Tin Tin died in 1932, Lee Duncan took the unusually gracious effort to pay for his dog's body to be returned to his birth country of France and buried in an animal cemetery in Paris. But if you think the legacy of Rin Tin Tin would die with his death, you would definitely be barking up the wrong tree with that theory. Duncan had already bred a healthy pack of Rin Tin Tin descendants who would perpetuate the movie career before going on to star in one of the biggest TV series of the 1950's.

Believe it or not, the franchise is still on the road today doing promotional appearances and, for the record, if you happen to run into him today, you would be looking at Rin Tin Tin XII. Animal Planet ranks Rin Tin Tin as #14 on its list of "50 Greatest TV Animals".

 # 4) SNOOPY, from *Peanuts* ~ From his debut on October 4, 1950, in the third *Peanuts* comic strip created by Charles Schulz, right through the modern day, Charlie Brown's beagle Snoopy has certainly ascended to the status of being one of the most famous fictional dogs in history. One of the more memorable motifs Schulz used with his character was to have Snoopy imagine himself in another role, that of being a WW I fighter pilot. We'll get back to that one shortly.

While he did occasionally make some dog noises, one thing that serves to differentiate Snoopy from most other cartoon dogs is that he never spoke. The manner by which his thoughts were articulated was through the use of thought bubbles. Schulz first employed this technique on March 16, 1952. Some other Snoopy milestones would be his first appearance standing upright (January 9, 1956), first depiction of his iconic sleeping on top of his dog house rather than inside it (December 12, 1958), and first adoption of the WW I fighter pilot persona (October 10, 1965).

In the mid-1960's, Snoopy found himself as the star of a string of hit songs. This began in 1966 when a group called the Royal Guardsmen began playing upon the premise that Charles Schulz had been incorporating a Snoopy-as-a-WW I-fighter-pilot theme into his comic strips. Their #2 tune "Snoopy vs. the Red Baron" was the first of four hit Snoopy songs.

How about we summarize some Snoopy numerology for you... Charles Schulz published a total of 17,897 *Peanuts* comic strips in his lifetime. There were also 2 TV series, 46 TV specials, and 7 movies. *TV Guide*'s ranking of "Greatest Cartoon Characters" has Snoopy at #8 and in Animal Planet's list of the "50 Greatest TV Animals", Snoopy is ranked #6. Keep in mind the above rankings include **all** cartoon animals, not just dogs.

#3) LASSIE ~ In honor of this #3 rating, how 'bout we lead with a trilogy of Lassie fun facts.

* In the collie's first movie *Lassie Come Home* the dog was paid twice as much as co-star Elizabeth Taylor.
* *Variety* magazine named Lassie as one of their "100 Icons of the Century", the only animal to make the list.
* Descendants of the original Lassie, all male by the way, have continued to play the part ever since. That being said, due to the fact that the storyline casts the character as a female, we will use the pronoun "her" throughout this component.

So now let's go back and take a look at the storyline that traces the path of our iconic collie over the past nine decades right through to the Lassie of today. Modern-day Lassie was essentially born with a 1938 *Saturday Evening Post* short story written by Eric Knight.

In that story, when financial desperation forces Lassie's family to sell her, the devoted dog, driven by her loyalty, undertakes the long and dangerous journey to find her way back to her family. The Knight story was adapted to make the first movie in 1943, hence that title of *Lassie Come Home*, which was the first of 20 Lassie movies.

Success on the big screen was followed by TV stardom which saw Lassie last for a 19-year run on CBS from 1954-1973. The trophy case in Lassie's doghouse is filled with 9 animal Emmys from the TV show and 2 animal Oscars from her movies. There's also a star on the Hollywood Walk of Fame, she was the original inductee into the Hall of Fame of the American Humane Association, and Animal Planet lauds Lassie as #1 on its list of "50 Greatest TV Animals".

#2) SCOOBY-DOO ~ First cruising into the hearts of middle-America in the Mystery Machine van in 1969, Scooby-Doo has maintained a ubiquitous media presence ever since. The number of films and TV series in which the character has appeared is mindboggling and we'll get to that in a moment, but how 'bout we lead with a series overview.

The primary cast consists of five crime-solving "meddling kids" who are employed by Murder Inc. and are constantly thrust into mysterious scenarios where it becomes their mission to solve the mystery and save the day. Of these main characters, the Great Dane Scooby-Doo is the only non-human. He is joined by the group's leader Fred (tall, handsome blonde dude); Daphne (adept sexy redhead); Velma (intelligent brunette w/glasses); and Shaggy (scruffy, long-haired surfer dude).

Scooby-Doo is anthropomorphic, walking upright, talking and carrying on human conversations. Scooby and his master Shaggy are often the most afraid of the five, perhaps showing the good judgment to be so in light of the dangerous circumstances in which they often found themselves. But despite the danger, the crew always got to the bottom of things by the end of the episode.

Before we return to some Scooby stats to validate that "ubiquitous" claim we issued in our first paragraph above, the legend of Scooby cannot be complete without the sharing of how the Hanna-Barbera studio seemed to have slipped one by the censors in the early years of the series. In the late 1960's Hanna-Barbera had come under criticism from parent groups because their cartoons were too violent… lots of sci-fi superhero fisticuffs and fighting.

So *Scooby-Doo* actually launched in 1969 as one of the replacement shows for the violent material. In retrospect, however, it seemed to be out with the violence but in with the drugs. The topical intrigue of this storyline is that, knowing what they were up against, Hanna-Barbera apparently used a very calculated approach to introduce a superbly subtle storyline whereby they could slip the smoky references past the parents and the censors. That being said, here is our long-story-short on how Scooby-Doo essentially could have translated into Scooby-Doobie-Doo.

Keep in mind the year was 1969… it was the year of Woodstock and the height of the hippie revolution which brought marijuana into mainstream America for the first time. Summoning that high-hippie vibe, the Mystery Machine van was painted in swirling psychedelic colors. There was always an abundance of billowing smoke when the van pulled out of any given scene and the source of the smoke was always left intentionally vague. Was it coming from the tailpipe or out of the window?

In terms of his appearance and speech, Shaggy certainly exuded the vibe of a pot-smoking stoner. The long disheveled hair, permanent trace of beard stubble, and rambling speech pattern all contributed to that vibe. Furthermore, Shaggy and Scooby spent significant portions of every episode in search of food, usually junk food. The obvious implication to go along with the rest of the clues was they had the "munchies" because they were high.

It's interesting to look at the modern-day websites and chat rooms where the consensus is, "How could they not have known?" and "How could they have missed this?"

As we go-to-fade with our list of Scooby-Doo accolades, check out the numerology on his media resumé. Over the years he had 13 different TV series, 12 TV specials and 46 movies. *TV Guide*'s ranking of "Greatest Cartoon Shows" has *Scooby-Doo* at #5, and "Greatest Cartoon Characters" has Scooby at #22. In Animal Planet's list of the "50 Greatest TV Animals" Scooby is ranked #13.

 # 1) TOTO, from *The Wizard of Oz* ~ When Dorothy says, "Toto, I've a feeling we're not in Kansas anymore," it confirms our entry into one of the greatest fantasy scenes in film history. The spot where *The Wizard of Oz* switches to Technicolor as Dorothy and Toto enter the land of Oz remains spectacularly spellbinding to this very day. In addition to serving as Dorothy's canine companion throughout the movie, there's one aspect of the film which cannot be overlooked. The entire storyline is predicated upon the fact that it is Dorothy's devotion to Toto that sets all the wheels into motion. That's an absolute truth.

Another fact that helps Toto rise to this transcendent level would be that Toto achieved all of his fame being played by just one dog. That's a lot of bang for your bark! While there were six Lassies and twelve Rin Tin Tins, there was only one Toto. And here's her backstory…

Toto (1933-1945) was a Cairn terrier, who was originally named Terry, and actually compiled quite an impressive film career resumé. Beginning in 1934, she appeared in 23 movies, (her first big break occurring with Shirley Temple in *Bright Eyes*), but obviously none rivaled the impact of her role in *The Wizard of Oz* which occurred when she was 6 years old in 1939. The success of *Oz* prompted her owner to officially change her name to Toto.

Speaking of her owner, Toto was not born with a silver bone in her mouth… she was abandoned as a puppy. Things, however, began barking up the right tree for her when she was adopted by Carl Spitz, the owner of the Hollywood Dog Training School. Spitz was credited with developing the training method of having his animals respond to hand signals rather than vocal commands. This was necessitated by the transition from silent films to sound because vocal signals would be picked up by the microphones recording the actors.

Upon landing the *Wizard of Oz* gig, Spitz pegged Terry/Toto for the part and began working on the behavioral nuances needed for the role. The casting was obviously a perfect fit and knowing how integral Toto's part was to the success of the film, the studio actually paid her $125 a week which was more than most of the human actors received. Adjusting for inflation, that would be $2,773.53 in today's dollars. That's a lot of doggie treats!

From the moment Toto's biting of Almira Gulch leads to the demand that she be euthanized, till the moment Toto pulls back the curtain exposing the fraud of the Wizard, she is a scene stealer. Judy Garland actually became so attached to the dog during the making of the film that she tried to buy Toto from Carl Spitz, but the animal trainer was not interested in selling.

One Toto fun fact was that she actually attended the debut of the film when it occurred at Grauman's Chinese Theatre on August 25, 1939.

We'll finish by recapping a few highlights from earlier in the book as we share our final poem...

The ark trip, Noah said, was a go-go
Smokey Bear said the fires were a no-no
But with dogs of renown
Number one must be found
Nowhere else, but in Kansas, with Toto

ADDENDUM #1
UNITED STATES ZOOS & AQUARIUMS

These are the responses from around the country to our three questions asking for your 1) Most Unique Animal, 2) Oldest Animal, 3) Cleverest Named Animal.

ALABAMA – Alabama Gulf Coast Zoo (Gulf Shores, AL)
Thank you for reaching out to us [literally on the Gulf of Mexico] with this opportunity. Below are our answers to your questions.
More unique animals: We have two Brazilian three-banded armadillos, Arti and Lucille Ball "Lucy". This armadillo species can roll themselves completely into a ball and are great animal ambassadors for the zoo.
Older animals: Our oldest animal is Chucky, an American alligator; he is over 40 years old and is the oldest resident of the zoo having lived here for over 30 years.
Animals at your zoo with a clever name: We have several… Bruce Quillis, the African crested porcupine; Kevin Bacon & Piggy Smalls, our miniature pigs; Quill Nye, the Prehensile-tailed porcupine. [kudos to GCZ for their celebrity puns]

ALASKA – Alaska Zoo (Anchorage, AK)
Unusual: The Alaska zoo started with a female Asian elephant that was won in a contest, but she passed away years ago and her companion, a female African elephant, we sent to a California sanctuary to join companions in a better climate.
Older: We have had a number of unusually old animals like "Jake" the Kodiak brown bear that lived to 39 and "Tiska" the bald eagle that lived to 45 but they are sadly no longer with us.
Name: P.W. is an orphaned black bear cub that came to us a couple of years ago. He was found swimming between the Southeast Alaska mainland and Prince William Island, mother nowhere in sight. A charter boat spotted him, he was out of energy and going down, they pulled him aboard and gave him CPR. He was given the name Prince William (PW for short). Alive and well, living here at the Alaska Zoo with his buddy Zayk an adult male black bear.

ARIZONA–Wildlife World Zoo, Aquarium & Safari Park (Litchfield Park, AZ)
Unique animal: Stabitha the black-tailed hairy dwarf porcupine.
Very few of these are found in zoos in the United States.
Older animal: Maggie the Andean condor, she is over 60 years old.
Clever name: Our striped skunk named Buffy the Vampire Sprayer.

ARKANSAS – Arkansas Alligator Farm and Petting Zoo (Hot Springs, AK)
Unique animal: Mandarin duck - a colorful duck species that comes from Asia.
Oldest animal: Alligator snapping turtle, over 50 years old.
Clever name: Male and female vervet monkeys, Bill and Hillary. Named after Arkansas natives, former President Bill Clinton and First Lady Hillary Clinton. Looking forward to seeing the finished product!

CALIFORNIA – Oakland Zoo (Oakland, CA)
Unique animals: Union Island dwarf gecko, black beauty walking sticks,

Malayan flying fox bats.
Older animals: We have two Aldabra tortoises that are over 100 years old.
Clever name: Alvin, Simon and Theodore are our guira cuckoos.

COLORADO – Denver Zoo (Denver, CO)
More unique animal: The Lake Titicaca frog.
Older animal: Groucho, the Asian elephant who is 53 years old!
Animal with a clever name: We have a pair of Asian small-clawed otter brothers named Rocket and Slinky for the way they look when they move in water, and we have a pair of capybaras named for Ted Lasso's Roy and Rebecca. We also have two red-flanked duikers [antelopes] named Chicken and Biscuit ☺.
Looking forward to seeing this book!

CONNECTICUT – Riverside Reptiles Educational Center (Enfield, CT)
More unique animals: Red spitting cobra, horrid king assassin bug, purple "Zombie" land crab, giant Hungarian "Dracula" leech, European legless lizard, Mbu pufferfish, electric catfish.
Older animals: We're a young zoo so we don't have any really old animals but we have a few that are getting up there. Ben (alligator snapping turtle 45), Legolas (European legless lizard – 40), Tank (African spurred tortoise 40), Brenda the American alligator - 38 years old, Pretty Boy the Gila monster - 30 years old
Clever names: Legolas (European legless lizard), Eel-lon Musk (electric eel), Spitty (red spitting cobra), Wyatt Earp (western diamondback rattlesnake), Art Garfunkel (alligator gar [fish]), [Ben] Franklin (electric catfish)

DELAWARE – 3 Palms Zoo (Townsend, DE)
Thanks for reaching out! We're excited to be a part of your book and can't wait to see the final result!
Unique animal is our Indian blue peacock (*Pavo cristatus*) named Elton John.
Oldest animal is Otis, the African Sulcata tortoise (*Centrochelys sulcata*), in his 50's
Animal at our zoo with a **clever name**: Little Jerry Seinfeld, the domestic chicken (*Gallus gallus domesticus*). The story behind Little Jerry Seinfeld's name is actually pretty funny. Just like in the sitcom, he came to us from a home that bought sexed pullets as laying hens, just like Kramer did in that hilarious episode. He is also the same breed of chicken as in the episode; they could have been twins! While our Little Jerry Seinfeld won't be entering any rooster fights, we found the similarity in the stories quite amusing, and that's how he got his name! Also [from *The Addams Family*] – Morticia and Lurch, the black vultures (*Coragyps atratus*); and Dominick, the Donkey (*Equus africanus asinus*).

FLORIDA – Zoo Miami (Miami, FL)
Most unique animal is our giant eland [an open-forest and savanna antelope].
Oldest animal is "Goliath", Galápagos tortoise estimated to be 105 years old.
Animals with clever names: Sea turtles named after cheeses – "Gouda" and "Swiss", as well as our two giant horned lizards, "Kevin Hart" and "The Rock".
Looking forward to seeing the book when it is published!

GEORGIA – Zoo Atlanta (Atlanta, GA)
Hello! We are happy to participate. Thanks for thinking of us. Thanks, -- Rachel
More unique animals: Naked mole rats – It's hard to beat a eusocial mammal species for uniqueness! [Eusocial means one female mates with several males.]
Older animals: Our Aldabra tortoises, Shuffles and Patches. Their actual hatch dates are not known, but we believe them to be in their 70's to 80's.
Animal at your zoo with a clever name: There are a few; take your pick. We have tawny frogmouths named Tater Tot and Hashbrown; a Chilean rose tarantula named Sparklemuffin; and a Hoffmann's two-toed sloth named Nutella.

HAWAII – Honolulu Zoo (Honolulu, HI)
Unique animals: Kamehameha butterfly, called pulelehua in Hawaiian and the Hawaiian land snail, scientific name *Amastra cylindrical* – each a native species of butterfly and snail found only in Hawaii, bred here for release back into the wild.
Older animals: Jaws, Charlotte and Kim, Galápagos tortoises – arrived in Honolulu in 1928 with the Charles Darwin expedition. They are over 100 years old. In 1954, the Honolulu Zoo was the first zoo to ever hatch this species!
Animal at your zoo with a clever name: Bounce, the ball python. A BIG mahalo for supporting and recognizing the conservation efforts of zoos! Aloha.

IDAHO – Zoo Boise (Boise, ID)
More unique animals: Our Gorongosa girdled lizards, named Peter Pan and Tinker Bell are endemic to Mozambique where we are affiliated with Gorongosa National Park. We have sand cats, Simba and Nala, which are a species of wild cats living in the Sahara Desert, house-cat-sized that can and will eat venomous snakes!
Older animals: Our Aldabra giant tortoise Mr. Mack was born between 1910 and 1920, so he's over 100 years old.
Animal at your zoo with a clever name: The donors of our new lions wanted them to have *Star Wars* names and chose the lesser known, more modern *Star Wars* names of Revan and Ahsoka.

INDIANA – Indianapolis Zoo (Indianapolis, IN)
Unique animals: Our southern giant pouched rats: Lawino, Winona and Bindi. In African and Southeast Asian countries, these rats are trained to detect the smell of TNT & land mines. Several of them have been hailed as heroes for this.
Older animals: Orangutan Azy, he is turning 46 years old this December. (Fun fact: He's also the oldest male orangutan in the U.S.)
Two Elephants: Tombi & Kubwa who both turned 47 in 2023.
Clever name: male red kangaroos: Billroo, Brootis, Roofus, Androo & Eddieroo.

IOWA – National Mississippi River Museum & Aquarium (Dubuque, IA)
More unique animals: The greater siren, an eel-like amphibian.
Older animals: American alligator, Mama – she turned 50 in July 2023 and was one of the River Museum's first residents when we officially became the National Mississippi River Museum & Aquarium in June 2023!
Clever name: Our North American river otters are named Tom Sawyer and Becky Thatcher! Tom & Becky are two of our most beloved visitor-favorites. 😊

KANSAS – Manhattan Sunset Zoo (Manhattan, KS)
More unique animals: We have an albino wallaby born in January of 2021 named Bruny. Bruny being all white is easy to spot out of the rest, but also needs more shaded areas. Albino wallabies hail from the island of Bruny in Tasmania.
Older animals: Susie, Sunset Zoo's oldest female chimpanzee celebrated her 69th birthday in 2023. Susie is the oldest living chimpanzee in human care in the U.S. She has been with Sunset Zoo since 1974 and has had three successful births. One at the age of 52! Susie gets along well with the troop and enjoys climbing & playing outdoors. She's exceeded the lifespan of chimps in the wild.
Clever name: We have peccaries [pig-like mammals], named Acorn, Squash, and Pumpkin. They are all related and have a wonderful home at Sunset Zoo.

KENTUCKY – Louisville Zoo (Louisville, KY)
Hey there! Here are a few ideas we had. As for our **oldest resident** we had one famous resident until last year. Helen, the Western Lowland gorilla, was the oldest known gorilla in North America and the second oldest in the world. Sadly, she passed away in October of 2022 at age 64. Would it be possible to talk about her posthumously? If not, Dot our Aldabra tortoise is 87 years old (born 6.15.36).
More unique animals: Louie, a rare white alligator; Qannik, wild-born rescued bear. We made a world discovery and headlines with the reticulate python parthenogenesis, [an asexual reproduction without fertilizing egg with sperm].
Animals at your zoo with clever names: Maverick the goose (*Top Gun*), Ariel, Aurora, Jasmine, Mulan (Disney princess black swans), Gibbs the zebra (*CSI*).

LOUISIANA – Audubon Zoo (New Orleans, LA)
Thank you so much for including Audubon Zoo in your upcoming project!
Unique Animals: Audubon Zoo's orangutan congress is a real family affair. Three generations of orangutans live in our Zoo including grandmother Feliz (age 34) her daughter, Menari (age 14) and Menari's little one, Roux (pronounced ROO, born Christmas Eve 2021). Roux, **cleverly named**, is a thickening base used to make gumbo, also the same reddish-brown color of an orangutan's fur.
Oldest animal: "Feldspar" a male Aldabra Tortoise is 99 years old!

LOUISIANA – BREC's Baton Rouge Zoo (Baton Rouge, LA)
Our **oldest animals** are 41-year-old Cassowaries, named Hondo and Grodi.
Our **most unique** animals are our pygmy hippopotamuses, Spencer and Ginger. There are about 20 in the zoos in the United States.
Unique name: a Lesser Madagascar tenrec [hedgehog], Tawanda Lu Prickles.
Thanks for reaching out to us! We look forward to seeing the book.

MAINE – York's Wild Kingdom (York, ME)
One of our more **unique animals** is a southern cassowary. This large bird looks a lot like a dinosaur, probably because they are descendants of them, hence the **clever name**, Raptor. Our bangled tiger, Moxy, joined us 6.23 at 10 months old. The **oldest animals** we have are our gibbons over 50 years old. Our female Gibbon is named Almondine, and the male Gibbon is named Jethro.

MARYLAND – Salisbury Zoo (Salisbury, MD)
Most Unique Animal: We have begun the process of building a new state of the art Andean Bear breeding facility. We are also acting partners in the red wolf and ocelot repopulating program. The Andean bear, or spectacled bear, is the only bear native to South America. It is a clever, arboreal animal that builds platforms and nests in trees for eating and sleeping.
Oldest Animals: We currently have several ducks that are over 20+ years old and a flamingo that was 53 years old.
Names: Bayou-Sloth, Nigel-Night Heron, Pinocchio, Inti, Raymi,-Andean Bears, Anahi-Ocelot.

MASSACHUSETTS – Southwick's Zoo (Mendon, MS)
Unique animal: It is our white rhino attraction that sets us apart from other zoos in New England. We offer a rhino encounter where visitors can interact with, and actually touch and pet them. This concept has generated over $100,000 for Project Rhino in South Africa.
Oldest animal: We had a chimp named Jingles who died at 53 in 2023.
Clever names: We had white rhinos named Bonnie & Clyde who lived to be 42 and 43 respectively. Our current resident rhinos are Thelma & Louise. They have been instrumental ambassadors to bring awareness to the rhinos' plight in the wild. We love our inclusiveness of entertainment with education. We bring them in thinking they're going to be entertained and then, while they're not looking, we educate them! Just like you do with your writing!

MICHIGAN – Detroit Zoo (Detroit, MI)
Thank you for thinking of the Detroit Zoo! Below are answers to your questions.
Unique animals: One of the more unique species to call the Detroit Zoo home is the Japanese giant salamander.
Older animals: Trixi the chimpanzee is one of the oldest animals who calls the Detroit Zoo home. While we don't know her exact birth date, she is estimated to be 53 years old.
Animals with clever names: There are so many! Please take your pick. A giraffe calf named Juhudi, which means hard work, effort and enthusiasm in Swahili, honors the dedication and effort of our staff to give this calf a proper start to life. Warren, a ring-tailed lemur, is named for the Michigan city from which he was rescued. Fitzroy and Stanley are two penguin chicks named after locations in the Falklands - this honors the conservation work our team engages in to protect wild penguins and sea birds in the Falkland Islands. There is also a trio of rescued bald eagles named after comic book heroes - Flash, Mr. America and Captain Marvel.

MINNESOTA – Como Park Zoo (Saint Paul, MN)
Unique: Eddie the Lungfish (lives in the giraffe barn) as a unique animal! He has 2 lungs and breathes air to survive. He can go about 3 years without eating anything.
Oldest: Neil (28) is the oldest male polar bear in North America, Nan (29) is tied for the oldest female polar bear; that's unique in my opinion, to have the 2 golden oldies at the same zoo. Schroeder the gorilla is 38 & Markisa the orangutan is 37.

Clever name: I vote "Sargent Skeeter Spaulding CPA" personally. He is one of our giraffes, and goes by "Skeeter". It's a bit of a convoluted story. Years ago we had a trivia contest at a full staff meeting where the winning team would get to choose his name. A table with some pretty creative people won and came up with it. Sargent was because he needed a title, Spaulding was a nod to *Castaway* (but it was Wilson in the movie), Skeeter was from the Muppets and CPA just because it sounded extra important. We call him Skeeter for short. We have since stopped these sorts of contests. HAHA! *Authors note: One of our favorite stories.*

MISSISSIPPI – Tupelo Buffalo Park & Zoo (Tupelo, MS)

Unique animal: We have three Linnaeus's two-toed sloths; the parents are named Molasses and Slorena, and their baby we call Mocha.
Oldest animal: Our most senior citizen is 31-year-old capuchin monkey Oliver.
Unique name: Our feisty female Burmese pythons are named Lucy Ricardo and Missy. We demonized Disney, going with Jafar as the name of our reticulated giraffe. We started as a 22-acre drive-thru safari with 52 buffaloes and later added the zoo.

MISSOURI – Kansas City Zoo & Aquarium (Kansas City, MO)

Unique animals: The scimitar-horned oryx, these majestic antelopes are extinct in the wild due to hunting and are truly a testament to the importance of conservation. The Wyoming toad, which in 1994 were virtually extinct in the wild. Thanks to AZA breeding efforts, Wyoming toads are being reintroduced back into the wild!
Oldest animals: Our Aldabra giant tortoises are oldest, Ray is 70 and Chip is 68.
Animals with a clever name: There are currently three chinstrap penguins at the KCZoo, all named after types of hats: Cowboy, Bonnet and Fez. The Burmese Python at the KCZoo is Louise, which is always a fun rhyme: Louise the Burmese!

MONTANA – Zoo Montana (Billings, MT)

Thank you for reaching out, what a fun premise! Here is the info requested:
More unique animals: Wolverines – We were fortunate to be one of only three zoos within North America to have kits this year. [kits would be baby wolverines]
Older animals: Currently, our oldest animal is Emelio the Bald Eagle at 33 years. Interestingly, we did just say goodbye to one of our Red Panda's named Taylor, who was the oldest living Red Panda in the world at 22, according to Guinness.
Clever Name: We have a few! A lynx named Optimus Prime, a king snake named Taco, a chicken named Colonel Sanders and a walking stick named Princess Pink Armpits (thanks to her pink underarms). You can pick the one you like most! Looking forward to seeing the end result!

NEBRASKA – Riverside Discovery Center (Scottsbluff, NE)

Unique animal: We'll go with our Yellow Niger Uromastyx lizard named Spike.
Oldest: That would be our black-handed spider monkey Scootie, 38 years old.
Name: Zaida, the zebra, named after exec. director Desiree's great grandmother.

NEVADA – Animal Ark Wildlife Sanctuary

Unique animal: Here at the Animal Ark we are choosing Santo the jaguar.
Oldest animal: Mr. Peabody the desert tortoise. His estimated hatch year is 1956.

Clever names: Mochi the green iguana and Mr. Peabody the desert tortoise.

NEW HAMPSHIRE – Squam Lakes Natural Science Center (Holderness, NH)
Unique animals: Ours are all native species, nothing exotic like tigers, elephants, or macaws. How about porcupines – do 30,000 quills on their body sound unique?
Older animals: The animals at the Science Center tend to live longer lives due to regular feeding, veterinary care, and lack of predation. We had a brother/sister pair of mountain lions who came to the Science Center in early 2003. The exhibit here at the Science Center was built specifically for them. The female passed away at 19 years old and her brother passed away at 20 years old. In the wild a mountain lion typically lives about 8 to 11 years. We had two new mountain lion cubs join us early in 2023 and hopefully they will live as long and healthy lives as their predecessors.
Clever name: Not here! The animals at Squam are named for their species and the year they arrived. For example, "Red Fox 14". Not very clever but it helps us identify them. The live animals here serve as valuable teaching tools to educate our audiences about each species' role in its environment. To reduce focus on the individual animal and the inherent risk of making wild animals appear as "pets," the Science Center does not use "pet" names for exhibit or program animals.

NEW JERSEY – Turtle Back Zoo (West Orange, NJ)
Most unique animals: Pygmy slow loris (*Xanthonycticebus pygmaeus*) is an animal [primate] many may not know we have at the zoo. They are nocturnal and secretive, but are one of the most threatened animals due to illegal wildlife trafficking. We work with the Species Survival Program for this species to ensure a sustainable zoo population and teach our guests about the conservation efforts for saving this species in their native habitat throughout Southeast Asia.
Oldest animals: Our Aldabra tortoise (*Aldabrachelys gigantea*), Andy is about 65 years old, born in 1959. He can be seen with his friends Patches (50 years old) and Delilah (22 years old) in their new habitat, Island Giants that opened in fall 2023.
Unique name: One of our cownose rays (*Rhinoptera bonasus*) born here at the zoo is named Sugar (Ray). We do monitor most of our animals individually, so many that you may not expect to be named or respond to their names actually do!

NEW MEXICO – ABQ BioPark (Albuquerque, NM)
Here you go, from the ABQ BioPark!
Unique animal: Tasmanian wombat (We're the only zoo in U.S. housing these).
Oldest: Aldabra tortoise. We don't really know how old, but over 100 years.
Any animal at our zoo with a clever name: McLovin' the red kangaroo, and our three cheetah "beans", Garbanzo, Pinto & Borracho.

NEW YORK – Buffalo Zoo (Buffalo, NY)
One of our more **unique animals** is our tufted deer. The unique feature of this animal is definitely the two fang-like canines that males have. They look like mini-vampire deer.
Timmy the box turtle is our **oldest animal** here at the Zoo! He was born in 1973 and is 51 years old!
Most **clever name** for one of our animals is Dr. Strangepork our Fly River Turtle.

NEW YORK – Rosamond Gifford Zoo (Syracuse, NY)

Most unique animals ~ The most unique animals at the Rosamond Gifford Zoo are the miracle Asian Elephant twins Yaad and Tukada. The little calves made history as the first recorded instance of surviving elephant twins born in an American zoo. * Arana, the Hoffmann's Two-Toed Sloth: Born on August 1, 2013, Araña is among the very few hand-raised sloths in North America and made an impact serving as an ambassador animal for zoo education programs as well as events. In 2017, Wall Street Journal videographer Adya Beasley came to Syracuse to do a story on the "slothmania" sparked by several movies including *Ice Age* and *Zootopia*. The WSJ.com video that Adya produced starred Araña and increased her fame in the world of slothdom. Arana was humanely euthanized in 2022. * Right as the Covid-19 pandemic forced shutdowns in spring 2020, an unprecedented situation developed at the Rosamond Gifford Zoo. Patas monkey Becca gave birth to a baby, but did not survive childbirth, so the newborn had to be hand-reared by our team. Named Iniko, she is the first baby patas monkey that we know of to be hand-reared in North America at an AZA facility.

Oldest animals ~ Siri the Asian Elephant is the eldest elephant in our herd at the zoo at 56 years old.

Animals with a clever name ~ Amur tiger cub Coba, born on April 19, received this exotic name due to a unique stripe pattern at the top of her head which uncannily resembles a barn owl. "Coba" (pronounced "so-va") is the Russian word for "owl". * Iniko the patas monkey's name means "born during troubled times". * In the Diversity of Birds Aviary, one resident isn't a feathered flier. That's Mortoise the Tortoise! The word 'mortise' means "a hole or recess cut into a part which is designed to receive a corresponding projection," sort of like the holes in Mortoise's shell which his head and limbs can poke in and out of! The 35-year-old radiated tortoise represents a critically endangered species. * Nueve the bird was born on September 9, 1999.

NEW YORK – Seneca Park Zoo (Rochester, NY)

Most unique animals: African elephants – Seneca Park Zoo is the only zoo in New York state that has them. There are only about 160 African elephants in AZA zoos in U.S. in total. Panamanian golden frogs – this species is believed to be extinct in nature. Conservation care is the only place to see them.

Older animals: Currently, our oldest animal is African elephant Genny C who is 46 [Genesee Cream Ale is a popular beer in the Rochester area], with the other two elephants, Lilac and Moki, right behind her at 45 and 41 respectively. Polar bear Anoki is getting up there at age 27.

Animals at your zoo with a clever name: Male Canada lynx Gretzky was named after Canadian former professional hockey player, Wayne Gretzky. Gretzky's son, Stanley, was named following this theme after the Stanley Cup, which the famous hockey player won 4 times in his career. The Zoo is also home to one red-footed tortoise named Koopa, a reference to "Koopa Troopa" a fictional turtle-like character in the popular Mario video game franchise. Toni the red-tailed hawk is named after the pro skateboarder and legend, Tony Hawk. Our African lions' names together mean "A beautiful life in Rochester" (Asha, Zuri & Chester).

NORTH CAROLINA – North Carolina Zoo (Asheboro, NC)
Unique animal: We have quite a few, including the red wolf (the world's most endangered wolf, only found in the wild in eastern North Carolina). The North Carolina Zoo plays a central role in efforts to save the red wolf from extinction.
Oldest animal: Maximus (affectionately known as "Max") is our resident centenarian. He is an alligator snapping turtle estimated to be between 100-120 years old! Max is also the largest freshwater turtle in the United States, weighing in at a whopping 158 lbs. Also, although he is not as old as Max, the oldest African bull elephant in North America (C'sar) also calls the North Carolina Zoo home! He turns 50 in 2024, which also coincides with the 50th anniversary of the Zoo.
Clever name: Many of our vampire bats are named after famous musicians, including one cleverly named Bat Benatar. Other living bats with musician names currently in our zoo include Bruce Springsteen, and Prince. Bats of ours that have passed away were named Jimi Hendrix and Johnny Cash. Also, we have a female bison named Pistol Annie (named after the country music group Pistol Annies).

NORTH DAKOTA – Dakota Zoo (Bismarck, ND)
Unique: Sichuan takin, the Beast from Disney's *Beauty & the Beast* is based on this takin, a cross between a bison & a mountain goat. Ours are Houdini & Dillinger.
Our oldest: A box turtle who is 63, named Myrtle.
Unique name: Our 2-toed sloth's name is Slash.

OHIO – Cincinnati Zoo (Cincinnati, OH)
Unique animal: Fiona the hippo, the only premature hippo known to survive!
Oldest mammal: Mai Thai, Asian Elephant. She just celebrated her 50th birthday!
Animals at our zoo with "clever" names: Little penguins named Mars and Rover, Bowie (after David Bowie), Cuppa Joe (after Joe Burrow), Larkin (after Barry Larkin). Gibbons named Skittles and M&M.

OKLAHOMA – Oklahoma Aquarium (Jenks, OK)
More unique animals: Bull sharks - One of the most fascinating species calls the OK Aquarium home! We are one of the only aquariums to house a population of bull sharks in managed care. While bull sharks have earned quite the reputation in the wild, being responsible for 30% of shark attacks, we spend a lot of our time debunking common myths that our guests may have.
Older animals: One of the oldest animals at the OKAQ is Grandpa, our alligator snapping turtle, who is approximately 125 years old! This species, a native of Oklahoma, grows about 1 pound every year. Thus, we can infer that he is around 125 years old based on his weight. He is even older than the state of Oklahoma!
Animal with a unique name: Seamore, our 28-year-old loggerhead sea turtle, whose name was voted on by the public back in 2019. He is a charismatic character who spends his day greeting guests and enjoying his delicious seafood lunch!

OREGON – Oregon Zoo (Portland, OR)
More unique animals: The Pacific lamprey is an eel-like fish with a jawless mouth and no scales. Predating dinosaurs and even trees, this 400-million-year-old fish has survived three ice ages and five mass extinctions, but populations have declined over the past 75 years due to habitat loss, climate change and food scarcity.
Older animals: A trio of fifty-something chimpanzees: Chloe (54), Jackson (51) and Delilah (50). Wild chimps typically live around 33 years, and the median life expectancy in zoos is 41.7 years for female chimps, according to the Association of Zoos and Aquariums. The zoo participates in AZA's Species Survival Plan for chimpanzees, which are nearing extinction in many of their range countries.
Animal with a clever name: Lots of "clever" names, but one that stands out might be a bontebok [antelope] named Tutula, selected by her care staff in honor of her "Tutu Tuesday" birthday (and also, perhaps, because she is too, too cute!) Looking forward to seeing the book!

PENNYSYLVAINA – Lehigh Valley Zoo (Schnecksville, PA)
Unique animals: Kordofan Aoudad [rare sheep native to Saharan Africa].
Older animals: Leopard tortoise, Audubon (38 years old) and a close second is our African grey parrot, Douglas (32 years old). Note: Douglas passed on 2/16/24.
Clever: Shiska bobcat & Dwayne the Rock Johnson (shingleback skink) [reptile].

RHODE ISLAND – Roger Williams Park Zoo (Providence, RI)
Unique animal: Komodo dragon (only zoo in New England to house this threatened species).
Older animals: Male Chilean flamingo - 54 years 1 month 16 days [mid-2023].
Animal with a clever name: Our scarlet ibises are named after the Pink Ladies in *Grease*: Rizzo, Frenchy, Marty, and Jan – very fitting due to their bright pink color.

SOUTH CAROLINA – Riverbanks Zoo & Garden (Columbia, SC)
Unique animal: We are one of only four zoos in the world (two in the U.S.) to house lesser green broadbills [bright green birds native to Malaysia].
Oldest: Of course, the tortoises will win this race. Bravo, our male Galápagos, was brought to the United States in 1921 when he was already classified as an adult. But we have had some of the oldest members of certain species within U.S. zoos living at Riverbanks over the years. Tigers, Diana monkeys, and lorikeets [bird].
Clever names: We have a rockhopper penguin named Antipodes, Dapper Dan the alpaca, and Kettle the corn snake.

SOUTH DAKOTA – Great Plains Zoo (Sioux Falls, SD)
Unique animals: Red wolves – This is the most endangered canid species in the world, with only 20-30 in the wild. Red wolves are the only wolf species to live entirely within the United States. Great Plains Zoo has a breeding pair – Camelia and Uyosi – who welcomed their first litter in May 2023. The litter of six is all healthy, and the first-time parents are doing an excellent job. Like other members of their species, they are owned by U.S. Fish and Wildlife Service as part of a reintroduction program. Eastern bongo – This critically endangered mountain antelope is native to central Kenya. Great Plains Zoo has a breeding pair – Zahara

and Beauregard – as well as their youngest offspring, Bingo. Bingo was born in 2022, and is Zahara and Beau's second calf. Their first moved to another zoo.

Older animals: The oldest Humboldt penguin at the Great Plains Zoo is Oliver, born at SeaWorld San Diego in 1991. He is very engaged with his zookeepers and has a great personality, although his eyesight is no longer the best. Oscar, our blue-fronted Amazon parrot is the oldest, more than 45. He's a very popular ambassador animal, and loves attention from his caregivers and members of the public.

Clever names: Uyosi (ooo-YO-see), Our adult male red wolf's name means "hungry" in Cherokee. He was born at Jackson Zoological Park in 2013. He arrived at Great Plains Zoo in 2022. Mandelbaum, African spurred tortoise is estimated to be 40 years old. He was found at a farm close to Madison, South Dakota, likely a pet that grew too large for its owners, now living with fellow sulcata tortoise, Heidi.

TENNESSEE – Nashville Zoo (Nashville, TN)

Thanks for thinking of Nashville Zoo for your next project.

Unique animals: Eastern hellbender [amphibian], Clouded Leopard, Maleo [bird], Axolotl [salamander], Rhinoceros Hornbill [bird], Sulawesi Babirusa [wild pig].

Older animals: We have one of the oldest white-cheeked gibbons under human care. Her name is Muffy and she is 54.

Animal with a clever name: We have a flamboyance [group] of Chilean flamingos named after chili peppers (Ahi, Poblano, Jalapeno, Cayenne, etc.). There's a Cape Porcupine named Jake Quillenhaal. Several of our red kangaroos are named with "roo" in the name like Rooben, Aroogula, Proodence, Gertrood and Roothie.

TEXAS – Caldwell Zoo (Tyler, TX)

More unique animals: The Attwater's prairie chicken, which happens to be a critically endangered native Texas species. (It's really a grouse!)

Older animals: Tonya, our beautiful 45-year-old African elephant.

Animal with a unique/clever name: Tua, Jalen and Patrick- our three adorable and athletic cheetah cubs named after young, star NFL football quarterbacks.

UTAH – Living Planet Aquarium (Draper, UT)

In a landlocked state, we refer to our aquarium as the "only ocean view in Utah"!

Most unique animals: We have an Asian Arowana [fish] and vine snakes.

Older animals: Since we are a younger aquarium, we have younger animals. I wanted to approach this from the quality of care that we provide where our animals are older than typical for their species. We have a mantis shrimp that is almost 10 years old, typical for zoos and aquariums in the AZA is 7 years old.

Clever names: Rhu (Clouded Leopard, short for "Rhubarb pie" as her birthday is March 14 or 3/14, "Pi" Day), Sharptooth (Cuban iguana), and Grinch (moray eel).

VERMONT – Vermont Reindeer Farm (Charleston, VT)

More unique animal: We specialize in reindeer, having the only ones in Vermont.

Older animals: Our Prancer is 14, and doing well, always in the holiday spirit.

Clever names: In addition to Prancer we currently have Dasher age 9 & Cupid 8! My grandson said, "We may not be rich, but we have the only reindeer in Vermont." The latest reindeer, Aurora Vixen, came in on Christmas 2023.

VIRGINIA – Virginia Zoo (Norfolk, VA)
Unique: The tawny frogmouth owl is known for its observant hyper-focused stare.
Oldest: Our most senior citizen would be our Aldabra giant tortoise A.J. who's 95.
Clever name: Our Masai giraffe is named Tisa which is Swahili for "9". Nine is her magic number as she was born on 9/9/22; Tisa was the 9th calf born to Imara.

WASHINGTON – Seattle Aquarium (Seattle, WA)
Unique animal: I'd say our giant Pacific octopus is one of the most interesting!
Oldest animal: Of the old-timers at the aquarium, our harbor seal Barney is 38.
Most unique names: Our two white-spotted boxfish are named Polka and Dot.

WEST VIRGINIA – West Virginia Wildlife Center (French Creek, WV)
Most unique animal: We have hellbenders which are giant aquatic salamanders. Also, fishers, carnivorous mammals that look and climb like cats (aka fisher cats).
Oldest: Our bison, Beatrice, born in 2007, and arrived here at 20 months old.
Animal with a unique/clever name: We have several! These include Lewis, the mountain lion, who came here with his brother Clark. Unfortunately, Clark has since passed but Lewis is still doing well. We also have Tony Hawk, a one-winged red-tail hawk who came to us from a rehabilitation center. He was named Tony because he never gives up on any task, and always gets up to try again. And finally we have French Creek Freddie, our resident weather forecasting groundhog, who always puts on a great show each February 2nd.

WISCONSIN – Milwaukee Zoo (Milwaukee, WI)
Most unique animal: We have a scimitar-horned oryx, a type of African antelope. This species became extinct in the wild in the year 2000.
Oldest animal: Amazon River turtle named Onassis, arriving here in 1969 from a fish market in South America. Her estimated birth year is between 1915-1935.
Cleverest named animal: Red panda Dr. Erin Curry – she was born at the Cincinnati Zoo and named after the zoo's reproductive physiologist who tracked the pregnancy, resulting in the female cub, via ultrasound.

WYOMING – Seedskadee National Wildlife Refuge (Green River, WY)
Unique animal from your refuge: Our greater sage-grouse (large beautiful bird).
Oldest: Our longest life expectancy would probably be a trumpeter swan (25 years).
Unique names/nicknames you have used: A pronghorn "speed goat".

ADDENDUM #2
INTERNATIONAL ZOOS & AQUARIUMS

In terms of the content you'll see here, we maintained the original wording for the most part. So, on occasion, you may notice some authentic native country language emerging in this global project. We actually thought that did add character to the content. Alternate English-language spellings (like color/colour) we left in, but we did correct obvious misspellings and made adjustments where we thought the meaning might be unclear.

Any use of brackets [like this] indicates that we have interjected our words and any use of parenthesis (like this) would be those used by the original contributors. As you see beginning with Albania below, for what we project to be a primarily English-speaking audience for this book, we have initially Anglicized the name of the zoo/aquarium and then followed that up with the native-language version.

ALBANIA – Zoopark Tirana (Parku Zoologjik i Tiranës)
Unique animals: two Siberian tigers, rescued from a Slovakian facility.
Oldest animal: bear Xhina, 28 years old. She came from the Tirana Circus when she was a baby and has been part of the zoo since then.
Smart name: lion cub Tuku - found abandoned. Name was given due to his character (quite frightened but nonetheless wanting to show he is a lion).

ARGENTINA – Ecological Complex of America (Eco de America)
Most unique animal: At the Ecological Complex of America, we focus on the conservation of endangered native species, such as the jaguar. Yboty, a beautiful mature female jaguar, whose name in Guaraní means "flower", is an emblematic figure. As the mother of several cubs, she plays a crucial role in the preservation of her species. In Argentina, the jaguar, declared a natural monument, finds a prominent representative in Yboty, symbolizing the importance of our work to guarantee the survival of these majestic creatures.
Oldest animal: 19 years ago, we received Aukan at the America Ecological Complex, an imposing Andean condor (Vultur gryphus) at that time, 14 years old from the Hurlingham Zoo, which closed its doors in 2004. This majestic animal, at 33 years of age, has been a fundamental part of our conservation mission since then, enriching the experience of our visitors with its unique presence.
Cleverly named animal: Homer, like Homer Simpson, is the name of our oldest hippopotamus. He entered the Ecological Complex of America on May 3, 2002, from the Mundo Marino Aquarium, where he had been born and baptized fourteen years before. At 35 years old and weighing an impressive 3000 kg [6614 lbs], Homer is a prominent figure in our institution.

ARMENIA – Zoological Garden of Yerevan (Yerevani Kendanabanakan Aygi)
Thank you for this amazing project and we are happy and excited to be included.
Unique animal: Cinerous vulture (Aegypius Monachus) Endangered species, from the first days of her life our workers had taken care of her with a special developed method. Her name is Fenix.

Older animal: Reticulated python (Malayopython reticulatus) 28 years old. Indian python (Python molurus) 28 years old.
Interesting name: Mandrill (Mandrillus sphinx) his name is Murzik once he fell in love with his caretaker since then he does not accept any females in his species. Also two lion sisters (Panthera leo) Zita & Gita from famous Indian movie.

AUSTRALIA – Adelaide Zoo (Zoos South Australia)
Unique animal: Snow White (f) – She is the only white Meerkat on record.
Older animal: Our female Sumatran Orang-utan Puspa, she is 48 years old.
Interesting name: Three Female Coati's – Cha Cha, Samba, and Rumba

AUSTRIA – Alpenzoo Innsbruck (Alpenzoo Innsbruck-Tirol)
Unique animals: Our wallcreeper (Tichodroma muraria) is well camouflaged in the rocks with his grey feathers. But when he is active on the rocks, he shows some reddish-pink feathers at his wings. So he looks like a butterfly. There are only 3 or 4 private keepers in Europe; we're the only zoo worldwide keeping such a couple.
Older animals: Our former pair of bearded vultures (Gypaetus barbatus) was more than 50 years old when they died in 2013. They had been one of the most successful breeding pairs within the EEP for the bearded vultures. 2014 born, a new couple came into our zoo and they had the first breeding success this year. The young vulture had been released in May this year.
Another one is our male lynx, Lynx Albert, who is nearly 20 years old. Most of the time he is lying in "his" tree, a giant spruce. But sometimes he must have been on earth (ground:-)), because food disappears and every year newborn Lynxes appear.
Animal at your zoo with a clever name: We keep our female European otter (Lutra lutra) "Azuki" which came from our co-partners and friends in Aquamarine Center Fukushima in Japan. The father of Azuki origins from our zoo.
We weren´t content with our former male Moose (Alces alces). His offsprings, the calves often were too weak to survive. So we exchanged the male. A young one came three years ago from Sweden. He always has strong and vital offsprings. This makes us happy and lucky! His name is Luke.

BELGIUM – Antwerp Zoo (ZOO Antwerpen)
I'm excited to send you the 'nominees' from the Antwerp ZOO in Belgium. We wish you all the luck with your project.
Unique animal: Amahoro (Grauer's gorilla – Eastern Gorilla) She is the last one of her species in captivity.
Older animal: Francky (Pygmy marmoset) [born] 06/Jul/2004 / [over 19 Years]
Fun fact: Amahoro belongs to the biggest ape species in the world, Francky is one of the smallest monkeys in the world ☺.
Interesting name: "De Jos" (Lactoria cornuta) / Longhorn cowfish, the only fish in our aquarium who has a name.

BELGIUM – Planckendael Zoo (ZOO Planckendael)
More unique animals: A slender-horned gazelle named Shafira: we are the only zoo in Europe who still has one.

Older animals: Our oldest animal is orang-outan Karo (linchen). She turned 50 on the 8th of December! [2023]

Animal at your zoo with a clever name: We have a few so feel free to choose one. One of our Asian small-clawed otters has the name Harry, so that's Harry Otter in full ☺. We have a Tasmanian devil that is named Tortellini. And Kordofan giraffes named Barbie and Diamant.

BRAZIL – Rio de Janeiro Bioparque Zoo (BioParque do Rio)

Unique: Oncillas, gold with black spots, are one of the smallest wild cats in Brazil, less than 2 feet long.

Old: The blue hyacinth macaw can live to 50 years old.

Name: Simba the lion celebrated his 15th birthday in December, 2023 with a cake made of meatballs, chicken and meat blood.

BULGARIA – Dubrich Zoo (Zoo Centre Dobrich)

It is a great honor to find out you want to include our zoo info in your book! I had a look at your books and they seem really interesting.

Unique animal: Ygor (Equus ferus przewalskii) – he's a 25-year-old Przwalski stallion and is one of our oldest and most important animals, as his blood is pure wild Takhi; he has had a lot of offsprings over the years and has helped in the breeding and comeback of his endangered species.

Older animal: We look after a record old spur-thighed tortoise (Testudo graeca) - The zookeepers call her "Babata", which means "The Granny" in Bulgarian. She was hit by a car and had her carapace [shell] cracked, so she arrived to us at an already very old age. She's been living in our zoo for three years now and is estimated to be over 100 years old, her carapace is 31 cm long [12.2 inches] and she weighs 5.7 kg [12.6 pounds].

Interesting name: Our female brown bear's name is Bernadette, shortly we call her Berna. She is 10 years old and was donated to us by the town municipality of Bern, Switzerland 8 years ago. Our coatis (raccoon family) names are Yin and Yang.

CANADA – Bird Kingdom

Bird Kingdom is the world's largest free-flying indoor aviary, located a 5-minute walk from Niagara Falls in Canada. Home to hundreds of tropical birds, this aviary connects people to the wonder of birds even when it's winter outside. Heated by energy-efficient heat pumps and powered by 95% non-carbon-emitting electricity. Come experience an adventure for all ages!

More unique animals: We have two Hyacinth Macaws which were donated from the pet trade. This vibrant blue and large species of parrot has declined by over 90% in the last 30 years due to habitat loss and illegal capture for the pet trade. We continue to get calls every day from people trying to give us parrots, because they are difficult to care for. So we help the wild parrot population by teaching people that while parrots are amazing, they are not good pets.

Older animals: Gronigo, the Moluccan Cockatoo, is 42 years old. Parrots are exceptionally long-lived, so he may live up to 20 more years!

Animal at your zoo with a clever name: Charles "Boom" the Chaco Chachalaca (pronounced CHA-kah-LAH-kah). It's so fun to say BOOM Chachalaca!

COSTA RICA – El Castillo-Arenal Butterfly Conservatory

Most unique species: It would be the Blue Morpho (Morpho helenor), the National Butterfly of Costa Rica. This butterfly is named Morpho, because it can morph into a different look to avoid predators. This happens because it has two sides, one is the blue attraction side which is basically reflecting the blue wavelength from the ambient light. The other side is its defensive side, which is designed to scare away predators, and when this butterfly turns against the sun the blue no longer reflects so it appears that only the defensive side is seen, which confuses and frightens the predator away.

Lives longest: We raise 35 different species during the year, the shortest living of those is about one week, and longest living is the giant Owl Eye butterfly (Caligo atreus) which can live up to 8 weeks.

Interesting name: Well the Red Eyed tree frog (Agalychnis callidryas) is an icon in Costa Rica. This frog has many colors on its body, and when a predator is sensed to be close, it stretches and makes a leap showing all these colors which startles the predator while the frog escapes. We call it the "Great Escape".

I hope these answers are of interest to your readers, giving them a surprise.

CROATIA – Osijek Zoological Garden (Osječki Zoološki Vrt)

Combining all three questions, our **unique** jaguar Micica whose beautiful **name** means "born during rain" lived to be the **oldest** jaguar ever. She was almost 30 when she died in 2017. Thanks to Tim for visiting our country in 1992 to speak at The World Festival of Animated Films which was held in Zagreb, Croatia that year. Nice to be able to return the favor.

CYPRUS – Pafos Zoo (Paphos Zoo)

Unique animal: hyacinth macaw.
Older animal: Aldabra giant tortoise 60 years old.
Interesting name: Dias & Hra (Zeus and Hera) our male and female white lions.

CZECH REPUBLIC – Plzeň Zoo (Zoologická a botanická zahrada města Plzně)

Unique animal: Young pair of spider-tailed horned vipers (Pseudocerastes urarachnoides); in public exhibit from spring 2023.
Older animal: Matamata Turtle (Chelus fimbriata); lives in Zoo since 1973 and is minimally 51 years old.
Interesting name: Female of Indian rhino (Rhinoceros unicornis) "Manjula" common female Indian name [meaning melodious, beautiful, likable].

CZECH REPUBLIC – Prague Zoological Garden (Pražská Zoologická Zahrada)

Unique animals: Mammal – Chinese Pangolin (*Manis pentadactyla*) [only mammal covered with scales]; Bird – pink pigeon (*Nesoenas mayeri*); Reptile – Iraqi mastigure (*Saara loricata*); Amphibian: Titicaca Water Frog (*Telmatobius culeus*).
Oldest animal: Male Western Santa Cruz Tortoise (*Chelonoidis niger porteri*) called "Eberhard". He is definitely more than 90 years old, which makes him undoubtedly

the oldest animal in the Prague Zoo. We do not know his age for certain as he came to Prague from Leipzig in 1996, but we can estimate as we possess a photo of him from 1967, where he is pictured as a fully grown adult.

Clever name: Šiška is the female Chinese Pangolin pup that was born in February this year being the first ever born and now reared pangolin pup in Europe. As it was a giant success of international relevance, she quickly became a "celebrity" of not only our zoo and the Czech visitors, but also among media outlets and zoos all over the world. Her story is being closely watched by multiple esteemed zoologists and conservationists, for example by the one and only Jane Goodall, who even sent her best regards through a video greeting when the pup was two months old. Regarding the name – when I saw the baby for the first time, she immediately reminded me of a spruce cone, so that is exactly what "Šiška" means in Czech. Please keep us updated about the birth of your book.

DENMARK – Aalborg Zoo

More unique animal: Two-toed sloth…

Older animal: Our male sloth is 44 years old, still reproductive and very active – for a sloth!

Clever name: He is called Willem ☺

DENMARK – Copenhagen Zoo

Unique animals: Tasmanian Devils… Threatened in their native Tasmania due to a contagious cancer called Devil facial tumor disease, devils are -despite what their name might imply- lovely and fascinating creatures. Copenhagen Zoo is the only zoo outside of Australia to have breed these animals, and their breeding habits are truly remarkable: First of all the mating. This takes place in the fall over 3 or so days with lots of screaming and growling. Fundamentally the male will grab hold of the female and drag her into a den. The pair then stays in there growling away for a couple of days until the male staggers out, typically somewhat chewed to pieces by the female. After an astonishingly short pregnancy of about 3 weeks the female gives birth to 20-30 tiny babies about the size of a corn. The youngsters will attempt to make their way to the pouch, for devils are marsupials just like kangaroos, only to find that there are only 4 teats to grab onto, meaning that most of the offspring are lost. Of the four that potentially manage to find a teat one or two run the risk of being kicked out by their stronger siblings, but after 4-5 months 1-4 lovely little devils emerge from the pouch. Just in time for spring.

Older animals: We have several flamingos that are in their forties, but in general we try to optimize life quality over quantity. Many zoos take great pride in keeping geriatric animals long beyond their life expectancy in the wild. Here we'd rather see the next generations talking over ensuring continuous turnover of the valuable gene pool over keeping post-reproductive animals for years and years on painkillers and dental diets. This may sound tough, but it allows us to actually live the mission that we share of maintaining healthy populations of endangered animals.

Clever name: We try to stay clear of human names to avoid too much anthropomorphism, and many animals are simply called red/red, blue/green or yellow/black based on leg bands or ear tags (left/right).

DENMARK – Givskud Zoo Zootopia
We have settled on the following:
More unique animals: Mountain Bongo (Tragelaphus eurycerus isaaci) With about 400 animals in breeding programs in zoo's worldwide, there are more captive bongos [a type of antelope] than there are bongos left in the wild.
Older animals: Plateosaurus trossingensis, 227 million years old (and can be found in our dinosaurpark ☺) or our white rhino "Sophie" who is 42 years old.
Clever name: Our pygmy hippo male is called "Microchip" His father was "Chip".

EGYPT – Hurghada Aquarium (Alghardaqat Akwarywm)
Unique animal would be sharks seen through the shark tunnel.
Oldest animal would be green sea turtle at 70 years.
Funniest name would be shovelnose guitarfish. [actually a kind of ray]

ENGLAND – Colchester Zoo
Unique animal: Tamandua (lesser anteater)
Older animal: Elephant Tanya is about 41 years old
Clever names: 4 vultures-Jekyll, Hyde, Morticia, Gomez [last 2 from *Addams Family*]

ENGLAND – Paradise Wildlife Park
Most unique animal: The Park's most unique animal is a Binturong (a bearcat).
Oldest animal: Newt, a Gibbon, would be the oldest in the park at 50 years.
Clever name: For a unique name, how about Optimus Prime, a Green Anaconda.

ESTONIA – Tallinn Zoo (Tallinna Loomaaed)
Unique: Przewalski's horse [named after Russian explorer] is extinct in the wild.
Oldest: The Tropic House has a crocodile that has reached the age of 45 years old.
Name: "Illu" (meaning beauty), a Finland lynx, was the zoo's first animal in 1939.

FINLAND – Ahtari Zoo (Ahtarin Eläintarha)
Unique animal: We have many unique animals but as an evolutionary biologist I have to say that I am amazed by our giant pandas. They are so well adapted to use bamboo as their food source and their reproduction biology is so unique.
Older animal: Our oldest animal must be our brown bear lady Mimmi. She is 32 years old now. And I say must be because we have some birds rescued from wild and who have been at our zoo about 20 years now, so we do not know their age for sure. But I am pretty sure Mimmi is the oldest one.
Interesting name: This is also difficult one. We have many interesting named animals, but maybe I choose Kasper, Jesper and Joonatan. The brown bear brothers who are sons of Mimmi. They are named after three happy robbers from Norwegian fairytale by Thorbjørn Egner.

FINLAND – Ranua Wildlife Park (Ranuan Eläinpuisto)
Unique animals: Most special/unique animal is the Wild forest reindeer called Sampo, who was captured from the wild during reintroduction project and is now

living in Ranua Wildlife park as a breeding male - he has a very special role as a new founder in the zoo population.
Older animal: The eldest animal in Ranua Wildlife park is Alexix, the great grey owl, who was born in 1998.
Interesting name: Our hawk owls are called Sunday and Saturday, reason being that also their parents are called weekdays, Tuesday and Thursday.

FRANCE – Beauval Zoo (ZooParc de Beauval)
[Billed as being the 4th most beautiful zoo in the world.] Thank you very much for reaching out to us, we're very excited to help you out in this endeavor. Answers…
Unique animal: Giant panda (Ailuropoda melanoleuca). We are the only French zoo presenting this species. Our reproductive couple had twins two years ago, we are proud of this achievement conservation-wise.
Older animal: one of the oldest animals we have is a female radiated tortoise. Her name is Didlina and she is around 54 years old.
Clever name: One of our Aldabra giant tortoises is named "table basse", which literally means "low table" or "coffee table" in French. We came up with this name because he is really big and his shell very rounded.
We remain at your disposal if you need any other information.

FRANCE – Biopark - Doué-la-Fontaine Zoo (Bioparc - Zoo de Doué-la-Fontaine)
Unique animals: Aardvark (*Orycteropus afer*), the Bioparc is the only zoo in France where this species can be observed.
Oldest animal: Chilean Flamingo, born in 1981 (43 years old)!
Clever name: Esmeralda, this giraffe was born on April 15, 2019, the day Notre-Dame Cathedral in Paris accidentally burned down. [Esmeralda was the heroine in Disney's feature *The Hunchback of Notre Dame*.]
We would love to see the inclusion of those pieces in your book if you're able to share this with us in due course!

FRANCE – Palmyre Zoo (Zoo de La Palmyre)
More unique animals: A pair of Roloway Monkeys (*Cercopithecus roloway*), listed as critically endangered on the IUCN Red List, among the World's 25 most endangered primates and with probably very few specimens left in the wild.
Older animals: Our male Aldabra Giant Tortoise named Maurice (we don't know his exact date of birth but he's probably between 70-80 y.o.) and then a male American Flamingo aged 45.
Animal with a clever name: Our femelle Common Hippopotamus named "Sucette" (which means "lollipop" in English) and our twins, Bearded Emperor tamarins named Tic and Tac, which are the French names for the famous Walt Disney characters Chip and Dale.
Would be great to see how these informations are featured in your book.

FRANCE – Wild Planet (Planéte Sauvage)
We are excited to participate in this project and here are our responses.
Unique animal: Philippine pelican. Only French park to present and raise them.

Older animal: white rhinoceros - 45 years old. Her name is Sana. [from the Arabic sana, meaning "to gleam" or "to shine"]
Interesting name: Marabou Stork (Loréal/Fructis/Dop). 3 cosmetic brands.

GERMANY – Berlin Zoological Garden (Zoologischer Garten Berlin)
What an exciting project! We are happy to join it and provide a few fun facts.
Unique: Short-beaked echidna (first hatched egg in Berlin in 115 years this year).
Older animal: A flamingo called Ingo (a great name too) is 75 years old. [Ingo means "protected by Yngvi," a deity to the Germanic Ingaevones people.]
Interesting name: Our two young Pandas Pit and Paule; these are typical Berlin names. It has long been a tradition to give certain animals a name. Almost every Berliner knows these animals, and on anniversaries people even travel to be there.

GREECE – Attica Park Zoo (Zoologikós Kípos Attica Park)
Unique animal: Sloths – Female: Vivia [lively] and Male: Tawa [harmonious]
Oldest: Aldabra tortoise – Atlas has reached the age of 133 years old.
Names: Persephoni and Adis [Persephone & Hades] two young African penguins.

GUAM – Guam Zoo
From Guam, "Where America's Zoo Day Begins!" … We are excited for the publicity and thank you for your help!
Unique animals: Mariana fruit bats, called fanihi in our Chamorro language, endemic to the Mariana Islands; there are fewer than 50 bats remaining on Guam. Habitat loss and degradation, along with illegal hunting, are the major threats to the fanihis. Guam Rail, (locally known as the ko'ko') a flightless bird found only in Guam [which appears in the Guam Zoo logo].
Older animals: Rhesus Macaque, [monkey] Makaka is 37 years old; Water Buffalo, Belle is 24 years old.
Interesting name: Green sea turtles… Suette meaning lucky in the Chamorro language and Lala'la' meaning live/alive.

GUYANA – Guyana Zoo & Wildlife Rescue Centre
Unique animal - Harpy Eagle – (*Harpia harpyja*).
Older animal - Jabiru Stork – (*Jabiru mycteria*) - approximately 35 years old.
Interesting names – We have three red-faced spider monkeys (Jack, Helen & Nelly) approximately 30 years old.

HAITI - Wynne Farm Ecological Reserve
I consider our musician bird the "Rufous throated solitaire" (Myadestes genibarbis) (indigenous)the **most unique** because as you take a walk through the reserve you can hear him sing from one pine tree to another. Although it is difficult to hear him, people always ask who is playing that flute?
Our **oldest** animal is our horse, Spirit. Children love to ride him. An even older former resident was the mule Panky who passed away 3 years ago at the age of 35. The **most clever** one is our German Shepherd tour guide dog "Zaro".

HONG KONG – Ocean Park Zoo (Hǎiyáng gōngyuán dòngwùyuán)
Combining questions – A **uniquely named** animal was An An, a giant panda who died at the age of 35, as the **oldest** living male in the world in July of 2022.

HUNGARY – Nyíregyháza Animal Park (Nyíregyházi Állatpark)
Unique: Sumatran tiger, Indian rhinoceros, Komodo dragon, Bornean orangutan
Older animal: Asian elephant (Yasmin, born at 1966, 58 years old)
Clever name: Kimani – African elephant calf: Kimani in the African origin means "One who is Beautiful and Sweet". Sand tiger shark – Joker because of her smile.

ICELAND – Reykjavik Zoo (Dýragarðurinn í Reykjavík)
In a frozen combination of answers, the **most unique** animal on the island is the Icelandic horse. Norse sailors brought the animals to the island late in the first millennium. One of the **oldest** and purest breeds on the planet, importing horses to Iceland is now illegal so as to preserve the purity of the Icelandic horse breed. In terms of longevity, they can reach over 40 years old.

INDIA – Delhi Zoo (Dillee Chidiyaaghar)
A **unique** animal was the chimp **named** Rita who arrived here at the age of 4 and died as India's **oldest** chimpanzee at the age of 59 in 2019.

INDONESIA – Surabaya Zoo (Kebun Binatang Surabaya)
Unique animals: Komodo dragon (*Varanus komodoensis*) Surabaya Zoo take care of more than 100 komodo dragons in our zoo. Some of them are bred and hatched in Surabaya Zoo. Komodo dragon is a protected animal in Indonesia.
Older Animals: There are 2 Female Sumatran tigers (Panthera tigris sumatrae) that are more than 21 years old (born in September 2002) named Rara and Rana. They are old but relatively healthy now. The keepers keep them active by routinely giving them various enrichment so they can stay active.
Clever name: This one is tricky… Let's try with our 13-years-old male elephant named Gonzales (Gonzales is not a usual name in Indonesia), the name Gonzales is taken from a famous football player Cristian Gerard Alfaro Gonzales (from Uruguay) that scores a lot of goals in Indonesian Football league back then, at the time Gonzales (elephant) was born in 2010.
Thanks for giving us the opportunity to be included in your book.

IRELAND – Dublin Zoo (Zú Bhaile Átha Cliath)
We are more than happy to contribute to your next wonderful book.
Unique animals: Aye-aye (we recently received a family trio, a 1st keeping this nocturnal species for Dublin) The aye-aye is a long-fingered lemur, a strepsirrhine primate native to Madagascar with rodent-like teeth that perpetually grow and a special thin middle finger. It is the world's largest nocturnal primate. Also, okapi (Dublin began caring for this rare and elusive species in 2013 and have successfully produced 2 calves). [aka "zebra giraffe" because they look like that combination.]
Oldest: Betty the chimp (61 years old, we believe is the oldest known in captivity).
Clever: Flash the sloth (ironic, as one of the slowest mammals on the planet).

ITALY – Living Biodiversity Park (Parco Natura Viva)
We asked Marketing Director Maria Ordinario how to Anglicize her Italian park title and enjoyed her response of, "Thanks Tim & Deb, very good question and my puzzle for marketing purposes for more than 15 years now ☺" The answer we collectively landed upon was "Living Biodiversity Park" which appears above.
Unique animal: Red-headed vulture (*Sarcogyps calvus*): we are the only zoo across European zoos hosting and breeding this species.
Older animals: Toby, white rhino (*Ceratotherium simum*): when he died (Autumn 2021), he was the oldest white rhino in the world, 54 years old.
Clever name: Chicks of red-crowned crane or Manchurian crane (*Grus japonensis*): Yuki (2018), Kino (2020), Kiki (2023) (the name of the 2023 chick is made by the end of the name of the first chick and the beginning of the name of the second chick). ~ All the best from Parco Natura Viva -Italy, all the staff and animals.

JAMAICA – Jamaica Zoo
Unique animal: Duck ant, Jamaicans call it (Chi-Chi) A white termite of Jamaica, of species (*Nasutitermes nigriceps*), which builds large nests in trees.
Oldest animal: Lion named Santa (fun fact: he is the first lion to be born in Jamaica) Santa is 22 years old.
Clever name: Boer goat by the name "89" When it was a baby kid, one day we were bottle feeding him and his cry sounded like the number 89.

JAPAN – Tama Zoological Park (Tamadōbutsukōen)
Unique: Japanese stork (*Ciconia boyciana*), Small Japanese mole (*Mogera imaizumii*)
Oldest: We are currently breeding Anura, the longest-lived Asian elephant in Japan, 70 years old.
Names: Azumi (f) and Hanzou (m), Japanese giant flying squirrels (*Petaurista leucogenys*) are named after the famous ninja. [In Japanese, ninja's plural has no "s"]

KAZAKHSTAN – Almaty Zoo (Almatı Xaywanattar Bağı)
Unusual Animal: Our African marabou stork, Mara is a large wading bird with a 9-foot wingspan. We have a venomous viper subspecies endemic to Asia.
Age: Zina, our female (*Caiman crocodilus*), [crocodile] was born in 1972 (and is now 52). We also have a steppe eagle (*Aquila nipalensisa*) born in 1976 (who is now 47).
Name: Himalayan bear named Budur which is a girl's name of Arabic origin [meaning full moon]. Our white-armed gibbon, Tabin, has a powerful hard-hitting punch that destroys/crumples whatever it hits. The most crucial punch known to man. Devastating, just devastating! *(Note: The Almaty Zoo tells the almighty truth!)*

LATVIA – Riga Zoo (Rīgas Zoodārzs)
Unique animals: Siberian flying squirrels (*Pteromys Volans*), Malagassy Ginat jumping rats (*Hypogeomys antimena*), Nile softshell turtle (*Trionyx triunguis*).
Older: Female white cockatoo (*Cacatua alba*), we estimate her age to be 48 years.
Clever name: all our Mishmi takins (*Budorcas taxicolor taxicolor*) are named after Greek Gods – Zeus (the breeding male), Perseus, Apollo, Athena and Aphrodite. Could you share snippets from the book, if our animals do make the cut and get included in the book? Wishing you a successful writing and publishing process!

LITHUANIA – Lithuanian Zoological Gardens (Lietuvos Zoologijos Sodai)
Unique animal: Hermit beetle (*Osmoderma barnabita*)
Older animal: European pond turtle (*Emys orbicularis*) is about 40 years old.
Interesting name: Popcorn, European bison (*Bison bonasus bonasus*)

MALTA – Malta National Aquarium (Akkwarju Nazzjonali ta' Malta)
Unique animals: 1) Casper, our albino stingray! He was caught by a fisherman here in Malta who got scared and cut off his tail, so the chances that he would be able to survive on his own in the wild would be very small! The Aquarium team takes care of Casper with love and dedication every single day. 2) Our couple of zebra sharks who like to sleep together every day in the same spot!
Older animals: blacktip reef sharks – 11 years old
Animal at your aquarium with a clever name: Casper, from above story.

MEXICO – Guadalajara Zoo (Zoológico de Guadalajara)
Unique: southern cassowary – huge black flightless bird from Indonesia
Oldest age and favorite name: Tequila, the hippo, who lived into the 40's.

MOROCCO – National Zooligical Parc of Rabat
Author's note: We celebrate this as our most passionate in-depth response from the Muslim world.
I am writing on behalf of the team at the National Zoo of Rabat in Morocco to express our sincere gratitude for considering our zoo in your project. We are eager to provide detailed information for your book about our diverse animal residents:
Unique Animal: Louiza, the nocturnal striped hyena in our zoo, stands out with her unique behavior. She is nocturnal, consistently staying outside her wildlife shelter at night. Despite efforts to entice her with food and pathways, she prefers the open enclosure area. In consideration of her well-being and preference, the zoological team has decided to let her remain outdoors during the night.
Older Animal: Clyde, the chimpanzee, who was born in 1989, forms a unique bond with Tarzan and Boris in our chimpanzee trio. Zookeepers rely on Tarzan's assistance when Clyde chooses to stay outside at night. Despite occasional disagreements with Boris, it's the protective nature of Tarzan that defines Clyde's attitude and relationships; Tarzan becomes Clyde's defender, showcasing a deep and endearing friendship.
Clever name: Izem, the Atlas Lion. One of our 32 Atlas lions is called "Izem," signifying "lion" in the Amazigh language, honoring Moroccan heritage. His name creates a meaningful connection between the animal and its indigenous roots. This approach reflects our commitment to fostering a deeper understanding of the diverse cultural tapestry surrounding these animals in the kingdom of Morocco.

Once again, thank you for including us in your upcoming book project. We look forward to the collective success of "Crowning The Animal Kingdom."

NEPAL – Central Zoo (Kēndrīya Ciḍiyākhānā)
Unique animal: Indian-crested porcupine, which can weigh up to 40 pounds.
Oldest animals: Elephants which roam free.
Unique name: "Barking deer", they make a bark-like sound to indicate danger.

NETHERLANDS – Apenheul Primate Park (Apenheul Primatenpark)
Most unique: Our blue-eyed black lemurs. In the wild, these critically endangered lemurs live on the African island of Madagascar. They are very rare in zoos. Extra special: in 2017, 2018 & 2022 blue-eyed black lemur babies were born in Apenheul.
Older animals: Pepi, she is the oldest primate in our park. Pepi is a brown-headed spider monkey that has lived in Apenheul since the very beginning: 1972! She's 55 years old now, which is very old for a spider monkey.
Clever name: Gorilla Kiango. He was born in 2021 during the COVID-19 pandemic. During that time, our zoo was closed for the public. His name was chosen by the public via an online name contest. Kiango means "light" in Swahili. He was a beacon of light in this time of the pandemic. He brings cheerfulness and a different dynamic to the gorilla group. The birth of his father's first offspring also signifies a bright future for the conservation of the species.

NEW ZEALAND - Victoria University in Wellington
Unique animal: Our elderly geriatric Maud Island frogs.
Oldest animal: Maud Island frog named Wellington, age 37.
Cleverest names: Frogs Gollum (The Hobbit) 35 and Xena (Princess Warrior) 34.

NORTHERN IRELAND – Belfast Zoo (Zú Bhéal Feirste)
Unique animal: Isa our tree kangaroo
Older animals: Delilah the gorilla (60 years) and Sandy the zebra (she's 41 years old, born on July 21, 1982). We believe she is the oldest zebra in Europe.
Name: Giraffe (BallyHenry) – all of our giraffes are named after places in Ireland

NORWAY – Kristiansand Zoo & Amusement Park (Kristiansand dyrepark)
Unique animal: Our chimpanzee, Julius, is the most famous animal in Norway!
Oldest animal: The radiated tortoise, George, is about 100 years.
Interesting names: European otters Hugin and Munin [representing "thought" and "memory" in Norse mythology]

PALAU – Palau Aquarium (Aquarium era Belau)
Our **unique animal** would be the Palau Nautilus (*Nautilus belauensis*), which is believed to be endemic to Palau.
Our **oldest animal** would be one of our giant clams (*Tridanca gigas*) which we estimate to be between 50-80 years old.
And for the **clever name**: we have a Picasso Triggerfish (*Rhinecanthus aculeatus*) which we have named Pablo.
Excited to see the end result! Please keep us in the loop once published.

PAPUA NEW GUINEA – **(Woodland Park Zoo/Tree Kangaroo Conservation Program)**
Unique animal: Matschie's tree kangaroos – kangaroos that live in trees! These live only on the Huon Peninsula of northeastern Papua New Guinea.
Older animals: Squint, a 57-year-old kea (alpine parrot native to New Zealand); a 50-year-old Egyptian tortoise.

Clever name: Finni, a baby Matschie's tree kangaroo (a baby kangaroo is known as a joey) whose name was inspired by the Finisterre Mountain range in the YUS (Yopno-Uruwa-Som) Conservation Area in Papua New Guinea.

POLAND – Płock Zoo (Płocki Ogród Zoologiczny)
We will be very pleased if you tell the story of our **unique** alligator **named** Marta, who is still in very good condition at the age of 93. We are currently trying to enter the Guinness Book of Records.

PORTUGAL – Lisbon Zoo (Zoológico de Lisboa)
Unique: White Tiger; **Oldest**: Chimpanzee is 50;
Name: Dolphin (golfinho in Portuguese) is named Soda.

PUERTO RICO – Kira's World Exotics Mini Zoo (Minizoológico Kira's Mundo Exoticó)
Unique: White-tufted-ear marmoset [monkey].
Oldest: Cockatoo is age 40. **Name**: Toucan named Toucan Sam.

ROME – The Colosseum
The Colosseum, which enjoyed its opening ceremonies during the years 80-81 A.D., was used to exhibit to the public a menagerie of animals which included, in addition to the combatants listed below; monkeys, giraffes, zebras, antelopes, gazelles, jackals, hyenas, Egyptian salukis (greyhounds), flamingos, parrots, and ostriches.

The wild animals were kept in caged areas in the cellar, underneath the arena floor. When it was showtime, the animals were moved into a system of 28 manually propelled elevators and lifted to the surface. The arena was permeated with trap doors, enabling dramatic calculated entrances at various locations. Because they were under the Colosseum floor and subsequently more protected, those original concrete animal cages survive as one of the more intact components of the ancient structure and tourists can still peer inside them today.

Specifics have become sketchy in the murky waters of time, and wide-ranging numeric boasts are documented by both Roman rulers and historians, but suffice it to say that literally tens of thousands of innocent animals, and thousands of humans, were slaughtered in the Colosseum for what was considered at the time to be entertainment. Here's our modern-day assessment of the three questions addressed by the current zoos participating in this project. Regarding the bloodletting at the Colosseum…

Unique animal: Humans. Reflective of the times we are describing, this is the only instance in the book where we are categorizing human beings as animals. In the Colosseum, Romans had human gladiators fight lions, tigers, bears, rhinos, cheetahs, panthers, bulls, elephants, and crocodiles in contests called venationes ("wild beast hunts"). Under that air of civilization, the Romans exhibited a bloodlust that rendered them as barbaric as the barbarians to whom they would eventually succumb.

Oldest animals: Based upon life expectancies of the creatures known to be exhibited, the parrots and the ostriches were both capable of reaching 50 years old.

Unusual name: As discussed earlier in the book, "cameleopard" was the name Romans assigned to giraffes based upon the fact that it combined the long legs of the camel with the spots of the leopard. The Roman name does survive in what is now the giraffe's actual scientific species name, "giraffa camelopardalis".

RUSSIA – Novosibirsk Zoo (Военi Hajvonoti Novosiвirsk)
Most **unusual** animal is a liger **named** Zita (lion father, tiger mother).
Oldest animal is 31-year-old mandrill.

SCOTLAND – Edinburgh Zoo
Unique animal: Brigadier Sir Nils Olav III – the only knighted penguin in the world! Nils, a king penguin, is regarded very highly among the Norwegian Guardsman and has received various honours and medals due to his outstanding service and good conduct! The Guardsmen like to visit Nils every few years while they are in the city performing at the Edinburgh Military Tattoo.
Older animal: Louis and Lucy (chimpanzees) are 47
Clever Name: Gentoo penguins - Maggie Hatcher [after former Prime Minister Margaret Thatcher], Benedict Cumberhatch [after actor Benedict Cumberbatch]

SERBIA – Belgrade Zoo (Beogradski zoološki vrt)
Unique – White lions, loved in Belgrade because city's name means "white city".
Oldest – Muja the Alligator is 87.
Name – When Sami the chimp arrived in 1988 he escaped his cage and wandered the city streets for an hour before zookeeper Vuk Bojović found Sami, put him in his car, and drove him back to zoo.

SLOVENIA – Sikaluzoo (Živalski vrt Sikaluzoo)
Unique animal: Barbary macaque (Macaca sylvanus).
Older animal: Our Greek tortoise (Testudo graeca) is about 76 years old.
Interesting names: The group of our ring-tailed lemurs called King Julian, Curious George, Katka, Slyvie and Chopin.
Thank you for including our zoo in your project.

SLOVENIA – Tropical House (Tropska hiša)
Unique animals: Big hairy armadillo (*Chaetophractus villosus*), Siamese spitting cobra (*Naja Siamensis*), Vietnamese mossy frog (*Theloderma corticale*).
Older animals: We're almost 3 years old and we mostly have younger animals. We have 15-years-old boa constrictor, 25-years-old yellow-spotted Amazon river turtle, 15-years-old violet turaco [bird], 13-years-old Pygmy slow loris [monkey].
Clever name: Shrek, Large hairy armadillo; Bella Veronika, Siamese crocodile; Fredy, Argentine horned frog

SOUTH KOREA – Everland Zootopia (Ebeolaendeu Jutopia)
The **unique** story for this year is how Everland's giant panda **named** Ai Bao, **age** 9, gave birth to twins for the first time in the history of South Korea on July 7, 2023. In twin panda births, both do not usually survive, but Rui Bao (Wise Treasure) and Hui Bao (Shining Treasure) successfully celebrated 100 days of life.

SPAIN – Barcelona Zoo (Zoologico de Barcelona)
Unique animals: Our group of Montseny brook newt, the last vertebrate discovered in Europe in the beginning of the 21st century.
Older animals: Our Rhino Pedro is 52 years old.
Clever name: Giraffe "Thembi" (Rhulani Thembi Siweya is a South African politician who served as the Deputy Minister in the Presidency since 2019.)

SWEDEN – Ystad Zoo
Unique: Sune the Catalina macaw who turns 30 years old in April this year.
Older animal: Blue-fronted Amazon parrot named Pancho is 47 years old.
Interesting names: The common marmosets [monkeys], Bonnie and Clyde.

SWITZERLAND – Tropiquarium
More unique animals: Lune - albinos Galágapos turtle (*Chelonoidis nigra*).
Older animals: Reptile: Sulcata turtle (*Centrochelys sulcata*) – 73 years old ~
Bird: Boat-billed heron (*Cochlearius cochlearius*) – 42 years old.
Clever name: three spectacled caimans *(caiman crocodilus)*: Paco, Rabanne et Gucci.

SYRIA – Damascus Zoo (Hadiqat Alhayawan Bidimashq)
Unique: French chicken chanticleer, **Older** sulfur-crested cockatoo (35 years)
Unique name A-Wolf.

TAIWAN – Taipei Zoo (Táiběi Dòngwùyuán)
Uniquely, the Taipei Zoo has 3 giant pandas, **named** Yuan Zai (born 2013), Yuan Bao, (born 2020); cubs of Yuan Yuan (19 years old on August 30, 2023) & Tuan Tuan (died in 2022). **Oldest animal** ever: elephant Lin Wang (died at 85 in 2013).

TAJIKISTAN – Dushanbe Zoo (Bogi Xajvonoti Duşanbe)
Unique animal: Corn snake named Zard (yellow).
Oldest animal: Our ostrich is 35 years old.
Clever name: We have a deer named Bambi.

TASMANIA – Tasmania Zoo
Where you can pet live kangaroos, even mothers with a joey in her pouch.
Unique animal nod would have to go to the Tasmanian devil because this is the only zoo that can call the animal endemic.
Oldest animal is the rose-breasted cockatoo, about 40 years old.
Clever name is the wombat, Roxy. When Roxy rocks he even lets you pet him.

TURKEY – Faruk Yalcin Zoo (Faruk Yalçın Hayvanat Bahçesi)
Unique: The zoo received its first pair of sloths, arriving from a German zoo.
Oldest: The tortoise, Tuki, turned 100 years old in 2020.
Name: First Indian rhino in Turkey is "Samir" meaning good friend or companion

UKRAINE – Mykolaiv Zoo (Mykolayivs′kyy zoopark)
In response to your letter, we would like to provide information about the animals of Mykolaiv Zoo: (*Authors' note: What a surprise to receive this from a war zone!*)
Unique animals: Amur leopards (*Panthera pardus orientalis*) are among the rarest animals kept and bred in our zoo. We have a pair of leopards, Rayo and Eva, who

have been breeding regularly in Mykolaiv Zoo since 2014. Even in March 2022, during the war, when Mykolaiv was actually under siege, during daily shelling, a male cub of the Amur leopard was born in our zoo, he was named Aldan.

Older animals: One of our old residents is a hippopotamus (*Hippopotamus amphibius*) named Kazymyr, who was born on January 19, 1978 in Kharkiv Zoo. On November 28, 1978, he came to Mykolaiv Zoo, where he still lives. He is the father of 6 children. Now he is kept together with a young girlfriend Rikki.

Our female chimpanzee (*Pan troglodytes*) named Ambi is also an old-timer. She was born in 1968. In 2004, Ambi came to Mykolaiv Zoo from the Netherlands as part of a group of chimpanzees. Now, in addition to Ambi, we keep her daughter Aliti, and Aliti's children Chilina (female), Ramina (female) and Sherman (very active and decisive, like his famous namesake, male). Ambi is a very caring grandmother and takes care of all her grandchildren.

Clever names: Steppe eagles (*Aquila nipalensis*), pair: Bald (male, born in 1975) and Baba Yaga (female, born in 1975). Bald is named so because he injured the scalp, feathers no longer grow there and baldness has formed. Baba Yaga is named after an old witch, a character from Slavic fairy tales. The bird has a characteristic feature of behavior, she moves hunched and croaking, like Baba Yaga, a character in fairy tales. Interesting "sweet, milky" names have our polar bears (*Ursus maritimus*). Their names are Sour Cream (Smetanka) and Marshmallow (Zephyrka).

UNITED ARAB EMIRATES – Zoo Wild Life Park (Hadiqat Alhayawanat Albariya)
Name: Habuba, a Bornean orangutan. (Name means "the loving one" in Arabic.)
Unusual animal: Lappet-faced vulture which has huge pink face.
Oldest animal: Our red-crowned crane is 24 years old.

VIETNAM – Vinpearl Safari (Vinpearl Cuộc đi Săn)
Thank you for your interest in Vinpearl Safari, I would like to send you the information you need and hope it can help you.
Unique animals: A pair of Sumatran Orangutans, Suaq (male) and Surya (female).
Older animals: A female Asian Elephant named Tuc, she is nearly 70 years old.
Interesting names: Three White Rhinoceros born in our zoo, named Cà Phê, Sữa, Đá (which means Coffee, Milk, Ice in English respectively).

WALES – Folly Farm Adventure Park & Zoo (Parc Antur a Sw Folly Farm)
Unique animals: Welsh wildcat - Ambassador animals for the potential release project of wildcats into the Brechfa Forest.
Older animals: Lightcap - Two-toed sloth. Earliest record dates back to 1982. At least 41 years old. Fifth oldest in Europe!
Clever name: Glyndwr – Eastern black rhino. First rhino born in Wales (represented by his Welsh name) and named after Folly Farm founder.
Hope this is ok? Looking forward to seeing the finished result.

ADDENDUM #3
WILDLIFE PRESERVES & ANIMAL SANCTUARIES

BOTSWANA – Kgalagadi Transfrontier Park (Kgalagadi Transfrontier Gape)
Unique: Secretarybird has a body like an eagle with legs like a crane.
Oldest: Eagle can live over 30 years.
Name: Blue wildebeest or white-bearded gnu.
Botswana has 38% of its land devoted to animal conservation.

BURKINA FASO – Arli National Park (Parc national d'Arli)
Arli is **unique** with 200 African elephants, 200 hippos and 100 lions.
Some **older** elephants reach 70.
Antelope called bushbuck, aka imbabala – both kind of funny **names**.

CAMBODIA – Phnom Tamao Wildlife Rescue Centre (Mochchhomondal Sangkroh Satvaprei Phnom Tamaw)
Thank you so much for thinking of Phnom Tamao and reaching out to us.
We would love to be included in the book! Answers below:
Unique animals: Sunda Pangolin – our current ambassador is named "Chanti" which is the Khmer language word for cashew nut, which they resemble when they roll up in their defensive position.
Older animals: This is a tricky one because we only have records for the animals for the last 20 years and many of the animals were rescued as adults so we don't know how old they are. There are definitely crocodiles and turtles on the site that have been here more than 20 years. In 2020, our Indochinese tiger, Map, passed away at 24 years old and in 2021, Cambodia's last captive Indochinese leopard, named Reap, passed away at 20 years old.
Clever name: Cambodia's only elephant with a prosthetic leg is named 'Chhouk', which is the Khmer language word for lotus flower. Lotus flowers represent purity, strength and resilience, all of which are important in conservation.

In case it is useful, here is a blurb about Phnom Tamao: Phnom Tamao Wildlife Rescue Centre (PTWRC) was created in 1995 by the Forestry Administration (FA) of Cambodia to care for rescued wildlife in need of a home. It also serves as Cambodia's only national zoo. In many ways it is an inspired choice of location for such a venture. Set in a large forest that is also managed by FA, rescued animals feel at home and thrive here.

There is also the opportunity to release appropriate wildlife back into the surrounding forest. Initially, the FA experienced a lack of funding and could not care for the animals properly. However, due to the excellent relationship that has existed in the past between Wildlife Alliance and PTWRC's FA Director, Mr. Nhek Ratanapich, the Centre has blossomed into perhaps the best of its kind in the region. Our proud boast is no wild animal is ever turned away and all would be dead without our intervention.

CAMEROON – Ape Action Africa (Ape Action Afrique)
Unique animal: Shufai – The rescue story of western lowland gorilla Shufai has touched the hearts of more people than that of any other orphaned primate in our care. Shufai arrived at Ape Action Africa in 2006 as a traumatised infant, badly injured by the bullets that had killed his mother. This does not make him unique – wounds like these are all too common amongst the orphaned apes and monkeys we rescue.

But for Shufai, the bullets lodged in his arm had caused irreparable damage to his bones and meant that amputation was unavoidable. After surviving the trauma of losing his family, Shufai proved himself yet again to be a fighter and was climbing and playing just one day after his operation. Shufai has grown into a stunning silverback, the leader of a family of six rescued gorillas.

His physical difference makes him immediately recognisable to visitors to our forest and is a unique reminder of the kind of trauma that all of our nearly 300 rescued primates have overcome. Shufai's strength and resilience are inspirational, and we couldn't be prouder of this very special silverback.

Older animal: Bertie – We first encountered Bertie, now 33 years old, in a tiny, dilapidated cage in a zoo, where he lived with female Ashmael. For an inexplicable reason, Bertie's ears had been cut off when he was younger, but what was even more striking about his appearance was the sadness in his eyes – the desperation and the loss of hope.

In 2006, we were finally given permission to bring Bertie and Ashmael to our sanctuary. After giving them time to settle following their transfer, the day came to open the door of their satellite cage. Bertie dashed out into the forest stamping his feet, calling, and eager to explore his new home. But Ashmael had been incredibly traumatised by her time in captivity and was too scared to leave the cage.

Every day Bertie would try to entice her out, but she remained where she was, cement and iron having been the only environment she'd known for many years. Eventually, Ashmael found the courage to overcome her fears and one morning rushed out to hug Bertie and to start her new life among the trees. A new life meant a new family and when these two brave chimps were comfortable in their forest, we introduced them to 15 juveniles – they became incredible surrogate parents.

We sadly lost Ashmael to illness a few years ago, but Bertie remains a loved and respected member of his group. We're delighted that these two incredible individuals got the second chance that they so thoroughly deserved, the chance to have a family, the chance to enjoy the forest and the chance to feel joy again.

Interesting name: Yeba – In 2005, researchers in a reserve in Cameroon stumbled across a tragic scene. A tiny two-week-old gorilla lay next to his mother, who was dead but showed no obvious signs of trauma. Fearing serious disease, the researchers called us for help. When we arrived, the baby had been alone for more than two days. Miraculously he had survived, but we discovered two dead adult chimps nearby and a necropsy later revealed anthrax as the cause of death.

Still at serious risk, the baby gorilla was transferred to an isolation facility under the care of our then senior gorilla keeper. The two remained alone in quarantine and became each other's entire worlds, so the caregiver named the baby 'Yeba', meaning 'universe' in his local dialect. Thankfully, Yeba never developed anthrax and was eventually able to join other rescued gorillas in our forest, where he's grown into a stunningly strong and handsome silverback.

CAMEROON – Limbe Wildlife Center (Centre de Faune de Limbé)
Unique animals: Lada is a unique chimpanzee – she has very short arms and legs. It is unfortunately due to malnourishment during the time she was kept illegally as a pet, but it doesn't stop her. She might be small but she has a big personality, and is a very active and playful member of our island group of chimpanzees.

Jumbo is a unique gorilla – some say she is the most intelligent gorilla in the world! She has many tricks, but her main ones are to steal things from people's pockets with sticks and to get mangoes from the trees using rocks & her good aim.

Older animals: Since the Limbe Wildlife Centre is entering its 30th year, many of the animals in our care are below 30 years of age as they often arrive as young orphans. However, we do have some very old residents in our care: two dwarf crocodiles that were residents at the former zoo from which the wildlife sanctuary was created.

We cannot be sure of their exact age, but estimate them to be at least 50 years old. Since they have been in captivity for so long, even before the zoo was turned into a wildlife sanctuary, it is not possible to release them. The LWC staff continues to provide them with the care they need, for as long as they shall live!

Clever name: Most of the animals at the centre are named after the place that they came from! Bonamoussadi the mandrill was being kept illegally as a pet in Bonamoussadi in the city of Douala until being confiscated by wildlife officials. Manowar the putty-nosed monkey was named after Man O'War Bay in Limbe, where he had been kept as a pet until his owner surrendered him to the LWC. One final one is Balinga, a western lowland gorilla who was born here at the LWC. He was named Balinga in honour of a conservationist and long-term advisor to Pandrillus, who used to manage the famous Korup National Park.

CANADA – Bear Creek Exotic Wildlife Sanctuary
Please do keep in mind that we are not a zoo facility. We are a sanctuary and we do not buy or sell animals. We also do not breed, but due to the fact that when we acquire a female animal of any species and are told that they are spayed, we have to take their word and in this case have been misinformed before. We now neuter all male animals that arrive at our facility.

More unique animals: We have a Kinkajou (tropical rainforest mammal) his name is Jivala (Full of Life) who was born in August of 2012. He was being attacked by his father and removed from the enclosure just in time and hand reared. For the last 8 years, Jivala has been insulin dependent.

We also have Jahzara. A female Jaglion. Mother lioness and father jaguar. Both parents grew up together but were separated when the lioness went into estrus. Depression became a large factor in both animals during this time. Although several years of separating during estrus, year seven turned out to be a failure and two cubs were born April 2006 and known to be the only living ones in the world.

Today, only the female [Jahzara] survives at the age of 17 years. The male [who was named Tsunami] passed away in 2023.

Our African fruit bats are not found anywhere in captivity but are rehabilitated in Israel. We have a colony of Ruwenzori long-haired fruit bats. They are a cave dwelling bat and do not require sunlight.

Older animals: We have had several older animals in our 34 years of operating as a rescue sanctuary. Mountain lioness that lived to 22 years. We currently have an Amur female tiger (Kyra) at 22 years and a male (Kamen) at 19 years. We also had a female spider monkey (Priscilla) live to 47 years.

Clever: We have a ring-tailed lemur named Rumel (Lemur spelled backwards). A kinkajou name Chilli who was purchased as a pet from Chilliwack. She suffered a two-week withdrawal from drugs due to the house she was living in.

An African serval cat named Zenyatta after one of the fastest thoroughbred horses who won 19 out of 20 races. Hope this is enough information for now. With all the animals being rescued at our facility, we have quite a few interesting and some sad stories.

Remember, until you have loved an animal, part of your soul will have remained dormant.

CENTRAL AFRICAN REPUBLIC – Manovo-Gounda St. Floris National Park (Manovo-Gounda St. Floris Pariki ya Ngoto)
Unique animal: Sudan cheetah.
Oldest animal: Elephant.
Unique Name: Red-fronted gazelle.

CHILE – Torres del Paine National Park (Parque Nacional Torres del Paine)
Unique animal: The Austral pygmy-owl is one of the smallest species of owl.
Oldest animal: The Andean condor can live to be 50 years old, sometimes older.
Name: Ferdinand Magellan was rewarded for sailing around Chile. This park is home to the Magellanic woodpecker, Magellanic goose, & Magellanic horned owl.

CHRISTMAS ISLAND – Christmas Island National Park
This scenario in place on this remote island in the Indian Ocean, halfway between Africa and Australia, is unique for a combination of reasons. Discovered by the British on Christmas Day, 1643, there were no native inhabitants, which remained the case for centuries.

An historic "fun fact" would be to note that, of all the places in the world that are currently inhabited by man, Christmas Island was one of the last locations to be populated, an event that didn't happen until around 1900, giving the British the time to plan the development with a somewhat more modern-day perspective on how best to do things.

Years of preparation preceded the process, and a full 63% of the island was devoted to the National Park which contains a tropical rain forest. Because of its remote location, the island finds itself home to a wonderfully diverse array of endemic flora & fauna species. In terms of animal questions, we have the following:
Unique Animal is the endemic red crab, 50 million of them, whose migration patterns dictate life on the island and provide the major source of tourism. Just

Google the scenes of a red sea of live animals flooding the beaches and roads during migration and you'll see why.
Oldest Animal is the coconut crab, the world's largest land crustacean, which can live more than 50 years.
Best Name: The red-footed booby, a bird with a blue bill, a white body & red feet.

COLOMBIA – Tayrona National Natural Park (Parque Nacional Natural Tayrona)
Unique: The oncilla is a spotted wild cat only 2 feet long also known as a tigrillo.
Oldest animal: Ocean sponges can live to be 100.
Name: Mantled howler is a monkey with long mantle-like hair guarding its sides.

CONGO D.R. – Friends of Bonobos (Lola ya Bonobo)
About us: Lola ya Bonobo is the only bonobo sanctuary and release site in the world. We save bonobos and their rainforest home. Lola ya Bonobo is the world's only rehabilitation center for bonobos. Its mission is to rescue, care for, and release endangered bonobos, while working in partnership with governments and NGOs to protect the forest habitat bonobos need to survive.
Unique animals: Omandja is a five-year old male bonobo who has remarkable chestnut hair which is much lighter than the darker coloring of the other bonobos.
Older: Semendwa came to the sanctuary in 1996 and is a great leader and matriarch at Lola ya Bonobo. She is mother to Elikya and grandmother to Molende. Fun fact! Semendwa's photo is the most shared photo of a bonobo online.
Clever: Interestingly, most of the bonobos at Lola are named after the place they were rescued. Take for example Tshimbulu, a seven-year-old male bonobo who was rescued from a place called Tshimbulu in Kasai Central Province in DR Congo.

CONGO D.R. – J.A.C.K. Primate Sanctuary.
(Jeunes Animaux Confisqués au Katanga Sanctuaire des Primates)
Note: The J.A.C.K. acronym translates from French to English as "Young Animals Confiscated in Katanga"
Unique animals: Djonga and Wata are very unique animals given their species. They are two lesula monkeys (*Cercopithecus lomamiensis*). The lesula is an endemic species of the Democratic Republic of Congo. It was discovered in 2007 in the heart of the current Lomami National Park. These animals live in an area crossed by the Congo River basin, and one of the greatest threats to their survival is poaching. J.A.C.K. is the only primate rehabilitation center in the world where these beautiful primates can be seen.
Older animals: Lulah, a female chimpanzee rescued from individuals in 2020, was kept as a pet for a long time. She was already an adult when she was rescued. Her age has been estimated at 22, making her the oldest animal in the entire Rehabilitation Center.

However, Chita, a male chimpanzee, was one of the very first primates at J.A.C.K. He was kept in the homes of private individuals who found it difficult to contain him due to his turbulent nature. He was abandoned at the Lubumbashi Zoo, until the founders, Franck and Roxane, were able to take him and annex him to the J.A.C.K project in 2006. He is the oldest primate rescued at J.A.C.K.

Clever name: At J.A.C.K., names are given depending on where the animal was confiscated or who made the confiscation. This means that we never keep the names given by the holders/poachers/traffickers and that we change the names of the newcomers. Zumba, for instance, was confiscated at the border between Zambia and DR Congo. Her holders named her *"Trump"*. Also, Monga, who was one of the three baby chimps kidnapped from our sanctuary last year, was named *"Obama"* by the traffickers that held her in horrible conditions.

COTE D'IVOIRE – Comoé National Park (Parc National de la Comoé)
Unique: Lesser spot-nosed monkey, which has distinctive round white nose.
Old: Yellow-casqued hornbill [bird] lives 35-40 years.
Name: Blue duiker – Small bluish-grey antelope.

EASTER ISLAND – Rapa Nui National Park (Parque Nacional Rapa Nui)
[For the record, this is the island with the giant stone head carvings]
Unique animal: Rat, not unique on a worldwide basis, but unique here because it's the only remaining indigenous mammal (domestic animals have been imported)
Oldest animal: Green sea turtles can live 70 years.
Animal name: Red-tailed tropicbird (white bird with long thin red tail).

ECUADOR – Galápagos National Park (Parque Nacional Galápagos)
Unique: Galápagos penguins are very unique in that they are the only species which lives in the northern hemisphere. To survive in the warm climate, they have evolved in a number of ways. They have far less body fat and feathers than their cold-weather counterparts. It's believed that storms and ocean currents carried over the first Galápagos penguins from Southern Chile to the islands. Despite being left stranded, they were able to survive and grow their population.
Oldest: Galápagos giant tortoises can live over a hundred years.
Name: Alternate jokes notwithstanding, the blue-footed booby is best known for the bird's bright blue feet.

ESWATINI (formerly Swaziland) – Hlane Royal National Park
Unique: After long absence, cheetah populations have been reintroduced in park.
Oldest: Some elephants in their 70's.
Name: Lappet-faced vulture a fold or hanging piece of flesh in some animals. So ugly they're funny.

GABON – Lékéid Biodiversity Foundation (Fondation Lékédi Biodiversité)
We would be happy to appear in this book alongside our friends from PASA [Pan-African Sanctuary Alliance]. The Lékéid Park is managed by the Lékéid Biodiversity Foundation which must appear in the book.
Unique: The park shelters two populations of habituated mandrills, one of more than 300 individuals and the other of 50. This is a unique example of a successful reintroduction of a highly endangered primate into the natural environment. The first reintroduction took place in 2003 with about 20 individuals that still form the nuclei of the largest group. They are monitored daily by an international team of researchers. The 2nd group was released in 2014; its population has now doubled.

Older animal: The oldest animal of the sanctuary is Billy a male chimpanzee 30 years old. Billy had a very special life; he was collected by the presidential family in Gabon. He has spent twenty years in a palace in Libreville before arriving at the Lékédi Park. Today he is in a large enclosure of 7 hectares with his friends, and he learns step-by-step the wild life.
Funny names: Bonnie and Clyde are two chimpanzees who arrived together. Also, Biscotte and his daughter Auber (word game in French bicotte and butter).

GHANA – Mole National Park
Animal Unique: Martial eagle. They have wingspans up to 8½ feet.
Animal Old: Crocodile can live over 70 years.
Animal Name: White-naped mangabey is monkey which is polygynandrous, so both males and females have multiple partners.

GREENLAND – Northeast Greenland National Park (Nordøstgrønlands Nationalpark)
We are the world's largest national park at 375,000 square miles. Depending on whether you'd prefer an American or a European frame of reference, that would be about the same size as France and Spain combined, and even larger than Texas and Oklahoma combined!
Unique * Polar bears are unique as the largest land carnivore.
Old * Beluga whales live 40-50 years.
Name * Pink-footed goose, sometimes shortened to "pinkfoot".

GUINEA – Chimpanzee Conservation Center (Centre de Conservation des Chimpanzés)
We are located in the High-Niger National Park near Faranah. My English is not perfect. I am available if you have any questions. Thanks for interest in our work.
More unique animals: All the chimpanzees at the centre are exceptional. They are survivors of poaching. They have an incredible will to live. One example is Max, who for us embodies that will to live and courage. He was being held by a military officer in Faranah, a town in Guinea. Max was malnourished and suffering from acute gastro-enteritis and gingivitis caused by a fungus that had exposed the roots of all his incisors. He had deep wounds on his hips caused by the rope that kept him tied up.

We weren't sure we could save him, such was his critical and pitiful condition. In July 2005, Max was transferred to the CCC. He let us take care of him and put all his trust in us. During the first month, Max was so weak that he stayed in bed for 2 weeks. He was under 24-hour surveillance to provide the care and medication he needed to recover. Max has come a long way. For several years he suffered from a serious heart problem which stunted growth. Today, he is a magnificent, confident male.

We can also mention Léonie, who arrived in 2011. She comes from Sierra Leone, a country bordering Guinea, hence her name. A Sierra Leonean soldier bought her from a poacher and sold her to a Guinean soldier. A Guinean Water and Forestry officer seized the little chimpanzee and had the soldier arrested at the border. When she arrived, Léonie was very small and had wounds on her head, a filling in her left cheek and almost complete paralysis of her entire right side.

Almost 10 days after her arrival at the Centre, Léonie developed an abscess over the bullet hole in her skull. After extensive treatment and constant monitoring, her condition improved. Smiling again, she began to move around better, was more alert and was able to regain some of the mobility in her right side. Unfortunately, her condition remained very precarious. In October 2012, a neurosurgeon kindly came to Somoria to operate on Léonie on the spot. The operation went very well and Léonie recovered very quickly. Léonie has a very strong character and a real zest for life despite her past suffering.

Older animals: The oldest chimpanzee at the CCC is Bobo. Aged around 29, Bobo arrived at the centre at a young age. He comes from a house in Conakry where expatriates used to live. He lived there in a tiny cage, pacing up and down and banging his head against the bars out of boredom. He was recovered in 1996 when his owner, a missionary, left Guinea. Bobo was in a bad way, suffering from a serious skull fracture.

It was very difficult to reintroduce him to the other chimpanzees, as he was terribly afraid of his fellow chimpanzees. After years of rehabilitation, Bobo was released in 2010, but he was unable to cope with the pressure of release and had to be taken back to the CCC. Back at the sanctuary, Bobo quickly recovered and found a smile and a zest for life. He's a very clever chimpanzee and also the biggest resident of the centre!

Animal at your facility with a clever name: Labé arrived at the CCC on 1 July 2012 after being confiscated in Conakry by the authorities. Labé comes from the town of Labé in Fouta Djallon. It was to be offered to a major drug dealer! Fortunately, the young man who was "looking after her" treated her well. She spent 6 weeks in quarantine and turned out to be in excellent health.

She quickly adapted to her new life at the CCC, happily rediscovering the forest, wild fruit and the joys of going out in the bush! Labé was affectionately nicknamed "Labétise" by the members of the team. It's a French play on words to describe Labé's fun-loving character. Labé was always cracking little jokes and loved to provoke the team into play. She is now the dominant female in her group and is very peaceful. Labé does not like conflict.

Here are my answers regarding the name. Labêtise is a play on words in French for "foolishness." I'm not sure of the English translation. It refers to the little things that children can do despite being forbidden to do so by their parents. For example, Labé could walk in the forest by turning around and closing her eyes. Of course, she'd end up bumping into a tree... Sometimes she'd just roll around. Or she would smear her face with earth. She particularly liked defying authority.

The CCC is the most isolated centre in Africa. Project Primates France was set up to help the centre raise funds, communicate...

THE HOLY LAND – By God, this one's a little bit different, and as quirky as it is, it's a better fit here than in the zoo addendum. By "Holy Land" we are referring to an area roughly located between the Mediterranean Sea and the eastern bank of the Jordan River which has been traditionally synonymous with the biblical land of

Israel, or in layman's terms, the setting of the Bible. Here's what happens when you apply our 3 questions to the animals found in the Bible.

Unique: We'll go with the unicorn on this one. The King James Version (KJV) of the Bible has nine "unicorn" references with one of the more common being found in Job 39: 9-12 where the question is posed, "Will the unicorn be willing to serve thee, or abide by thy crib? Canst thou bind the unicorn with his band in the furrow? or will he harrow the valleys after thee? Wilt thou trust him, because his strength is great? or wilt thou leave thy labour to him? Wilt thou believe him, that he will bring home thy seed, and gather it into thy barn?"

Age: Depending on the species, Jonah's whale could have been over 100 years old. Jesus compared his own burial to Jonah's entombment in the whale's stomach.

Unique Name: "cameleopard" – In the KJV of Deuteronomy 14: 5, a giraffe is referred to as a cameleopard, the name first attributed to giraffes by the Romans because the animal had the long legs of a camel and the spots of a leopard.

LAOS – Lao Conservation Trust for Wildlife (Mooniti Anoulack Saat Pa Lao)
Thank you for reaching back out and we have discussed it within our team and here are the answers to the questions you have asked.

Unique animal: Red-shanked douc langur [monkey with bright red legs (shanks)]; Hannah (adult female), Verbena (orphaned baby), IUCN: Critically Endangered.

Older animal: Asian elephant, Keaw Khun, 48 years old. Keaw Khun was a logging elephant, later a riding elephant, zoo elephant, and eventually transferred to LCTW's care, where she was freed from her chain and given an enclosure. Last year, she was transferred to the specialized Elephant Conservation Center (ECC) where she is part of a reintroduction program, learning to live in the forest and live with other elephants. If all goes well, she will be fitted with a radio collar and live as a free elephant for the remainder of her life.

Names: Keeled box turtles, (*Cuora mouhotii*), named Voldetort, Turtellini, Tortilla. In terms of a series of thematic plays on words, we found the naming efforts of the team at the Conservation Trust for Life in Laos to be a particularly stellar rock 'n roll revival. With zoos around the world making music a common theme for intriguing names, we felt a need to wax poetic, writing the following global analysis

> *While the musical names were a common endeavor*
> *We found those Laotians exceedingly clever*
> *With those pun battles raging all over the house*
> *There were none could compete with those punsters from Laos*
> *Challenging wordplays were conquered like hurdles*
> *With ingenious musical names for their turtles*

Prompting a promenade down the path from
Elvis Presley→Elton John→Alice Cooper→Alice in Chains→Shania Twain, those musical magicians from Laos coined a turtle shell shellacking shining the spotlight on their turtles named...
Shellvis→Shellton John→Shellice Cooper→Shellice in Chains→Shellia Twain.
Please do let us know if we end up in your book as we would like to see it.

LESOTHO – Sehlabathebe National Park (Mhlabathebe National Park)
Unique: Maluti redfin, a critically endangered fish which is endemic to the park.
Older: Cape vulture lives 20-25 years.
Name: Bearded vulture sounds funny.

LIBERIA – Sapo National Park
Animal Unique - Liberian Mongoose - endemic to Liberia and Ivory Coast.
Animal Old - Crocodiles live longest in park.
Animal Name - "Pygmy hippopotamus" is a contradiction of terms, what you call "oxymoron" in English.

MADAGASCAR – **Masoala National Park (Parc National Masoala)**
More unique: If those cute lemur eyes are starring at you from the wild, the only place in the world you could be is in Madagascar.
Old animal: The humpback whales, which visit Antongil Bay for breeding during their migration can live to be 90 years.
Name: The tomato frog lives up to its unique name; bright red, round, and four inches in diameter.

MALAYSIA – **Bornean Sun Bear Conservation Centre (Pusat Pemuliharaan Beruang Madu Borneo)**
More unique animals: Bornean Sun Bear Conservation Centre only takes care of sun bears rescued across Sabah. Currently, there are 44 rescued sun bears at our centre. I will always claim that sun bears are unique in the sense that they are the smallest bear species in the world. They have the smallest ears compared to other bear species and they can climb one of the tallest trees in the world!
Older animals: Amaco is our oldest rescued male sun bear, age 30-years-old at Bornean Sun Bear Conservation Centre. He was rescued in 2011 from a mini-zoo owned by an oil palm plantation after being kept in a small cage for 18 years. He is healthy and enjoying his senior age at the sun bear centre.
Clever name: Mamatai is our old female sun bear age 22 years old. The name "Mamatai" in the local Dusun language means "die you!". She was named with such a name because of her aggressiveness when she was young. However, her personality changed a lot and now she is adorable and downright cute with her big grey beautiful eyes. Due to her poor dental condition, Mamatai has moved to the quarantine area. Even there, Mamatai is a happy go lucky bear who loves to greet the forest in the morning! She loves to stay in the basket facing the forest.

The Bornean Sun Bear Conservation Centre (BSBCC) was founded in 2008 by wildlife biologist Dr Siew Te Wong to conserve sun bears through holistic and pragmatic approaches that incorporate improved animal welfare, education, rehabilitation, and ecotourism.

The centre was created under a partnership among Sabah Wildlife Department, Sabah Forestry Department, and a local NGO LEAP. Over the past 15 years, BSBCC has received 69 sun bears rescued by the Sabah Wildlife Department. Twelve of them have been successfully rehabilitated and released back into the wild. Currently, BSBCC is home to 44 rescued sun bears.

MALDIVES – Fuvahmulah Dive Tiger Zoo (Fuvammulah Daiv Taigar Zoo)
That's funny that we got attention from the party who were interested in ZOOs, indeed! :))) We are not a "Zoo" like a formal zoo, however the name is given with a big meaning. Let me explain…

Seven years ago we found out this place is full of tiger sharks, and opened the first diving centre on this island. The island at that time was totally abandoned and unknown. and there was NO tiger shark diving in the Maldives ever before. Tiger sharks are widely distributed in temperate waters all around the world. Here in the Maldives as well. But, there are not so many places where you can freely dive with them. There was only one place – Tiger Beach in the Bahamas, when conditions are more or less pleasant. But also seasonable.

When we discovered this place, we were so excited, and my husband named it "ZOO", "Tiger Zoo". We call it "Zoo" because in this dive site you can see tiger sharks everyday with no exception. Many of them. More and more, day by day. There are no seasons. Same as at the zoo. You can dive any time and predictably see the animal. But we have no cages, no captivity.

We have permanent marine biologists in our team and we carry out lectures and shark education for the guests during their stay. We carry on official government research of tiger sharks and other elasmobranch [endangered shark species] in Fuvahmulah. Our database includes more than 300 tiger shark individuals, which is a unique and ultimate occasion in all our planet. You cannot find the place better if you like tiger sharks.

As per nowadays, we already have many diving facilities on the island, many accommodation providers, and more and more tourists. Fuvahmulah is becoming a world famous place, because of the Tiger Zoo. This is one of the excellent examples of how sharks raise the economy of all region. And definitely, it is one of the unique places and zoos on our planet.
Unique animal: Tiger sharks
Older: Silver tip sharks, turtles, napoleons, barracudas, surgeon fishes, trigger fishes and many more reef dwellers. Some of our tiger sharks are 50 years old.
Interesting names: So many. Even J.Lo and Rihanna we have. :))

MONTENEGRO – Montenegro Animal Sanctuary (Utočište za životinje Crne Gore)
Unique: The animals, except the bear and wolf cubs, roam freely through the sanctuary and visitors are completely free to interact with them. This of course does require a certain amount of common sense, not always a given!
Oldest: Emus who roam free and run with visitors, okay maybe "chase visitors" sometimes, can live to be 35. They were abandoned by a traveling Italian circus.
Name ~ Two former circus camels, Budimir and Milutin, named after a Croatian soccer player and a Serbian king. How's that for a unique combination?!

MOZAMBIQUE – Gorongosa National Park (Parque Nacional da Gorongosa)
Gorongosa National Park is perhaps Africa's greatest wildlife restoration story. In 2008, the Government of Mozambique and the Carr Foundation formed the "Gorongosa Restoration Project", a 20-year Public-Private Partnership for the

joint management of the park and for human development in the communities near the park. In 2018 the parties signed a 25-year extension.

By adopting a 21st Century conservation model of balancing the needs of wildlife and people, we are protecting and saving this beautiful wilderness, returning it to its rightful place as one of Africa's greatest parks, a position enjoyed prior to the Mozambican Civil War (1977-1992).

Nelson Mandela was the inspiration behind the impeccable planning that pervaded this project, perpetuating health, education and human welfare. Medical facilities used to support the park also serve the community. Revenue has been used not only to build schools, but also to deliver a gender equitable curriculum which seeks to support and empower female student opportunities.

In 2008 Gorongosa had 10,000 animals and today about 15 years later there are over 100,000.

On August 1, 2019 a historic ceremony was held in Gorongosa to celebrate the Cessation of Hostilities Accord between the leaders of the Government of Mozambique and the opposition Renamo Party. This peace accord established Gorongosa National Park as a "Peace Park", delivering human development to the communities that share the greater landscape.

We are showing the world an example of what a national park can be.

After contacting them, Gorongosa also wanted us to acknowledge their passion for the pangolin saying, "We received your email and request about the invitation for us to be part of your upcoming project on a zoological book.

We are excited to inform you that we would be more than happy to share with you about our efforts towards the protection and conservation of the beautiful unique animal – the pangolin, for which we have even created a country-only [the only one in Mozambique] rehabilitation center here in the park's main camp of Chitengo."

"The pangolin is believed to be one of the most trafficked non-human mammals in the world and so it is very important to raise awareness around this issue. Pangolins are hunted for meat, for use in traditional medicine and as fashion accessories, particularly in China and Vietnam. The large-scale illegal trade in Asian pangolins is drastically driving down their numbers, and pangolin trafficking is a now huge (and illegal) business!"

On August 1, 2019 a historic ceremony was held in Gorongosa to celebrate the Cessation of Hostilities Accord between the leaders of the Government of Mozambique and the opposition Renamo Party. This harmonious landmark accord established Gorongosa National Park as a "Park for Peace", delivering human development to the communities that share the greater landscape.

We are showing the world an example of what a national park can be.

MONGOLIA – Khustain Nuruu National Park
(Khustain Nuruuny Baigaliin Tsogtsolbort Gazar)
Funny name and animal: The Pallas's cat is a small furry round animal that looks like a moving dust mop with ears placed unusually low on the side of their head.
Oldest animal: Black storks can live over 30 years.

NAMIBIA – Namibia Wildlife Sanctuary
Unique animal: Kudu: Africa's graceful antelope with spiral horns.
Oldest animal: Baboon 40 years old.
Unique name: The hartebeest antelope has a short neck and pointed ears.

NIGERIA – Gashaka-Gumti National Park
Here are some colorful answers from Nigeria!
Unique Animals: African golden cat – black with gold spots, 30" long.
Older animals: Black-and-white colobus monkey (20 yrs), roan antelope (17 yrs).
Colorful Name: Yellow-backed duiker, small antelope with yellow back.

RWANDA – Akagera National Park (Parc National de l'Akagera)
Here's our animal restoration story since the 1994 Tutsi genocide. In 2015, seven lions were reintroduced to the park from South Africa, the first lions in Rwanda in 15 years. In 2019, five eastern black rhinos were reintroduced from zoos in Europe, and in 2021, thirty southern white rhinos were reintroduced from South Africa.

SENEGAL – Fathala Wildlife Reserve (Réserve Faunique de Fathala)
Unique animal: The lion cubs are the cutest on our lion walks.
Oldest animal: Tortoises live the longest here.
Unique name: On lion walks, you can meet Tara (m) and Lisa (f).

SIERRA LEONE – Tacugama Chimpanzee Sanctuary (Tacugama Chimpanzi Sanktua)
Thank you for your reply. We would be very grateful if Tacugama can appear in this project. Even though Tacugama was created as a sanctuary, it has evolved to a unique conservation project that aims at protecting the Western Chimpanzee, a critically endangered species. We work in different areas in Sierra Leone to protect the wild chimpanzees and their natural habitat, and educating and supporting the communities at the same time.
Most unique animal: Chicha (2 years old. Arrived at the sanctuary in 2022). Chicha was confiscated from a small village in Loma Mountains National Park. We found out about her existence after we received an alarming call from people that had seen a very small chimp being held as a pet. We were able to locate Chicha through our outreach network in the area and it took our rangers more than two days to find her.

But we did, thanks to our long-term relationship with the Loma Mountain Communities. Chicha was in a very bad condition when we found her. She was deeply traumatized, malnourished and dehydrated. We feared that she would not make it, but thanks to the hard work of our vet team and love and care of surrogate mother Mama P, Chicha survived.
Older animal: Tom (41 years old. Arrived at the sanctuary in 2013). Tom was handed over to Tacugama in 2013 when his "owner" realized that keeping a chimp as a pet was illegal. Unfortunately, Tom had been kept in a cage for 30 years and the region where he is originally from is unknown. Although the cage was large and Tom was able to move around, he lacked the ability to socialize with other chimps and climb and swing from trees, 3 of the most important chimpanzee behaviors.

He did not know he was a chimp and suffered from psychological trauma. Since Tom had not had any contact with other chimps for the majority of his life, he had a lot of difficulty integrating at Tacugama. He did not know how to climb or defend himself, and was often getting beaten up by more dominant males.

However, with the commitment and determination of Tacugama care staff, Tom started gaining more confidence and learning how to be a chimp since he had plenty of space to roam, play, and climb. He was able to find a friend named Nico and the two like playing together and grooming each other.

Animal with a clever name: Somebody (16 years old. Arrived at the sanctuary in 2012) & Someone. Somebody arrived at Tacugama when she was approximately 4 years old. She was caught in a snare close to Makeni (Northern Province of Sierra Leone) and then sold to a couple who moved her to Bo (Southern Province of Sierra Leone). This couple kept her for almost two years, until they visited the sanctuary and realized she would have a better life with her peers.

When Somebody was initially caught in the snare, her right hand suffered severe damage and only one finger is left. despite her handicap, she is quite skillful at building nests, holding cups and fishing "termites" out of fake termite mounds in the enclosures. In 2017, Somebody was featured in a small clip on NatGeoWild showing off her ability to use a stick to fish out honey from man-made "termite" mounds.

 In 2019, Somebody was the featured animal on the "Chimpanzee" episode of BBC Two's "Big Animal Surgery". The episode shows world renowned wildlife vet, Romain Pizzi, removing a large hernia on Somebody's abdomen. The initial surgery was performed at Tacugama in September 2018 and Somebody recovered without issue. Somebody came into the spotlight yet again in 2019 when she gave birth to a healthy baby boy who care staff named Someone!

On 13 September 2019, Somebody gave birth to a beautiful boy, Someone. Although TCS vets were anticipating his arrival, Somebody's pregnancy came as a surprise due to implant failure. This happens in chimpanzees just like it does in humans. Someone is one of the luckier chimps at the sanctuary because he gets to grow up with his mom.

Despite Somebody's handicap, she is a great mom. From the start, she allowed Someone to explore on his own for periods of time and he has been seen engaging in gentle play sessions with some of the other adults in the group including his suspected father, Zack. Somebody is never far away and always keeping a watchful eye on him.

SOUTH AFRICA – Vervet Monkey Foundation

More unique animals: We have a group of Samango monkeys… Mango (first orphan to arrive in 2015), Zea (ex-pet who had a broken arm), Nino (found being sold on the side of the road), Satchmo (orphan found alone), Zayda (found alone with concussion and had health problems for first year of life) & Lili (found clinging to dead mum by the side of the road, Zea is her foster mum).

We have a few blind monkeys who live in the Calypso's Corner group, many of these were shot by pellet guns but have now been fostered by a couple of seeing females. Shanti-Ray arrived when he was around one year old, shot in the head but thankfully survived and was carefully guided in his enclosure by his foster mum Frenchie who took such good care of him.

We also have some monkeys such as Fiona who has had both arms amputated as she got into too many fights but amazingly is still able to climb, groom, eat and play and still going strong.

Older animals: Our eldest animal was Whitey who lived to 33 years old, she fostered babies until she was 29 years old and was still living in a troop until her last few months of life. We have many monkeys over the age of 20 years:

* Armies 26 years old, his mum was hit by a car when he was young, he now has some arthritis in his hands and gets some additional special foods, supplements and juices to make his days easier but he does very well with his friend Bainne who he lives with next to the Royal troop, one of the oldest troops at the sanctuary.

* Chippy 26 years old, her mum was shot by a farmer; she is a gentle but feisty lady in the Robert troop.

* Seuntjie is 19 years and also lives alongside the Royal troop, his mother was hit by a car and sadly he fell into the wrong hands where he was abused and kept in a small cage for the first few years of life. He has had a few monkey companions over the years, one of whom was an old female called Sparkle who passed away around a year ago.

* Murray – lives alongside the SAAV troop with his female friend called Colin. He is 21 years old and had a cancerous growth in his cheek pouch a couple of years ago that was removed; he hasn't had any further problems since but did lose most of his sight. He still manages to get around in his enclosure and climb very well.

Animal with a clever name: Mr. Miyagi lives in Engeltjie troop; he has a distinctive look about him and is quite the character. He was an orphan, then kept as a pet before arriving here. Others: A construction team of Irish vols decided to name one baby Bob the Builder. We also have Leakey named after Lois Leakey.

SWITZERLAND – Geneva Bioparc (Genfer Bioparc)

Unique animal: All of the Bioparc Genève furry, feathery, or covered with scales friends are unique in many different ways! But Robin, our almost 15-years-old ring-tailed lemur dominant female (Lemur catta), has been chosen as our totem animal. She gave birth to six babies since 2018, becoming then the very first lemur mother here in Geneva! Through her story, she is helping us raising our visitors' awareness of species and biodiversity conservation, natural habitat protection, or else wild animals traffic. In our park, Robin is her wild cousins' ambassador.

Older animals: As a refuge, the Bioparc Genève is welcoming confiscated animals, abandoned animals, or wild and injured animals, with often no available background information. But, as far as we know, our oldest friend here is Aldo, our sulphur-crested cockatoo (Cacatua galerita). Aldo was born on May 15th, 1962 and will turn 62 in 2024! The Bioparc team is lucky enough to take care of him since October 18th, 2017.

Clever name: One of the Bioparc Genève red-crested turaco (Tauraco erythrolophus) has been baptized "Imba". Imba means "to sing" in Umbundu, an autochthonous language of Angola, where this species is originally from. But, fun fact, red-crested turacos actually bark more than they sing!

The Bioparc Genève, created in 2018, is the only place in the canton of Geneva where you can observe more than 250 animals, from close to 85 different species. Most of these animals arrived in the Bioparc through seizure or abandonment and nearly 40% of them belong to threatened species in the wild.

The Bioparc Genève is dedicated to protecting biodiversity through four key missions: conservation, research, environmental awareness and education, and animal-assisted therapy. As the Embassy of Biodiversity in Geneva, the Bioparc Genève aims on connecting humans and animals, nature and culture, and citizen population and wilderness.

TANZANIA – Ngorongoro Conservation Area (Hifadhi ya Ngorongoro)

The Ngorongoro Conservation Area spans vast expanses of highland plains, savanna, savanna woodlands, and forests. Established in 1959 as a multiple land use area, with wildlife coexisting with semi-nomadic Maasai pastoralists practicing traditional livestock grazing, it includes the spectacular Ngorongoro Crater, the world's largest caldera. This property has global importance for biodiversity conservation due to the presence of globally threatened species, the density of wildlife inhabiting the area, and the annual migration of wildebeest, zebra, gazelles and other animals into the northern plains.

Extensive archaeological research has also yielded a long sequence of evidence of human evolution and human-environment dynamics, including early hominid footprints dating back 3.6 million years. Ngorongoro is thought to have formed about 2.5 million years ago from a large active volcano whose cone collapsed inward after a major eruption, leaving the present vast, unbroken caldera as its chief remnant

Unique animal: The "Grant's zebra" is the smallest species of zebra in the world.
Oldest animal: The black rhinoceros can live 50 years
Unique name: East African wild dog or "painted dog", both image-evoking names, is the continent's largest wild canine. The African wild dog, also known as the painted dog or Cape hunting dog, is a wild canine native to sub-Saharan Africa.

TOGO – Fazao Malfakassa National Park (Parc National de Fazao Malfakassa)
Unique animal: The firefinch, a brilliant red bird.
Oldest animals: Elephants, chimpanzees, hawk eagles – 30 years.
Unique name: Red-flanked duiker [medium-sized antelope]

TRINIDAD & TOBAGO – Samsara Nature Park
Unique animal: Red-rumped Agouti (large South American rodent)
Older animal: Blue and Gold Macaw – "Uncle" is believed to be about 65 years old, was given to park.
Interesting name: Four donkeys (Sugar, Jaggery, Honey and Manuka)

UGANDA – Ngamba Island Chimpanzee Sanctuary

This year, 2023, marks 25 years of existence for the sanctuary. Over the last 25 years, Ngamba Island has received a number of orphaned and rescued chimpanzees with a few born at the sanctuary. Currently, the sanctuary is home to 53 chimps.

The 25th-anniversary celebrations will raise awareness about the importance of conserving chimpanzees and their natural habitats. The theme for this celebration is "Partnerships for co-existence", to promote the need for humans and wildlife to live in harmony in shared environments. The celebrations will be graced by the founder of the Jane Goodall Institute, Dr. Jane Goodall; a world-renowned ethologist and UN peace ambassador and a focal person in the establishment of the sanctuary as a project of the Uganda Chapter of the Jane Goodall Institute.

To celebrate this remarkable 25-year journey and set the stage for the next quarter-century, we have launched a unique fundraising campaign we have dubbed "25 for 25 years" under our celebratory theme – partnerships for co-existence. Our goal is to raise $250,000 through donations in multiples of 25, symbolizing the incredible progress made and the continued impact we can achieve together.

Unique animal: Natasha is the most intelligent chimp at Ngamba island.
Oldest animal: Kidogo, Nagoti and Sunday are the oldest chimps at Ngamba island, all around 40.
Unique name: Peace, who says, "I am quite famous for being the only chimp to 'testify' in court against the illegal possession of chimpanzees."

VENEZUELA – Canaima National Park (Parque Nacional Canaima)

Unique animal: The Tyler's mouse opossum qualifies as the smallest, and one of the only, marsupials in the Western Hemisphere.
Old: Red-shouldered macaw can live to be 50 with red patches on yellow shoulders
Unique name: The yellow-banded poison dart frog is a deadly, but beautifully-colored brilliant yellow and black amphibian.

ZAMBIA – Chimfunshi Wildlife Orphanage Trust

Sorry for the delay, but we've been very busy over the last few weeks, celebrating Chimfunshi's 40th anniversary in Lusaka and then Chimfunshi. I hope you're still thinking of adding Chimfunshi, the oldest and largest sanctuary in Africa.

Who are we: Chimfunshi Wildlife Orphanage Trust (CWOT), located in the northern Copperbelt region of Zambia, is one of the largest chimpanzee sanctuaries in the world. In an area of over 10,000 hectares of Miombo forest on the banks of Zambia's 2nd largest river, the Upper Kafue River, over 150 endangered chimpanzees and other wild animals in need have found a place to be rescued and rehabilitated in species-appropriate, semi-captive enclosures.

CWOT was established in 1983 to provide a home for a growing population of seized chimpanzees. Together with the local population, CWOT takes responsibility for the endangered chimpanzees as well as the wildlife species native to Zambia and works to protect them. CWOT provides employment opportunities, develops local partnerships to decrease poverty, and creates new sources of income by developing ecotourism activities. Lastly, CWOT is an effective tool for communication, awareness and education on local and international biodiversity, conservation, and animal welfare.

Our missions: CWOT's missions are 1) to support wildlife law enforcement and to rescue and rehabilitate orphaned chimpanzees and other wildlife by providing long-life care, 2) to engage children and the community to protect chimpanzees, local wildlife and the Miombo forest through education and 3) to reduce poverty and improve local community well-being through medical care, gender equality, alternative income community-based projects (e.g., organic farming) and capacity building.

Unique story of Pal, the first Chimpanzee who arrived at CWOT: Pal, the first chimpanzee, was smuggled into Zambia from Zaire (RDC now) and discovered being sold by poachers in a local market. Pal was in terrible condition, showing signs of abuse and malnutrition. He had severe injuries to his face, including an open laceration and his back teeth had been deliberately broken.

Initially, it was thought that Pal would not survive, but with the constant care and love of Sheila Siddle, Pal managed to win his fight for life. Although Pal's physical wounds healed relatively quickly, his drooping jaw remains a permanent reminder of the trauma he endured. Pal's rescue marked the birth of the Chimfunshi Wildlife Orphanage. Inspired by Pal's resilience, Sheila and David Siddle worked tirelessly to create a sanctuary for chimpanzees and other animals in need.

Over the past forty years, the orphanage has become one of the largest and most successful primate sanctuaries in the world. Today, Pal lives a peaceful life with other rescued chimpanzees at Chimfunshi Wildlife Orphanage. He spends his days exploring the lush forest (80ha) and enjoying the freedom he was once denied. Pal's journey from captivity to freedom is a poignant reminder of the importance of organisations like the Sanctuary. Through their tireless efforts, they continue to ensure a brighter future for chimpanzees and other captive animals.

Unique story of Mila, the oldest Chimpanzee at CWOT: Reflecting on Mila's early life fills our hearts with sorrow as we learn of the illegal purchase she endured as a baby in Cameroon and the subsequent years of abuse she suffered. At just three years old, Mila was taken to Tanzania and placed in a bar, where she gained a reputation as the chimp who enjoyed beer and cigarettes. For 18 long years, Milla's sole purpose was to entertain the public.

In 1990, Dr. Jane Goodall made a life-altering discovery at this bar in Tanzania when she stumbled upon Mila, who was in desperate need of a new home. Moved by the distressing situation Mila found herself in, Dr. Jane Goodall knew she had to intervene. However, releasing Mila back into the wild was not an option. Jane reached out to Sheila Siddle, and together they arranged for Mila to be transferred to Chimfunshi.

On June 9th, 1990, accompanied by Dr. Jane Goodall, Mila embarked on a journey to Chimfunshi, breaking records as the oldest chimp ever to arrive there. Mila faced numerous challenges during her transition to a new life. She experienced withdrawal symptoms as she was gradually weaned off her addictions, but eventually, she adapted well to her new environment.

Despite her traumatic history, Mila showcased her gentle and intelligent nature, often reaching out to her keepers for water and treats. Over time, she grew to appreciate her new sanctuary, and she is now recognized as one of Chimfunshi's most senior and intelligent residents. Today, at the impressive age of 51, Mila thrives in a life of happiness and security. She resides in one of Chimfunshi's forested enclosures, surrounded by fellow chimps who have become her chosen family. Mila's journey from a life of exploitation to a place where she has found love, care, and a true sense of belonging is truly awe-inspiring.

Unique story of Nikky, our blind Chimpanzees at CWOT: After being used as a tourist attraction for 9 years and being chained at a restaurant in Bangui, Central African Republic, a chimpanzee named Nick, affectionately known as Nicky, was finally rescued and brought to Chimfunshi in 2000. Nicky found a new home at Chimfunshi where he thrived and became the dominant male in Enclosure 4 for a period of time.

However, two years ago, during the transition of dominant males in Nicky's group, he was injured in a fight and lost his sight while trying to assist another chimpanzee. Despite our veterinary team's best efforts to save his vision, it was determined that Nicky would never be able to see again. As a result, a difficult decision was made to keep him inside an enclosure where he can be closely monitored on a daily basis. Luckily, Nicky's group still visits him regularly, showering him with affection and love. However, he yearns for a life outside once more.

To address his longing, we are currently raising funds to construct a smaller facility for Nicky, which will allow him to have access to the outdoors and be with his group. In the meantime, since losing his eyesight, enrichment activities have become essential in Nicky's daily routine. These activities help keep his mind engaged and his spirits lifted until his new enclosure is completed. Despite his blindness, Nicky remains a highly intelligent chimpanzee and still excels at solving the complex mazes we provide him with as part of his enrichment.

ZIMBABWE – Lion Park Harare

Thank you so much for reaching out to us at the Lion Park Harare. If I could introduce myself, I am Georgie Bristow the Social Media Manager for the Lion Park as well as the daughter of the owners of the park Graeme & Julie Bristow. Below are our answers to your questions and thank you very much for thinking of us to include in your new book.

More unique animals: Two of our unique big cats at the park are Leo and Lola our two resident white lions. White lions are a genetic mutation caused by a recessive gene, and not a form of albinism. Leo and Lola both have bright blue eyes proving they are not albino. White lions are a very rare occurrence with there, only being no more than 20 white lions in the wild.

White lions do occur naturally in the wild but have only been sighted in the Greater Timbavati area and southern Kruger National Park. The Shangaan people of the Timbavati region believe that the presence of a white lion in the area is a message from the Gods and their presence in their tribal lands ensures peace and prosperity for all.

Older animals: Tommy the Aldabra tortoise was rescued in the 1950s by a couple of friends of Ossie Bristow, the founder of this park. He was thought to be a Galápagos tortoise aging somewhere in his 70s, he needed a home to live out the rest of his years, so thanks to the kindness of the friends, Tommy travelled from

Mozambique to Rhodesia [now Zambia and Zimbabwe]. He was given to Ossie in 1960 for safe keeping.

When the Lion and Cheetah Park was opened in 1974, Tommy was given a forever safe home, where he has become the main attraction! After many years of Tommy being a Galápagos tortoise, the Bristow's reached out to the Indian Ocean Tortoise Alliance (IOTA) in the Seychelles, to help identify him correctly.

Tommy's case was an intriguing one as he had features of a Galápagos tortoise **and** an Aldabra, the eyes of an Aldabra but the upper lip of a Galápagos. The confusion in his identity came with his upper lip area, Tommy's beak is wide and flat. The IOTA suspected this unusual appearance was the result of a beak deformity Tommy had since hatching (hence the misidentification). It is Tommy's eyes that give away that he is an Aldabra giant tortoise as they are slightly positioned above his nostrils. The top of Tommy's head is also slightly rounded (like an Aldabra) not flat like that of a Galápagos.

Tommy is also not as old as he is believed to be, however this can only be determined after he passes away unfortunately due to the lack of knowledge about Tortoises. Therefore, we cannot accurately say how old he is, all we know is we have had him since 1960. And so, at the Lion Park Harare, Tommy is the living legend that connected the Seychelles, Mozambique, Rhodesia and Zimbabwe, reminding all who encounter him of the beauty that can flourish when kindness and conservation come together!

Animal with a clever name: We have a "Captain Jack Sparrow" and "Elizabeth Swan" our resident ostrich pair. We also have "Happy" and "Snappy" a pair of charming crocodiles; just don't put any of your limbs close to them!

We look forward to seeing Lion Park Harare featured in your book and we hope that this will bring more attention to the importance of wildlife preservation. We also hope that it will inspire readers to take an interest in the rich and diverse wildlife that Africa has to offer. Thank you for considering us for this exciting project. We're eager to see the final product and how it will contribute to the cause of wildlife conservation globally.

Should you need any more info please do not hesitate to contact me.

With thanks and kind regards,
Georgie Bristow

ADDENDUM #4
ANIMAL ADVOCACY GROUPS

We would like thank and acknowledge the following organizations who lent a hand in our research. Here they are with their mission statements…

ALL ABOUT RABBIT RESCUE ~ All About Rabbits Rescue is a nonprofit organization focused on rabbit rescues based in Queens, NY.

AMPHIBIAN FOUNDATION ~ The Amphibian Foundation is dedicated to connecting individuals, communities and organizations in order to create and implement lasting solutions to the global amphibian extinction crisis.

AMPHIBIAN SURVIVAL ALLIANCE ~ We are a global partnership strengthening and consolidating the impact of effective conservation actions to mitigate and prevent amphibian declines. The Amphibian Survival Alliance vision is to build a future where amphibians thrive in nature.

AUSTRALIAN PLATYPUS CONSERVANCY ~ The platypus is one of the world's most remarkable animals. The Australian Platypus Conservancy is working hard to unlock some of the key scientific mysteries which still surround the species, and also conducts a wide range of conservation programs and environmental education initiatives.

AUSSIE ARK ~ Aussie Ark is dedicated to creating a long-term future for Australia's threatened wildlife. Our mission is to protect Australia's threatened species with robust insurance populations; to create healthy ecosystems within Aussie Ark sanctuaries and through rewilding; and to have long-term tangible outcomes for the species in our care.

BEAR CONSERVATION ~ Bear Conservation is a non-profit organization advocating and campaigning for the welfare, conservation and protection of bears and their environments, both in captivity and the wild. Our vision is a world where bears are given the necessary protection and space to live out their lives in their natural habitats.

BETTER CHICKEN COMMITMENT ~ The BCC demonstrates a commitment to the most important standards required for chicken welfare, including breed, housing environment, and slaughter. This commitment enables companies to meet customer expectations regarding product quality and the more humane treatment of animals.

BIG CAT RESCUE ~ Big Cat Rescue operates an animal sanctuary in Hillsborough County, Florida, U.S., which rescues and houses exotic cats, and rehabilitates injured or orphaned native wild cats.

CROCODILE RESEARCH COALITION ~ A nonprofit organization devoted to promoting conservation of crocodiles and their habitats throughout Central America through community involvement, research, and education.

ELEPHANT AID INTERNATIONAL ~ EAI's mission is to end the worldwide suffering of elephants by creating innovative approaches to the care and management of elephants in captivity.

GIRAFFE CONSERVATION FOUNDATION ~ The Giraffe Conservation Foundation (GCF) is the only organization in the world that concentrates solely on the conservation and management of giraffe in the wild throughout Africa. GCF is dedicated to a sustainable future for all giraffe populations in the wild. GCF is a voice for giraffe.

HEALESVILLE SANCTUARY ~ Located in Australia, our mission is fighting extinction and creating a future rich in wildlife. We will protect the ecosystems and biodiversity which belongs to us all.

HELPING RHINOS ~ Helping Rhinos is forging innovative conservation, community and education initiatives to ensure the long-term survival of the rhino and other endangered wildlife in their natural habitat. We are improving livelihoods by investing in local communities and leading conservation education initiatives.

HOUSE RABBIT SOCIETY ~ House Rabbit Society is a global network that provides educational materials to the public, shelters, and others. Working with our supporters, our own shelter, veterinary professionals, and other rescue groups, we collect and share current, accurate care information. We advocate for the health and care of all domesticated rabbits and that they be cared for as the social and intelligent individuals they are.

INTERNATIONAL FUND FOR ANIMAL WELFARE ~ The International Fund for Animal Welfare (IFAW) is one of the leading voices in the recovery efforts for the critically endangered North Atlantic right whale and is one of the only conservation groups to take an interdisciplinary approach to save the right whale through on-the-ground efforts, scientific research, and regulatory change with a team spanning the entire eastern seaboard.

INTERNATIONAL WOLF CENTER ~ The International Wolf Center advances the survival of wolf populations by teaching about wolves, their relationship to wildlands and the human role in their future.

LION GUARDIANS ~ Lion Guardians is a conservations organization dedicated to finding and enacting long-term solutions for people and lions to coexist. We are committed to workable solutions that are scientifically-driven and transferable across areas.

OCEAN ALLIANCE ~ Ocean Alliance's mission is to protect whales and their ocean environment through research, scientific collaboration, public education, and the arts.

OCEANIC PRESERVATION SOCIETY ~ The Oceanic Preservation Society is a California-based 501 non-profit organization that promotes marine conservation and environmental protection by combating complex global issues such as biodiversity loss, climate change, illegal wildlife trading, deforestation, and unsustainable fishing through documentary, film and media.

OUR BREATHING PLANET ~ Our Breathing Planet delivers visually compelling information about unique and amazing species and places to inspire and make caring about our planet a viral cause. The organization was founded in 2010 to raise awareness on environmental challenges.

PINNIPED ENTANGLEMENT GROUP ~ The Pinniped Entanglement Group was formed in 2009 by four U.S. marine mammal biologists and has since grown into a worldwide effort. There are currently 144 members from 18 different countries dedicated to the safety and welfare of pinnipeds.

PET SKUNK ADVOCATES & RESCUE ~ Pet Skunk Advocates & Rescue was formed to give people a legal option to safely surrender their domestic, exotic pets when they can no longer be kept in their original home. Pet Skunk Advocates & Rescue believe all animals' welfare should always come first.

SAVANNAH PIG RESCUE ~ The mission is to provide a lifetime sanctuary for Pot Belly Pigs & Farm Pigs who have been neglected, abandoned or no longer able to live in their owner's house due to being too big or aggressive.

SAVE THE FROGS! ~ This organization protects amphibian populations and empowers ordinary citizens to make extraordinary contributions to the betterment of the planet. We work in California, across the USA and around the world to create a better planet for humans and wildlife.

SAVE THE HIPPOS ~ The Turgwe Hippo Trust is about saving the lives of families of hippos whose very existence would have ended way back in 1992, and helping those hippos to breed, have calves and live the lives they were born to lead as wild African animals.

SAVE THE TASMANIAN DEVIL PROJECT ~ aims to create a resilient wild devil population that needs limited management intervention.

SEAL CONSERVANCY ~ The mission of the Seal Conservancy is to preserve and protect the La Jolla harbor seal rookery for the enjoyment and educational benefit of children, and for the ecological, scientific, historic, and scenic benefits to all.

SECOND CHANCE BIRD AND REPTILE RESCUE ~ We are a non-profit exotic bird & reptile rescue serving Rochester, NY & surrounding areas.

SHARK & MARINE RESEARCH INSTITUTE ~ Our goal is to advance the understanding and conservation of sharks and marine ecosystems through innovative research, education, and community engagement. We're committed to conducting comprehensive studies that illuminate the complex lives of sharks, their habitats, and the interconnectedness of marine life.

TURTLE FOUNDATION ~ The Turtle Foundation is an NGO that has devoted itself to the protection of all seven species of sea turtles and their natural habitats worldwide. With seven national offices we follow the vision of a future where sea turtles and their habitats are sustainably protected.

ADDENDUM #5
BEST ZOO LOGOS

One fun aspect of this project was taking in the beautiful logos of many of the participating zoos and aquariums. We can't bring the beautiful artwork into this book and these need to be experienced in glorious color, so we'll provide you the list. Next time you're in the mood for an amazing slide show, go through and look these up.

3 Palms Zoo (Delaware)
ABQ BioPark (New Mexico)
Alabama Gulf Coast Zoo (Alabama)
Alpen Zoo (Austria)
Alaska Zoo (Alaska)
Audubon Zoo (Louisiana)
Bird Kingdom (Canada)
Buffalo Zoo (New York)
Cincinnati Zoo (Ohio)
Dakota Zoo (North Dakota)
Denver Zoo (Colorado)
Detroit Zoo ~ (Michigan)
Great Plains Zoo (South Dakota)
Guam Zoo (Guam)
Hogle Zoo (Utah)
Honolulu Zoo (Hawaii)
Kansas City Zoo (Missouri)
Indianapolis Zoo (Indiana)
National Mississippi River Museum & Aquarium (Iowa)
North Carolina Zoo (North Carolina)
Oakland Zoo (California)
Oklahoma Aquarium (Oklahoma)
Oregon Zoo (Oregon)
Pafos Zoo (Cyprus)
Palau Aquarium (Palau)
Planete Sauvage (France)
Tacugama Chimpanzee Sanctuary (Sierra Leone)
Turtle Back Zoo (New Jersey)
Vermont Reindeer Farm (Vermont)
Virginia Zoo (Virginia)
Wildlife World Zoo, Aquarium &Safari Park (Arizona)
York's Wild Kingdom (Maine)
Zoo Atlanta (Georgia)
Zoo Boise (Idaho)
Zoo Miami (Florida)
Zoo Montana (Montana)

ADDENDUM #6
LONGEST-LIVING ANIMALS

In this addendum we are going to tackle those animals that are really into it for the long haul. Any animal who makes this elite list has to be capable of celebrating at least 200 years of life. Suffice it to say that you and I will not be attending these parties.

We cued up four websites to collaborate on this consensus countdown, averaging out any slight differences of opinion to provide a polished perspective on this list of longevity.

When we Googled what animals lived the longest the four websites, (followed by the acronym we'll heretofore use to identify them), that came up at the top of the list were Live Science (LS), One Kind Planet (OKP), Ocean Conservancy (OC), and Adventure Canada (AC).

Almost all of this addendum will take place underwater validating the Disney dictum that, "Everything's better, down where it's wetter, under the sea." But we will start things off on land with…

 # 12) ALDABRA GIANT TORTOISE (*Aldabrachelys gigantea hololissa*) **– 200+ YEARS** ~ Okay, we hate to do this to you, but we're going to start out with a bit of an asterisk on this one. The unofficial story of record-breaking age goes to Adwaita, a tortoise said to have reached the age of 255 upon his death at the Alipore Zoo in Calcutta, India on March 22, 2006. Guinness World Records recognizes the oldest tortoise ever to be Jonathan, a turtle living on the British island of St. Helena in the South Atlantic, who will be 192 years old in 2024.

So what's the story on Adwaita? Anecdotal records have him as one of four tortoises arriving at the estate of British diplomat Robert Clive in northern Calcutta after the Battle of Plassey in 1757. Estimated to have been born around 1750 at the time, Adwaita lived at the Clive estate until being transferred to the Alipore Zoo in 1875 where he lived until his death.

For whatever reason, the anecdotal dates involved with Adwaita do not meet the Guinness standards for official recognition. Who are we to criticize Guinness because they've been doing what they do for a long time, but even if you throw a little give and take into those dates in the 1750's, it's hard to construe a scenario where they're off by more than 55 years. So we're going to allow the giant tortoise to crawl into our 200 club. Hopefully in the 2032 edition of this book, Jonathan will be joining us.

 # 11) RED SEA URCHINS (*Mesocentrotus franciscanus*) **– 200+ YEARS** ~ These small round red spine-covered invertebrates live in shallow coastal waters from Alaska to California. It's the ones in the colder water that live long enough to pass that two-century mark and, ready for the really good news… when they hit 100, they maintain the health and reproductive skills of their youth. No little blue pills for these little red guys! Radiocarbon dating confirms that, if they can avoid disease and predators, some of them eclipse the 200-year mark.

 # 10) BOWHEAD WHALE (*Balaena mysticetus*) **– 200+ years** ~ These Arctic and sub-Arctic dwelling creatures are the second largest mammal on the planet, weighing in at between 75 and 100 tons while reaching 60 feet in length. The fact that they live at such depths complicates the process of scientific study, but DNA testing and also the ability to date harpoon fragments in recovered bodies has confirmed that some bowhead whales have lived over 200 years.

 # 9) ROUGHEYE ROCKFISH (*Sebastes aleutianus*) **– 205 years** ~ Lurking around the caves and crevices of the ocean floor, 500-1,500 feet deep, the rougheye rockfish can be found in the coastal waters of the Pacific rim from the west coast of the U.S. around the rim to Japan. They can grow to lengths of 38 inches and weigh 15 pounds. The longest documented life span is 205 years, not too rough at all.

 # 8) KOI (*Cyprinus rubrofuscus*) **– 226 years** ~ These fish are actually a domesticated variety of the common carp. Under normal circumstances, their life expectancy is 30-40 years, but if provided with the perfect environment, these koi can keep kickin' it for a long time. What is perfection for a koi? That would be an extremely clean, deep dark pond. It was under those conditions that a koi called Hanako set the longevity record for the species, making it to the amazing age of 226 when she died in Japan in 1977.

 # 7) FRESHWATER PEARL MUSSEL (*Margaritifera margaritifera*) **– 280 years** ~ These animals are the only ones on our list who find themselves on the IUCN Red List of endangered species. The reason for this is basically that the poor mussels live too close to man. Their habitat is in streams and rivers in Europe and North America where the oldest documented life occurring was 280 years. Human-related factors have altered their living conditions in ways ranging from not-surprising factors like encroachment of their habitat, to totally twisted tales like the one you'll find if you Google the article "Seattle Mussels Test Positive for Opiods".

 # 6) GREENLAND SHARK (*Margaritifera margaritifera*) **– 392-512 years** ~ We'll explain this large range in a minute, but first a brief description. As the name implies, Greenland sharks live in the North Atlantic around the large island after which they're named. They grow to a size of 25 feet long and weigh over 2,000 pounds as they slowly cruise through the deep Arctic waters at an average speed of three quarters of a mile per hour. Here are the age ranges indicated by our four website sources...

* AC: The oldest living vertebrate: A 392-year-old shark!
* LS: Researches suggested that the sharks could have been up to 512 years old.
* OC: Scientists discovered a 400-year-old female Greenland shark that set a new record for the oldest living vertebrate.
* OKP: Greenland sharks live for between 300 and 500 years.

As we mentioned in our shark chapter, one quirky way to look at this would be to say that a Greenland shark who saw the Pilgrims land at Plymouth Rock in 1620 could still be out there swimming around today!

 # 5) COLD-SEEP TUBEWORM (*Escarpia laminata*) **– 300+ years** ~ The longest living members of this species live around cracks or fissures in the seafloor called cold seeps where chemicals oozing through the cracks create a cold stable environment where a slow metabolism can extend life expectancy. On the ocean floor of the Gulf of Mexico, these creatures have few predators and can grow up to 10 feet long.

On the list of things they don't have also appears "a mouth" and "an anus" – no intake or output valves available. So how do they survive? The chemicals seeping through the seafloor are absorbed through the tubeworm's skin and mix with the bacteria inside their bodies to create the sugars which provide the nourishment needed to live. A 2017 study published in the journal *The Science of Nature* found that they regularly live up to 200 years, and some specimens survive for more than 300 years.

 # 4) OCEAN QUAHOG CLAM (*Arctica islandica*) **– 507 years** ~ When they dredged him off the ocean floor near the coast of Iceland in 2006 they named him "Ming" because this particular clam was 507 years old, having been born in 1499 during the reign of the Ming Dynasty in China. What else was going on in 1499? Well, France conquered northern Italy causing Leonardo Da Vinci to flee from Milan to Venice and Christopher Columbus was in the midst of his third of four voyages to explore the New World.

Meanwhile, Ming was growing his first of the 507 rings which enabled scientists to pinpoint his age. For the next five centuries plus, this edible hardshell clam would be chillin' in the cold waters off Iceland which slowed down the clam's metabolism enabling it to achieve such lofty life-span longevity. After making it through more than half of a millennium, Ming's final musings might have been, "Who knows how much longer I might have lived if they hadn't harvested me?"

 # 3) BLACK CORAL (*Leiopathes glaberrima*) **– 4,265 years** ~ This one is kind of a team effort with the black coral reef being formed by the exoskeletons of invertebrate creatures known as polyps continually multiplying so as to make the underwater structure larger and larger. The components of the black coral structure spend their lives lying low, over a mile beneath the ocean surface where even their days are dark and quiet.

Using radiocarbon dating, a black coral structure located near Hawaii was determined to be 4,265 years old according to Life Science. That being said, scientists estimate that the species could live for 11,000 years, not the blackest future that could be projected for any living creature.

2) GLASS SPONGE (*Monorhaphis chuni*) – **10,000 years** ~ The year was 1987 when the glass sponges, thought to be extinct for 40 million years, showed up in Canada. Apparently they had been hiding at the bottom of the ocean for all that time, allowing us to assume the 40-million-year-old fossils we found on those European cliffs were just parting gifts the glass sponges left for humanity.

Yep, the sponges were back and it was good to know they'd never left. All the while they were just solidly attached to the sea floor, pumping water through their porous bodies in order to extract the minute particles of nourishment needed for survival.

The glass sponge reef discovered in Canada is dated as being over 9,000 years old and scientists predict they'll be good for another millennium at the least. Unless there's another group of them hiding out somewhere else on a remote ocean floor, the Canadian glass sponges are the only ones in the world.

1) JELLYFISH (*Turritopsis dohrnii*) – **immortal** ~ This jellyfish reigns as the Earth's only species known to have mastered immortality. Obviously if this were an easy task, other species would have followed suit and mastered it as well, so that being said, we'll offer up our layman's term explanation of how this happens.

This extremely small jellyfish, which measures less than .02 inches across, has two basic forms in life. It starts as a polyp, just lying on the ocean floor with its fellow polyps. Then it develops into its medusa form… think classic jellyfish with the dome and multiple tentacles, albeit much smaller than that first jellyfish image that pops into your head.

If at any time this jellyfish, in its medusa form, becomes injured or stressed, it can revert to its polyp form and start the cycle of life all over again. This process can be repeated any number of times so the caveat that must be mentioned is that while this creature can be eaten by other animals, in non-predatory conditions, the Turritopsis dohrnii can live forever.

So not only are the immortal jellyfish a tough act to follow, they are able to follow up their own act, time after time, until the end of time. Seems like there must be a song in there somewhere.

ADDENDUM #7
ANIMALS IN THE OLYMPICS

There's a good chance this is one you've probably not previously pondered. In the entire history of the both the Summer and Winter Olympics, how many events do you think have involved live animals? We'll go sideways for a sentence or two and provide you with the opportunity to give this a little thought before locking in your answer.

THE POSSIBILITIES ~ Here's our one hint for you… of the possibilities in the queue of this quiz, there's really only a few that, if they don't immediately occur to you, will seem obvious when you hear them. Dwell upon it if you must, but if you'd rather avoid the 800-pound gorilla in the room, fear not as the answer awaits just over the horizon and if we have managed to lure your brain astray with the primate reference, rest assured that no gorillas have ever participated in the Olympics.

We'll lead this paragraph by sharing with you that the total number of Olympic events which have included live animals is five, with the breakdown being three in the summer games and two in the winter games. The ones to which we previously alluded as being those that will provide the "Oh, yeah" moment as the Olympic sports you could picture with live animals would be polo and equestrianism where horses are participants.

POLO ~ Of the sports with animals that have been discontinued at the Olympics, none were competed as many times as polo which appeared in the summer games in 1900, 1908, 1920, 1924, and 1936. For the record, of the five gold medals awarded, England took home three and Argentina two.

So why did the Olympics pull the plug on polo? It actually was not due to declining popularity; it was rather a factor of finances and logistics. The area required to accommodate a polo field and the required buffer around the area is equivalent to nine football fields.

And then there are the horses. While there are only four players on a polo team, each player requires 6 to 12 horses per match. The concept of transporting such vast numbers of large animals on a global basis was definitely daunting. It was those pragmatics that precluded the possibility of polo persevering as an Olympic pursuit.

So, let' regroup here and note that now we have four Olympic events left with animals competing, two from the summer games and the remaining two from winter Olympics past. At this point we'll stick with horses in the summer and trot on toward…

EQUESTRIANISM ~ There are actually multiple categories of horseback riding which are rewarded with Olympic medals during the summer games. We've all seen them. Depending on how much of a horse person you are, the Equestrian Dressage may range from a must-see to a must-switch-channel event. But as we've said, the equestrian gig is one Olympic animal act most everyone is aware of.

MODERN PENTATHLON ~ This is a logical topic to tackle next, because it is still being competed and it has a clear connection with our previous component. The "traditional pentathlon", first competed in 708 B.C. included the five sports of running, the long jump, discus throwing, javelin throwing, and wrestling. The modern pentathlon features fencing, freestyle swimming, cross country running, pistol shooting and equestrian show jumping. The latter is an event which falls under the umbrella of equestrianism, so while that overlap does exist, equestrianism and modern pentathlon are two distinctly different medaling events at the Olympics.

So at this point, now down to our final three, we can reset the game board with the knowledge that we have two animal events in the winter games, and one other animal event in the summer games. Next, let's get our collective chill on and direct our focus toward the critters we might find at the winter games because that last summer event which included animals is one of the most bizarre to ever be held at the Olympics and a knock-it-dead grand finale! (There may be a pun hidden in that last descriptor – keep it in mind.)

In resetting this piece for the live-animal portion of the two Winter Olympic events that have actually involved live animals, we will set you up with the following lead-in. For each of these events we will share with you the fact that they have not been mainstays of the Olympics. And as we often do in the audience-participation mode of our interaction with our readers, we'll offer up the teaser that one of these events you have absolutely heard of, and the other one, unless you are some kind of Olympic sport research freakazoid, you will never have heard of.

SKIJORING ~ Here's the story on the one that is virtually unknown. It's called skijoring and here's the concept. The sport of skijoring involves skiing while being pulled by a horse or dogs. The rules in this one can vary slightly, but they are not very complicated.

The participating human-animal teams compete in a straight-line race that can range from three to fifteen miles. The animals, on foot, propel the humans, on skis, across a course which combines snow and ice in whatever configuration is dictated by the logistics of any individual course. As long as the terrain is the same for everybody, it's game on!

So while very few know this as an Olympic sport, it does seem kind of fun. And if you have the right animals at home, it's an Olympic sport that you could actually try yourself. Skijoring made its only Olympic appearance in the 1928 games in St. Moritz, Switzerland, and in this one, it was horses that pulled the people. Skijoring was a demonstration sport with no medals awarded.

SLED DOG RACING ~ The other winter sport that involved animals, and the one you may have actually thought of on your own, would be sled dog racing. It was an Olympic event at only the 1932 games and the concept is pretty straightforward. Because sled dog racing can be competed in such varied locations, there is never a totally standardized set of rules.

Here are the nuts and bolts of the 1932 Olympic event. The race consisted of two runs over a 25.1 mile (40.5 km) long course. With six dogs per sled, each sled took off at three-minute intervals, and intermediate times were given to the mushers at 4 miles (6.44 km), 10.6 miles (17.06 km), and 22.46 miles (36.14 km). Canada had the lowest combined times and won the gold.

While it is no longer an Olympic event, the sport of sled dog racing still retains a fairly significant level of fame, in our minds in large part because of the annual media coverage afforded the Iditarod sled dog racing event held in Alaska.

The Iditarod Trail Sled Dog Race is an annual long-distance run in early March from Anchorage to Nome, Alaska. Mushers (the sled drivers) and a team of 14 dogs cover the distance in 8 to 15 days. The Iditarod began in 1973 as an event to test the best sled dog mushers and teams and evolved into today's highly competitive race which attracts worldwide attention.

So now, let's cue up a final drum roll before we reveal our last Olympic sport involving live animals. At one point we wrote an article for our local paper where we counted down the Top 10 Most Bizarre Olympic Events ever, with animal-involvement being an absolute non-factor, and this next event came in at #1 on our list. Craziest ever.

An element that certainly contributes to the bizarrerie of the event is that while it involved live animals at the outset, the event resulted in about 300 dead animals. Where was PETA when we needed them?! Brace yourself for…

LIVE PIGEON SHOOTING ~ The event to which we are referring was the Live Pigeon Shoot which, thank the Lord, occurred only once in the Olympics, at the 1900 games in Paris. Leave it to those funky Frenchmen to incorporate an event into their Olympics which would leave the following tallies on the scoreboard…

Dead Pigeons: 295
Dead Frenchmen: 0

Here's how it all went down and we offer this with the tangential thought that it would have probably been much more sporting, not to mention a ratings bonanza, if they could have figured out a way to enable the birds to shoot back. And how 'bout for effect, we cue up the soundtrack to the musical *Bye Bye Birdie*…

With the gunman locked and loaded in firing position, 6 pigeons were released at a time, from a distance of 27 meters in front of the shooter. The challenge of each participant was to kill as many birds as possible during a rampage that was allowed to continue until the shooter had missed 2 birds. So theoretically the massacre could have continued indefinitely; there was no time limit.

The gold medal was taken home by Belgian Leon de Lunden who made his kill of 21 pigeons a permanent part of ignominious Olympic history. All told, nearly 300 birds sacrificed their sweet-singing souls for Olympic glory.

In the original before-Christ Olympics, even those grizzly Greeks did not kill animals for the sake of competition and thankfully, the Live Pigeon Shoot in 1900 was the only modern Olympic event in which animals were killed for sport.

It's hard to leave this one without a final visual image of the killing grounds. The field was left with hundreds of birds, both dead and dying. (If the bird dropped from the sky, it was considered a "kill" even though it might have only been winged.)

It's not like they had veterinarians sally forth into the fray to confirm a cold-blooded heartbeat, or lack thereof, on the part of the imperiled pigeons. The backdrop of the award ceremony was a disgusting display of pigeon guts, bird blood and frayed feathers.

High above the ceremony we're picturing the two birds that de Lunden missed swooping celebratory circles above the pathetically precocious party proceeding below. We're thinking they'd probably agree with the thinking in our poetical take on this fiasco which we offer below…

This pigeon shoot's way out of whack
We cut the Olympics no slack
So here's what we say
Let's figure a way
To enable the birds to shoot back

ADDENDUM #8
HOW FAST CAN THAT ANIMAL MOVE?

If you've always been the competitive type and found yourself wondering who would win a race between a lion and tiger, or whether or not you could outrun a particular animal if it were chasing you, then this addendum is for you. Please allow us to explain our take on how we've framed this up.

We took the fastest speed attainable by each animal and that's the first figure in each of the two columns below. Then, displaying our competitive side, we set up the lanes for a hypothetical 100-yard dash race between all the animals on our glorious planet. The second figure provides the time it would take each animal to cover that traditional distance.

A couple caveats on our competition… While most of these times are achieved by animals running on the ground, some are obviously achieved while flying in the air and others while swimming in the water. Also, as stated, the indicated speeds are the highest attainable and, in some cases, they could not be maintained over a 100-yard distance. So enjoy these numbers for what they're worth as we take a look at the comparative rates of speed in the animal kingdom.

The template below is… **Fastest MPH/100-YDT–Animal**

242/0.8–Falcon (peregrine descent)
105/1.9–Swift (bird in straight flight)
100/2.0–Bat (Brazilian free-tail)
80/2.6–Marlin (fastest fish)
70/2.9–Cheetah (fastest on land)
60/3.4–Gazelle
60/3.4–Dragonfly (fastest insect)
55/3.7–Duck (flying)
55/3.7–Horse (quarter horse sprint)
50/4.1–Jaguar
50/4.1–Lion
50/4.1–Puma
50/4.1–Reindeer (Santa speed)
50/4.1–Wildebeest
45/4.5–Hare
45/4.5–Shark
45/4.5–Tiger
45/4.5–Zebra
44/4.6–Dinosaur (ornithomimus)
44/4.6–Horse (race horse w/rider)
43/4.8–Coyote
43/4.8–Donkey
43/4.8–Kangaroo (red kangaroo)
43/4.8–Ostrich (fastest land bird)
42/4.9–Dog (racing greyhound)

42/4.9–Fox
40/5.1–Camel
40/5.1–Deer (mule deer)
40/5.1–Ferret
40/5.1–Hyena
40/5.1–Lynx
38/5.4–Ocelot
37/5.5–Giraffe
37/5.5–Meerkat
36/5.7–Leopard
35/5.8–Alligator
35/5.8–Bear
35/5.8–Buffalo
35/5.8–Dolphin
35/5.8–Flying Squirrel
35/5.8–Moose
35/5.8–Moth (sphinx moth)
35/5.8–Prairie Dog
35/5.8–Robin (average bird)
35/5.8–Wolf
34/5.9–Porpoise
31/6.6–Anteater
30/6.8–Armadillo
30/6.8--Bobcat
30/6.8–Cat

30/6.8–Dog (collie or shepherd)
30/6.8–Rabbit
30/6.8–Sea Lion
30/6.8–Wolverine
27/7.6–Horse (galloping)
26/7.9–Roadrunner (bird)
25/8.2–Aardvark
25/8.2–Cattle
25/8.2–Elephant
25/8.2–Octopus
25/8.2–Polar Bear
25/8.2–Seal
25/8.2–Sheep
25/8.2–Whale
25/8.2–Wombat
23/8.9–Red Panda
22.2/9.23–Human (Usain Bolt best)
22/9.3–Crocodile
22/9.3–Turtle (swimming)
22/9.3–Walrus
21/9.7–Chipmunk
21/9.7–Lizard (spiny-tailed iguana)
20/10.2–Bee
20/10.2–Chicken (wild)
20/10.2–Koala Bear
20/10.2–Manatee
20/10.2–Mongoose
20/10.2–Penguin
20/10.2–Squirrel
19/10.2–Badger
19/10.2–Flying Fox
19/10.2–Hippopotamus (on land)
18/11.4–Shrew
16/12.8–Gopher
16/12.8–Tasmanian devil
15/13.6–Chinchilla
15/13.6–Goat
15/13.6–Housefly
15/13.6–Otter
15/13.6–Boar
15/13.6–Raccoon
15/13.6–Squid
15/13.6–Weasel
12/17.0–Butterfly
12/17.0–Kimodo Dragon
12/17.0–Scorpion

12/17–Snake (black mamba)
11/18.6–Lobster
11/18.6–Pig
10/20.5–Crab (ghost crab)
10/20.5–Frog
10/20.5–Skunk
10/20.5–Spider (camel spider)
9/22.7–Chicken (domestic)
9/22.7–Groundhog
8/25.6–Duck (walking)
8/25.6–Mink
8/25.6–Mouse
8/25.6–Rat
7/30.5–Gerbil
6/34.1–Beaver
6/34.1–Guinea pig
6/34.1–Hamster
6/34.1–Insect (tiger beetle)
6/34.1–Porcupine
5/41.0–Frog (swimming)
5/41.0–Hippopotamus (in water)
5/41.0–Shrimp
5/41.0–Toad
4/51.1–Hedgehog
4/51.1–Human (walking)
4/51.1–Mole
4/51.1–Possum
3/1 min, 8 seconds–Muskrat
2.1/1:37 seconds–Sea Cucumber
1.9/1:48–Ant (Saharan silver ant)
1.5/2:16–Gila Monster
1.5/2:16–Platypus
1.4/2:26–Echidna
1.2/2:50–House Spider, Tarantula
0.84/4:20–Goldfish
0.63/5:24–Tortoise (small land)
0.19/17:56–Giant Tortoise
0.18/18:56–Slug
0.17/20:06 seconds–Sloth
0.04/1 hr, 25:12–Sea Star (Starfish)
0.03/1:53:01 second–Snail
0.009/6:18:36–Sea Horse
0.0052/10:55:48–Clam
0.0020/1 day, 4:24:30–Sea Urchin
0.00006/39days–Sea Anemone
0.0–Oyster–stays affixed to rock

ADDENDUM #9
THE BIBLE'S TOP 6 ANIMAL ACTS

Here is our countdown of the most significant animals in the Bible. It all ends up the way the book started back in the Chapter 1 "Storyline Sampler" but before Noah's Ark pulls into dock, be prepared to sleep in the cave of the lion, enjoy Egyptian plagues, experience a firsthand view of a whale's innards, and partake of forbidden fruit. First however, let's light up the biblical tale that could serve as the inspiration for the internet browser Firefox.

 # 6) SAMSON'S FOXES (Judges, 15) ~ In the Old Testament, Samson catches 300 foxes, pairs them in two's, ties their tails together and sets them on fire. They are subsequently released into the land of the Philistines as an act of revenge. Obviously there is no PETA in the Old Testament.

This storyline can't help but leave one wondering what the vengeance being sought was for. Turns out it was those flagitious Philistines who sent that diabolical Delilah to cut off Samson's hair, which of course was the source of his power.

 # 5) DANIEL'S LIONS (Daniel, 6) ~ This was quite possibly the worst sleepover ever, and it went down in Persia, about 250 B.C. The era is pre-Jesus and pre-Muhammad, so there's no Christians or Muslims. Your two teams in the game are the Jews and the Pagans, so you can pretty much guess who Vegas has listed as the early favorite in this one.

Long-story-short, the Jewish Daniel is set-up by the Pagans in a scam resulting in Darius, King of Persia, sentencing Daniel to spend a night in a cave full of man-eating lions. The odds don't look good, but Daniel does have one heavenly ace up his robe which we detailed earlier in the book.

 # 4) THE EGYPTIAN PLAGUE ANIMALS (Exodus, 8-10) ~ Holy Moses indeed! In biblical times, Moses was the leader of the Hebrews who had been enslaved by the Egyptian Pharaoh Ramses II. Repeated demands on the part of Moses to, "Let my people go," were ignored by Ramses II leading to God imposing a series of 10 plagues upon the Egyptians.

Consistent with the theme of this book, we will share with you just the plagues where God was assisted by animal accomplices in plaguing those pesky Egyptians who found themselves targeted by lice, flies, locusts, and frogs. Certainly a daunting quartet of adversaries, and who among us has not felt the nightmarish fear of frogs flopping around in our beds?!

The biblical plague list includes that "throughout the land of Egypt the dust will become lice." Then it is noted that, "the houses of the Egyptians will be full of flies." Next the locusts will "cover each and every tree of the land and eat all that is there to be eaten." Finally, "the Nile will teem with frogs; they will come up into your palace and your bedroom and onto your bed."

Turns out, those Egyptians are a stubborn lot. Even through the frog infestation, Ramses II holds firm, and holds on to his Hebrews. It's only the last plague where God takes the first-born son of every living being, including the son of Ramses II, that the decision is finally rendered to send the Hebrews on their way home.

 # 3) JONAH'S WHALE (Jonah, 1) ~ The story starts with Jonah turning down a preaching gig that God gave him. We'll call that Bad Move #1. Then, rather than face God's wrath, Jonah runs. Bad Move #2. C'mon, Jonah, it's God... are you really thinking he's not going to find you? Then, of course, comes the retribution and you know there's nothing like spending a few dark days in the belly of a whale to give a man cause to reflect upon a few of the decisions he's made. Full details are available in the whale chapter.

 # 2) THE GARDEN OF EDEN SERPENT (Genesis, 3) ~ After setting up Adam and Eve with some divine digs in the Garden of Eden, there's really only one clause in the lease that the new tenants must strictly adhere to. There is to be no eating of the forbidden fruit from the garden's most impressive piece of landscaping which God identifies to the couple as "the Tree of Knowledge of Good and Evil." But of course the Devil is in the details or, in this case, the form of a tempting serpent and, as we all know, there's an eviction hanging on the horizon here. A more complete version of this account can be found earlier in our snake chapter.

 # 1) THE NOAH'S ARK ANIMALS (Genesis, 6-9) ~ This group ascends to the #1 position on the basis of collective majesty. Due to the circumstances dictated by the storyline, never before and never after would there be such an assemblage of God's creatures and, coming full circle somewhat like the animals did in eventually returning to land, we'll close with our opening comedy bit about the hoof-written note Noah found upon returning home which read...

Dear Noah,
We could have sworn you said you were leaving at 2:00.

Sincerely,
The Unicorns

ADDENDUM #10
ANIMAL ACCOLADES

Coming out of our Bible addendum, we'll acknowledge that animals are honored in various avenues of life. Three such "Bibles" of modern society would be *TV Guide,* The Hollywood Walk of Fame and Grauman's Chinese Theatre. Here are their respective takes on the all-time greats…

TV Guide's 50 Greatest Cartoon Characters of All Time

Okay, this poll is over 20 years old, but it was generated by the Bible of television, and it has been referenced by many subsequent polls. We think you'll enjoy it and we'll take the liberty of sharing a few thoughts regarding our perspective on this poll, with two decades in the rear-view mirror.

There are definitely a few examples in this poll of the rankings becoming too caught up in the popular trends of the times. Examples of this which we feel sure *TV Guide* will dial down next time they tackle this topic will be the overrating of then-current favorites such as SpongeBob, Pikachu, and Ren & Stimpy.

Some classics such as Mickey Mouse, Donald Duck, and Tom & Jerry are probably underrated, but we do appreciate the acknowledgement of sometimes-overlooked classics like Woody Woodpecker, Underdog, and Felix the Cat.

After sharing some pre-publication drafts of this, one suggestion that came back was for us to assign a "greatest omission" designation. After pondering the possibilities, one in particular popped. Where's Garfield?! That cat was nominated for 7 Emmy Awards and won 3! Definitely coulda, shoulda, made the list.

But without further ado, here are *TV Guide*'s rankings of the greatest cartoon characters of all time, with the non-animals omitted, hence the missing numbers…

1 ~ Bugs Bunny	27 ~ Winnie the Pooh
3 ~ Rocky and Bullwinkle	28 ~ Felix the Cat
8 ~ Snoopy	31 ~ Ren and Stimpy
9 ~ SpongeBob SquarePants	33 ~ Tweety and Sylvester
14 ~ Daffy Duck	36 ~ Yogi Bear and Boo Boo
15 ~ Pikachu	37 ~ Mighty Mouse
18 ~ Top Cat	38 ~ Wile E. Coyote & Road Runner
19 ~ Mickey Mouse	43 ~ Donald Duck
22 ~ Scooby-Doo	44 ~ Alvin (& the Chipmunks)
23 ~ Underdog	46 ~ Woody Woodpecker
25 ~ Heckle and Jeckle	47 ~ Porky Pig
26 ~ Arthur	50 ~ Tom and Jerry

HOLLYWOOD WALK OF FAME

Our next assessment of animal accolades is to take a look at how many of our furry and feathered friends have been enshrined on the Hollywood Walk of Fame. Here's some quick background. A walk down the Walk will take you over a 1.3 mile, 18-block length of sidewalk lining Hollywood Boulevard and Vine Street. The course of this hallowed route is embedded with over 2,700 brass stars saluting the pillars of the entertainment industry including actors, musicians, directors, producers and fictional characters.

Of those 2,700 stars, only 14 animals have been so honored, so they're not exactly handing these things out like doggie treats. Speaking of dogs, of the 14 animal stars only 3 have gone to real-life animals and they are all canine. Those would be Strongheart, a German shepherd considered to be the first movie star dog, achieving fame during the silent era of the 1920's; Rin Tin Tin, also a German shepherd; and Lassie, a border collie. Both Rin Tin Tin and Lassie were played by multiple dogs over the years.

Compiled below is the complete list, in alphabetical order, followed by the year the star was awarded.

Alvin & Chipmunks (2019)
Big Bird (1994)
Bugs Bunny (1985)
Donald Duck (2004)
Kermit the Frog (2002)
Lassie (1960)
Mickey Mouse (1978)
Minnie Mouse (2018)
Muppets (2012)
Rin Tin Tin (1960)
Winnie the Pooh (2006)
Snoopy (2015)
Strongheart (1960)
Woody Woodpecker (1990)

ANIMALS HONORED AT GRAUMAN'S CHINESE THEATRE

Being honored by having your hand or footprint preserved for posterity in the Forecourt of the Stars at Grauman's Chinese Theatre at 6925 Hollywood Boulevard is even a tougher task than making the Walk of Fame. Only six animals have been so honored, three real-life and three fictional. All three of the live animals are horses from the Golden Age of Westerns and they were all co-inducted alongside their cowboy co-stars.

The honorees are listed below and if the name doesn't immediately click for you, Leo would be the MGM lion whose roar resonates during the opening credits of that studio's films. Also, for the record, while Leo was officially recognized by Grauman's, there is no actual imprint anywhere in the courtyard. Rather than fake a footprint, they decided to just officially enshrine the iconic lion.

For the record, there are just shy of 200 handprints, footprints and autographs imprinted in the courtyard, so if you were to extrapolate the comparison between the Hollywood Walk of Fame and Grauman's, while the number of animals is lower at Grauman's, the percentage of animals is actually higher. Also, in 2013 the Chinese electronics manufacturer TCL bought the naming rights to the theatre, but in our heart of hearts it will always be Grauman's. The honorees are listed alphabetically below.

Alvin & the Chipmunks (2011)
Champion (1949) with Gene Autry
Kermit the Frog (1989) with Jim Henson
Leo the Lion (2014)
Tony the Wonder Horse (1927) with Tom Mix
Trigger (1949) with Roy Rogers

ADDENDUM #11
TOP 10 ENDANGERED SPECIES COMEBACK STORIES

Throughout this book we have endeavored to deliver a straightforward assessment of the realities of endangered species across the animal kingdom, even when the news hasn't been great. We thought we'd counterbalance that to some degree in this addendum where we'll share some good news about the most successful stories of animals who have made the most celebratory comebacks in terms of their endangered species status.

These success stories are exciting to share not only for the victories in and of themselves. Perhaps even more important than each victory, is what can be learned from the success and how that knowledge might be applied to the endangered species still in peril.

If you're a holiday person, or even if you're not, we've got a suggestion to add to your calendar next spring. Pencil in the 3rd Friday in May as Endangered Species Day. It's the day designated to celebrate the stories we're about to share, and also strategize about how to slide some of the "in peril" stories from that column of concern into this collection of comebacks.

For the record, this addendum started out as the "Great 8 Endangered Species Comeback Stories". Our Liaison Lindsey turned it into a "Top 10" by including the black-footed ferret and the grizzly bear, both deserving additions, and we want to acknowledge Lindsey for doing the heavy lifting on the writing of those two components.

AMERICAN ALLIGATOR ~ They've been around for 150 million years and managed to survive the extinction of their reptilian cousins, the dinosaurs, 65 million years ago. But by the 1950's, habitat loss and unregulated hunting had driven the animal to the verge of extinction. By 1967 federal protection had been afforded to the alligator making the hunting of the animal illegal.

Aided by captive breeding programs, enhanced enforcement of hunting regulations, and habitat protection, the alligator has been enabled to not only survive, but thrive. Nowadays there are 5 million gators prowling the freshwater marshes, swamps, lakes and rivers of the Southeast, ranging from Texas to North Carolina. The highest populations exist in Florida and Louisiana.

BALD EAGLE ~ Obviously this one takes on a symbolic significance for all Americans as the extinction of the animal that serves as the national symbol would have been an environmental failure of epic proportions. When the bald eagle landed at its lowest point in 1963, there were under 500 breeding pairs in the continental United States due to the combined effects of hunting, habitat loss, and pesticide use.

Significant dates in the comeback story include 1972 when the pesticide DDT was banned. This chemical compound had been linked to causing thinness of eagle eggshells, endangering the species' survival rate. The Endangered Species Act of 1973 put into place further safeguards protecting the bald eagle and aiding in the repopulation efforts.

By 1995 numbers had risen sufficiently to allow the IUCN (International Union for the Conservation of Nature) to reclassify the bald eagle from "endangered" to "threatened" and in 2007 it was removed completely from the endangered list and given "least concern" status by the IUCN. Today, there are an estimated 15,000 breeding pairs soaring over the skies of North America.

BLACK-FOOTED FERRET ~These ferrets are different than the ones you would find in a pet store. In 1964, the species was thought to be extinct, but a small population was found in South Dakota! These ferrets were studied for a while but shortly their population began to decline. Scientists captured 9 BFFs and took them into captivity in hopes of starting a breeding program. This attempt was unsuccessful and the last known ferret died in 1979. Once again, the species was declared extinct. BUT the story does not stop there!

In 1981, a ranch dog in Wyoming brought his owner a dead black-footed ferret, which lead scientists to confirm that there were wild black-footed ferrets still out there! At first scientists attempted to leave the ferrets, but ultimately history repeated itself, and the population started declining. This was due to a few different things, but mostly because of a loss in their primary prey source, prairie dogs. The population of prairie dogs was decreasing due to humans and the Sylvatic plague (which ferrets can also contract).

In 1987 scientists captured the 18 remaining ferrets and transferred them to breeding facilities. That left the fate of the species up to 18 individuals, and they were successful! Currently there are 6 breeding facilities across the U.S., and now there are 300 wild BFFs! Though this story is incredible, they are still facing threats in the wild, including disease, loss of habitat, and loss of their main prey, those aforementioned prairie dogs.

BROWN PELICAN ~ This bird's story mirrors that of the bald eagle in some significant regards, namely declining numbers due to habitat loss and DDT weakening their eggshells. Native primarily to Louisiana, brown pelican population loss led to its being added to the endangered species list in 1972.

The banning of DDT and intensive captive breeding programs reintroducing the brown pelican to the wild contributed to an extremely successful comeback. There are currently about 18,000 nesting pairs of brown pelicans living in Louisiana and the bird was removed from the endangered species list in 2009.

CALIFORNIA CONDOR ~ Standing tall as North America's largest bird, we thought the California condor warranted a shout-out here, even if its comeback has not been the overwhelming success of the previous few components of this addendum. Hunting, habitat loss, DDT, and lead poisoning from bullet fragments in carrion all contributed to the decline of the condor.

By the early 1980's, the population had dropped to the point where there were only a few dozen of these condors left in the wild. An ambitious captive breeding program and stringent conservation have led to a significant turnaround. The numbers for the California condor are now at around 500.

GRAY WOLF ~ Before the arrival of the European settler colonizers, over two million gray wolves populated North America and had coexisted with indigenous peoples for millennia. Europeans brought with them their fear of wolves and their cultural practices which led to eradication campaigns and bounty systems. The population had been reduced to a few hundred animals by the 1970's and in 1974 it was placed on the endangered species list.

The restoration plan for the gray wolf featured some strategic approaches. The animal was reintroduced into calculated locations like Yellowstone National Park in the 1990's. Also, programs were put in place to compensate ranchers for livestock killed by the wolves, subsequently making the wolves less likely to be killed by the ranchers. Wolves are also excellent dispersers and have slowly recolonized part of their historical range.

The gray wolf population has increased since then, but they are still protected under the Endangered Species Act (with the exception of the Northern Rocky Mountain population). Current population estimates are around 6,500 in the contiguous 48 states, and 7,000-11,000 in Alaska.

GRIZZLY BEAR ~ Grizzly bears are one of the most iconic species in the west and, at one point, they only occupied about 2% of their former range in the lower 48 states. Their historic range spanned most of the western U.S. – from all the way up to Alaska (where they still live today), down to Mexico! At the peak of this population, there were about 50,000 bears, but by 1975 the population in the lower 48 had dropped to under 800 individuals. In 1975 they were placed under the Endangered Species Act. Most of their decline can, not unexpectedly, be attributed to humans, but they have made a great recovery!

As of 2021, there are at least 1,923 grizzly bears in the lower 48, with most of them living in the Greater Yellowstone area (northeastern Wyoming, north-central and southwest Montana), the Northern Continental Divide (north-central Montana), the Cabinet-Yaak area (northwestern Montana and Idaho), and the Selkirks (northern Idaho, northeast Washington, and southeast British Columbia).

HUMPBACK WHALE ~ We'll lead with the numerical roller coaster ride on this one. The world has seen its population of humpback whales peak at around 125,000, dip to 1200, and subsequently recover to that original level of 125,000. The international ban on commercial whaling in 1986 was obviously good news as for centuries the hunchback was hunted for its oil, meat, and blubber. The humpback pragmatically rose to the top of the whalers' want list because of their huge size and slow speed.

The humpback whale has benefitted from protections afforded by the International Whaling Commission, the Marine Mammal Protection Act, and the Endangered Species Act. Known for their lengthy migration route, the humpback whales now swim the seven seas deterred only by inadvertent adversaries such as vessel strikes and entangling pollution.

PEREGRINE FALCON ~ We were glad we didn't lose these guys when we did Addendum #8 above, because on the speed chart we found them at #1 on the list. Yep, no animal on the planet can move faster than the peregrine falcon which can reach speeds of 242 mph while rapidly descending toward prey. Unfortunately, the peregrine population also took a precipitous plunge with roller coaster numbers rivaling that of the aforementioned humpback whale.

In the 1940's it was estimated that the U.S. population of peregrine falcons was around 4,000. That number had dropped to 324 in 1975 with pesticides cited as the primary culprit. A captive breeding program proved extremely successful with a current population of around 6,500 in the U.S. today. They live in cities as well as the wild with their primary habitat goal being height. They nest at the top of tall buildings in the city while cliffs or mountains are their habitat of choice in the wild.

SOUTHERN SEA OTTER ~ How 'bout we make the transition from the fastest animal on the planet to the furriest. In assessing the pros and cons of achieving that status, a pro would be that you would stay very warm in cold weather. A con would be that you become the humans #1 choice for that fur trade which formerly flourished. That would be the primary reason why the southern sea otter, which once numbered over a million on the coast of California, was hunted and trapped to near extinction by the mid-1900's.

That large population was reduced to several hundred and in 1977 the southern sea otter was listed as endangered, falling under the auspices of the federal Endangered Species Act. Protections now being offered the species have led to a significant increase in the California population with current numbers approaching 3,000. Now if we can just avoid any fur coat comebacks!

WHOOPING CRANE ~ In 1800 there were an estimated 20,000 whooping cranes throughout the southern U.S. Then the people started showing up and the birds' habitat began to disappear. Their population had decreased to 1,500 by the mid-19th century and continued to spiral downward to the point where in 1941 you could pretty much hand count the 21 that remained.

That number had crawled back up to 50 birds when official "endangered" status was declared in 1967. Subsequently, progress facilitated by the Endangered Species Act has led to more substantial gains. The Louisiana Department of Wildlife and Fisheries has monitored a program which has bred whooping cranes in captivity and reintroduced them to the wild with the current population having grown to around 600. Good thing humanity reacted before these guys were too pooped to whoop!

ADDENDUM #12
PRESIDENTIAL PETS

Here's our rundown of all the animals who inhabited the White House, or other presidential abodes, along with some of the subsequent stories that sprung to life because of their presence on the property. Hitting a high with Teddy Roosevelt's menagerie of 40 critters everything is covered right down to the bottom of the litterbox where you'll find the Polk and Trump households, the only two who harbored no love for animals whatsoever.

GEORGE WASHINGTON had about 10 dogs (foxhounds, coonhounds, and a greyhound). Perhaps revealing his fondness for an occasional alcoholic beverage, the first president had a quartet of boozily-named coonhounds who answered to the calls of Tipsy, Taster, Tipler and Drunkard. He also had seven horses including his two Revolutionary War mounts Nelson and Blueskin, who for the record was primarily white.

One interesting pet that Washington was able to add to his stable was an Andalusian donkey which was a gift from King Charles III of Spain, offered as a gesture to cement the friendship between the two countries. The donkey arrived on September 26, 1785 amidst much public pageantry and acclaim across America. The naming committee did not set the creativity bar very high settling on "Royal Gift" as the donkey's moniker.

First Lady Martha Washington was known to be a bird lover with multiple houseguests making general comments about the size of her aviary. Only two names seemed to have survived, parrots named Polly and Snipe.

JOHN ADAMS had three dogs, one of whom he devilishly named Satan. He also had a pair of horses upon whom he bestowed the historically classic names of Caesar and Cleopatra. Romance clearly running rampant.

THOMAS JEFFERSON comes in near the top of the list of presidential pet owners. Let's start with the extreme and then we'll dial it down; for a time he had two pet grizzly bears. The grizzlies had been a gift from explorer Zebulon Pike and, full disclosure, they were just cubs when they were living at Monticello. They had a cage and at times were allowed to freely roam Jefferson's garden. When they got older the bears were donated to a museum.

His menagerie also included peacocks and partridges and he had pet mockingbirds that he trained to eat out of his own mouth. Jefferson's favorite mockingbird was named Dick. Tame deer also roamed the garden and he kept pockets full of dried corn to feed them.

More mundane members of the menagerie included two French shepherd dogs, three horses and a herd of forty sheep. The sheep grazed at his Monticello home, never making the trip to the White House.

Mammoth Mania ~ When it comes to Thomas Jefferson's deep storyline regarding animals there is a rather intriguing side story that we feel compelled to tell. Even though it wasn't even a word when he was alive, Thomas Jefferson was really into paleontology. He loved the history of animals that could not easily be found and if you combine that love with one of his religious beliefs, you end up with a perplexing paradox. He believed that all of God's creations were divinely perfect so, in his mind, it was impossible for any animal to become extinct. If an animal had ever existed, it was still out there somewhere; you just had to find it.

While dinosaur bones had been discovered before Jefferson's time, it would not be until the 1820's that scientists began to coalesce around the theory that dinosaurs were an extinct species of reptile, a realization that would have burst the bubble of Jefferson's anti-extinction theory, but there was one ancient animal that totally fascinated him. What was it? Jefferson was totally intrigued by the wooly mammoth and he was just sure that some were wandering around somewhere, very possibly in the unexplored western territories that would eventually become part of the United States.

So, when the Louisiana Purchase became a reality, Jefferson viewed the sale with double-edged enthusiasm. Not only was it zoned for "Western Expansion", there could be wooly mammoths in them thar hills! From a real estate perspective, it was a hell of a deal; we got all or part of 15 states for just $15 million as France was conducting its going-out-of-business-in-the-New-World sale. It's hard to buy a state for a mere million dollars these days.

The second reason for Jefferson's jubilation was that he genuinely thought that by the end of his second term there could be a live wooly mammoth frolicking within the gate enclosures of the south lawn of the White House. We're thinking that this was a possibility that had not been run by the presidential grounds crew.

So, when Lewis and Clark were sent to explore the Louisiana Purchase, they had one quirky presidential passion placed in the back of their minds. If they could find a wooly mammoth out in the west, it would score big points back in Washington. When the mammoth mission malfunctioned, Lewis and Clark did come up with a consolation prize. They sent Thomas Jefferson a prairie dog.

JAMES MADISON, along with his wife Dolley, had a pet parrot named Polly. When the White House burned during the War of 1812, Dolley rescued the portrait of George Washington and her pet parrot who, as it turned out, outlived both James and Dolley.

JAMES MONROE owned a Siberian husky named Sebastian and his youngest daughter Maria had a pet spaniel whose name is not recorded.

JOHN QUINCY ADAMS was the first president to have a pet alligator, which he kept in a tub in the East Room for a few months. It was allegedly a gift from Revolutionary War hero the Marquis de Lafayette perhaps answering the question, "What do you get the man who has everything?" About the alligator, Adams was supposed to have said, "I love the spectacle of guests fleeing from the room in terror."

In a squirmy additional note, First Lady Louisa Adams raised silk worms whose silk she actually spun.

ANDREW JACKSON was known for being a little rough around the edges and his presidential pet portfolio seems to substantiate that storyline. He had a grey parrot named Polly who emulated Jackson's propensity to swear like a sailor. Polly outlived Andrew, attended the funeral, and had to be removed because of her persistent and prolific profanity. He also had 4 horses and gamecocks for cock fighting.

MARTIN VAN BUREN was following a dictum that even in the first half of the 19th century it was considered unwise for politicians to snub the leaders of Arab countries. Perhaps that was why Van Buren accepted the gifts of two tiger cubs from the Sultan of the Arabian Peninsula country of Oman. Soon after their arrival, the tigers were donated to a museum.

WILLIAM HENRY HARRISON only served a month in office before his death from pneumonia, but he did have two pets during his short tenure. Those brief White House guests were a Durham cow named Sukey and a goat whose name is not recorded.

JOHN TYLER did bring some unique naming strategies to his pet portfolio; when his second wife Julia gave him a pet canary, he named it after himself, Johnny Ty. He had a horse called General and he also couldn't resist the urge to give an Italian animal a French name. He named his Italian greyhound dog Le Beau.

JAMES K. POLK gets a zero on the pet animal list. The only other president who will replicate this status, is Donald Trump.

ZACHARY TAYLOR presided over a White House stable that housed two horses. One was Old Whitey, the mount he rode as a general during the Mexican-American War. The other was a circus pony named Apollo which had been given to Taylor's daughter Betty.

MILLARD FILLMORE stabilized the number of horses in the White House stable at two. Not-so-subtly, with the Civil War looming on the horizon, Fillmore named his two horses Mason and Dixon.

FRANKLIN PIERCE had his pet portfolio driven by the fact that the Perry Expeditions of 1852 and 1854 had opened up new diplomatic channels with Japan. Gifts bestowed upon Pierce as part of the project included seven Japanese "teacup" dogs and two birds.

The type of birds is undocumented and the dog info is only slightly more detailed. The term "teacup" dogs refers to the fact that they were miniatures who might actually fit into a large teacup. Two of the dogs were noted as being of the Japanese chin breed.

JAMES BUCHANAN owned an unnamed eagle and two dogs. This pair consisted of a Newfoundland named Lara and a toy terrier named Punch.

ABRAHAM LINCOLN was a true animal lover and his resumé is sprinkled with several sparkling storylines. He had two dogs named Jip and Fido and noteworthy in this regard is that "Fido" had never been a standard go-to dog name before Lincoln's Fido.

He also had two goats named Nanko and Nanny and a white rabbit, name unknown. There was a White House turkey named Jack who was actually intended to be on the table for Christmas dinner prior to an intervention by Lincoln's son Tad.

When it came to animals however, Lincoln's greatest animal passion was that he was a connoisseur of cats. According to the U.S. National Park Service, when Mary Todd Lincoln was once asked if her husband had a hobby, she replied, "Yes, cats!" From his feline fascination, only two names can be documented, Tabby and Dixie. A related quote from Lincoln himself espoused the theory that, "Dixie is smarter than my whole cabinet."

He also had a favorite driving horse called Old Bob who went the distance with the president. He served Lincoln prior to his presidency and participated in the funeral upon Lincoln's death.

ANDREW JOHNSON had no traditional pets, but there are multiple accounts of his feeding white mice which resided in his bedroom. Not much better than a zero, but not an impeachable offense.

ULYSSES S. GRANT was a horse guy; his White House stable was occupied by eight horses and two ponies. The most unusual of the names was that of his Civil War mount Jeff Davis, ironically named after Confederate President Jefferson Davis.

He also had two dogs, a Newfoundland named Faithful and a second, of unspecified breed, named Rosie.

RUTHERFORD B. HAYES had a double-digit list of pets in his White House which included a first-ever overseas story we'll get to in a minute. Some of the quirkier characters in his collection included canaries, Jersey cows and a goat.

Hayes was definitely a dog lover with a desire for diversity. His kennel included a cocker spaniel, Dot; English Mastiff, Duke; Greyhound, Grim; Newfoundland, Hector; mongrel, Jet; hunting dogs, Juno and Shep; and miniature Schnauzer, Otis. Having documented the dogs, we'll move on to certainly the most unique animal story of the Hayes administration.

First Lady Lucy Hayes was also a renowned cat lover, originally heaping her affections upon her cat Piccolomini (who had been named after an Italian general). In an effort to endear himself to the President, the American consul in Bangkok, Siam (now Thailand) created some international theater by orchestrating a grandiose gesture whereby the United States would be blessed with its very first Siamese cat.

Here is the cat's itinerary. She would travel by train from Bangkok to Hong Kong, then by boat from Hong Kong to San Francisco, then by train from San Francisco to Washington. The sojourn, which began in late 1878, was not completed until early 1879. Lucy was said to be thrilled with her exotic feline and named her, appropriately, "Siam".

Later a second Siamese cat would be gifted to the Hayes White House which Lucy named Miss Pussy.

JAMES GARFIELD had a horse named Kit and a black Newfoundland dog with the cleverly presidential name of Veto. It was Veto who definitely had the more interesting side story. This involved a pet and president performance shtick which the pair practiced and used to entertain guests arriving at the White House.

Veto, would initiate the reception by launching into a series of barks and howls which the president would then proceed to echo. It is kind of a funny scenario to picture. You're standing at the front door, about to enter the White House, and you've got the President and the First Dog performing a canine duet.

CHESTER A. ARTHUR had a rabbit and three horses. Two of the three horses were a source of particular presidential pride in that they were beautiful reddish brown bay horses. Arthur sought to show them off by commissioning the construction of an ornate presidential carriage. In the resulting presidential promenade, flashy silver harnesses were employed to accent the brilliant red color of the horses.

GROVER CLEVELAND stands out in this addendum as being the first presidential fish aficionado having an aquarium filled with dozens of imported fish. It was certainly something most folks would not have seen at the time.

From there the menagerie took a bit of a more mainstream approach, although in sheer quantity he probably would land at #3 on the presidential list behind only Cal Coolidge and Teddy Roosevelt.

The roll call would include a dozen dogs from at least six different breeds, ponies, Shawineck game chickens, canaries and mockingbirds.

BENJAMIN HARRISON certainly took advantage of his office to keep his grandkids entertained when it came to pets. The safer of these examples would be the goat, Whiskers, who was known to be a favorite of the kids. A more unusual option would be the two alligators who lived in the White House conservatory until reaching the size where they were donated to the local zoo.

The more traditional pet would have been the Harrison collie, Dash, who was joined in the White House by two opossums. The quirky names for these critters were Mr. Protection and Mr. Reciprocity, monikers which were culled from an 1896 Republican party platform line which read, "Protection and reciprocity are twin measures of Republican policy and go hand in hand."

WILLIAM MCKINLEY was the proud owner of a Mexican double-yellow-headed parrot named Washington Post. Among the parrot's most crowd-pleasing acts, the patriotic fan favorite was hearing Washington Post whistle "Yankee Doodle Dandy".

Perhaps ironically, because he presided over the Spanish-American War, McKinley had two angora cats which he named Valeriano Weyler (Spanish general) and Enrique de Lome (Spanish ambassador).

THEODORE ROOSEVELT and Calvin Coolidge would be the two White House patriarchs in the discussion as to who could lay claim to being at the pantheon of presidential pet owners. If you wanted to give the nod to Roosevelt, you could tip the scales by acknowledging that as the more charismatic of the two, there are more entertaining stories and quotes appearing in the realm of Roosevelt.

In the Roosevelt roll call could be found a badger, barn owl, black bear, garter snake, hen, horned frog, hyena, lion, macaw, pig, rabbit, rat, rooster, two cats, two ponies, five guinea pigs, and nine dogs.

As promised, here are some rosy animal stories from the Roosevelt era. In 1902, Roosevelt was invited on a black bear hunting trip to Mississippi, but came up empty. Hating to have his president return to the capital disappointed, one member of the hunting party used dogs to corner an older bear and tie it to a tree for Roosevelt to shoot. Obviously there was no sport to be had in this opportunity and the president refused.

The story went viral and a toymaker in New York asked Roosevelt if he could make and market a stuffed animal black bear which would be called a "Teddy Bear". Roosevelt gave his blessing to the initiative and the success of the Teddy Bear became the impetus for the formation of the Ideal Toy Company.

Go Ask Alice~ Alice, the oldest Roosevelt child, was in the White House during her late teens and early 20's and she certainly brought a bizarre flair to the festivities. One of her favorite shticks would be performed when she knew guests were being anticipated.

She would hide beneath the main staircase by the White House front door, lying in wait for her victim(s) arrival. Then she would emerge with her pet snake Emily Spinach wrapped around her neck and her head wreathed in cigarette smoke. Picture a combination of Alice Cooper and Cruella Deville!

After successfully setting the mood of bizarrerie which she sought, she would approach the startled guest(s) and proceed to share the revelation that Teddy Roosevelt beat his children every day. Welcome to the White House!

Roosevelt was always ready with a rationale regarding the antics of Alice. "I can be president of the United States," he said, "or I can govern Alice, but I cannot possibly do both." We have a favorite quote from First Lady Edith regarding the playfulness of her husband. "I have six children," Edith would say, "of whom Theodore is the youngest."

WILLIAM HOWARD TAFT brought some interesting twists to his single term in the White House. We have some animal stories including a possum, a cow and a horse.

In a two-sided animal story, Taft was the last president to keep a cow at the White House and the first president to get rid of all the horses. Let's do the cow story first. Named Pauline, she was a gift from a Wisconsin senator and she produced eight gallons of milk a day. At this point we'll mention that, in addition to Pauline, there was a second cow at the White House named Mooly Wooly, but Pauline was the star of the show.

Pauline was so popular she actually went on tour, a tour that came perilously close to a tragic ending. The train tour was to travel from Washington to Milwaukee with multiple whistle stops where the people were afforded the opportunity to come out and meet the presidential cow. Who says the entertainment wasn't top notch back in the day?!

A Pauline Panic ~ It was the stop in Chicago where disaster was narrowly averted. We're thinking some heads probably rolled on this one because somehow they lost Taft's cow! How does **that** happen? A frantic search eventually located Pauline at the Chicago stockyard lined up for the slaughter. Cow catastrophe canceled.

Fleshing out the Taft pet storyline, they did also have a dog named Caruso who comes with some quick comedy. After the Italian opera singer Enrico Caruso performed at the White House, his takeaway impression from the visit was that cows were not appropriate pets for a little girl, so he gifted Taft's daughter Helen with a dog which was appropriately named Caruso.

Taft was the first president to have a car at the White House. The age of the automobile was upon us. In accordance with that societal shift the White House stables were converted into a garage. Farewell to the horses.

Playing Possum ~ Here's our final Taft animal story. The previous president, Teddy Roosevelt, had a stuffed animal named after him and the "Teddy Bear" had become immensely popular. In an attempt to emulate that success using William Taft as a model, Ideal Toys came out with the "Billy Possum". As evidenced by the total lack of any Build-a-Possum workshops at the mall, it can accurately be surmised that this new toy idea pretty much flopped.

WOODROW WILSON had two dogs, a cat and a variety of songbirds which were kept at the White House, but the most significant animal aspect of the Wilson administration would be the flock of sheep led by the ram Old Ike. Ike was actually known to be a prolific chewer of tobacco.

Truth be told, Wilson was actually playing politics with his sheep. The flock which peaked at the number of 48 grazed on the White House lawn to such a degree that the grass never had to be cut. Wilson sold this practice as an example of the austerity that Americans were encouraged to exhibit during the years when WW I was being waged in Europe. The wool was even sold to benefit the Red Cross.

WARREN G. HARDING presided over a relatively calm White House when it came to animals, especially in comparison to what was to follow him. He had two dogs, an Airedale terrier and a bulldog, as well as two other pets. In a scenario which was a certain source of confusion when summoning the pets, the Hardings also had a squirrel named Pete and a canary named Petey.

CALVIN COOLIDGE was a dog lover, who once said, "Any man who does not like dogs and want them about does not deserve to be in the White House." In the category of more common domesticated pets, the Coolidges also had cats and birds in their White House. But these more common household companions were just the beginning of this administration's menagerie.

There's actually a website devoted specifically to the Coolidge animals and it reads like a veritable zoo. Of the domestic variety they had 9 dogs, 4 cats, 13 ducks, and 7 other birds. In the exotic category they had 2 raccoons, an antelope, a wallaby, a black bear, and a pygmy rhinoceros. That gives us a grand total of 39!

As we noted back in the Teddy Roosevelt section of this addendum, Calvin Coolidge was not known for his flamboyant personality. Perhaps operating on the dictum that if you personally are not very funny, you could at least surround yourself with funny people, Coolidge was a close friend of actor and humorist Will Rogers, who was a frequent visitor to the White House. Rogers called Coolidge to task for allowing his animals to roam free range throughout the presidential abode.

Rogers' Response ~ "Truth be told," Rogers wrote, "the president seems more comfortable around animals than people. Frequently he looks the other way as his collies help themselves to morning sausages, and lick the sugar out of the bottom of his empty coffee cup." Rogers went on to add that the dogs were treated so much better than the human guests, he often considered getting down on all fours in order to gain the maximum favor of the president.

HERBERT HOOVER was a dog lover who, according to his presidential library, had no less than 15 dogs during his White House tenure. The most famous of those was a Belgian shepherd named King Tut who was frequently featured with the president in public appearances. Hoover felt that cavorting with King Tut made him come off as more approachable to the public.

In addition to the dogs, they also had a Persian cat named Kitty and a roller canary named Caruso. The other most renowned Hoover pet was Billy Possum who moved into a tree house previously inhabited by the Coolidges' raccoon Rebecca and was subsequently adopted by the Hoovers.

FRANKLIN ROOSEVELT had animal preferences that resembled his predecessor in that he was a dog lover, sharing the White House with eight different dogs from eight different breeds. The most notorious was a German shepherd named Major who had to be returned to the Roosevelt home in Hyde Park, New York "after a number of White House biting incidents." This of course serves to foreshadow the Joe Biden story which is upcoming.

In his final campaign of 1944, rumors were spread that FDR had left his Scotch terrier Fala in Alaska and then sent the Navy on an expensive rescue mission to retrieve the pooch. The president adeptly turned the potentially dangerous accusations into a positive by passionately countering with the comments that, "I don't resent attacks, and my family doesn't resent attacks, but Fala does resent them. You know, Fala is Scotch, and … his Scotch soul was furious. I am accustomed to hearing malicious falsehoods about myself … But I think I have a right to resent, to object, to libelous statements about my dog."

HARRY S. TRUMAN did not preside over one of the more pet friendly eras in the White House. The Trumans had two dogs, an Irish setter and a cocker spaniel which was actually given away to the Truman family physician.

DWIGHT EISENHOWER also has a short pet storyline. His White House was home to a Weimaraner dog named Heidi and a parakeet named Gabby. When Gabby died in 1957 the bird was buried by the southwest corner of the White House.

JOHN F. KENNEDY reversed the trend of his two predecessors opening his White House up to a menagerie of animal life. The Kennedy White House accommodated a canary, cat, horse, rabbit, 2 parakeets, 2 hamsters, 3 ponies, multiple ducks, and 11 dogs.

There are a few interesting names and storylines. The rabbit was named Zsa Zsa after popular Hollywood actress Zsa Zsa Gabor. One of the ponies was named Leprechaun, a gift from Irish President Eamon de Valera. Despite the Kennedy administration occurring at the height of the Cold War, one of the dogs named Pushinka was a gift from Soviet Union Premier Nikita Khrushchev and actually a puppy of Soviet space dog Strelka.

LYNDON B. JOHNSON did have some hamsters and lovebirds in his White House but he was primarily a dog guy and within that realm he was more specifically a beagle guy. Of the six dogs who lived in the LBJ White House, four were beagles, the most famous being a pair named Him and Her.

Turns out that one of the reasons for his beagles' fame managed to stick in Johnson's craw, an appropriate Southern expression indicating a source of annoyance. At one of his press engagements in April of 1964, LBJ was photographed picking up Him by the ears, causing the dog to yelp. Maybe they did that sort of thing in Texas, but it did not play well in most of the rest of the country.

Next day headlines included... "Barking Beagles Get LBJ in SPCA Trouble" and "LBJ's Beagle Hoist Arouses Ire of Humane Society". Modern-day historical retrospectives refer to the incident as "Beagle-gate" even though the Watergate affair, which brought "-gate" into common usage as a suffix, hadn't even happened yet.

LBJ spent most of the next week trying to back track and deflect which of course only served to confirm how much the incident had gotten under his skin. To his press secretary he complained that, "They've got every dog lover in the country raisin' hell thinkin' I'm burning 'em at the stake."

RICHARD NIXON had three different dogs during his time in the White House, a poodle, an Irish setter and a Yorkshire terrier. That being said, however, far and away the most famous animal moment in the history of Richard Nixon was the "Checkers speech" which he delivered on September 23, 1952. Here's the scoop...

The year was 1952 and Nixon had been chosen by Dwight Eisenhower to be his running mate in the upcoming election. Meanwhile Nixon had come under public criticism because of questionable fundraising practices and his acceptance of gifts from political donors. As the criticism mounted, Nixon decided to take advantage of the fairly new medium of television and deliver a national speech in an attempt to rally viewers to his support and maintain his position on the ballot.

In an attempt to humanize himself, Nixon said that regardless of the outcome of the controversy the one gift that he would never return was Checkers, a black and white cocker spaniel to whom his daughters had become deeply attached. While the speech had the desired effect at the time, historical retrospective does not shine favorably upon it. A "Checkers speech" has come to be defined as "any superficially emotional speech, which actually lacks material substance."

GERALD FORD shared his White House with three dogs and a cat. The most well-known was a golden retriever named Liberty who actually gave birth to a puppy named Misty while in the White House. Their cat was a Siamese named Shan.

JIMMY CARTER had two dogs, a border collie and an Afghan hound and daughter Amy had a Siamese cat she named Misty Malarky Ying Yang. But by far the most heralded animal story of the Carter administration was one that did not involve a pet.

Various circumstances led to labels which acknowledged him as the "Rock and Roll President" who killed off the "Killer Rabbit". If you're thinking that would be a lot of hats to wear, you would be correct. Ever hear about the attack of the "killer rabbit?"

Rabbit Revealed ~ So here's what happened. April 20, 1979 was a beautiful spring day in Plains, Georgia where Carter resided. What do southern peanut farmers do on warm spring days after the chores are done? Well, certainly one possibility would be to head for the fishing hole and that's just what Jimmy did on that day.

As he sat alone in his boat, Carter noticed something moving toward him in the water. As the moving object began to draw closer, he realized that there was a rambunctious rabbit headed right for his rowboat. Using the paddle he had on board, Carter redirected the rabbit toward the opposite shore.

Upon returning home, Carter shared the story with his staff who gave him some good-natured ribbing about the event, embellishing the danger of the "attack rabbit" and espousing the theory that rabbits can't swim in the first place. For the record, just to clarify what's really going on here, there are swamp rabbits in the south that can indeed swim and this particular one had hit the water because it was being chased by dogs.

And there was some documentation of the event. As you would suspect, while Carter was alone in the boat there was some security staff on the shore to monitor the president's safety. One staffer even managed to snap a picture of the President battling the rabbit so we do have a confirmed sighting.

Rabbit Returns ~ After some good-natured guffaws at the President's expense, the incident was pretty much forgotten until Carter's press secretary Jody Powell mentioned it to reporter Brooks Jackson several months later. On August 30, 1979, Jackson's story about the incident was published on the front page of the *Washington Post* under the headline "Bunny Goes Bugs: Rabbit Attacks President".

At that point, for whatever quirky reason, the story just seemed to catch fire with the public and the media, enveloping the country in a collective case of rabbit fever. One 1970's megahit movie was at the core of the comedy. A popular meme became to take movie posters from the shark-attack movie *Jaws*, change the shark to a rabbit, and retitle the movie as *Paws*.

RONALD REAGAN of course rode to fame as an actor, with many of his films being westerns, so it's not surprising to confirm that he was a horse guy. He had a dozen that resided at his California ranch during his presidency. He also had two tortoiseshell cats who never left Cali.

Reagan also had six dogs, some of whom did spend time in Washington. The one with whom he is most often pictured at the White House was a King Charles spaniel named Rex.

GEORGE H.W. BUSH had a springer spaniel named Millie who gave birth to a puppy named Ranger during the years when Bush was in the White House.

BILL CLINTON had a cat named Socks who lived in the White House for all eight years of his presidency and a chocolate Labrador retriever named Buddy who was around for most of the second term. Socks received and also responded to a considerable amount of fan mail prompting the probably overzealous reaction of Republican Dan Burton of the House Oversight Committee. Burton complained that the use of government stationery and postage for Socks' correspondences was a misuse of taxpayer money. Cat owners were not in Burton's corner.

GEORGE W. BUSH had three dogs and a cat at various times in the White House. He also had several animals back at his ranch in Texas.

BARRACK OBAMA facilitated the first high profile appearance of the Portuguese water dog. Of his many campaign promises, one that he could never forget was that he promised his daughters Malia and Sasha that he would get them a dog whether he won or lost. Always a man of his word, Obama made doubly good on the promise presenting his daughters with two Portuguese water dogs, Bo and Sunny.

DONALD TRUMP had no love for animals.

JOE BIDEN had three dogs, all German shepherds, and one cat in the White House. The cat was a gray tabby named Willow who endeared herself after jumping on stage during a 2020 political rally in Pennsylvania.

The most notorious Biden pet storyline emerged as that of Major who became involved in multiple White House biting incidents. These were serious enough where Major did not just get sent to the doghouse, he got sent to a Delaware doggy rehab. When that didn't take, Major was sentenced to permanent relocation. Unfortunately Major's plight was replicated by another Biden shepherd named Commander.

Further compromising the Biden K-9 conundrum was that their third dog Champ died while he was in office. So, bottom line, it's a good thing the cat jumped on stage.

ADDENDUM #13
TIMELINE OF ANIMAL HISTORY

Here are some dates that resonate in the annals of animal history; saddle up for some informative fun.

4.1 billion B.C. ~ The earliest form of life is documented in fossils which were discovered in Australia. Yeah, it goes way back but let's face it, you wouldn't be reading this book if it hadn't happened.

2.8 billion B.C. ~ Life moves on land occurs for the first time. Time to hit the beach.

550 million B.C. ~ Corals, sponges and sea anemones appear in the earth's oceans. Little do these sponges know they will someday become common household cleaning implements.

530 million B.C. ~ The first fish appear. Lucky for these guys the human concept of frying them up every Friday is still way down the road, or up the river, so to speak.

511 million B.C. ~ The first crustaceans appear; the concept of becoming "crabby" is given birth.

500 million B.C. ~ The first jellyfish appear.

485 million B.C. ~ The first vertebrates appear, fish with actual bones.

479 million B.C. ~ The first insects appear; don't let it bug you.

380 million B.C. ~ The first spiders appear; the ascribed species initiation motto of, "If the insects have six legs, we're going to have eight" remains disputed.

368 million B.C. ~ The first amphibians appear; **somebody** with just four legs has to overcome the fear of coming out of the water.

365 million B.C. ~ A type of fish called a tetrapod grows legs and walks on the land.

360 million B.C. ~ The first crabs appear; now we have animals that can walk on the land sideways.

350 million B.C. ~ The first sharks appear, cue up the spooky music.

225 million B.C. ~ The first dinosaurs appear. Enjoy the party because 160 million years will be over before you know it.

210 million B.C. ~ The first mammals appear, small shrew-like creatures.

187 million B.C. ~ The platypus diverges from other mammals, egg-laying mammals join the party.

150 million B.C. ~ The first birds appear, worms beware.

114 million B.C. ~ The first bees appear, who wants to get stung first?

100 million B.C. ~ The first ants appear, who wants to march in line?

95 million B.C. ~ The first crocodiles appear; see ya later alligator.

90 million B.C. ~ The first snakes appear, Garden of Eden sequence notwithstanding.

65 million B.C. ~ Dinosaurs become extinct; be sure to hang on to those replicas you had as a kid.

62 million B.C. ~ The first penguins appear; guest villain roles in the Batman franchise loom in the distant future.
52 million B.C. ~ The first bats appear, completing the penguin-foreshadowing scenario suggested in the previous entry.
40 million B.C. ~ The first butterflies appear, enjoying a net-free world.
38 million B.C. ~ The first bears appear; those bees that have been around since 114 million B.C take new measures to protect their honey.
37 million B.C. ~ The first alligators appear, joining their crocodile cousins.
35 million B.C. ~ The first dogs appear, although it will be millions of years before they allow themselves to be domesticated.
24 million B.C. ~ The first pinnipeds appear; this species includes seals, sea lions and walruses.
23 million B.C. ~ The first ostriches appear, destined to become the world's fastest two-legged animals.
20 million B.C. ~ The first giraffes appear, although their future looks spotty.
15 million B.C. ~ The first kangaroos appear; Australia celebrates.
12 million B.C. ~ The first cats appear; mice be forewarned.
5 million B.C. ~ The first elephants, lions, hippos and zebras appear; Africa celebrates.
1 million B.C. ~ The first coyotes appear; road runners beware.
600,000 B.C. ~ The first polar bears appear. What would they do for a Klondike Bar?
28,000 B.C. ~ Humans make cave paintings in western Europe depicting animals, the first being mammoths.
15,000 B.C. ~ The first dogs are domesticated. Make room in the cave for that food bowl.
10,000 B.C. ~ Humans arrive at the party. Things will never be the same again.
8,000 B.C. ~ The Chinese first domesticate wild boars. Pulled pork, anyone?
7,500 B.C. ~ The first cats are domesticated in the Middle East. They might have succumbed earlier, but it was in their nature to spend a few thousand years looking down upon the dogs who first embraced the humans.
6,500 B.C. ~ Ancestors of domestic cattle, called aurochs, first appear. Don't have a cow, man!
6,400 B.C. ~ A man and his pet dog are buried in the same grave in Sweden.
5,200 B.C. ~ The silkworm is domesticated in China.
4,000 B.C. ~ The first horses are domesticated.
3,500 B.C. ~ In the Fertile Crescent area of Mesopotamia, new uses of horses and donkeys are developed. In agriculture they are used to pull plows. In the military, mounted soldiers become the first cavalry and horse-drawn chariots are used in battle.
3,500 B.C. ~ The Hierakonpolis menagerie in Egypt houses over 100 animals including baboons, elephants, hippopotamuses and wildcats. Archaeological evidence suggests the animals were well-kept.
2,000 B.C. ~ The silkworm is domesticated in China.

2,000 B.C. ~ Egyptians domesticate cats as a strategy in controlling their snake population.

1,475 B.C. ~ Egyptian Queen Hatshepsut's menagerie features giraffes, monkeys and rhinoceroses.

1,250 B.C. ~ Egyptian pharaoh Ramses the Great had a lion named "Slayer of his Foes" which he took into battle with him.

1,150 B.C. ~ The Chinese Empress Tanki founds China's first zoo, the "House of Deer".

1,100 B.C. ~ Chinese Emperor Won Chang of the Zhou Dynasty establishes an imperial zoo stocked with birds, deer, fish, and goats from all over the known world.

1,000 B.C. ~ Camels are first domesticated.

750 B.C. ~ According to legend, Lupa, a mother wolf, discovers the abandoned royal twins Romulus and Remus along the banks of the Tiver River. She nurses them back to health and subsequently Romulus would kill Remus before going on to found Rome.

540 B.C. ~ Indian philosopher Buddha espouses the intrinsic value of animals, his teachings characterized by the acknowledgement that animals should be treated kindly and have value above and beyond their usefulness to man.

500 B.C. ~ The Greek philosopher and theologian Xenophanes first determines that fossils are animal remains and also, the fact that where aquatic fossils could be found on land, that land had once been underwater.

500 B.C. ~ By this year many Greek city-states have assembled their own menageries. In subsequent centuries their collections will be enhanced by Alexander the Great whose interest in the concept leads him to send animals back home from conquered lands.

427 B.C. The Greek philosopher Plato advocates for animals, writing that man mistreating animals would lead to man mistreating man.

330 B.C. ~ During time off from conquering the world and tending to his horses and elephants, Alexander the Great introduces the peacock to Europe. Alexander was awestruck by the beauty of the bird.

100 B.C. ~ The Roman philosopher and historian Plutarch states that animals' behavior is motivated by reason and understanding.

46 B.C. ~ The first giraffe sets foot on the European continent, one brought back by Julius Caesar after his conquest of Egypt. This has been a good year for Caesar and he stages a parade in Rome to impress his subjects with the menagerie of animals he has been able to assemble.

4 A.D. ~ As corroborated in the classic Christmas tale, the three Kings: Melchior from Europe, Caspar from Arabia, and Balthazar from Africa travel to Bethlehem by horse, camel, and elephant respectively, to present the newborn baby Jesus with the symbolic gifts of gold, frankincense and myrrh. And yes, Jesus was actually born 4 A.D.

80 A.D. ~ The Coliseum is completed in Rome and becomes the home of an array of animals including bears, crocodiles, elephants, giraffes, hyenas, lions and tigers. Some of the animals were primarily for the purpose of public exhibit but, Roman mentality being what it was, many of the animals became the victims of bloodsport.

211 ~ During the reign of Roman Emperor Marcus Aurelius, zebras are noted to be a component of the animal exhibits available to the public. There will be no further documentation of zebras in Europe until the 19th century.

800 ~ The Muslim theologian and scholar from Basrah (modern-day Iraq) writes his most famous work *Al-Hayawan, (The Book of Animals)*.

900 ~ The use of horses for agricultural purposes becomes more prevalent in Europe with the advent of crop rotation practices.

1275 ~ Marco Polo's travels bring Europeans a greater awareness of Asian animals. He reports seeing unicorns in China which were, in all likelihood, rhinoceroses.

1487 ~ The Medici giraffe becomes the most notable to set foot on European soil since Caesar's giraffe, more than 1,500 years earlier. The Sultan of Egypt gives it to the Italian Prince Lorenzo de Medici who maintains a menagerie of animals for public viewing in his hometown of Florence.

1492 ~ Christopher Columbus, sailing for Spain, introduces cattle, horses and pigs to the New World.

1519 ~ In chronicling Cortez's conquest of Mexico, Spanish historian Bernal Diaz del Castillo details Aztec ruler Montezuma's menagerie of animals which includes armadillos, bears, jaguars, monkeys, parrots, pumas, rattlesnakes, sloths, and wolves.

1523 ~ Spanish historian Gonzalo Fernández de Oviedo y Valdés becomes the first to describe multiple New World animals such as anteaters, hummingbirds, iguanas, manatees, opossums, pelicans and tapirs.

1588 ~ British naturalist Thomas Harriot publishes his *Brief and True Report of the New Found Land of Virginia*, which includes descriptions of the black bear, gray squirrel, hare, horseshoe crab, opossum, otter, raccoon, skunk, turkey, and the Virginia & mule deer.

1635 ~ Ireland passes the first animal protection legislation which was "An Act against plowing by the tayle, and pulling the wool off living sheep".

1641 ~ The Massachusetts colony's "Body of Liberties" includes regulations against "Tirranny or Crueltie" toward animals.

1657 ~ In an ironic follow-up to the previous entry, the last wolf in Massachusetts is killed.

1668 ~ The Royal Menagerie at the Palace of Versailles opens in France.

1681 ~ The last dodo bird is seen on Mauritius Island, where the species was endemic.

1752 ~ The Schönbrunn Zoo in Vienna, Austria opens and remains the world's oldest continuously operating zoo.

1755 ~ The last preserved dodo bird, a rotting relic, was burned at Oxford England.

1780 ~ British philosopher Jeremy Bentham advocates for better treatment of animals.
1822 ~ The British Parliament passes an "Act to Prevent the Cruel and Improper Treatment of Cattle".
1824 ~ The Society for the Prevention of Cruelty to Animals is first founded at Old Slaughter's Coffee House in London, directed by Arthur Broome.
1825 ~ British geologist Gideon Mantell identifies the first dinosaur fossil, labeling the reptile as an "Iguanodon".
1826 ~ John James Audubon begins his "Birds in America" project, a series of engravings that will take him 12 years to complete.
1826 ~ Zarafa becomes the first giraffe to set foot on the continent of Europe since 1487.
1828 ~ The Zoological Society of London opens an animal observation opportunity which would evolve into the London Zoo. A hippopotamus is viewed on European soil for the first time since the first century AD.
1835 ~ The first Cruelty to Animal Act is passed in England.
1837 ~ Giraffes first appear in traveling shows in the United States.
1844 ~ The Berlin Zoo opens.
1859 ~ British geologist and naturalist Charles Darwin publishes *On the Origin of Species* explaining the process of evolution by natural selection.
1862 ~ San Francisco lawmakers exempt the city's best rat-catching dogs, Lazarus and Bummer, from the newly adopted muzzle law. Bummer for the rats.
1864 ~ The Central Park Zoo opens in New York City.
1864 ~ The Moscow Zoo opens.
1866 ~ The American Society for the Prevention of Cruelty to Animals (ASPCA) is founded in New York.
1868 ~ Lincoln Park Zoo opens in Chicago.
1872 ~ Giraffes made their first appearance in Central Park in New York City; Philadelphia follows suit two years later.
1874 ~ The Philadelphia Zoo opens.
1875 ~ The Cincinnati Zoo opens.
1875 ~ The National Anti-Vivisection Society is established in England with a goal of ending harmful, flawed and costly animal experiments.
1885 ~ Jumbo, the elephant whose name became a common noun for the concept of huge, is killed in Ontario, Canada after being struck by a train while being transported into a circus carriage.
1889 ~ The National Zoological Park opens in Washington, D.C. as part of the Smithsonian Institution.
1889 ~ The Cincinnati Zoo is home to the first giraffe born in captivity in the United States.
1898 ~ The world's first officially designated game reserve opens in Sabie, South Africa.
1898 ~ During the construction of the Uganda Railroad, the Tsavo lions kill 30 workers in British East Africa (now Kenya).
1899 ~ The Bronx Zoo opens in New York.

1900 ~ At this time, prior to the advent of the automobile, the count of horses pulling vehicles numbered 300,000 in London and 100,000 in New York City.

1903 ~ Annie Edson Taylor sends her cat Lucky over Niagara Falls to test the durability of the barrel which she herself will take over the falls two days later. Both survive, and subsequently pose side-by-side, with Lucky on top of the barrel. One lucky Lucky.

1905 ~ The American Bison Society is established.

1906 ~ Upton Sinclair's novel *The Jungle* focuses attention upon the cruelty and appalling conditions of the Chicago meatpacking industry.

1906 ~ The Beijing Zoo opens in China.

1907 ~ Russian scientist Ivan Pavlov demonstrates conditioned responses with salivating dogs.

1916 ~ The San Diego Zoo opens.

1919 ~ Thoroughbred Man o' War begins his record-breaking career.

1922 ~ German shepherd Rin Tin Tin begins a Hollywood film career that will last a decade and encompass a total of 26 films. The Warner Bros. star receives 10,000 fan letters a week.

1925 ~ Fighting a diphtheria outbreak, dog sled teams are called upon to deliver a vaccine from Nenana, Alaska to Nome. The longest leg of the 674-mile route was covered by Leonhard Seppala with his lead dog Togo, the greatest fame would fall upon Gunnar Kaasen and his lead dog Balto who covered the final leg, and were in position to take advantage of all the photo ops.

1926 ~ The last gray wolf disappears from Yellowstone Park.

1927 ~ The last U.S. whaling ship, the John R. Mantra, is sent out from New Bedford, Massachusetts.

1929 ~ The first seeing-eye dog school is chartered in the U.S. in Morris Township, New Jersey.

1934 ~ German Nazi party official Herman Goering approves a request from the forestry service to introduce North American raccoons into the wild. The animals thrive with over a million in Germany today.

1936 ~ A giant panda visits the U.S. for the first time when Su-Lin arrives in San Francisco.

1937 ~ William Randolph Hearst's private zoo closes in San Simeon, California, and his zebras escape into the wild. They survive and thrive and come to comprise the largest wild zebra herd outside of Africa.

1938 ~ Lofty & Patches embark upon their arduous journey from Uganda to the San Diego Zoo to become the first breeding pair of giraffes in the U.S.

1938 ~ Lassie debuts in a *Saturday Evening Post* story written by Eric Knight, a long movie/TV career to follow.

1938 ~ From a group of five "applicants" Roy Rogers chooses Trigger to costar in the film *Under Western Stars*. The pair would work together for the next two decades.

1939 ~ After a horse is forced to leap to its death during the making of the film *Jesse James* (starring Henry Fonda and Tyrone Power), the American Humane Association's Film and Television Unit is formed to monitor the use of animals in movies.
1944 ~ British animal rights advocate Donald Watson founds the Vegan Society.
1944 ~ The first Smokey Bear posters are created as part of a national firefighting campaign.
1948 ~ The International Union for the Conservation of Nature (IUCN) is founded in Fontainebleau, France. It will go on to become the world's preeminent environmental conservation organization.
1948 ~ Citation wins the Triple Crown.
1950 ~ As a result of a forest fire in the Capitan Mountains of New Mexico, an injured but surviving bear becomes the first real-life Smokey Bear.
1952 ~ Cheetahs become extinct in India after decades of hunting and habitat loss.
1960 ~ British anthropologist Jane Goodall begins her chimpanzee research.
1961 ~ The chimpanzee Ham becomes the first primate in space, taking a 16-minute flight aboard a NASA rocket ship in Cape Canaveral, Florida as part of the Mercury program.
1964 ~ The International Union for Conservation of Nature issues its first IUCN Red List of endangered species.
1966 ~ The U.S. Congress passes the Endangered Species Preservation Act.
1966 ~ A black bear named Gentle Ben gets his own TV series, co-starring with Dennis Weaver.
1970 ~ The first Earth Day is celebrated with Pogo Possum serving as mascot on the official poster.
1970 ~ Secretariat wins the Triple Crown.
1973 ~ The Iditarod dog-sled race is first run along the 1,159-mile route from Nenana to Nome, Alaska to commemorate the dog-sled relay team that successfully delivered a diphtheria vaccine in 1925.
1975 ~ The U.S. Food and Drug Administration issues a ban on the sale of turtles with shells less than 4 inches long. The popular kids' pet was identified as a major carrier of salmonella bacteria.
1975 ~ The U.S. Department of the Interior establishes the grizzly bear as an endangered species in the lower 48 states.
1976 ~ Smokey the Bear dies at the age of 26 at the National Zoo in Washington.
1976 ~ The U.N. Convention in International Trade in Endangered Species bans the trade of rhino horn. A full 90% of the world's rhino population would be gone by the mid 1990's.
1980 ~ The organization People for the Ethical Treatment of Animals is founded, adopting the acronym PETA.
1983 ~ The Farm Animal Rights Movement establishes World Day for Farmed Animals to be acknowledged on October 2.
1985 ~ The first annual Great American MeatOut is organized by the Farm Animal Reform Movement.

1986 ~ Fur Free Friday is established as an annual nationwide fur protest to be acknowledged on the day after Thanksgiving.
1989 ~ Avon becomes the first major company to stop testing its products on animals; followed by Revlon in 1990.
1993 ~ When drug Lord Pablo Escobar is killed in a shoot-out, his abandoned hippos begin the herd that is currently inhabiting Colombia.
1996 ~ Dolly the sheep becomes the first mammal to be successfully cloned.
2001 ~ The British House of Commons votes 387-174 to ban fox hunting. It's the end of an era.
2001 ~ The first cat is cloned by scientists at Texas A & M. It is named CC for "carbon copy".
2004 ~ Clothing chain Forever 21 stops selling fur.
2007 ~ Atlanta Falcons quarterback Michael Vick is convicted for his involvement in an illegal dog fighting ring.
2015 ~ Ringling Bros. and Barnum & Bailey Circus announces that it will remove the elephants from its traveling show.
2015 ~ SeaWorld announces it will end its orca shows and breeding program.
2015 ~ Cecil the lion is killed in Zimbabwe by American dentist James Palmer who paid two natives $50,000 to lure the lion off protected land. International outrage ensues and the world shames James, deservedly so.
2017 ~ Giraffe mom April and daughter Tajiri achieve internet fame when April becomes the first giraffe to give birth on live TV, doing so in front of 1.2 million viewers on YouTube at the Animal Adventure Park in Harpursville, New York.
2018 ~ Nabisco changes its 116-year-old package design for Animal Crackers. The new box is cage-free but the residual problem still lingers… the elephants and giraffes still seem to taste exactly the same.
2019 ~ California becomes the first U.S. state to ban the sale and manufacture of new fur items.
2019 ~ New York becomes the first state to ban the declawing of cats.
2020 ~ Tasmanian devils are reintroduced to mainland Australia for the first time in 3,000 years, looking to adapt to their new accommodations in the thousand-acre Barrington Tops Wildlife Refuge in the state of New South Wales.

ADDENDUM #14
SPORTS MASCOTS

When it comes to sports mascots and nicknames, animals rule. In this addendum, we've scoured the rosters of all the major professional sports and college teams to provide this alphabetical overview. Our spacing strategy was to keep things concise as you could list these at incredible lengths if you included all the minor league teams and small colleges. That being said, if we'd already started a line and had some room to spare, we did throw in some examples from lesser-known arenas.

ACRONYMS:

MLB-Major League Baseball
NBA-National Basketball Assoc.
NFL-National Football League
NHL-National Hockey League
NCAA-National Collegiate Athletic Association

AGGIES ~ NCAA: Texas A & M, Utah State, New Mexico State, North Carolina A&T, University of California – Davis
ANTEATERS ~ NCAA: University of California – Irvine
ANTELOPES ~ NCAA: Grand Canyon University; Soccer: Netherlands Antilles
BADGERS ~ NCAA: Wisconsin
BANANA SLUGS ~ NCAA: University of California – Santa Cruz
BARRACUDAS ~ Hockey: Jacksonville (Southern Hockey League); Soccer: Brownsville (Major Indoor Soccer League)
BATS ~ Baseball: Louisville (International League), Hockey: Austin (Ice Bats- Central Hockey League)
BEARCATS ~ NCAA: Cincinnati, Sam Houston, State University of New York at Binghamton (hereafter SUNY)
BEARS ~ NFL: Chicago; NCAA: Baylor, Cal (Golden Bears), Brown, Maine (Black Bears) Northern Colorado, Coast Guard Academy, Arkansas Central, Mercer, Missouri State, Morgan State, SUNY-Potsdam; Negro Baseball: Milwaukee (1923); Hockey: Hershey (AHL), Smiths Falls (CCHL)
BEAVERS ~ NCAA: Oregon State, Caltech; Baseball: Portland (Pacific Coast League); NHL: Quebec (1926-28)
BEES ~ Baseball: Salt Lake City (Pacific Coast League)
BENGALS ~ NFL: Cincinnati, NCAA: Idaho State, Buffalo State; Soccer: Bangladesh (Bengal Tigers)
BISON ~ NCAA: Bucknell, North Dakota State, Howard, Lipscomb (Bisons); Baseball: Buffalo (International League-Bisons)
BLACKBIRDS ~ NCAA: Long Island University (1935-2019)
BLUE JAYS ~ MLB: Toronto; NCAA: Creighton, Johns Hopkins
BOBCATS ~ NBA: Charlotte (2004-2014); NCAA: Ohio, Montana State, Quinnipiac, Southwest Texas, Texas State
BOLL WEEVILS: NCAA: Arkansas-Monticello
BRONCOS ~ NFL: Denver; NCAA: Boise State, UC – Santa Clara, Western Michigan, Rider; Hockey: Swift Current (International Hockey League)
BRUINS ~ NHL: Boston, NCAA: UCLA, Belmont; Hockey: Providence (AHL)

BUCKS ~ Milwaukee (NBA)
BUFFALOS ~ NCAA: Colorado, Marshall (Thundering Herd)
BULLDOGS ~ NFL: Canton (1920-26); NCAA: Georgia, Gonzaga, Mississippi State, Yale, Butler, Fresno State, Citadel, Drake, UNC Asheville, Louisiana Tech, Gardner Webb, Alabama A & M, Western Illinois, Samford, Bryant;
Hockey: Hamilton (American Hockey League)
BULLS ~ NBA: Chicago; NCAA: South Florida, Buffalo;
Hockey: Birmingham (1976-79-WHA), Baseball: Durham (International League)
CAMELS ~ NCAA: Campbell; Soccer: Western Sahara (Dromedaries)
CANARIES ~ Soccer: Brazil; Baseball: Sioux Falls (American Association)
CARDINALS ~ MLB: St. Louis; NFL: Arizona, Chicago (NFL 1922-59), St. Louis (NFL 1960-87), NCAA: Louisville, Ball State, Lamar, SUNY-Plattsburgh
CATAMOUNTS ~ NCAA: Vermont, Western Carolina
CHANTECLEERS ~ NCAA: Coastal Carolina; Soccer: France
CHEETAHS ~ Soccer: Iran
CHICKS ~ All-American Girls Professional Baseball League: Milwaukee (1944), Grand Rapids (1945-54)
COLTS ~ NFL: Indianapolis, Baltimore (1947-1975); MLB: Houston (1962-64)
CONDORS ~ Basketball: Pittsburgh (ABA 1970-1972),
Hockey: Bakersfield (East Coast Hockey League)
COUGARS ~ NCAA: Houston. Brigham Young, Washington State, Southern Illinois, College of Charlestown, Chicago State; Hockey: Detroit (NHL-1926-30), Chicago (WHA-1972-1975), Basketball: Carolina (ABA 1969-74)
COYOTES ~ NHL: Phoenix
CROCODILES Soccer: Timor-Leste (East Timor)
CUBS ~ MLB: Chicago
DOGS ~ Baseball: Charleston Riverdogs (Carolina League), Portland Sea Dogs (Eastern League), Batavia Muckdogs (PGCL)
DOLPINS ~ NFL: Miami, NCAA: Jacksonville University, LeMoyne (in Syracuse, NY)
DOVES ~ MLB: Boston (1907-10) franchise subsequently goes to Milwaukee (1953-1966), then Atlanta (1967-present), now the Braves
DUCKS ~ NHL: Anaheim, AHL: Cincinnati; NCAA: Oregon;
Baseball: Akron (Rubber Ducks-Eastern League)
EAGLES ~ NFL: Philadelphia, NCAA: Boston College, Florida Gulf Coast, Marquette (Golden Eagles), Georgia Southern, Eastern Michigan, North Texas, Eastern Washington, Southern Mississippi, Niagara (Purple Eagles), American U., Oral Roberts (Golden Eagles), North Carolina Central, Morehead State, Winthrop, Coppin State, SUNY-Brockport (Golden Eagles); NHL: St. Louis (1934-35); Negro Baseball: Newark (1936-48), Brooklyn (1935);
Soccer: Syria, United Arab Emirates
ELEPHANTS ~ Negro Baseball: Denver (White Elephants – 1915-1935)
Soccer: Laos, Thailand
FALCONS ~ NFL: Atlanta; NCAA: Air Force, Bowling Green;
NHL: Detroit (1930-32); Soccer: Saudi Arabia, Pakistan, Kyrgyzstan

FLAMINGOS ~ Baseball: Miami (Florida International League – 1940-1954)
FOXES ~ NCAA: Marist (Red Foxes), Sweet Briar (Vixen – women's college in Virginia)
FROGS ~ Basketball: Quebec (Jumping Frogs – American Basketball Ass.); Baseball: Florida (Fire Frogs – Florida State League)
GAMECOCKS ~ NCAA: South Carolina, Jacksonville State (Alabama)
GATORS ~ NCAA: Florida;
Hockey: Louisiana (Ice Gators – Southern Hockey League)
GILA MONSTERS ~ NCAA: Eastern Arizona;
Hockey: Tucson (West Coast Hockey League)
GOPHERS ~ NCAA: Minnesota;
Baseball: St. Paul (Negro League – Colored Gophers – 1907-1914)
GREYHOUNDS ~ NCAA: Loyola (Maryland)
GRIZZLIES ~ NBA: Memphis, Vancouver (1995-2001); NCAA: Montana, Southwest Missouri State; Oakland (Golden Grizzlies);
Baseball: Fresno (California League), Football: Memphis (World Football League); Fairbanks (Indoor Football League); Hockey: Utah (WCHL)
HAWKS ~ NBA: Atlanta, St. Louis NBA (1955-1968), Milwaukee (1951-1955); NCAA: Indiana (Jayhawks), Miami (of Ohio – Red Hawks), Louisiana Monroe (War Hawks), Monmouth, Hartford, Lehigh (Mountain Hawks), Montclair State (Red Hawks), Southeast Missouri (Red Hawks), U. Mass – Lowell (River Hawks), Tennessee Martin (Sky Hawks), Laurier (Golden Hawks),
Roberts Wesleyan (Red Hawks)
Lacrosse: Rochester (Knighthawks-NLL); Baltimore (Bay Hawks-MLL);
Hockey: Waterloo (Black Hawks-USHL), Winston-Salem (ECHL)
HENS ~ NCAA: Delaware (Blue Hens);
Baseball: Toledo (Mud Hens-International League)
HOKIES ~ NCAA: Virginia Tech
HORNETS ~ NBA: Charlotte; New Orleans (2002-2013);
NCAA: Alabama State, Delaware State, Sacramento State; Soccer: Brunei;
Negro Baseball: Charlotte (Black Hornets – 1950-51);
Football: Charlotte (World Football League – 1974-1975)
HUSKIES ~ NCAA: Connecticut, Washington, Northern Illinois, Northeastern; NBA: Toronto (1946-1947)
JACKRABBITS ~ NCAA: South Dakota State
JAGUARS ~ NFL: Jacksonville; NCAA: South Alabama, Southern University, I.U.P.U.I. (Indiana)
KANGAROOS ~ NCAA: Missouri-Kansas City, Soccer: Australia
LEOPARDS ~ NCAA: Lafayette; Soccer: Zanzibar, Zaire
LIONS ~ NFL: Detroit; NCAA: Penn State (Nittany Lions), Colombia, Loyola-Marymount, North Alabama, Southeastern Louisiana, Arkansas-Pine Bluff (Golden Lions)
Soccer: England, Iraq, Afghanistan, Tajikistan; CFL: British Columbia
LIZARDS ~ Lacrosse: Long Island (Major League Lacrosse);
Hockey: Jacksonville (Lizard Kings–East Coast Hockey League)

LOBOS ~ NCAA: New Mexico
LONGHORNS ~ NCAA: Texas
LYNX ~ WNBA: Minnesota; Hockey: Augusta (East Coast Hockey League)
MAMMOTHS ~ Lacrosse: Colorado (National Lacrosse League); Hockey: Winston Salem (Southern Hockey League)
MANATEES ~ Hockey: Miami (Southern Hockey League)
MARLINS ~ MLB: Florida
MAVERICKS ~ NBA: Dallas, ABA Houston (1967-69); Hockey: Missouri (Central Hockey League)
MOOSE ~ Hockey: Manitoba (American Hockey League)
MUSKIES ~ Basketball: Minnesota (ABA – 1967-1968)
MUSTANGS ~ NCAA: SMU, Cal-Poly; Soccer: Chicago 1968 (NASL)
ORIOLES ~ MLB: Baltimore
OWLS ~ NCAA: Temple, Rice, Florida Atlantic, Oregon Tech (Hustling Owls)
PALADINS ~ NCAA: Furman (Purple Paladins)
PANTHERS ~ NFL: Carolina; NHL: Florida; NCAA: Pittsburgh, Wisconsin-Milwaukee, Florida International (Golden Panthers), Georgia State, Birmingham Southern, East Illinois, Prairie View, High Point; Football: Michigan (USFL)
PARROTS ~ Hockey: Winston Salem (Southern Hockey League)
PEACOCKS ~ NCAA: Saint Peter's (New Jersey)
PELICANS ~ NBA: New Orleans; Baseball: Myrtle Beach (Carolina League), Negro Baseball: New Orleans (Black Pelicans – 1926-1950)
PENGUINS ~ NHL: Pittsburgh; NCAA: Youngstown State; Hockey: Wilkes-Barrie Scranton (AHL)
POLAR BEARS ~ Soccer: Greenland; Hockey: Orlando (Solar Bears-International Hockey League)
PREDATORS ~ NHL: Nashville
PRIDE ~ NCAA: Hofstra; Soccer: Orlando (National Women's Soccer League)
RACERS ~ NCAA: Murray State
RAMS ~ NFL: Los Angeles, Cleveland (1937-45), St. Louis (1995-2015); NCAA: Colorado State, Rhode Island, Fordham
RAPTORS ~ NBA: Toronto
RATS ~ Hockey: Albany (River Rats – American Hockey League)
RATTLERS ~ NCAA: Florida A&M
RAVENS ~ NFL: Baltimore (NFL)
RAYS ~ MLB: Tampa Bay (Devil Rays 1998-2007); Women's Soccer: San Jose (Cyber Rays 2001-2003)
RAZORBACKS ~ NCAA: Arkansas
RED SNAPPERS ~ Soccer: Maldive Islands
REDBIRDS ~ NCAA: Illinois State
RETRIEVERS ~ NCAA: Maryland-Baltimore County
ROADRUNNERS ~ NCAA: Ramapo, Texas-San Antonio
SAND GNATS ~ Savannah Minor League Baseball (later changed to Savannah Bananas)

SEAHAWKS ~ NFL: Seattle; NCAA: University of North Carolina at Wilmington (Sea Hawks), Wagner (Sea Hawks)
SEALS ~ NHL: California (1967-1976); Pacific Coast League Baseball: San Francisco (1903-1957); Hockey: Florida (Southern Hockey League)
SHARKS ~ NHL: San Jose; Football: Jacksonville (World Football League); NCAA: Long Island University; Baseball: Wilmington (Coastal Plain League)
SPIDERS ~ NCAA: Richmond; Baseball: Cleveland (MLB 1887-99), Texas (Black Spiders – Negro League – 1932-1937)
SQUIRRELS ~ NCAA: Haveford College (Black Squirrels), Mary Baldwin (Fighting Squirrels, Oberlin (Albino Squirrels)
Baseball: Richmond Flying Squirrels (Eastern League)
STAGS ~ NBA: Chicago (1947-50), NCAA: Fairfield;
Hockey: Michigan 1974-75 (World Hockey Association)
STALLIONS ~ Football: Birmingham (USFL) Augusta (Arena Football)
T-REX ~ Hockey: Tupelo (Central League)
TERRAPINS ~ NCAA: Maryland
TERRIERS ~ NCAA: Boston University; St. Francis (of New York), Wofford
TIGERS ~ MLB: Detroit (MLB), NCAA: Clemson, LSU, Auburn, Missouri, Memphis, Princeton, Pacific, Towson State, Savannah State, Texas Southern, RIT; NHL: Hamilton (1920-1925); Baseball: San Diego (Negro League – 1946), Lakeland (Flying Tigers – Florida League); Soccer: Malaysia
Football: Hamilton (Tiger Cats – Canadian Football League)
WHALES ~ MLB: Chicago (1914-1915), Hockey: Connecticut (AHL)
WILDCATS ~ NCAA: Arizona, Kentucky, Kansas State, Villanova, Northwestern, New Hampshire, Weber State, Davidson
WOLFPACK ~ NCAA: North Carolina State, Nevada (Wolf Pack); Hockey: Hartford (American Hockey League)
WOLVERINES ~ NCAA: Michigan
WOLVES ~ NBA: Minnesota (Timberwolves) NCAA: Alaska Anchorage (Sea Wolves), SUNY–Stony Brook (Sea Wolves); Arkansas State (Red Wolves), Keuka; Hockey: Chicago (AHL), Mississippi, (ECHL); Soccer: Mongolia, Uzbekistan; Baseball: Detroit (Negro League – 1932)
YELLOW JACKETS ~ NCAA: Georgia Tech, University of Rochester

ADDENDUM #15
OLDEST ZOOS IN THE U.S.

The list of oldest zoos in the U.S. can actually be a subject of controversy, a fact that may surprise you. Why would that be? Well, there are a few factors at play in this equation and, while there is some overlap, we'll wrap our ratings around the following four questions in the equation.

1) When did the zoo get its charter?
2) When did the doors actually open to the public?
3) When did the first animal(s) arrive?
4) When did the zoo cross the admittedly murky boundary of having enough animals to be considered to be a zoo by modern-day standards.

There is an acknowledged overlap between #3 and #4 above, so to calibrate that gap, let us throw out the following example. The origins of the Buffalo Zoo occurred when someone dropped off two deer. At this point, it's obviously **animals – yes; zoo – no**. And the answers to all the questions above may be in flux for various periods of time in various scenarios.

In all of our years of extended research on this project, the most astute analysis of this concept we found to be one written by Kyle Glatz for the website AZ Animals and last updated on 7.17.23. They counted down their Top 10 which we are replicating here in the same order, combining their words with ours for the specifics.

#10 - (1888) Oregon Zoo (formerly Metro Washington Park Zoo) ~ This one starts when pharmacist Richard Knight begins taking in animals from sailors who have brought them into port. The 1888 start date is established by the Portland City Council accepting the gift of a grizzly bear and making Charles Myers the first zookeeper. By 1894, there were over 300 animals at this zoo. Today that number stands at 1,800 animals.

 # 9 - (1882) Cleveland Metroparks Zoo (formerly Cleveland Zoological Park) ~ The original facility opened in 1882 at the present-day site of the Cleveland Museum of Art. This zoo began by exhibiting various local animals before expanding to various exotic African species such as monkeys and elephants. Today, the zoo is home to over 600 species, including over 3,000 animals.

 # 8 - (1876) Maryland Zoo (formerly Baltimore City Zoo) ~ Here is a perfect example of how these dates can become so blurred. As early as 1860, the superintendent of the Druid Hill Park in Baltimore began caring for animals abandoned by local residents. So the concept of "zoo" is established, but the reality – not yet. However, this charitable effort, through time and love, emerged into the Baltimore City Zoo which opened on April 7, 1876 and remains open to this day. The zoo had financial trouble in the early 2000's but made a remarkable comeback in the early 2020's.

 # 7 - (1875) Ross Park Zoo (Binghamton NY) ~ Of the three zoos who show opening dates of 1875, this is slotted into the 7-hole as descriptions of the grand opening picnic on August 27, 1875 make no mention of any animals yet being on the premises and details of when they actually arrive remain murky. Ross Park has experienced a roller coast ride in recent years, losing AZA accreditation in 2005, regaining it in 2009, then losing it again in 2014. These days, the zoo focuses on teaching stewardship and conserving the surrounding area.

 # 6 - (1875) Cincinnati Zoo and Botanical Garden ~ Founded in 1873, the Cincy Zoo opened to the public on September 18, 1875. At the opening roll call, the animals present included birds (100's of them), buffalos, an elephant, elk, grizzly bears, a hyena, monkeys, and more. In *USA Today*'s 2023 poll of "10 Best Zoos in the U.S." the Cincinnati Zoo came in at #2. The facility is noted for its conservation efforts and breeding programs.

 # 5 - (1875) Buffalo Zoo ~ The Buffalo Zoo traces its history to 1870, when Jacob E. Bergtold, a prominent furrier, presented a pair of deer to the City of Buffalo. The deer were housed on a small piece of land in Delaware Park. Five years and a few animals later, the first permanent building was erected, signifying the establishment of the Buffalo Zoological Gardens in 1875. Over the next fifteen years, a flock of sheep, a pair of bison, and eight elk were added. In 1890, development continued with the construction of a bear exhibit and a larger animal house. With these additions, public awareness began to grow and, as a result, many animals were donated to the zoo. Due to the rapidly growing animal collection, the city hired Frank J. Thompson as the zoo's first curator in 1895, an era when Buffalo appears in the list of 10 biggest cities in the U.S. Currently the 24-acre zoo exhibits a collection of 1,400 animals in a wide variety of species. With 400,000 annual visitors, the Buffalo Zoo is the second largest tourist attraction in Western New York, behind only Niagara Falls.

 # 4 - (1874) Philadelphia Zoo ~ This rating comes with an asterisk and here's the story. The very first charter to operate a zoo issued by an official government organization in the U.S. occurred on March 21, 1859 when such a charter was issued to the Philadelphia Zoo by the Commonwealth of Pennsylvania. This is the fact that enables the zoo to lay claim to being the oldest zoo in America. So why the delay? Well, that pesky Civil War broke out and in the years after the charter was issued, there was a lot more Pennsylvania traffic through the battlefield at Gettysburg than there was through the future site of the zoo in Philadelphia. By the time Philly threw open the gates on July 1, 1874, the turnstiles were spinning at three other U.S. zoos. See below.

 # 3 - (1872) Roger Williams Park Zoo (Providence, Rhode Island) ~ This one got started when, in 1871, Betsey Williams bequeathed her 102-acre farm to the city of Providence in memory of her great-great-great-grandfather, Roger Williams, the founder of Providence. Hence the city had Roger Williams Park and in 1872 the first zoo there opened with a line-up of small animals including, alphabetically: anteaters, guinea pigs, hawks, mice, peacocks, rabbits, raccoons, and squirrels. If you were looking to save time, word has it that the line to view the mice cages was quite short. In 1986, it became the first zoo in New England to earn accreditation from the Association of Zoos and Aquariums. We thank the Roger Williams Park Zoo for being the oldest zoo in the U.S. to contribute to this project.

 # 2 - (1868) Lincoln Park Zoo (Chicago, Illinois) ~ The beginnings were humble, initiated with the donation of a few pairs of mute swans in 1868, but within a few years the collection had grown to include eagles, elk, pumas and wolves. In 1870 the first permanent structure was built. Other acknowledgeable milestones include the first bear arriving in 1874, and the first American bison born in captivity in 1884. Lincoln Park lives on, in the heart of Chicago, as one of the few admission-free zoos in the U.S. Currently it houses about 1,100 animals from over 200 species.

 # 1 - (1864) Central Park Zoo (New York City, New York) ~ Granted, it's relatively small, but it's the original and it's still there and located on 6.5 acres on the southeast corner of Central Park on the island of Manhattan in NYC. The assemblage of animals began in 1859 when a menagerie came together as people started dropping off their unwanted animals at the current site, even though there was no charter in place. By the time the Philadelphia Zoo opened in 1874, there were over 400 animals at the Central Park Zoo. Who could have known at the time that this zoo would become the centerpiece of the greatest animated film franchise, namely *Madagascar*, where the entire franchise begins with the core of animal actors breaking out of the Central Park Zoo.

ADDENDUM #16
TOP 35 OVERALL RANKINGS
(FAME, HUMOR, IMPORTANCE, INTRIGUE, INFLUENCE)

35) CURIOUS GEORGE ~ After the man in the yellow hat found Curious George in Africa in 1941, the monkey starred in 87 books and 199 videos.

34) NEMO AND DORY ~ In fish films, *Finding Nemo* (2003) and *Finding Dory* (2016), Dory sallies forth under the mantra of "Just keep swimming".

33) ALVIN & THE CHIPMUNKS ~ Beginning in 1958, these guys have chalked up 50 albums, 14 chart hits, 8 movies, 3 TV series. Chipmunks rule!

32) TWEETY ~ "I Tawt I Taw a Puddy Tat... I Did, I Did, I Did Taw a Puddy Tat!" Although he had a speech impediment to die for, this bird never did.

31) THE TROJAN HORSE ~ The Greeks tricked the Trojans with this ploy, and three millenniums later you still hear, "Beware of Greeks bearing gifts."

30) THE JAWS SHARK ~ The classic 1975 Stephen Spielberg movie thriller *Jaws* spawned a pop culture tsunami unequaled by any other animal movie ever.

29) SAN DIEGO CHICKEN ~ As a general rule of thumb, this book avoided sport mascots, but we give deference to the first and arguably the best.

28) TASMANIAN DEVIL ~ When Bugs Bunny needed a new adversary Taz was created as the perfect combination of ferocity and character innovation.

27) KERMIT ~ From his hit Muppet song "The Rainbow Connection", it was "the lovers, the dreamers, and me" leading Kermit the Frog's rise to fame.

26) TEENAGE MUTANT NINJA TURTLES ~ With Italian Renaissance painter names, the "Cowabunga" dudes achieved iconic 1990's superhero fame.

25) DUMBO ~ In the 1941 Walt Disney classic, this endearing elephant uses his oversized ears to take flight, simultaneously enabling him to save the circus.

24) DAFFY DUCK ~ Accounting for the lisp and the quirky somewhat sloppy speaking nuances, Daffy spits out a catch phrase of, "Youuu're deththpicable!"

23) THE COWARDLY LION ~ Here *The Wizard of Oz* provides us with the ultimate jungle paradox, a scaredy-cat lion who ventures forth seeking courage.

22) BIG BIRD ~ Appealing to both adults and kids, Big Bird made his 1969 *Sesame Street* debut as the most multi-talented 8 foot, 2 inch costumed bird ever.

21) SCOOBY DOO ~ Beginning in 1969 this canine, and his four human sidekicks, have been ubiquitously solving mysteries on TV and in the movies.

20) JURASSIC PARK/JURASSIC WORLD ~ This franchise, beginning in 1993, spanned 2 trilogies, 6 movies, that made dinosaurs pop culture phenoms.

19) GARFIELD ~ Star of the comics, television, and film, this food-crazed feline lasagna lover famously pointed out the word "diet" is "die" with a "t".

18) THE BIG BAD WOLF ~ The evil villain of "The Three Little Pigs" was a star of movies and music who could huff and puff and blow your house down.

17) BAMBI ~ In the annals of Walt Disney movies, no animal title character comes with more name recognition than the star of the classic 1942 film *Bambi*.

16) MOBY DICK ~ In the Melville novel, Captain Ahab's whale obsession led to his demise, spawning the idiom of a fatal flaw being a "white whale".

15) MAN 'O WAR ~ He was the consensus greatest racehorse of all time. During his incredible 1919-1920 career, he won every race he ran, except one.

14) SIMBA ~ In this story of redemption, the "Circle of Life" in *The Lion King* takes Simba from Pride Rock, before ultimately returning his rightful throne.

13) TIGGER ~ There's no such thing as a tiger in Winnie the Pooh in Milne or Disney. It's "T-I-double 'guh' - er! That spells Tigger!" Bouncing all the way.

12) GARDEN OF EDEN SERPENT ~ No biblical animal, not Daniel's lions, nor Jonah's whale, looms larger than Adam and Eve's sinister snake.

11) PUSS IN BOOTS ~ Riding a crest-of-fame wave stretching from 1550's fairy tales to 2022 movie releases, let's crown Puss in Boots our King of Cats.

10) PUNXSUTAWNEY PHIL ~ Since 1887, Groundhog's Day has been highlighted by the possibilities of the Pennsylvania rodent seeing his shadow.

9) DONALD DUCK ~ In apropos wording from Walt Disney himself, "Like many large families, we have a problem child. You're right, it's Donald Duck."

8) MISS PIGGY ~ While Kermit was pegged as "top frog" when *The Muppet Show* debuted in 1976, it was actually Ms. Piggy who ended up stealing the show.

7) BUGS BUNNY ~ After emerging from his rabbit hole in 1940 to deliver his first line of, "What's up Doc?" this "wascally wabbit" garners great glory.

6) TOTO ~ As real animals go, the permanent pop culture impact of the pairing of Toto and Dorothy in *The Wizard of Oz* (1939) remains unrivaled.

5) KING KONG ~ Having launched a successful 13-movie career in 1933, this 8th Wonder of the World ascends to the status of our most iconic primate.

4) EASTER BUNNY ~ Originally popping out of a German rabbit hole in 1682, the Pennsylvania Dutch brought him to America in the mid-18th century.

3) WINNIE THE POOH ~ Created by A. A. Milne in 1926, this bear's greatest fame would come after Walt Disney took over his career in 1966.

2) RUDOLPH THE RED-NOSED REINDEER ~ Since joining Santa's original team of 8 in 1939, he's been playing reindeer games & leading the way.

1) MICKEY MOUSE ~ Regarding the icon of his entertainment/theme park franchise, Walt Disney reminded us to never forget, "that it was all started by a mouse." Thanks, Mickey and thanks, Walt.

ADDENDUM #17
CHYNNA'S EULOGY

As shared in our Dedication, our cat Chynna Cat Sunflower Smith unexpectedly died of cancer the day after we finished this book. We had written several eulogies for our local paper over the years, but this one was unique. Yes, this one was different because it was for an animal, but we thought it would be an appropriate manner in which to close this book. All good things come to an end, and here's what wrote as our send off to Chynna...

We'd never seen the whites of her eyes before and it was the first time we felt that wave of concern that maybe something was really wrong. It was just before 9:00 that morning and we were taking our beloved 1½-year-old cat Chynna to the vet because she had been limping.

With Deb driving, and Tim in the passenger seat with the patient on his lap, we noticed her looking at us out of her pet-carrying case. Under normal circumstances, she would move and look us directly in the eyes. Confined to her carrier, she could not achieve her preferred angle and was trying to make eye contact with us, without moving her head. In the effort, she showed us those never-before-seen whites of her eyes. Perhaps we should have known.

We came home, worked out, ate breakfast, and started to lay out the cover of this animal book, *Crowning the Animal Kingdom,* having just finished the last bit of writing the night before. It had been an 18-month project, so a major plateau had been achieved. Everything in the house was prepared for our girl to come home and begin her road to recovery. At 1:00 we got the call letting us know that our beautiful Chynna Cat Sunflower Smith was dying of cancer. She would not be coming home and there would be no road to recovery.

The loss of a pet is always traumatic, and while we'd each lost pets before, this one was so damn devasting because neither of us had ever had a pet taken at such a young age, and, neither of us had ever lost a pet that been our companion 24/7 for its entire life.

Earlier pets were equally important, but they had been shared with kids and jobs and the foibles of youth. In our retirement, we had spent most of our time writing our articles for the local paper and our books for the world. Chynna's bed was always comfortably perched on our desk, between us and our computer screens. She was with us when we worked, with us when we worked out, and with us when we slept.

But that was never going to happen again. We spent the day asking God why, without receiving an answer. But that night Chynna came back and spoke to us, providing at least some partial answers. Here is our transcription of the words that we heard from the female feline who had become the love of our lives…

"There is a reason that God make pets' lives shorter than humans'. For those able to hear the music, each pet sings a song intended to be a life lesson. It is the lesson which is meant to be the blessing that animal was sent to bestow upon the human who was willing to trade love for wisdom. Tim & Deb, you two traded wisely. And the song upon which we collaborated will resonate through time as long as the printed word. The *Sentinel* did not dub you "The (Word)Smiths" without reason.

I was your muse and you will hear my music in the sound of every word you write, for the rest of your lives. Did it dawn on you that my life coincided precisely with the work window for our animal book? My leg was hurting and I know we all thought it would get better but that was not God's plan. That last night you had to pick me up and lay me in my bed was the night we finished the book and my work was done.

That being said, you two still have work to do with the cover, the publishing process, the promotional efforts, and following up with the connections to all the zoos, aquariums, and wildlife sanctuaries we heard from. I know I'm purring for perpetuity here… but finish strong with our animal book. That will always be my legacy through you, and to you, and yours to the world. You couldn't have done it without me which is what puts the muse in the music. That was the reason why God put me in the position to be rescued by you when I was abandoned as a baby. I know we three see that so clearly now.

Yes, we three, were meant to be; we were something else together. I accepted your love with open arms, and legs, and every time I laid, at length, peacefully on my back with all four limbs extended, it was because I was taking in your love, and I could tell how endearing it was for you to see me in that position. I knew I was somehow, in my own way, converting your love into wisdom and channeling it back to you. Truth be told, that position wasn't all that comfortable, but hearing you talk about how adorable I was just made me try and stretch my legs out a little bit further.

I know I'll never forget the toys, and the treats, the early morning greets, the nuzzling of feets. Deb, or "Mom" as you called yourself, I know I watched your every move, to the point where you must have felt like you were performing your motherly duties under a microscope. I know you would have pristinely prepared my water, food and litter even if I weren't watching intently. But I know it made you feel good that I was, because I heard you walk out and tell Dad about it every time you finished.

And Dad, every time you walk on that hardwood bathroom floor, I'll know there will be one memory I've left with you. Me, clinging with my teeth and feet to the softness of your sock, Mom watching in the doorway, as you gently spun me around in circles on the floor in what you called "Chynna's

Cat-a-Whirl" Okay, I admit that sometimes I humored you. I felt like you were actually having more fun than me, but I thought, "Hey, you guys are so good to me, you're entitled to this moment."

And what was up with those dog tricks you taught me? They're already giving me grief up in kitty heaven about how I was willing to sit like a statue, willing to obey the repeated demands of, "Chynna stay, Chynna stay, Chynna stay" until those monotone words would end with a vigorous shout of, "On your mark, get set, go!" which of course was my cue to charge across the floor at breakneck speed for that dollop of Cheez Whiz that I would get to lick off your fingers. What I didn't do to please you two!

But now my work with you is done and God has other plans for me. So while I won't be back in body, the three of us know my soul will never leave. God will be sending you your next muse in due time and I will be moving on to my next assignment. That way God can have us working on separate songs simultaneously, so to speak. I hereby charge you with an ongoing commitment to bless lives on this planet with your work. If you ever find yourself stuck and in need of inspiration, just pray and I'll be there. I can see and hear things from my side that you cannot.

In your human minds, you always bestowed intellectual qualities upon me that exceeded the bounds of earthly possibilities. But now, as I speak to you from heaven, in this culminating one-time opportunity, I want you to know that I know. I loved every rub and I felt all the love. When you rescued me, it was meant to be. There was an intensity to our short earthly time together that God meant to exceed the power of us having had the opportunity to grow old together. Harness that power and passion and allow it to drive you through your remaining years. Nothing could be finer, than to do it for your Chynna. You guys were always magic on the "mantras." So there's mine for you. Don't let me down on this one. I know you won't.

My time with you grows short, so I must share my closing thoughts. I wish I could have grown old with you and I know you wish it too, but alas, that was just not meant to be. If you want a silver lining, take solace in the fact that I am no longer in pain. Remember how you carried me around from room to room, during my final days when I struggled to walk? You will no longer have to pick me up literally, but I will always have the ability to pick you up figuratively. While I charged you with your mission in life, I accept this as my charge in the afterlife."

Then Chynna gave us final purrs and kisses and directed us to go to the computer and write. We started this at 4:00 am on a cold February morning and it's now 5:30. It's our 90-minute memory menagerie for one Chynna Cat Sunflower Smith, the source of love and inspiration that powered a poignant period of our lives. Remember, until you've loved an animal, a part of your soul will remain unfulfilled.

ABOUT THE AUTHORS

We have a rather unique back story, most of which is set in upstate New York. We met on the first day of high school, brought together by the merger of two neighboring school districts. We ended up dating for all four years of high school, then went to different colleges and, as fate would have it, we ended up not seeing each other again for literally 40 years.

When Tim's mom passed away, Deb heard about it through the grapevine in Virginia Beach where she was teaching. She sent him a sympathy card, he wrote back, one thing led to another and Tim ended up going down to Virginia Beach at the end of that school year to pick Deb up and bring her back home to New York.

The thing Deb remembers most from that courtship period when she was in Virginia, but longing to be back in New York, was that every day at school when she went to her mailbox, there was an envelope from Tim. And each one contained an original letter Deb had written to him 40 years ago. He had saved every one. His go-to line regarding that part of the story is to say, "Yeah, it took me a long time to play those cards!" Sometimes the best things in life are worth waiting for.

We got engaged on Deb's mother's birthday (December 4) and we got married on Tim's mother's birthday (June 12). Because we both have Native American ancestry, we had the ceremony performed at the Ganondagan Historic Site by the Native American leader there; also presiding over the ceremony was a former student of Tim's.

So how did we get into this writing gig? Well, as fate would have it, we happen to live right next door to the newspaper office in our town. After hearing some of our stories, the publisher of the paper, Chris Carosa, suggested we write about our background and share it with the community. So we started by telling the personal story of our relationship, and we haven't stopped writing since. Currently our weekly feature comprises the entire back page of the *Mendon-Honeoye Falls-Lima Sentinel*, we have a second column that always runs on page 2, and we frequently contribute additional pieces. Contributing to the community is a passion of ours.

We write about an eclectic variety of topics including entertainment, sports, travel, history and human interest. Chris Carosa, who we mentioned above, had been encouraging us to write a book since we first began writing for the paper. That first book came to fruition with the publication of *The Beatles, The Bible & Manson: Reflecting Back With 50 Years Of Perspective* during the summer of 2019. We hope you've enjoyed *Crowning The Animal Kingdom* so much you'll be interested in checking out the rest of our work. Listed below is our entire catalog of published books…

2019 ~ *The Beatles, The Bible & Manson: Reflecting Back With 50 Years Of Perspective*
2020 ~ *Tit For Tat Exchanges ~ Tim & Deb's Greatest Hits*
2021 ~ *What's In A Name? ~ Your Geography Hall of Fame*
2022 ~ *Blacks Facts ~ An Ultimate Primer To The Historical and The Hysterical*
2023 ~ *Walking In A Women's Wonderland ~ An Ultimate Primer Of The Historical And The Hysterical*
2024 ~ *Crowning The Animal Kingdom*

Please feel free to email us at TSmith40@Rochester.rr.com

Made in the USA
Coppell, TX
30 March 2024

30677036R00203